INTERCOLLEGIATE DEBATES VOL-XIV
YEAR OF BOOK OF COLLEGE DEBATING

You are holding a reproduction of an original work that is in the public domain in the United States of America, and possibly other countries. You may freely copy and distribute this work as no entity (individual or corporate) has a copyright on the body of the work. This book may contain prior copyright references, and library stamps (as most of these works were scanned from library copies). These have been scanned and retained as part of the historical artifact.

This book may have occasional imperfections such as missing or blurred pages, poor pictures, errant marks, etc. that were either part of the original artifact, or were introduced by the scanning process. We believe this work is culturally important, and despite the imperfections, have elected to bring it back into print as part of our continuing commitment to the preservation of printed works worldwide. We appreciate your understanding of the imperfections in the preservation process, and hope you enjoy this valuable book.

PUBLIC LIBRARY
KANSAS CITY
MO

Intercollegiate Debates

(Volume XIV)

THE YEAR BOOK OF COLLEGE DEBATING

YALE — OXFORD — PRINCETON — UNIVERSITY OF WISCONSIN — UNIVERSITY OF MICHIGAN — UNIVERSITY OF SOUTHERN CALIFORNIA — UNIVERSITY OF GEORGIA — UNIVERSITY OF ARIZONA — NEW YORK UNIVERSITY — MARQUETTE UNIVERSITY — BELOIT — WOOSTER — BUCKNELL — COLGATE — OCCIDENTAL — FRESNO STATE TEACHERS COLLEGE — DELTA SIGMA RHO

EDITED BY

EGBERT RAY NICHOLS
Professor of English Language and Literature
University of Redlands, California

NOBLE AND NOBLE, *Publishers*
76 FIFTH AVENUE   NEW YORK CITY

Copyright, 1933

By NOBLE AND NOBLE

PRINTED IN U.S.A.

EDITOR'S FOREWORD

THE title of this little dissertation might be "Debating under the Depression," or perhaps it should be, "Debating Surmounting the Depression," for, after all, that is what it seems to be doing. The testing point is, of course, the debate trip. If the colleges have no money for debate, there can be no trips, and, as is generally known, all of the colleges have been forced to retrench during the past two years. It is a good testimony to the value placed upon debating that the colleges have not sacrificed it in these difficult times. There has been, during the past season a surprisingly large number of debate trips on a commensurate scale with those of the prosperous days before 1929. Lack of money did not prevent or gainsay them, and these trips were in addition to the regular debate schedule maintained with neighboring colleges.

Perhaps one of the interesting episodes arising out of the lack of funds for debate came when the Weber College team from Ogden, Utah, scheduled a trip to Southern California on what they called "official hitch-hiking." The trucking companies were interviewed and arrangements were made for the debate team to travel to its debate engagements on freight trucks. The trip to Los Angeles from Ogden was made on an onion truck. From Los Angeles various side trips ing. Those who have entered the tournaments are enthusiastic for this new form of debating, and the possibility of getting so many debates concentrated in one place has encouraged trips in spite of the depression.

When the first big tournaments were introduced by Pi Kappa Delta the conservative debate world held its breath and said, "Impossible." However, the movement succeeded. The more aggressive colleges sent teams, liked their experience, and the tournament was ushered in to stay. Now, all sorts and types of tournaments are being conducted. First, there is the Practice Tournament. This type is held early in the debate season before any of the colleges have solidified their debate cases. In fact, the tournaments following one upon another during the season have encouraged teams to keep their cases in a growing and developing state until the very end of the season. Tournaments of this type originated at Southwestern College, Winfield, Kansas, where an annual meet is held in December when the teams are beginning to study the season's debate question seriously. They learn much from one another, and as the season progresses are ready for other debates and tournaments with re-constructed arguments and cases. This idea has spread over the country and several colleges are holding annual Practice Meets.

Second, there is the Novices Tournament. Only inexperienced debaters who have never competed in league and conference contests are eligible to take part. The prime motive of this tournament is to train and develop new debaters. It was first used by the Los Angeles Junior College during the last debate season.

Third, The League or Conference Tournaments. These meets are designed to take the place of the old schedule of debates maintained by colleges associated together. Holding a tournament to decide the League winner is more economic in time and money and is growing in popularity. The meeting promotes good fellowship and sportsmanship.

Fourth, there is the Mixed Tournament. In this type Junior colleges, and four year colleges send both men's and women's teams to compete in the same meet. The usual thing is to separate the two types of colleges and to allow no mixed competition.

Fifth, Regional Invitational Tournaments. These meets, open to all comers, usually divided into classes of competition, are held toward the end of the debate season as a sort of climax or goal to work toward. Cases and arguments are pointed toward such meets unless there is a National meet in the offing in which case they are a part of the program of preparation.

Sixth and final, the National Convention Tournaments. These meets are held annually by some organizations and biennially by others—the high school and junior colleges favoring the annual tournament and the colleges the biennial meeting. As many as a hundred teams have met in one division of these National Contests, notably that held by Pi Kappa Delta.

The debate tournament may use any type of debating—Oregon Plan, University Plan, Non-decision or Decision, or what you will. In several instances the first part of the tournament has been non-decision followed by a decision meet. Various plans of rounds and eliminations have been tried. Usually the coaches do the judging assisted by persons available where the tournament is held. The adaptability of the tournament plan has been demonstrated. It serves a small group and a large group of teams equally well.

The tournament has taken the emphasis off of winning to a very great extent and has placed the stress on training received by competition and on good sportsmanship. These large meetings generate considerable enthusiasm, extend acquaintanceship, and teach the debaters very rapidly many things they could not obtain from their coaches. The economy of the movement enables the coaches to enter a much larger squad on the same amount of money, an amount spent a few years ago on a single intensively trained varsity team. It has become the practice of many colleges and junior colleges to enter as many teams as the rules permit, and to beg for a chance for more debaters to attend. This, in itself, takes the emphasis off of winning. The whole squad goes now, debates and learns what it can, while in the past only the champion gladiators of the platform were allowed to travel or to compete with rival colleges. This extension of the benefits of debate training to more students at no additional cost is another of the explanations why the tournament is popular and is here to stay. For these many reasons the educational value of the tournament is now unquestioned.

The depression has, of course, hastened the abandonment of that older aid to the debate trip—the guarantee. Now, as a rule, no cash guarantees are given; only twenty-four hours entertainment is offered, the entertaining school defraying the other expenses of the debate. It was felt that the contract involving guarantees amounted to paying one's own expenses anyway, when a return debate was agreed upon for the succeeding season on the same terms. The only advantage was that the traveling team had the use of the money when it was needed. This slight advantage was given up on the thought that each college should pay the expenses of its own traveling teams. The frequency and the generality of the long trip made the interstate debate or the inter-sectional debate so common that no college would pay any longer for the privilege of entertaining a team from a distance. The novelty of receiving the far travelers wore off, and the demand centered on obtaining the most debates for the money. More training could be gained for more people on the same expenditure with less cost per debate. The depression was not entirely responsible for this attitude. Debate managers were forced to economize. At best their expense account was only grudgingly tolerated on the balance sheet of the Associated Students, and graduate managers and the demands for larger athletic programs obliged the debaters to get the most out of the allotment assigned them. The influence of Scotch blood in student affairs was evident before the depression came, and restriction of funds since the depression accelerated an already growing tendency. It remains to be seen what effect this economy attitude is going to have on the international debate. It has not destroyed the debate schedule or the debate trip, so perhaps it will not greatly affect the international debate schedules.

The depression has had a marked effect also on the subjects under discussion. A few years ago debate subjects became scarce—that is—good ones. The process of collecting debates for a book such as this forced one to take note of that fact. In addition the custom of naming a single subject for almost the entire country by such large organizations as the Pi Kappa Delta Forensic Honor Society and the National Forensic League of the high schools reduced the available debates considerably. The depression has brought in a considerable number of new subjects, some of which will be found in this volume, and has re-popularized many old subjects such as Socialism, and Government Ownership. Among the new subjects are Limitation of Wealth (by income and inheritance taxes), Controlled Inflation of Currency, Control of Industry, Unemployment Insurance, Reduction of Wages, Capitalism, Control of Banks, Domestic Allotment Plan of Farm Relief, Dictatorship, and Methods of Taxation. Most of these discussions bear a direct relationship to depression problems, and are born of hard times.

The survey of the debate season taken last fall (1932) indicated that approximately fifty subjects would be discussed among the American colleges. This was a larger number of different subjects than had been used during the immediate preceding years. It is true, of course, that more different subjects are used in years when the large conventions of the National Forensic Societies are not held. On years when the National Conventions meet the colleges concentrate more on the main or National subject chosen. When there are no National Conventions in the debate season, the local conferences break away from the National choice of subject more freely. The many interesting subjects arising because of depression conditions added to the tendency to break away from the National Subject this year.

The leading subjects debated the past season have been Taxation of Invisible or Intangible Property by the High Schools, and Cancellation of War Debts by the Colleges and Junior Colleges. Control of the Banks, the Mid-West subject, was perhaps next in popularity with the colleges. Some of the Universities in the Middle West debated the Taxation question. The Ohio colleges discussed Limitation of Wealth through Inheritance and Income Taxes. A Third Party Movement was debated in Illinois and Occupational Representation in Legislatures and in Congress was used in Michigan. Also State Police Force was discussed in Michigan. The other subjects had only scattering adherents, and were used as additional or supplementary subjects to the main one—Cancellation of War Debts which was almost universally discussed.

Next year the conventions of the National Forensic honor societies are due again. The National subjects are either chosen or forecast by preliminary vote. The National Forensic League or the National High School question is concerned with Radio Broadcasting for next season. Pi Kappa Delta and Phi Rho Pi will probably discuss Control of the Banking System. At least this subject has won in the spring vote, with Currency Inflation in second place.

Since the depression has not stopped the debate trip, the sectional tournaments, nor dulled debate enthusiasm, the prospect for next year's conventions is good. In 1932 all agreed that the conventions would be poorly attended but that did not prove to be the case. This past season the National High School and Junior College organizations held successful conventions and tournaments. It is likely that the conventions scheduled for next year will be largely attended, and much more successful than the times warrant. The virility of debating must be quite a shock to the howling Cassandras who have been heralding its death for lo these many years! Much has been written concerning debate that has not been abreast of the times. The debating activity has just marched off and left some unobserving people marooned with an outlook ten years out of date. One of the marked things about college debating since it began in the early nineties at Harvard and Yale has been its constant change, growth, and development. Each decade it presents an entirely new face. Some persons have mistaken change for decay, transition for demise, and new forms for the final abandonment of the entire activity, but the true story is one of progress and improvement, and the future is full of hope—hope guaranteed by present realization and vigor.

EGBERT RAY NICHOLS

TABLE OF CONTENTS

	PAGE
FOREWORD	iii

REVENUES FROM INTANGIBLE PROPERTY *(Western Conference Debate)* 3
    University of Wisconsin vs. University of Michigan
    Bibliography

SOCIALISM *(An International Debate)* 77
    Yale University—Oxford University (England)
    Bibliography

CANCELLATION OF WAR DEBTS *(Pacific Coast Pi Kappa Delta Province Tournament Championship)* 121
    Fresno State College vs. University of Southern California
    Bibliography

WAR DEBTS 167
    Delta Sigma Rho Public Discussion

AMERICAN LEGION SHOULD BE CONDEMNED . . . 203
    Princeton University vs. University of Georgia
    Bibliography

GOVERNMENT CONTROL OF THE BANKING SYSTEM . 251
    Beloit College vs. Marquette University
    Bibliography

LIMITATION OF WEALTH 325
    College of Wooster Affirmative and Negative
    Bibliography

JAPAN'S POLICY IN MANCHURIA 369
    Bucknell University Affirmative and Negative
    Bibliography

CONTENTS

	PAGE
A PRESIDENTIAL DICTATORSHIP	419
Colgate University vs. New York University	
Bibliography	
RADIO BROADCASTING	467
Occidental College vs. University of Arizona	
Bibliography	
APPENDIX I	507
List of Subjects covered in Intercollegiate Debates, *Volumes I-XIV*	
APPENDIX II	517
List of Colleges represented in Intercollegiate Debates, *Volumes I-XIV*	
INDEX	521

REVENUES FROM INTANGIBLE PROPERTY
Western Conference Debate

REVENUES FROM INTANGIBLE PROPERTY

UNIVERSITY OF WISCONSIN AFFIRMATIVE VS. UNIVERSITY OF MICHIGAN NEGATIVE

The Western Conference Debates, held in December, were upon a question much discussed throughout both Colleges and High Schools in the 1932-33 Debating Season. The question was stated: *Resolved, that at least one half of all state and local revenues should be derived from sources other than tangible property.*

The speakers for the Affirmative in this debate were David August, O. Glenn Stahl and Harry L. Cole of the University of Wisconsin. Negative speakers were James Moore, Victor Rabinowitz and Nathan Levy of the University of Michigan. Dean G. C. Sellery of the University of Wisconsin presided at the debate and introduced the speakers.

Professor Rexford Mitchell, of Lawrence College, acted as Critic Judge and gave his decision to the University of Wisconsin Affirmative Team.

These speeches were contributed by Professor H. L. Ewbank, Coach of Debate at the University of Wisconsin.

Introduction, Dean G. C. Sellery

It gives me very great pleasure as a member of the faculty of the University of Wisconsin to play the honorary rôle of presiding officer. It gives me also great pleasure as a Professor of Medieval History to see debating still going strong. Debating under the medieval name of *disputatio* was the most characteristic activity, the most marked pedagogical device, of medieval universities. A man secured his degree by debating, by arguing, by demonstrating a thesis. Unfortunately, debating no longer occupies the central curricular position it had in the medieval ages, although it still survives in connection with the doctor's degree, when the candidate has to defend his thesis before the presiding judges or professors.

That the debate was very important in the medieval ages I think I can illustrate rather neatly by referring to a circular sent out by the University of Toulouse in 1229, a trifle over 700 years ago. The University of Toulouse had been recently founded in the old Albigensian territory. Its sponsors were very anxious to secure a good attendance, so they sent a circular out among the European Universities advertising the advantages at Toulouse. After explaining that the wine was very good there, that the rents were low, that the girls were pretty, they said, "Moreover disputations are held at Toulouse twice as frequently as they are held at the University of Paris." That was supposed to demonstrate to every one, that if he was an up and coming student he should come to the University of Toulouse.

I have been asked, before calling upon the first speaker to make two announcements to the audience. First, that the coaches and members of the debating squads of the nearby high schools are invited to attend a meeting of these debaters and other interested persons in Tripp Commons in the Memorial Union Building immediately after the conclusion of this contest. The judge and a number of the varsity debaters will discuss the details of the question.

The second notice relates to the ballots which are appended to the program. There are two types. Don't be worried if you haven't both; you are supposed to have only one. On one of these ballots you are requested to mark your decision as to the successful team. Those who receive the second type are asked to decide and record their judgment as to the relative success of the debaters, to rank the six debaters in the order of their merit.

Ladies and Gentlemen, I have the honor to call upon Mr. David August to open for the Affirmative.

First Affirmative, David August
University of Wisconsin

LADIES AND GENTLEMEN: Today marks exactly one month since you went to the polls in the presidential election, and in that campaign no issue was so widely discussed as the question of taxation. We have been particularly anxious to have the privilege of discussing the subject with the Gentlemen from Michigan. It has been well said that the power to tax is the power to destroy. Obviously no nation deliberately uses taxation as a method of destruction, but rather as an instrument to encourage industry and initiative among its people. In working out a satisfactory tax system, we face the difficult problem of finding the fairest and most enlightened means of meeting the cost of government, a plan which will not overburden those least able to pay. It is this consideration which moves us to suggest that at least one-half of all state and local revenues should be derived from sources other than tangible property.

At present, state and local governments are making a futile attempt to raise three-fourths of all their revenue from a single source, namely tangible property; whereas they collect only one-fourth from sources other than tangible property, including income taxes, inheritance taxes, motor vehicle and gasoline taxes, and the like. What we are proposing here tonight is that we should redistribute the tax burden and so proportion it as to lighten the heavy load which now rests upon the owners of tangible property and thus raise a proportionate share from other sources. At present, by consulting expenditures on state and local budgets, we find that public welfare and public education costs fifty-eight per cent of the total revenue collected. The construction and maintenance of public highways represents twenty-four per cent, and protection only eighteen per cent.

Our proposal is that we should raise the fifty-eight per cent needed for state and local education and welfare by means of a state income tax. We also propose to maintain our highways, twenty-four per cent, by means of a motor vehicle and gasoline tax. Thus we would rely on real estate for the eighteen per cent needed for protection. Now, this is a rather complicated proposal; so that we may keep perfectly clear on this, I will furnish the opposition with a copy of this plan. We urge this reapportionment, first of all because the present situation is intolerable; second, because the proposed shift is perfectly feasible; and third, because it will produce a more equitable situation than at the present time; a situation which is overburdening the farmers and the home owners and the business men.

At one time in our nation's history tangible property was the only form of taxable wealth, but the latest report from the Minnesota Tax Commission gives this statement: "The rapid growth of intangible wealth in recent years in the form of stocks, bonds and other credits, affords new opportunities for the investment of the salaried group who contribute but little to the expenses of the government under which they live and prosper." Now, this failure to extend the tax base to meet new social and economic conditions has resulted in a long list of flagrant inequities, a list so long we are forced to bring in a general indictment of the property tax. In one case here we have four Wisconsin farmers who barely made ends meet in 1930. This is a Wisconsin example but it applies to the precise situations in Michigan, in Minnesota, and other states of the union. On the other hand we have twenty-five Wisconsin residents who sat at home and did nothing but clip coupons. The farmers were taxed twelve hundred dollars,—the combined bill of those four farmers; but what did the twenty-five Wisconsin coupon clippers who clipped three million dollars worth of coupons pay? They paid forty-one cents less than the combined tax bill of the four farmers. Situations of this nature compel us to say that there is an unjust and unequal burden placed upon the farmer and home owner.

Here again we have the situation of a Green County farmer who made little or no net income from the farm in the year 1930 but was taxed two hundred seventy dollars. Then we have the case of a Wisconsin newspaper man who in the year 1930 received a half million dollars in dividends. What did he pay? He paid not one cent toward the cost of state and local government on those stock dividends. Is it fair to tax a farmer who toils on his land two hundred seventy dollars, so that we can exempt a man with a half million dollars of dividends? This is precisely the reason why economic authorities condemn the property tax as being unjust and intolerable. To point out the intolerable conditions imposed by a property tax I need merely point southward to the city of Chicago. In this municipality they have been unable to pay school teachers for the past two years, and yet the city does not hesitate to sue the teachers on delinquent property taxes. No wonder President Hutchins of the University of Chicago called the property tax "preposterous and unjust."

The Michigan Committee for Inquiry Into Taxation gives a very interesting piece of evidence on tax delinquency. They say, "Tax delinquency is not tax delinquency, but represents an excess levy of taxes beyond the ability of the people to pay." Let us look at the tax delinquent situation in Detroit, Michigan. The City of Detroit is twenty-seven per cent delinquent in its property taxes. Buffalo is thirty-two per cent delinquent, and in rural districts the rate runs from thirty per cent to sixty per cent. Only recently the State of Mississippi took over twenty-five per cent of all its farm lands for delinquent property taxes. This is the work of property tax that is being upheld by the Negative this evening.

There is good reason for this: the whole theory behind the property tax is erroneous. All economists lay down two fundamental doctrines which should be applied to systems of taxation. These are, first, that citizens should be assessed according to their respective abilities to pay; second, citizens should be assessed according to the amount of benefit they receive from the government.

But let us see what the National Industrial Conference Board said in its latest study of the relation between the rate of the property tax levy and these two fundamental doctrines. They say, "Usually there can be found no such direct relationship between the performance of the governmental functions and the market values of property, and it is only to the extent that such direct relationships do exist, that the property tax satisfies the benefit principle of taxation." Secondly, "As regards the ability principle, the deficiencies of the property tax are more evident and more serious. In the final analysis there can be only one source of tax payments, namely, income, and the usual meaning of the ability principle of taxation is that with some minor exceptions taxes should be apportioned according to the income received by different taxpayers."

This is from the most authoritative source on this subject, the latest report of the National Industrial

Conference Board. When President Hoover addressed the twenty-fifth annual conference of the National Tax Association last October, he said, "Along with the necessity for drastic tax reduction, the most pressing fiscal problem of the day is to adjust the state and local taxes to modern conditions so as to relieve the burden which now presses so inequitably upon the farmer and small home owner," and this is what we are trying to do with our proposal, to reapportion the tax burden so as to get a greater and greater proportion of taxes from intangible property.

You all want your tax burden to be as light as possible. Naturally tax reduction is imperative. It is a thing which must come. At the last election you went to the polls and voted for that party that promised a twenty-five per cent cut in taxes. If every time we have a cut in taxes we apply that to the property tax, we achieve a double purpose. We relieve the owners of tangible property from an unfair burden, and automatically approach the goal of raising a fair amount which should be levied from sources other than tangible property.

Before this debate continues much further you will want to know precisely how the opposition stands on certain fundamental issues. We should like to ask, first of all, do our opponents favor tax reduction, and if so, what taxes do they propose to cut? Second, do they accept the principles of ability to pay and benefits received? If so, do they maintain that the ownership of tangible property is a fair and accurate measure of either a person's ability to pay or the benefits received from the government? If they do not accept these fundamental principles, how do they answer the unanimous testimony of economic authorities which substantiates these two fundamental doctrines, and last, do our opponents favor a state income tax?

Ladies and Gentlemen, we have come here tonight to discuss one of the most pressing problems of the day. We have come here not to cry our eyes out and tell you of the sufferings of the poor farmers and home owners, but the fact remains, that they are now bearing an unfair and intolerable burden which is demanding more than they can possibly produce. We have come here tonight to ask you to put into the background a system which has been found to be deficient in every respect. We come here to condemn a system which was tried in all European countries and entirely discarded. Now, we ask you to put the present system into the discard and to take the proposition which we are presenting tonight, which would place a fair and equitable amount of taxes upon those people who are best able to pay.

First Negative, James Moore
University of Michigan

LADIES AND GENTLEMEN: First permit me to express the gratification of both Coach McBurney and the team of the University of Michigan on being able to come up here this evening to debate the University of Wisconsin. We have had the most wonderful treatment and we hope we will see our opponents down in Ann Arbor in the near future.

In so far as the efforts of the Affirmative this evening are directed toward modernizing or perfecting the status quo, in so far as their tax suggestions are made, I think they had an idea of curing administrative difficulties, or revising existing systems, of classifying property according to type; in short, of bringing more order into the entire state and local government. So far the Negative is willing and even anxious to go. If the Gentlemen of the Affirmative are interested in clearing out the graft, the extravagance and the waste that is so much an apparent part of the difficulties of state and local government, here too they will find willing acquiescence on the part of the Negative. Efforts along these lines will do much to decrease the difficulties complained of by the preceding speaker, but, not only has he failed to take proper cognizance of these matters, but he has, in his zealous efforts to portray a picture of present conditions, overstated their importance. Of the fourteen billion dollars tax burden raised in this country every year, thirty per cent is raised by the federal government, and the federal government raises all of its taxes from intangible property. This is a significant fact. It is so significant that any tax suggestion or any tax analysis which fails to take it into consideration is not only incomplete, but most misleading. The suggestions which I point out might go, together with this fact, to put the picture in a brighter light and undoubtedly in a more accurate manner.

REVENUES FROM INTANGIBLE PROPERTY   13

The Gentlemen of the Affirmative have given us certain questions asking whether we wish to lighten the tax burden, whether we favor tax reduction, what taxes we wish to have reduced, whether we accept ability to pay and the benefit theory. The Negative wishes to make perfectly clear its stand on the use and adoption of taxes designed to broaden the tax base. The Negative admits the tax base can be broadened in some states and in some manner, but that any system or any tax suggestion made with that idea in mind must be thoroughly tested in the light of local conditions, possible future needs, and strong scientific tax principles. We of the Negative admit there are many scientific tax principles: fiscal adequacy, equity, simplicity, diversity, and many others. But obviously the proper order to take them up is fiscal adequacy first and equity second; for it is merely theorizing to talk about equity if a tax does not meet the primary object of every tax, to raise sufficient money to run the government. It is on this line that we will draw issue this evening.

For we feel that the Affirmative tax suggestion as presented to you does not meet the first real test of any tax, fiscal adequacy. We are not alone in our opinion. Professor Lutz, noted Professor of Princeton, who wrote his book on public finance, says on page 165: "This requirement (fiscal adequacy) is of such supreme importance from the practical viewpoint of the treasury that it should be placed first. To be sure mere fiscal adequacy or productivity is not enough. A tax system to be thoroughly sound and enduring must be something more than productive of sufficient revenue to meet the needs of the state. But there is little practical advantage in considering any other qualifications either of a specific tax or the tax system as a whole, unless it will produce revenue. Many beautiful schemes have been formulated on paper for the satisfaction of the states' financial needs, and some of these have attained to quite dizzy heights of idealism in the theoretical justice and equity of their provisions for the distribution of the burden of taxation. But some of these schemes have never had a chance from the outset for the simple reason that they have clearly been incapable of producing a sufficient revenue."

We feel that the Affirmative tax suggestion in the first place can not provide sufficient revenue. In the second place it can not provide a satisfactory method of distribution of the revenue, and in the third place it can not provide for a certain and reliable revenue.

In support of the first contention I am going to discuss a group of states geographically situated around the United States, all of them with a different proportion of intangible wealth, all of them drawing wealth from different sources, all of them with different local problems; but they have one thing in common and that is they make use of all the tax suggestions which the Gentlemen of the Affirmative have advocated this evening. The first state I will discuss is New York, the greatest industrial state in the Union, and the state with the greatest pile up of intangible wealth in the Union or in the civilized world. Of New York's combined state and local revenue, seventy per cent is derived from a tax on tangible property; twenty per cent from intangibles, and nine per cent from licenses and permits. Applying the Affirmative's tax suggestion this evening, which says they are only going to raise eighteen per cent of the taxes, combined state and local taxes from tangible property, we will deduct from the seventy per cent which is now raised in the city of New York the eighteen per cent, which means a shift of fifty-two per cent over to the intangible column. The Affirmative, by their various tax systems, are going to raise seventy-two per cent of their income in New York from intangible sources. New York today has all the taxes you can think of, but the Affirmative hopes to raise over four times as much by taxation of intangibles as has been done heretofore. This would mean, among other things, a sixteen cents a gallon tax on gasoline.

I bring up the State of New York for one other reason. In 1930, according to the Federal Income Statistics, we find New York paid thirty-four per cent of all money which the Federal Government raised on income tax in the United States. This income is in easily available form; it is in stocks; it is in mortgages; it is in banks; and you can get at it to tax. Contrast this, however, with the State of North Dakota, which is ninety-five per cent rural. Ninety-five per cent of their income is derived from tangible property; ninety-five per cent of their wealth is in tangible property; and, in 1929, eighty-four per cent of their taxes, combined state and local, came from tangible property, three and thirty-six hundredths from intangibles, and twelve and fifty-two hundredths from licenses and permits.

Here we have a different local situation. They don't have any high incomes in North Dakota. By Federal Statistics we find they paid two hundredths of one per cent of the Federal taxes in 1930, one seventeen hundredth as much as New York. According to the National Industrial Conference Board, the per capita current income of the farmers in North Dakota is lower than that of the New York farmers. A substantial portion of the farmer's income is received in most cases in items consumed by the farmer's family and therefore never reported as taxable income. Remember in New York they could get their taxes because they could find the sources of intangible wealth, but in the agricultural states you can not do that because the wealth is represented in bags of potatoes, bushels of wheat, and shocks of corn. The farmer may use it in his family or to feed his stock. At any rate it isn't available for taxing under the Affirmative plan.

Let us apply their plan to North Dakota. To subtract eighteen per cent from the present seventy per cent means a shift of fifty-two per cent over to the intangible column. Sixty-nine per cent is the total now to be raised on the intangibles, nineteen times as much as is raised today. They have a three per cent corporation tax in North Dakota. Under their tax it will mean a fifty-seven per cent corporation tax. It will mean a fifty-seven cent tax on gasoline. And remember the farmers are going to evade it as much as they can. Here is a local condition which the Affirmative's arbitrary plan can not meet.

Going down to the State of Mississippi we find another condition. Mississippi is seventy-five per cent rural; seventy-three per cent of their income comes from tangible property; five per cent from intangibles, and twenty per cent from licenses and permits. They contributed seven hundredths of one per cent to the Federal income tax. According to Governor Connor, "We have a local condition of few large incomes and no great industry. In order to get the Negroes, who constitute fifty-two per cent of our population to contribute anything we have had to adopt a general business tax."

This is another local condition. Applying the Affirmative's plan in the State of Mississippi, we find they would have to raise all taxes by from eight to twelve times their present amount. If they add on the taxes they contemplate, it would mean a twenty-four per cent sales tax, and a seventy-two cent tax on gasoline, where they now pay six cents. That is another local condition. Who bears the burden there? The colored people can't. The poor white man must.

I can take you out to the State of Utah. The same condition is true out there. Who will bear the burden there? The miners, because the farmers can evade the income tax. The miner can't evade and he only works one hundred days a year. Obviously the Affirmative's plan could not work in the state of Utah.

North Carolina is another example. North Carolina, by means of their income tax, supplies thirty per cent of their school fund. If they were going to supply the entire school fund they would have to raise their income tax three hundred per cent. To adopt the entire

Affirmative plan, they would have to raise the tax rates on intangibles twelve hundred per cent. So we conclude from a survey of our states around the Union that the Affirmative plan can not work because it can not get sufficient revenue; because these intangibles can not be taxed in such a manner as to assure collection of the tax.

We of the Negative in presenting our analysis have propounded a question for the Affirmative. We wish the Gentlemen would explain to us what substantial reasons they can give for setting fifty per cent as the maximum amount to be derived from tangible property in each of the forty-eight states? Why must a state like North Dakota be allowed no opportunity to obtain no more than fifty per cent from tangible property, why not sixty per cent, or seventy per cent? Why do they have any maximum of any per cent? We wish the next Affirmative speaker to answer this question: what substantial reasons can the Affirmative give for setting fifty per cent of revenue as the maximum to be derived from tangible property in each of the forty-eight states?

Second Affirmative, O. Glenn Stahl
University of Wisconsin

LADIES AND GENTLEMEN: The preceding speaker has just propounded the question, "What substantial reasons do we present for setting fifty per cent as the maximum revenue to be derived from tangible property in each of the forty-eight states?" That is like asking us why we are debating the Affirmative side of this question. In the course of my speech it is my purpose to point out just exactly what the opposition seems to want. They want to know how our plan is going to work; is it going to be practical? First of all, you notice they went over every state they could possibly find that they thought might be a good illustration of where our plan would not work, and among these was North Dakota. They forgot to pick out another agricultural state, North Carolina. North Carolina is an agricultural state as much as North Dakota, as much as the rest of these are, and yet it has been able within the last year to get forty-eight per cent of its state and local revenue from sources other than tangible property. It happens that North Dakota has three times the per capita wealth of North Carolina and four times the per capita income of North Carolina, according to the *World Almanac*.

The Gentleman of the Opposition very casually mentioned our questions but he did not answer them. He did not say whether or not they actually agreed with these fundamental principles of ability to pay or benefits received. He said nothing about how the present property tax is bearing too heavily on property owners, and leading to tax delinquency and the exemption of many forms of taxable ability.

Our program, already explained to you by my colleague, calls for a little more amplification. We are approaching this from the standpoint of where the state and local costs go, what they are being expended for. First of all, we found that the governmental services going to people in general; education, public welfare, publicly owned utilities and the like, represent fifty-eight per cent of state and local costs. Highways represent twenty-four per cent of the state and local costs, while general government and personal protection to property represent only eighteen per cent. On the basis of this we have arranged our program, and that my opponents may be perfectly clear as to what this program is, I present them with the copy which my colleague promised.

The first item is to retain the real estate tax, as my colleague pointed out, to the extent of eighteen per cent, to cover the last group of costs. The second item is motor vehicle taxes, gasoline and auto licenses, to cover the cost of highways. Highways represent twenty-four per cent of state and local costs. The third item is to cover those wider costs of government, education and public welfare, fifty-eight per cent, with a direct tax on the people. The authors of the Model Plan of the National Tax Association, the greatest body of experts on taxes in this country, speak of the personal income tax in this regard as a direct tax on the people: "It is better fitted than any other to carry out the principle that every person having taxable ability shall make a reasonable contribution to the government." The business and personal income tax, supplemented by the inheritance tax, is our means of supporting those general costs of government which go to people in general. It would mean, then, that in the average state at least eighty-two per cent of the revenue would be derived from sources other than tangible property. Of course, within each state this could be varied to fit particular conditions.

But what about the productivity, what about the sufficiency of the revenues of which the Gentleman of the Opposition speaks? Motor vehicle taxes at the present time are already supporting highway systems in several states. North Carolina, for example, with a six cent gasoline tax, is supporting every highway in the state; county, state and local. The gas tax has particularly shown itself to be an easy and cheaply administered source of revenue. The gas tax throughout the United States costs for administration only three tenths of one per cent of its total yield. The State of Virginia is getting twenty-one and one-half per cent of its revenue from motor vehicle taxes; South Carolina is getting twenty-five and one-half per cent of its state and local revenue from motor vehicle taxes. Obviously, gas and auto licenses are perfectly adequate to be applied in any state to cover their entire highway program. In this respect our program has shown itself capable of raising sufficient revenue in any state in the union, whether agricultural or industrial.

The income tax requires a little more explanation. The Gentleman of the Opposition who has just spoken has confused you by seeming to think that when we take the burden off property, we can't get the income in any other way. May I remind you that in the long run, no matter what kind of tax is assessed, the tax has to be paid out of income. The North Carolina Tax Commission says, "In the ultimate analysis it is income which circumscribes the limits of taxation and determines tax paying capacity." Richard T. Ely, the famous economist whose textbook is used in all parts of the country, says, "Nearly all taxes must be paid out of income. The specific tax employed is merely a device for distributing the tax." Why, then, should we employ a poor method of distribution? Why measure the capacity of a person to pay according to the so-called "market value" of a piece of property he happens to own? If there is any income from that property the income tax will get it; if there is no income, the income tax will get the revenue where income is being derived. If there is any income in the community at all the income tax can get it, since practically all taxes have to be paid out of income. The income tax can get at the income as well as, if not better than, any other tax.

Our proposal, then, would involve the extension of the income tax base further than it is now being used in the several states. It would mean two things: lowering the exemption from income tax, and bringing in other forms of income not now used. If we lower the exemption in accordance with the Model Plan of the National Tax Association, we will have this extension. The Model Plan brings exemption down to six hundred dollars for a single man, twelve hundred dollars for the head of a family, or two hundred dollars for each dependent. There are only one or two states in the entire union which have even approached these exemptions. It would widen the base to a sufficient extent so we could get revenue. Many states exempt dividends from domestic corporations, and yet dividends and interest throughout the United States represented twenty-four per cent of the total taxable personal incomes in 1928, the latest year for which the figures were available. Incomes from copyrights and patents have been made taxable by a decision of the Supreme Court, and this could be included as a form of income, and, may I remind you, the Model Plan says: "The personal income tax shall be levied in respect of the citizen's entire income from all sources."

Again to summarize our program, it means we will support those actual protection and general government costs, eighteen per cent of the state and local revenue throughout the country, with a real estate tax; secondly, to cover support of highways, twenty-four per cent of state and local revenue, with gasoline and auto license taxes; and third, to cover expenditures going to the people in general, like education, social welfare, sanitation, fifty-eight per cent of the state and local costs, chiefly with business and personal income taxes supplemented by the inheritance tax. As I already pointed out, the program which we are upholding is not only practicable from the standpoint of what it could do. It is already being done. I have mentioned that the State of North Carolina is getting forty-eight per cent of all state and local revenue from sources other than tangible property.

Governor Gardner in 1931 pointed out: "An important consideration is the fact that the greatest relief is given where relief is needed,—that is to agricultural lands." North Carolina, a predominantly agricultural state, is not the only example. There are other states.

South Carolina has gone to the extent of getting forty-five per cent of state and local revenue from sources other than tangible property, and it is even more of an agricultural state. That was true in 1930, and yet at the end of December 1931 South Carolina had a cash balance on hand of six million five hundred thousand dollars. This plan is certainly bringing in the revenue in South Carolina.

Here is the State of Virginia. At the end of 1931 it was getting fifty-two and one-half per cent of its state and local revenue from sources other than tangible property, and finally we come to the State of Delaware, which in 1930 already was getting seventy-two per cent of its state and local revenue from these sources other than tangible property. It is clear then, that our program not only by all indications would be practicable—it is already being put into actual operation and is producing the sufficient revenue of which the Gentleman of the Opposition has spoken.

The State of Wisconsin raises only thirty per cent of its state and local taxes from sources other than tangible property. The State of Michigan gets not quite twenty per cent from those sources. The new program might well be extended here as elsewhere.

Now, in view of the fact, as my colleague has pointed out, that the present system has resulted in an intolerable burden on property owners; has resulted in this tax delinquency, which the opposition has so far not mentioned; and has resulted also in the exemption of many forms of taxable ability: in view of the fact that this program is already practicable and put into operation in several states of the union, it is only right to assume that it is time for recognition of the soundness of the program we are advocating, as well as the justice of that program,—of the practicability of that program, the feasibility of getting at least fifty per cent,—if not as much as eighty-two per cent, although we are willing to go that far,—at least fifty per cent of all state and local revenues from sources other than tangible property.

Second Negative, Victor Rabinowitz
University of Michigan

LADIES AND GENTLEMEN: There seems to be a number of questions flying back and forth here. I would like first to repeat our question which the Gentlemen of the Opposition stated by saying or suggesting—I will read the question again first: "What substantial reasons can the Affirmative give for setting fifty per cent of revenue as the maximum to be derived from tangible property in each of the forty-eight states?" The Gentlemen answered the question by saying they were debating the Affirmative. What reason is that for believing fifty per cent of revenue can be raised from tangible property? Is it merely because they have to do this, because they were assigned to the Affirmative side of this proposition?

Their questions,—there are quite a number of them and we didn't get all of them,—but they can be all answered finally as my colleague answered them, by saying that all of those questions depend on local conditions, depend on conditions in the state. A blanket answer can not be given to any of those questions. We favor a state income tax where a state income tax, in view of local conditions, is desirable. In New York state, for instance, a state income tax is desirable. It has been working to some extent for some time. It has not been working nearly to the extent the Gentlemen of the Opposition advocate, but it has been working there for some time. In the State of Wisconsin you have your income tax. In the State of North Dakota we believe any substantial increase in their present income tax would be highly inadvisable. They have also spent quite a bit of time on North Carolina. North Carolina is getting forty-eight per cent of their income from tangible property. Well, in the first place that is North Carolina's plan for the next year. They have not collected that yet. In the second place I might point out the state debt in the State of North Carolina has increased from ten million to one hundred seventy million in the last ten years, so perhaps North Carolina has not an ideal tax system at the present time.

They quoted a number of other states. I believe some of these states were raising seventy-two per cent from sources other than tangible property. If the Gentlemen of the Opposition will either add their figures over again, or give a bit more detail we will discuss it, but the figures we have down do not anywhere approach that. Finally, the Gentlemen of the Affirmative have cheerfully assumed all the way through that an income tax and an ability-to-pay tax was synonymous. They have made no attempt to prove an income tax is a tax on ability to pay. It is quite obvious a man with an income of two thousand dollars living in the city of Madison has less ability to pay than a man with an income of two thousand dollars living in a rural community where the cost of living is much lower. That is one of the many problems.

This problem of shifting taxes is another problem that must be considered in deciding that an income tax and tax on ability to pay are synonymous. The Gentlemen of the Opposition should spend a bit of time in proving this assumption.

Our first speaker pointed out that the Affirmative tax suggestion can not provide a sufficient amount of money in all forty-eight states. He showed how high the income tax would have to be increased in the States of North Carolina and North Dakota. They want to raise fifty-eight per cent of their taxation from an income tax. At the present time North Carolina raises one per cent of its taxes from an income tax. They suggested a minimum exemption of six hundred dollars. That means, if the income tax was increased in North Carolina fifty-eight times, as it would have to be at the least, they would have a rate of fifty-eight per cent on an income of six hundred dollars. We believe that a tax as high as that in an agricultural community where taxes are easily evaded can not possibly be collected. There is no way of checking how much a farmer uses every year. There is no way of checking what a farmer's income is, and throughout the entire middle west everywhere from the Mississippi River to the Rocky Mountains those are all agricultural states where your incomes are farm incomes and they can not be checked. Attempting to place such an exorbitant tax on farm incomes will result in evasion. I will proceed to prove that the Affirmative tax suggestion can not provide a satisfactory method of disposition of whatever revenue they do collect.

It is quite obvious a tax must not only collect enough money, but must collect money in a form that it can easily be used. Mere collection of money is not sufficient. At the present time the states collect on an average of thirty per cent of the total state and local government. Under the Affirmative proposal they would collect on the average, eighty-four per cent of the state and local revenue. That means the states will be collecting fifty-four per cent more than they are collecting at the present time. Now, one of two things must happen to that fifty-four per cent. Either the money must be redistributed to the localities so that they can use it, or it is used by the state, resulting in an increased centralization of state and local functions.

We would like to point out that this problem has risen in two or three states at the present time where an attempt is made to redistribute funds. We would like to point out no state has solved that problem at the present time, and no state attempts to redistribute more than ten per cent of the state and local revenue. The Gentlemen of the Opposition are increasing that ten per cent to eighty-four per cent. The problem has not been solved at the present time. New York and Wisconsin both have the problem and both tax commissions complain that the problem has not been solved. The Gentlemen of the Opposition in proposing this tremendous increase must propose some satisfactory method of solution. There are two possibilities here. Either the state will redistribute this eighty-four per cent to the local units, or the state will use the additional fifty-four per cent itself. I will discuss both of those possibilities briefly.

If the state redistributes this additional fifty-four per cent to the localities, some method of redistribution must be devised. There are three methods of redistribution in common practice today: redistribution according to the amount received, redistribution according to the population of the community, and redistribution according to the need of the community. We believe that none of these methods has proved satisfactory. In the first place, redistribution according to the amount received from the locality—it is impossible to set a rate that will provide both rural and urban units with enough money. If your rate is large enough to supply the rural unit with enough money from the income tax, it will be so large you will have a tremendous surplus in the cities; on the other hand, if the rate is small enough to get the cities what they need, the rural units will have nothing. As regards the income tax, the State of Wisconsin has found this method results in unsolved administrative difficulties, since it is impossible to tell where any large corporation or individual gets his income. In what locality, for instance, does a railroad or public utility get its income. Finally, it will afford no relief to the rural areas because most of these taxes will come from the cities, and, as the Gentlemen of the Opposition have pointed out, the difficulties and alleged evils are greatest in the rural areas.

Secondly, since population bears no constant relation to the need of the community or amount received, redistribution according to the population is wholly irrational. Finally, redistribution according to need would seem at first sight to be the most likely; each community to get what it needed. There are, however, some very fundamental difficulties. It involves entirely too great an amount of discretion on the part of the distributing official, whether that be the governor, the budget commission, tax commission, or legislature. Whoever they may be, some person or group of persons must decide on the needs of each community. Granting the most favorable conditions possible—assuming that these men are honest and capable and sincere, it is impossible for a rural legislator or rural administrator to estimate the needs of an urban community. He can not do it. His point of view is different. Likewise an urban administrator can not say what a local unit needs. He doesn't know what the needs of a rural unit are. And when we realize that in some cases the administrators are not always perfectly sincere and not always perfectly capable, and in some cases not honest, this difficulty increases a thousand fold.

The second difficulty is that the communities get money they don't raise and don't get money they raise. That has been found to be true in communities where large communities raising a great deal of money get very little, while poorer communities contributing little get a great deal back. And finally the increasing rural-urban conflict in the legislature, a problem very great in all states at the present time, a problem that will be increased many times by the Affirmative's proposition.

The other possibility is that the state take on some of the local governmental functions. We believe that the Gentlemen of the Opposition have not advocated this and we are not going into it in great detail until they do so, but it results in increased centralization, a dogged backing away from the present principle of home rule which has been growing so rapidly in the United States for the last fifty or sixty years.

It results in all the evils of increased centralization, the evils of log rolling in the legislature, deciding what the salary of the dog catcher or school teacher shall be. All of these difficulties will be increased many times by a revision of our present policy, a backing away from home rule. This problem, even where the state distributes so small an amount as ten per cent, has not been satisfactorily solved in any state in the United States today. The Gentlemen of the Opposition are proposing to return not ten per cent, but fifty-four per cent. The problem will obviously be greatly increased. What is your solution?

Third Affirmative, Harry L. Cole
University of Wisconsin

LADIES AND GENTLEMEN: The first Negative speaker began by saying there were certain improvements needed in tax administration, and they would not object to certain improvements which would go a long way to correct the injustices of the present situation, and then he proceeded to object to the chief improvements which have been made in the last two years and are being made now in the tax system. In the States of North Carolina, Virginia and Delaware they have already worked out these problems of administration which the Gentlemen of the Opposition are telling you can not be worked out. Moreover, in European countries, where they take a much larger proportion of the people's income in taxes, they have for years successfully taken that large share through the process of taxation of intangibles and not through the use of the property tax.

The whole argument of the Negative so far in this debate,—their whole objection to our program of raising eighteen per cent of the taxes needed for local revenue from real estate taxes, our proposal to raise twenty-four per cent for highways from a motor vehicle and gas tax, and the fifty-eight per cent needed for general welfare and educational activities from income and inheritance taxes,—their whole objection has been a matter of administrative impracticability, and our answer to this is that it can be done because it is being done. It is being done in Delaware, Virginia, and North Carolina. But the Gentlemen say it isn't being done in North Carolina. Your statistics are not right on that. Our authority for our statistics on the percentage of revenue raised or derived from tangible property in these states is the work on *Federal and State Tax Systems* by the Tax Research Foundation published by the Commerce Clearing House of Chicago in January, 1932. All of these statistics for all the states may be found in this document.

However, that is not the only source of this information which is generally known throughout the whole world of people who are at all informed on this tax question. For instance, in the *Saturday Evening Post*, Governor Gardner of North Carolina discusses in some detail tax reforms and centralization and lifting the burden from tangible property in North Carolina. Governor Gardner discussed in some detail what they accomplished in 1931. In 1931 they raised forty-eight per cent of their total state and local revenue from sources other than tangible property, and since that time they have increased their gas tax and they have reduced their property taxes so there is no doubt at all but that today North Carolina has taken its place with Delaware and Virginia and is already raising more than half of its state and local revenue from sources other than tangible property. And this centralization, this reform in taxation procedure which the first speaker said they were going to agree to, and the second speaker objected to, this reform in North Carolina has resulted in a total tax reduction and total saving to the people of seven million dollars and has resulted in a reduction in the levy on real estate of twelve million dollars.

We asked the Gentlemen some questions and they said they must interpret them in the light of local conditions, and that they couldn't make a blanket answer. We are perfectly willing that they interpret them in the light of local conditions. We don't require a blanket answer. We would be glad to have them answer each one separately, and they are of matters where the Negative stand on fundamental issues which should be considered. First, we ask, do they favor tax reduction? They have not told us. We asked them, do they accept ability to pay as the test of a just tax system—and they have not answered. And we say, do they favor a state income tax? The Commission appointed in Michigan to investigate the status of taxation in that state recommended a state income tax. The people in the State of Michigan a month ago today voted for a limit of one and one-half per cent on their property levy, and with that limitation the communities of Michigan are going to be faced with very drastic reduction of revenue, and their schools are going to be closed, as they are in Indiana with a similar limitation in effect, and if the Gentlemen don't adopt this which their State Commission recommends they are going to be in pretty hard financial straits—just as they are this winter but not so badly as they will be next.

They have asked us a question—Why do we favor a fifty per cent limit, why do we believe that more than half of all state and local revenues should be derived from sources other than tangible property? We believe this because the present burden on tangible property is intolerably unjust and can not be justified either in theory or by the way it works out in practice. We believe it should be more than fifty per cent because such a plan is feasible and practical as shown where it is already working, and we believe this should be done because we will have a more equitable tax system when it is done.

I will now consider the comparative equity or justice of the tax apportionment defended by the Negative and the tax apportionment which we advocate. Professor F. G. Crawford of Syracuse says, "Relief from the burden on realty is imperative. All tax commissions without exception agree to this statement." Now, this lopsided apportionment stands indicted by the grand jury of the world economists and tax experts on four counts: *First*, injustice in share of income taken; *second*, injustice to the farmer; *third*, injustice of tax delinquency; and *fourth*, injustice to home owners. Let us consider the evidence upon these four indictments and see what way our program would eliminate these injustices.

Indictment Number One: Injustice in the share of income taken. You recall the instance of the four Wisconsin farmers with practically no net income who were taxed more than twenty-five coupon clippers. That is an example of the inequity in the share of income taken when you compare those who derive their incomes from intangible property as compared with those who derive their incomes from tangible property. Professor Jens Peter Jensen, Professor of Economics at Syracuse University, says: "The property tax often requires contributions where there is no income but fails to reach a great deal of income capable of paying taxes."

The National Industrial Conference Board in its

impartial study of the *State and Local Taxation System,* page 6, says, "Studies of taxation invariably indicate that property taxes take widely varying proportions of the income from different types of property." In 1931 the percentage of the rent taken in taxes varied from nineteen to ninety per cent, a variation of sixty-one per cent, and in the State of North Carolina, before the reform which we advocate was put into effect, in one county, the percentage of the rent taken was five per cent. In another county, two hundred seventy-seven per cent, a variation of two hundred seventy-two per cent in the percentage of rent was taken in taxes. Is an injustice like that going to be remedied by the reformed administration such as the first Speaker of the Opposition suggested?

We submit there is no correction for such injustice as this without a fundamental reapportionment of the whole burden such as we advocate.

Indictment Number Two: The injustice to the farmer. President Hoover said, "The farm relief most needed is tax relief." The farmer with one-tenth of the national income pays one-fifth of the national taxes. In the middle west there have been mortgage foreclosures by hundreds of thousands of dollars, robbing farm families of their homes and livelihood, and sending them to join the ranks of our cities' unemployed, feeding on charity in the cities.

Henry I. Harriman, president of the United States Chamber of Commerce, speaking to the American Farm Bureau Federation in Chicago, day before yesterday, said taxes take more than the farmer's net income in many fertile areas today. Sixty per cent of agricultural land has been forfeited in one state. In 1914, agricultural taxes took one-third of the value of the total wheat crop. In 1931 they took twice the value of the total wheat crop. Will an injustice like that be corrected by a technical administration in the reform of the property tax? The reform we advocate would lift half the burden from the backs of the farmer.

Indictment Number Three: Tax delinquency. Tax delinquency is simply a result of demanding taxes from people who are unable to pay them. When we redistribute the major part of the burden according to the people's ability to pay each year by their income, we will have done away with that.

Indictment Number Four: Injustice to property holders and home owners. According to the committee on taxation of President Hoover's Conference on Home Building and Home Ownership, the overburdening tax on real estate discourages and materially restricts home ownership.

Now, by readjusting the major portion of the tax burden on the basis of ability to pay as indicated by income, we do away with a great portion of these injustices, and we take a great burden from the farmer's back.

We do away with tax delinquency and protect the home owners, thus facing the four injustices which tax experts have condemned, the overburdening of the property tax, injustice of share of income taken, injustice to the farmer, and injustice of tax delinquency, and injustice to the home owner.

In conclusion I will again state the fundamental

propositions of the Affirmative case. They are these: *First,* the heavy tax burden on tangible property is unjust, both in theory and practice. It is not justified by the benefit theory or the ability-to-pay principle of taxation. It is condemned by our leading tax authorities and in practice it puts an intolerable burden upon certain incomes, and during a period of economic stress there are a large number of tax delinquencies, and a serious curtailment of government service when it is most desperately needed. *Second,* the plan is adequate and practicable as proven by the fact that in Europe larger proportions are taken by income tax, and by the fact that in America during the past two years nearly every state has come to derive an increased share of its revenue from income tax. *Third,* the apportionment of the tax burden we advocate is more equitable than the apportionment defended by our opponents as evidenced by the fact that we would reapportion the tax burden according to the income of the citizens by their ability to pay, as indicated by their income. For these reasons we advocate at least a fifty per cent limit in an effort to get at a more just tax system.

Third Negative, Nathan Levy
University of Michigan

LADIES AND GENTLEMEN: It would appear offhand that the questions are running around here without any owners, without any backers, without any sponsors. Both sides are trying to give the idea that the other side has not answered the questions. Do you want to reduce the taxes? Is there anybody who would say, "Increase them right away. Let's step this trouble up about one hundred per cent." I wish to point out, as did my colleague the first speaker, as far as the Opposition wish to do away with waste and extravagance they will find us hand in hand with them. They say, do you recognize the ability to pay? We have been demonstrating first of all you have got to place a good share of the burden upon those able to pay. Therefore, I would conclude from that we are in some measure backing up the benefit theory.

If the Gentlemen of the Opposition remember, my colleague said, that we advocate a state income tax, which by the way they have not proved is an ability-to-pay tax, in a state if it can use it and to that degree in which it seems wise to use it.

So much for these questions. And will the Gentlemen please tell us what substantial reasons—I don't want them to say the reasons are equity and adequacy, those are words—we would like to know the reasons they have for advocating fifty per cent as the maximum of dependence to be placed on intangible property as a source of revenue in each of the forty-eight states. Well, the Gentlemen of the Opposition in the first speech told you about how troubled the times were, and how heavy the tax burden is on certain people. We thought after they had finished that talk of that matter we would be through with that part, but no, the third speech also was devoted to telling you about the injustices of these various things. Two speeches have now been devoted in full, and the other speaker got in a good many mentions of the injustices of this tax burden.

We have been trying to talk to you about fiscal adequacy. When they can show you they collected in 1932 a gas tax in the State of Utah on this eighty-two per cent basis—that may vary from state to state, but they didn't tell us because they don't know, but approximately eighty-two per cent in Utah for 1932 on each and every gallon of gasoline sold in that state— they will say we can't do that, we will have just a little tax on gasoline. If they do they will put it on some other tax that will approach fifty per cent, or sixty per cent, or seventy per cent on income. It has to be gotten from some place.

They have quoted the National Industrial Conference Board so much perhaps it would not be a bad idea for us to do that. The National Industrial Conference Board published that book on that table. That book concerns doing away with a burden of four million dollars additional revenue in Missouri. That whole book is a fight. The experts are weighing the possibilities, the probabilities, the practicalities, and the injustice of making out of increase of income tax enough to collect four million dollars more, which is about eight per cent of the total state and local revenue in the State of Missouri. They don't say you can do it. They say, no, you can't, just by increasing income tax. Evasion in Missouri is too great and too easy, so we will try in part, little by little, and find out if we can. If we can and we find it is fair, perhaps we will increase it. But "equity" has been here before you so much you probably think by this time that the Negative has no care—we don't care about how fair, how just, how equitable a tax system is, and that the farmer who pays two hundred seventy-seven per cent of his income from land in taxes gets no sympathy from us.

We told you first of all the Gentlemen overstated their case. They didn't tell you about the Federal tax burden of four billion dollars a year. If I only had a portion of it, I would be willing to pay taxes on it any time. The Gentlemen of the Opposition have now set up their scheme and they are committed to this much, at least fifty per cent, but their scheme says eighty-two per cent. They have got to prove that is fair and just. They have said ability to pay is a good basis. The benefit theory is a good basis. We are going to consider just a few taxes that amount to eighteen per cent or less on ability to pay, on motor vehicle taxes and gas taxes. In other words, they have reduced the problems of taxes by a snap of the fingers. The ability-to-pay tax is a simple thing. All you do is tax incomes—taxes on all kinds of income—but how tax them; how make any allowance for difference in purchasing power? They talk about the difficulty we are having at the present time about the farmer whose wheat is not worth anything. Do they forget in the income tax you are not paying this year's money, you are paying last year's tax this year, and if you haven't got any income this year and last year you had a good one, where are you going to get the money to pay that. You have got to borrow.

The point is this. You can demonstrate cases of

hardship under peculiar and stressing circumstances in any tax system for the simple reason that perfection is not as easy to obtain as the Gentlemen would have you believe. You simply can't wiggle waggle your hands at two theories and say, "We will prove it," and I am going to prove that to you in the state most favorable to the Gentlemen of the Opposition, the State of New York. If their proposition of fifty per cent or more on intangible property is not just in the state of New York where the greatest pile up of intangibles known in the history of the human being is to be found, then it isn't equitable, fair or just anywhere in the country, in any single state in this Union. And so we turn to the report of the New York State Commission for the revision of the tax laws published in 1932. May I point out that on this Commission was the man recognized as the greatest authority in the United States, Professor Seligman of Columbia, Commissioner Haig, the gentleman who draws up most of these reports, and other men of equal caliber in the State of New York. Before I go into this report I want to quote this Model Plan of state taxation they have referred to so much. I wish to point out this Model Plan is based on three kinds of taxes, tangible property tax, personal net income tax, and business tax.

The experts did not attempt to set any percentage of dependence which should be placed on those taxes in all states because they recognized the divergence of local conditions. However, our Friends have been putting specific percentages on each one of those taxes. I quoted from the report of this Tax Commission in

New York to demonstrate exactly how the Gentlemen of the Opposition approached this question in discussing the proposition of inequity and injustice, and to give you the idea the experts have with respect to that approach. "If it can be shown that the owners of real estate pay heavier taxes than owners of other property, is this to be considered a demonstration that the burden on real estate is disproportionate?" The Commission goes on, "The answer to this question seems to be definitely 'no.' An affirmative answer to this question seems to assume that the equitable tax system is one which imposes a levy at a uniform rate on all classes of property. It ignores the shifting of taxes, which may distort completely the initial appearance of equity. It denies the validity of benefit as a test for certain forms of taxes. It does not take into account the possible funding or capitalization of taxes. It leaves no place for the introduction of progression. An indictment based on any one of these points would be sufficient to discredit the use of this test of disproportion."

The single norm of property or income is not the only norm for approximate ability to pay. A combination of several norms is superior to the use of any single norm.

So when this Tax Commission set to work out what would be equitable distribution in the State of New York, they came to this conclusion. The majority felt that real property in the State of New York, tangible property, should bear a burden of fifty-three and two tenths per cent in order to have an equitable distribution of a tax in that state. The minority in that state felt real estate should pay fifty-five and six tenths per cent—fifty-three and two tenths per cent the majority, —fifty-five and six tenths per cent the minority,— among whom was Professor Seligman of Columbia. Professor Seligman goes on further to say if any real appreciation were had of the shifting of taxes in that state the percentage of the dependence of the tax on real estate would be greater than that. That is the situation in the State of New York, the state most favorable to the Opposition.

I am not arguing about fifty-three and two tenths per cent or fifty-five and six tenths per cent. My point is that if the percentage is in favor of taxes on tangible property in the State of New York, the percentage increases and increases in other states of the Union. If the Gentlemen can not show its equity in that state, they can not show its equity in any one of the forty-eight states. If we admit this five per cent is not the thing we are basing our case on, we do not admit anything at all, because in the other forty-seven states, the pile up of intangibles is not nearly as great as in the State of New York.

I did not get around to my constructive speech, but since you all read the *Saturday Evening Post* you know how far behind the Federal Government is in their tax collection, placing their full dependence upon the sources which the Gentlemen of the Opposition advocate.

First Negative Rebuttal, James Moore
University of Michigan

LADIES AND GENTLEMEN: The debate has developed along very interesting lines this evening. We attempted in our first speech to lay out what we thought was the cardinal principle for any system of taxation, fiscal adequacy. The Affirmative have failed to meet us on any portion of it, but have been talking about equity or ability or anything else but fiscal adequacy. My colleague, the second speaker, brought before you for your attention, a very vital portion of the tax situation facing the states today, involving the disposition of all revenue collected. The Gentlemen of the Affirmative passed it off as a mere detail. Yes, it was a mere detail! It is a mere detail which involves an expenditure of fifty-four per cent of all tax money. It is a mere detail but it has not been solved by a single state in the Union today. We do wish the Gentlemen would get a little further down into the details of the matter because it is a vital fact that must be answered.

Now, the Gentlemen have been talking about two things. On one side they have told you about income tax. They have not yet shown income tax to be correlated with ability to pay, and on the other hand they have been advocating a very heavy gas tax, or a gas tax which amounts to fifty-eight per cent of the state revenue. They say we pick out just a few states where it might seem bad. If you will recall my words, these states are representative of different geographical groups throughout the United States. I took them because they were states favorable to the Affirmative. They are representative states from each group. The State of New York by their plan will put in a tax of forty-four cents a gallon on gasoline. They now have a tax of seventeen dollars upon motor vehicles. Under the Affirmative plan it would be sixty dollars per motor vehicle. Is this an ability-to-pay tax or is this equity? The State of North Dakota would pay fifty-seven cents gas tax. They would charge you one hundred ninety dollars a year to run a motor vehicle in the State of North Dakota. In Illinois it would cost two hundred fifty-eight dollars a year. In Utah it would cost two hundred dollars a year, in Mississippi one hundred fifty dollars a year, and in Oregon one hundred fifty-two dollars a year.

Now, the Gentlemen also told you they were going to raise a given proportion of the income by income taxes, and apply this to education. Just think of it. Education is the one thing that we can't fool with in any state and local government. It is the one thing you must safeguard; it is the one thing for which you must guarantee money, so that the children can be educated, so that schools can go along. The Gentlemen are going to put education at the mercy of a tax in North Dakota which will be fifty-eight per cent on an income of six hundred dollars, and they expect to raise the money that way to run the school system. Not only the State of North Dakota, but I can give you twenty states which are in analogous situations, where the twenty states together only contributed eight per cent into the total Federal income in the year 1930.

Therefore we know that in those twenty states they do not have large incomes. The Gentlemen have set their own arbitrary mark as to the exemption of the income —six hundred dollars. In the State of North Dakota it would be taxed fifty-eight per cent, a correspondingly heavy tax in the others, and they expect to gain the money in spite of the fact that the door is open for evasion. They are going to use taxes that the Federal Government regards as extremely problematical, and put the education system at the mercy of it.

They say some of our system would not work. They were mere details too, and yet Governor Connor of the State of Missouri in the *Saturday Evening Post* of July 27 says that at a single legislative session, without disturbing any governmental function or legislative function, we cut our budget and reduced our expenses thirty-three and one-third per cent. Now, I think there is probably a pretty big point in sitting down and paying attention to correcting a little bit of the waste and graft and extravagance rampant in most state and local governments. We do wish the Gentlemen would give us an answer to our first question, would pay a little more attention to my colleague, the second speaker, regarding the distribution of the revenue.

First Affirmative Rebuttal, David August
University of Wisconsin

LADIES AND GENTLEMEN: Our opponents have asked the question why, with a slight change and readjustment can we not maintain a sufficiently good tax system to remedy the present evils without going over to the plan presented by our side of raising at least one-half of all state and local revenues from sources other than tangible property. Would a slight change improve the situation of four Wisconsin farmers who have to pay forty-one cents more than the combined tax bill of twenty-five coupon clippers who sit at home and clip three million dollars of coupons? Would a slight change remedy that situation?

They have accused us of overstating the case, of making an emotional appeal. Ladies and Gentlemen, I have understated the case. If I could only tell you of the suffering that goes on in our country, not merely because of an inadequate tax system, but also because of the vicious circle of tax delinquency! If you will be so kind as to remember as far back as my first speech, I want to point out again the fact of tax delinquency, which the Gentlemen have failed to answer, which is twenty-seven per cent in Detroit, thirty-two per cent in Buffalo, and in rural districts from thirty per cent to sixty per cent. And they come to us and say the main issue in this debate is fiscal adequacy--how are you going to raise sufficient revenue? We answer by saying this, "You are not raising sufficient revenue at the present time, and we have proposed to you a system which will work out as is shown by the state of Delaware, which is now raising seventy-two per cent of its revenue from sources other than tangible property; Virginia, fifty-two per cent; North Carolina, forty-eight per cent; and South Carolina, forty-five per cent."

REVENUES FROM INTANGIBLE PROPERTY 49

Ladies and Gentlemen, the third speaker came before you and said we are coming before you and *(snapping fingers)* just like that settling all the questions. No, not just like that! *(snapping fingers)*. We have taken a thorough and careful analysis of this situation, and have shown you first of all that the present situation is intolerable, that tax delinquency is eating a hole out of the revenue which the Gentlemen of the Opposition want to get from the property tax, a system which has been discarded by every single European nation. Then we went on to show the feasibility of our plan; the states in which it is working, and proved it is producing a more equitable situation.

What are the objections which the Gentlemen raise to our fundamental proposition? They say that income taxes can be shifted. Let us see what the Minnesota State Tax Commission says about this after a thorough analysis and study. The Commission says:

"Can an income tax be shifted? While some hold to the view that such taxes cast a burden on the consuming public, most students of taxation hold to the theory that the burden of a general income tax ordinarily rests upon the taxpayer upon whom the tax was first imposed. Only in very rare cases can the burden of an income tax be shifted to others. This conclusion is quite generally concurred in by tax administrators in states having effective income tax laws." *(Minnesota Tax Commission—1930. Page 137.)*

This conclusion is quite generally concurred in by tax administrators in states having effective income tax laws!

Ladies and Gentlemen, I can not help stressing the fact of the vicious circle of tax delinquency. If you have tax delinquency such as Detroit and Buffalo you necessarily impose a heavier share upon the people who must pay the taxes, and the higher the taxes the more tax delinquency and the bigger the hole you put in the revenue. Gentlemen, I will say again, we have not come here tonight to overstate the case or to make an emotional appeal to you, to say, "This is a wonderful tax, a good tax, and you should take it." No, Gentlemen, we are not coming with a Utopia. We are not saying we are going to cast aside all evils, but I will say this, and this is not an overstatement: if we can present a system which will through the progress of the years bring us a little further toward our goal; come a little closer to fundamental doctrines and principles, and bring about a more equitable situation of the burden, I feel that we can rightfully ask you to vote "Yes" on the motion before the house.

Second Negative Rebuttal, Victor Rabinowitz
University of Michigan

LADIES AND GENTLEMEN: I would like to say one or two things about these coupon clippers in Wisconsin who are sitting at home clipping coupons and are not paying any money to the upkeep of the government. They cut, according to the first speaker, a total of three million dollars and didn't pay a cent for it. Those twenty-four coupon clippers paid seven hundred thirty-one thousand four hundred sixty dollars to the Federal

Government in federal income tax alone; a total of, well a bit over twenty-five per cent of their total income went to the Federal Government. The Gentlemen of the Opposition have said they don't pay anything at all to the state government, we are going to plaster another twenty-five per cent on them. Well, then, you are taking entirely too much from these poor coupon clippers and perhaps next year the Opposition will come up here and say, why, the farmers in Wisconsin are paying so much money on their property, and the poor coupon clippers are paying fifty per cent of their income in income tax, let us reduce the income tax, we are putting too much on intangibles.

The Gentlemen have completely failed to take into consideration the federal situation. They have assumed all the way through that the only taxes we pay are to the state and local governments yet the Federal Government levied not a cent on taxable property, and these coupon clippers pay now twenty-five per cent of their income to the Federal Government. Do the Gentlemen of the Opposition favor increasing this burden to a considerable extent in Wisconsin? Obviously, your tax burden on the intangible property would then be too heavy.

I would like you to note that the National Industrial Conference Board pointed out that a tax as high as thirty per cent on an income to three hundred thousand dollars is too high because it results in evasion; yet the Gentlemen of the Opposition are going to levy a fifty-eight per cent tax on an income of six hundred dollars in North Dakota, and make it pay the expenses of education in that state. If thirty per cent on three hundred thousand dollars leads to evasion, what about fifty-eight per cent on six hundred dollars in an agricultural state?

The Gentlemen of the Opposition have said a great deal about fiscal adequacy. They have spoken about the tremendous delinquency in the State of Michigan. Arthur W. Bromage, who is a present member of the Michigan State Tax Commission discusses the problem of tax delinquency. Does he say the amount of tax delinquency in Michigan is due to too heavy a tax? No. He says it is due to waste and extravagance in county government. That is the reason for the tremendous tax delinquency in the State of Michigan.

Whereas in the beginning the Gentlemen of the Opposition were moving with tremendous strides toward this Utopian plan, they are now beginning to weaken in their claims. My colleague pointed to the State of New York, certainly a state most favorable to the Gentlemen of the Opposition; certainly the state with the greatest amount of taxable intangible wealth, and showed that there the Tax Commission, composed of the best talent available finds that at the most, fifty-five per cent, or at the least fifty-three per cent should be raised from tangible property. That leaves only forty-seven per cent from intangibles, and not eighty-four or eighty-five per cent as the Gentlemen of the Opposition have advocated this evening. That is the equitable situation in the State of New York.

What about the State of North Dakota? What about all of those states between the Mississippi River and the west coast; all of the southern cotton and agricultural states?

In addition the Gentlemen have continued to ignore completely those "little details" of the distribution of several hundred millions of dollars a year; several billions of dollars a year it would amount to,—redistributing that to the local units or using by the state governments themselves. They have one more speech in which to do that. It isn't a mere detail. It is a problem that no state in the Union has satisfactorily solved when those states are redistributing only ten per cent to the local governments. The Gentlemen of the Opposition would have them redistribute fifty-four per cent.

Second Affirmative Rebuttal, O. Glenn Stahl
University of Wisconsin

LADIES AND GENTLEMEN: The speaker has claimed we paid no attention to their statement as to how we stand on the distribution argument; how we will distribute the amount of revenue we derive. As a matter of fact it is not necessary for us to present an exact program of distribution for every state, but we certainly do favor any method of state centralization of tax administration or state centralization of locally-shared taxes; and when they keep on contending it isn't being done successfully, how do they answer the fact that North Carolina is supporting all highways with a motor vehicle and gas tax, and all schools with a state income and state inheritance tax? How do the

Gentlemen meet this? Virginia is doing it even more than North Carolina, and Delaware even more than Virginia. In our own State of Wisconsin they redistribute income taxes in this way: ten per cent to the counties, fifty per cent back to the community it comes from, and the other forty per cent goes to the state. The state redistributes that forty per cent according to need, and the system seems to be working very nicely.

The speaker quoted one man's opinion on this tax delinquency argument. They have avoided it all during the debate and finally quote one man who says that tax delinquency is due to graft and extravagance. The inability of a person to pay taxes because he has got property and no income—here's what the State Commission of Michigan on Tax Inquiry says: *"Tax delinquency is not tax delinquency, but represents an excess levy of taxes beyond the ability of the people to pay."* That is exactly the situation in the city of Detroit with twenty-seven per cent of its property tax delinquent at the present time.

He says twenty-five coupon clippers getting over three millions of dollars paid seven hundred thirty-one thousand dollars to the Federal Government and the poor coupon clippers should not be taxed any more. Do we favor increasing the tax? You bet we do. If those twenty-five coupon clippers pay only that to the Federal Government they still have two million three hundred thousand left, and still the Gentlemen claim they should not be taxed, in face of the fact that four farmers, on the other hand, are together paying twelve hundred dollars, when they have practically no income at all and can barely scrape enough together to pay these taxes.

They claim the Federal Government is pre-empting all these sources of revenue. Richard T. Ely answers this, and I will read the direct statement:

"We see no reason why the states should renounce the income tax and use substitutes which are manifestly inferior, merely because the Federal Government is employing the same tax. Nearly all taxes must be paid out of income. The specific tax employed is merely a device for distributing the tax. Why, then, should the state employ a poor method of distribution, such as that embodied in the personal property tax, when it might employ a tax which with substantial accuracy lays the burden in accordance with ability to pay?"

The Gentlemen refer to the Model Plan of the National Tax Association as not being in favor of our program. They admit it presents three main types: first, real estate, second, personal property; third, business income. This quotation is from the Model Plan. It says: "Under a system by which the *same amount of revenue is collected from separate taxes levied upon income, property, and business,* it is clear that such inevitable inequalities as arise in the working of any one tax may be . . . offset or mitigated by inequalities arising under the others." Clearly, the Model Plan contemplated getting approximately the same revenue from each of these three forms of revenue, and since business income and personal income are two-thirds of the program, then it favors getting at least two-thirds from sources other than tangible property.

The Gentlemen of the Opposition have misconstrued our case by trying to claim that you would have to multiply gas and income tax so much in order to get the revenue, but have they taken into consideration the lowering of exemption and inclusion of other forms? They take the income tax as it is now being applied under the present exemption and multiply that by so much to reach the proportions we are advocating. They don't consider the extension of the income tax base so that it would cover more people and tax according to a personal income. In the State of New York they claim it can't be done and yet the income tax in that state is only one and one-half per cent on the first ten thousand dollars above a four thousand dollar exemption and finally gets up to four and one-half per cent on incomes above forty thousand dollars. What an income tax! They could lower that and include other forms of income and get the revenue.

Third Negative Rebuttal, Nathan Levy
University of Michigan

LADIES AND GENTLEMEN: The preceding speaker says we are wrong. All you have to do is extend income. In Mississippi they are down to seven hundred fifty dollar incomes, in North Dakota they are down to one thousand dollars. Extend the base and go down to fifty dollar incomes, or ten dollar incomes, I don't care where you go on the income. You can't go up because there are not very many higher. Even if you took the coupon clippers of North Dakota for everything they got, you would not have enough to run even a small share of the government. You can run a tax as low as you want. You have still got to get a tremendous portion of that, and that money happens to be in a form that is easily hidden, and every single addition of dependence upon that type of income adds an incentive to evasion, with an income that is easy to use and evade the tax.

It isn't so simple. Just saying, "Broaden the tax base," does not increase returns by ten per cent, or twenty per cent, or thirty per cent, or even with the Gentlemen's two or three hundred per cent increase on the returns of some of those taxes. You can't get that much of an increase merely by saying "broaden the base." As to the Model Plan—because it names three types of taxes to be used, the Gentlemen assumed the planners were going to place one-third equal dependence on each. You can't find the state, and this has been pointed out by many authorities, where they are agreed as to what percentage dependence shall be placed upon each one of those taxes because they frankly admit they don't know and couldn't figure it out until they had local situations in mind and knew first what would be equitable and correct in meeting tax principles of simplicity and diversity. In Wisconsin, after nineteen years of thus distributing income taxes, the Wisconsin Tax Commission is advocating a change.

The Gentlemen of the Opposition say, "Sure, you can

pass it back," but they are doing it in ways that they are not satisfied with. They are doing it with ten per cent of state and local taxes, and the Gentlemen of the Opposition want to increase that to handle a distribution of state and local taxes of about five billions of dollars a year in the United States, and they have not demonstrated to you any means—we don't want just a general means, we want to know a general method that can be used that will be satisfactory, and they have not brought one out.

Now, the Gentlemen of the Opposition have talked about this delinquency. This man we quoted happens to be a member of the State Tax Commission who was put on the Commission for the purpose of getting his particular information in that particular line, because he happens to be the outstanding authority on state and local taxes in the United States, and has made special studies of counties of the State of Michigan. That is the conclusion he reaches, that the waste and extravagance we spoke of in our first speech is the thing that causes delinquency. They quote the Michigan Tax Report, "Tax delinquency is not tax delinquency. It represents an excess of taxation over ability to pay." That does not mean what they think it means. It represents an excess over what the county should get and not an excess on any particular source —too much money, not too much with respect to those particular sources. Counties in the State of Michigan waste money "high, wide and handsome," because of their particular organization. And so far the Gentlemen have not attempted to take up and discuss the findings of the New York State Tax Commission, a Commission which has studied the problem more carefully than any group of men has ever studied it. That happens to be the state most favorable to the Gentlemen of the Opposition. The conclusion there of the tax authorities, giving attention to the ability to pay and benefit theory, is that a tax in New York to be equitable must have at least fifty-three and two-tenths per cent of the total revenue's dependence placed on a tax on tangible property. That, as we have said, is in the state most favorable to the Gentlemen of the Opposition. The equity about which they complain so bitterly would be more and more apparent in each of the other states of the Union as they applied this proposition of theirs to new states.

Third Affirmative Rebuttal, Harry L. Cole
University of Wisconsin

LADIES AND GENTLEMEN: The preceding speaker has closed with a reference to the special report of the New York Commission on Tax Revision. That report is very important because it represents the findings of a body of experts who were called together specifically to study this question, and it should be given great weight in deciding this matter. The Gentlemen who just preceded me said that the Tax Commission did not presume to set definite percentages upon this sort of tax or upon that sort of tax, but proposed it should be adjusted to local communities. As I said before, we are in favor of adjustments to local conditions, and agree with the Gentlemen of the Negative and the New York Tax Commission that the percentages will need to be adjusted to the differences in different communities. But we do not agree with them that if you keep the large part of the burden on tangible property the situation will be met. We contend you must have a large part of the burden distributed according to ability to pay if you are going to have a more equitable tax system.

Now, the New York Commission, as they have indicated, advocates various substantial increases in the revenue derived from intangibles and advocates these increases shall be applied to reduce levies on property. We are also in accord with the New York Tax Commission in that respect. They unanimously report in favor of increased revenue to the amount of one hundred twenty-seven million dollars in a normal year in order that the taxes on property should be lightened, but a majority of the committee said to lighten it one hundred twenty-seven millions was not enough. To quote the exact words of the Commission, whose report I hold in my hand, Part 1, page 48:

"The majority submits that, whether one takes property values or income as the test of fairness in the distribution of the tax burden, the portion of the aggregate tax burden which falls upon real estate is so great that the inequity will not be eliminated by the adoption of the revenue proposals listed in Class A."

The revenue proposals listed in Class A are to decrease property taxes one hundred twenty-seven million dollars by an increase chiefly in income taxes, and these income taxes are not anything like the rates they think would be necessary to raise revenue from intangibles: one per cent up to five thousand dollars, and a rate of two per cent on incomes up to ten thousand dollars. These are the terrific rates which they are so afraid of on the incomes! We have not begun to scratch the surface of the possibilities of raising revenue from income tax in this country.

The Gentlemen made the statement that there isn't sufficient revenue in the State of North Dakota to pay the income tax. According to the United States Government return, total revenue in the State of North Dakota was over one hundred forty million dollars in 1930. The expenses of the government were something like thirty million dollars, and yet they tell you there isn't sufficient income to pay their government costs. That is an absurdity. In any state the total expenses of government have to be a small percentage of the income of the people. Our fundamental contention is that we can readjust the major part of the tax burden and apportion it upon people in proportion to their incomes. And when you do that you will be getting at the ability to pay, you will be putting your tax system on a foundation of justice, and you will be curing these inequities whose existence the Gentlemen have not denied but which they have proposed nothing to correct. In conclusion, if we are to accomplish anything constructive in the way of improving our tax system, and doing away with the inequities which the Gentlemen have not denied, we must work out a program in every state as it is already worked out for Delaware, Virginia, and North Carolina, and thereby raise more than half of the state and local revenues from sources other than tangible property.

Decision, Professor Rexford Mitchell
Critic Judge

LADIES AND GENTLEMEN: Debaters are often told that they should regard the judge as one of the audience, and judges are frequently admonished to remember that they are one of that group. I am going to assume, therefore, this evening that you are willing to accept me as one of the group, and since I am the only member of the audience who has a chance to talk, I am going to presume to speak for you in saying to these men from Michigan and these men from Wisconsin that we have enjoyed this splendid discussion of this timely question. I think you will all agree that it has been an interesting and profitable evening.

I think you understand what I am asked to do. I am not asked, fortunately, to decide who is right, and I am not asked to decide the tax problem. We are going to let the Democratic Governors and Legislators which the State of Michigan and State of Wisconsin have elected so recently deal with that matter. I am simply asked to tell you which of the two teams I think has done the better debating, and I sure that after listening to the debate you don't envy me that task because it is a rather difficult one, I think.

Those of you who are in educational work are

familiar with the phenomena known as questionnaires. Some of you have been deluged with them from time to time. In order to be up-to-date and in step with the times, I have devised a questionnaire for use in analyzing this debate and in explaining the basis for my decision. But unlike most perpetrators of questionnaires, I am going to make myself the victim of the device and try to answer the questions. I think as the process proceeds you will discern what my decision is, and the basis for it. May I say further in disparagement of this questionnaire that in it I have separated factors that I know are inseparable.

The *first question* is this: Which team showed throughout the debate greater skill in analysis? My answer is that there was no perceptible difference.

Second: Which team showed a more complete knowledge of the question? Again I will have to say that to the best of my judgment there wasn't much difference.

The *third question* is: Which team showed superior skill in using argument backed up by evidence in building up a logical case? There I am going to fool you by having an opinion as to difference. I say the Affirmative had a slight edge in that respect. I felt that they had a little more closely knit case and that it was a little easier to follow them all the way through their argument.

The *fourth question:* Which team was superior in refutation and rebuttal? My answer is that I think the Affirmative had a slight edge.

I listed the questions that it seemed to me had developed out of the clash of argument as a result of the constructive speeches, the matters I felt each side must deal with, and I felt that the Affirmative followed the ball, so to speak, that is, kept their eye on the main issues, just a little bit better than the Negative did.

Fifth: Which team was superior in rhetorical organization? I think the Affirmative had the edge.

Which team was superior in delivery? I say the Negative was.

Which team was superior in persuasiveness? I say the Negative was.

Where did the weight of evidence seem to rest at the close of the debate? I felt it was with the Affirmative.

The last question: Which team on the whole did the more effective debating? My answer is the Affirmative, and thus ends the questionnaire.

BIBLIOGRAPHY: REVENUES FROM INTANGIBLE PROPERTY

Books

Adams, H. C.—*Science of Finance.* 1898. Holt.
Betters, Paul V.—*State Centralization in North Carolina.* 1932. Brookings Institute, Washington, D. C.
Brown, Harry G.—*The Economics of Taxation.* 1924. Holt.
Brown, Harry G.—*The Economic Basis of Tax Reform.* 1932. Lucas Brothers, Columbia, Mo.
Buehler, Alfred D.—*General Sales Taxation.* The Business Bourse, 80 West 40th Street, New York. $5.00.
Bullock, Charles J.—*Selected Readings in Public Finance.* 1924. Ginn and Company.
Comstock, Alzada P.—*Taxation in The Modern State.* 1930. Longmans. $2.00.
Dalton, Hugh—*Principles of Public Finance.* 1923. Knopf.

Hunter, Merlin H.—*Outlines of Public Finance*. 1926. Harper & Brothers.
Hutchinson, Ruth G.—*State-Administered Locally-Shared Taxes*. 1931. Columbia University Press.
Jensen, Jens P.—*Problems of Public Finance* 1924 Crowell.
Jensen, Jens P.—*Property Taxation in the United States*. 1931. University of Chicago Press.
Leland, Simeon E —*The Classified Property Tax in the United States*. 1928. Houghton Mifflin.
Loman, Harry J.—*Taxation*. 1927 D. Appleton & Company.
Lutz, Harley L.—*Public Finance*. 1924. D. Appleton & Company.
Lutz, Harley L —*The Georgia System of Revenue, Its Problems and Remedies*. 1930.
Mellon, Andrew W.—*Taxation: The People's Business*. 1924. Macmillan.
Peck, Harvey W.—*Taxation and Welfare*. 1925. Macmillan.
Plehn, Carl C.—*Introduction to Public Finance*. 1926 Macmillan.
Mill, John S.—*Principles of Political Economy*. 1900. Colonial Press, New York.
Robinson, M. E.—*Public Finance*. 1922. Harcourt, Brace & Company.
Schalkenbach, Robert—*Significant Paragraphs from Henry George's Progress and Poverty*. 1928. Doubleday, Doran & Company
Seligman, Edwin R. A —*Studies in Public Finance*. 1925 Macmillan.
Seligman, Edwin R. A.—*Essays in Taxation*. 1925. Macmillan.
Seligman, Edwin R. A.—*The Shifting and Incidence of Taxation*. 1927. Columbia University Press.
Seligman, Edwin R. A.—*Double Taxation and International Fiscal Cooperation*. 1928. Macmillan.
Shoup, Carl S.—*The Sales Tax in France*. 1930. Columbia University Press.
Shultz, William J.—*American Public Finance and Taxation*. 1931. Prentice-Hall. $5.00.
Silverman, Herbert A.—*Taxation: Its Incidence and Effects*. 1931. Macmillan $3.00.
Simpson, Herbert C.—*Tax Racket and Tax Reform in Chicago*. 1930. Institute for Economic Research, Chicago. $2.50.
Smith, Adam—*The Wealth of Nations*. 1776. Everyman's Edition or Harvard Classics.

Stamp, Sir Josiah—*Wealth and Taxable Capacity*. 1922. P. S King & Son, Ltd, London

Stauffer, William H.—*Taxation in Virginia*. 1931. The Century Company.

Taussig, F. W—*Principles of Economics*. 1920. Macmillan.

Young, Arthur N—*The Single Tax Movement in the United States* 1916. Princeton University Press.

Cost of Government in the United States. 1929-1930. National Industrial Conference Board, New York. $3.00.

Current Tax Problems in New York State. 1931. National Industrial Conference Board, New York.

Sales Taxes: General, Selective and Retail. National Industrial Conference Board, New York. $2 00.

The Shifting and Effects of the Federal Corporation Income Tax. Vol. 2. 1930. National Industrial Conference Board, New York

State Income Taxes. Vol. 1. 1930. National Industrial Conference Board, New York.

State Income Taxes. Vol. 2. 1930. National Industrial Conference Board, New York.

State and Local Taxation of Business Corporations. 1931. National Industrial Conference Board, New York.

State and Local Taxation of Property 1930. National Industrial Conference Board, New York.

BULLETINS, REPORTS, SPEECHES

Tax Research Foundation—*Federal and State Tax Systems.* Third Edition, January 1, 1932. Commerce Clearing House, 205 West Monroe, Chicago. $9.00.

Graves, Mark—*Making One Government Grow Where Two, or a Dozen, Grew Before.* United States Chamber of Commerce, Washington, D. C.

Studies in Taxation. December 1928. Extension Bulletin, University of North Carolina.

Taylor, Harry A.—*Relieving the Burden on Real Property.* New Jersey Association of Real Estate Boards.

Garnett, Burt P.—*New Sources of State and Local Revenues.* 1932. Editorial Research Reports, Washington, D. C.

Groves, Harold M.—*Speech on Taxation.* 1932. Wisconsin Tax Commission, Madison.

Englund, Eric—*Tax Relief, Reform, Revision, Reduction.* 1931. United States Department of Agriculture, Washington, D. C.

Current, Conflicting Views on Property, Income, Sales Taxation. 1932. National Research Bureau, 238 East Erie Street, Chicago. $2.25.

Blakey, Roy G.—*State Income Taxation.* 1930. Publication No. 31. League of Minnesota Municipalities, Minneapolis.

What Leading Retailers and Newspapers Have to Say Concerning the Proposed New York State Sales Tax. National Retail Dry Goods Association, 225 West 34th, New York

Cooper, Walter G.—*The Sales Tax.* 1931. National Retail Dry Goods Association, 225 West 34th, New York.

Sheridan, George V.—*Growth of Sales Taxing in the United States.* 1931. National Retail Dry Goods Association, 225 West 34th, New York.

Luxury Taxation and its Place in a System of Public Revenues. 1931. Special Report of the State Tax Commission, Albany, New York.

Crawford, F. G.—*The Administration of the Gasoline Tax in the United States.* 1932. Municipal Administration Service, 309 E 34th, New York.

An Address Delivered by Paul E. Hadlick. 1932. American Petroleum Institute, 250 Park Avenue, New York.

Walker, John E.—*Highway Tax Costs.* National Automobile Chamber of Commerce, 366 Madison Avenue, New York.

Facts and Figures of the Automobile Industry. 1932. National Automobile Chamber of Commerce, New York.

Fact Analysis of Oklahoma Gasoline Tax. 1932. Oklahoma State Chamber of Commerce, Oklahoma City. (And Supplement)

Hadlick, Paul E —*The Gasoline Sales Tax.* American Petroleum Institute, 250 Park Avenue, New York.

Schon, Pierre—*Motor-Vehicle Legislation and Taxation.* National Automobile Chamber of Commerce, New York.

Owsley, Roy H.—*Our Cities and the Gasoline Tax.* 1930. University of Kentucky, Lexington.

Special Taxation for Motor Vehicles. 1931. Motor Vehicle Conference Committee, 366 Madison Avenue, New York.

Martin, James W., and Stephenson, C. M.—*Taxation of Private and*

Common-Carrier Motor Vehicles by Municipalities. 1931 Municipal Administration Service, 309 East 34th Street, New York.

Final Report of California Tax Commission. 1929. State of California.

Jensen, Jens P.—*Survey of Colorado Tax System.* 1930. Denver Chamber of Commerce, Denver, Colorado.

Klemmedson, G. S.—*Taxation and Public School Finance in Colorado.* 1931. Colorado Agricultural College.

Report of Indiana Tax Survey Committee to Seventy-Seventh General Assembly, January 15, 1931.

Brindley, John E., and Zorbaugh, Grace S. M.—*The Tax System of Iowa.* 1930. Iowa State College of Agriculture and Mechanic Arts.

Report of Joint Legislative Committee on Taxation and State Board of Assessment and Review. 1930. State of Iowa.

Report of Kansas Tax Code Commission. 1929. Topeka, Kansas.

Leland, Simeon E.—*The Taxation of Intangibles in Kentucky.* 1929. University of Kentucky.

Leland, Simeon E—*Observations Upon the Minnesota Tax System.* 1932. Minneapolis.

Reports of the Commission to Investigate County and Municipal Taxation and Expenditures. Legislature of New Jersey.

Seligman, Edwin R. A.—*The Fiscal Situation in New Jersey.* Trenton Times Newspapers.

Message of Governor Franklin D. Roosevelt to Legislature. January 6, 1932. Legislative Document No. 3. Albany, New York

New York State Commission for the Revision of the Tax Laws. Report submitted February 15, 1932.

Melton, Judge Harve L.—*A Treatise on Oklahoma ad Valorem Tax and Oklahoma Conditions.* Oklahoma Chamber of Commerce.

Reconstruction of Virginia's Tax System. Virginia State Chamber of Commerce.

Haas, Judge T. N.—*Virginia Taxation, Its Defects and the Remedy.* 1931. Harrisonburg, Virginia.

Blakey, Roy G—*Report on Taxation in West Virginia.* 1931. University of Minnesota.

Groves, Harold M.—*Ability to Pay and the Tax System in Dane County, Wisconsin.* University of Wisconsin.

Groves, Harold M.—*The Wisconsin Income Tax.* 1929. Minnesota Municipalities, Minneapolis.

Blough, J. Roy—*The Wisconsin System of Taxation.* Wisconsin Tax Commission, Madison.

Blough, J. Roy—*The Geographical Problem in Wisconsin Taxation.* 1930. Wisconsin Tax Commission.

Groves, Harold M.—*Memorandum on the Migration of Industry from Wisconsin to Escape Taxation.* Wisconsin Tax Commission.

Leffler, George L.—*Wisconsin Industry and the Wisconsin Tax System.* 1930 University of Wisconsin.

Survey of Bank Taxation in the United States. 1931. American Bankers Association, Kansas City, Missouri.

Jackson, Donald—*Land Tax Delinquency a Growing Problem.* United States Department of Agriculture.

Englund, Eric—*Burden of Farm Taxation.* 1930. United States Department of Agriculture.

Englund, Eric—*Recent Trends in Farm Taxes.* 1930. United States Department of Agriculture.

Englund, Eric—*Why Farm Taxes Are Heavy and What Should Be Done About Farm Taxes.* Department of Agriculture, Washington, D. C.

Allin, Bushrod W.—*Possible Farm Tax Reduction Through Changes in Local Government.* 1931. United States Department of Agriculture.

Olcott, Margaret T.—*Taxation and the Farmer, A Selected and Annotated Bibliography.* 1928. United States Department of Agriculture.

Coombs, Whitney—*Taxation of Farm Property.* 1930. United States Department of Agriculture.

Rosa, Charles D.—*The Farmer in Wisconsin's System of Taxation.* 1927. Wisconsin Tax Commission, Madison.

Undeveloped Sources of Municipal Revenue—1932. Municipal Administration Service, New York.

Rightor, C. E.—*Comparative Tax Rates of 290 Cities.* 1931. Governmental Research Municipal Administration Service.

Bird, Frederick L.—*The Present Financial Status of 135 Cities in the United States and Canada.* 1931. Municipal Administration Service, New York.

A Ten-Year Plan For Public Improvement in Kansas City. Civic Improvement Committee, City Hall, Kansas City.

Williams, Percy R.—*Pittsburgh's Graded Tax in Full Operation.* 1925. National Municipal Review.

Collins, Clem W.—*Taxes and the Taxpayer.* 1931. Denver City and County Council.

Final Report of Committee on Taxation and Public Expenditures. 1932. Philadelphia Chamber of Commerce

Stutz, John G.—*Probable Effects Upon Cities by Recommendations of Kansas Tax Code Commission.* League of Kansas Municipalities, Lawrence, Kansas.

Can General Property Taxation Be Reduced? April 1931. Massachusetts Institute of Technology.

Local Fiscal Problems. 1929. United States Chamber of Commerce.

Assessments. 1930. United States Chamber of Commerce.

Taxation Activities. 1931. United States Chamber of Commerce.

PERIODICALS

American Bankers Association Journal.—26 No. 1:97-8ff. *Progress Toward the Goal of Fair Taxation.*

American City.—45 No. 3:107. *Britain To Tax Land Values.* September 1931. 46 No. 1:100-2. *Delinquent Real Estate Taxes— Prevention and Collection.* January 1932.

American Economic Review.—21:672-81. *A Mediaeval Tax Problem.* December 1931.

American Political Science Review.—25:996-1003. *State Centralization in North Carolina.* November 1931. 25:1004-7. *State Supervision of Local Fiscal Officers in Virginia.* November 1931.

Annals of American Academy.—153:238-45. *Problems of Taxation in Tennessee.* January 1931. 129:9-15. *Ways and Means Toward Equitable Adjustments of State and Federal Taxes.* January 1927.

Atlantic Monthly.—127:849-854. *Adventures in Taxation—The Sales Tax.* June 1921.

Bulletin, Milwaukee Association of Commerce.—11 No. 17. *Milwaukee's Increasing Tax Trends.* November 24, 1931.

Bulletin, National Retail Dry Goods Association.—*An Analysis of Present State Sales Tax Laws.* August 1930. *Retail Sales Taxing An Active Issue in One-Half of the States.* September 1931.

Bulletin, National Tax Association.—16 No. 5:137-8. *Excise and Income Taxes in Oregon.* February 1931. 15 No. 9:258-262. *The General Sales Tax As a State Revenue.* June 1930. 16 No. 4:105-114. *How Business Corporations Should Be Taxed* January 1931. 16 No. 9:269-275. *How Existing Methods of Income Taxation May Be Improved.* June 1931. 16 No. 6:165-7. *Measuring the Intangible Tax Base.* March 1931. 17 No. 1:9-15. *The Mechanics of a Tax Reduction Study; Points to be Considered by Chambers of Commerce.* October 1931. 16 No. 1:8-9. *More Research and Analysis Needed.* October 1930. 15 No. 4:109-117. *North Carolina Tax Problems.* January 1930. 15 No. 9:255-8. *Ohio's Opportunity in Taxation* June 1930. 15 No. 6:162-6. *The Reorganization and Consolidation of Local Units and Functions of Government and the Resulting Effect on Taxes.* March 1930. 16 No. 1:14-18. *Sales Tax in France—Simplicity?* October 1930. 14 No. 4:106-110. *Some Queer Provisions of Former Tax Statutes.* January 1929. 17 No. 4.96-101. *Status and Certain Tests of Uniformity in Allocating Corporate Income.* January 1932. 15 No. 6:166-178. *A Survey of the Remedies that are Possible Under the Classification Amendment in Ohio.* March 1930. 17 No. 1:15-20. *The Taxation of Business Enterprises.* October 1931. 16 No. 8:231-2. *Taxation of Financial Institutions in Kansas.* May 1931. 16 No. 7:213-7. *Taxation—The Position of the Banks.* April 1931. 16 No. 9:275-7. *The Tax Burden upon Industry in New York.* June 1931. 15 No. 7:200-3. *Tax Problems and a Tax Program for Real Estate.* April 1930. 12 No. 6:181-4. *Ten Years of the State Income Tax.* March 1927. 14 No. 2:45-8. *The Trend in State Revenues.* November 1928. 16 No. 2.37-9. *What Part of our Wealth is Real Estate?* November 1930. 17 No. 3.78-81. *Why Increased Taxes are Unavoidable.* December 1931.

Business Week.—*Illinois Taxes Incomes to Relieve Property-Holders.* February 24, 1932. *Mandatory Control of all Taxes in North Carolina Successful.* July 15, 1931. *Mississippi Shows How to Apply a Sales Tax.* May 18, 1932. *Tax Reduction in Ohio Attracts Manufacturers.* August 19, 1931.

Christian Science Monitor.—*Hoover Seeks State and Civic Aid to Halt Mounting Tax Tide.* April 28, 1932. *Tax Reforms In-*

augurated by Oklahoma. May 7, 1931. *Tax on Incomes Thought Best.* February 14, 1931.

Citizens' Bureau, Milwaukee.—*Comparative Tax Burden on $1,000,000 Manufacturing Corporation.* May 30, 1931.

Congressional Record.—Vol. 66, Part 5:5510. *Duplication of Taxes.* March 4, 1925. Vol. 66, Part 2:1189. *Income Taxes and the Price Level.* January 3, 1925.

Current History.—34·448-50. *Land Taxation in Great Britain.* June 1931. 33 244-6. *A New Source of State Revenue.* November 1930.

Forbes Magazine.—*How Racketeers Steal Millions in Bootlegging of Gasoline.* December 15, 1931.

Forum.—*Pittsburgh Has a Plan.* April 1928.

Gas Tax News.—*Gasoline Tax Payments Soar and Make New Record*—1 No. 7, 1932. American Petroleum Institute, New York.

Harlows Weekly.—38 No. 10.4-6. *Humphrey Briefs New Tax Theory* September 5, 1931. *Taxation In Oklahoma.* September 26, 1931.

Illinois Journal of Commerce.—*Reorganization of Local Government.* November 1931.

Journal of Political Economy.—*The General Property Tax and the Farmer.* January 1930.

Manufacturers News.—*We Save at Washington and Waste in the States.* November 1926.

Manufacturers Record.—*Gas Tax Diversion and Evasion.* January 7, 1932.

Nation.—134:484-6. *Toward a New Tax Program.* April 27, 1932.

National Municipal Review.—20 No. 9:518-522. *Brain Muddle in Chicago.* September 1931. 20 No. 10:584-8. *County-Municipal Segregation Plan Proposed for New Jersey.* October 1931. 21 No. 2:101-6. *Has the Indiana Plan Been a Success?* February 1932. 20 No. 6:328-334. *North Carolina's New Plan for Controlling Local Fiscal Affairs.* June 1931. 20 No. 9:527-530. *State Centralization in North Carolina.* September 1931. 20 No. 9:523-7. *Tax Investigations in Twenty-Six States.* September 1931. 20 No. 3:136-8. *Tax Reforms in Tennessee.* March 1931.

National Petroleum News.—24 No. 26:16. *Memphis Gasoline Broker Accused in Gasoline Tax Evasion Case.* June 29, 1932.

24 No. 17. *Tax Evasion is Menace to Government.* April 27, 1932. 24 No. 26:13-4. *Taxoline, a Fitting Name.* June 29, 1932.

Nation's Business.—19 No. 2:29. *Chicago Teaches a Tax Lesson.* February 1931. 19 No. 10:31-3. *How North Carolina Cut Its Cost.* October 1931. 20 No. 2:46-50. *It's the Poor Who Pay a Sales Tax.* February 1932. 19 No. 7:46. *Taxes Threaten Retail Growth.* July 1931. 20 No. 6:33. *Ten Governors Discuss Taxes.* June 1932. 19 No. 5:31. *Throwing Light on the Sales Tax.* May 1931. 20 No. 5:25-7. *Your Part in Tax Reduction.* May 1932.

New York Times.—*Use Here of British Tax Plan.* May 1, 1932. *Excessive Cost of Local Government.* July 7, 1931. *Mississippi Giving Sales Tax a Trial.* May 8, 1932. *State Legislatures Consider Income Tax.* March 22, 1931.

Nineteenth Century.—109:637-47. *The Taxation of Land Values.* June 1931.

North American Review.—232:33-42. *The Landowner's Lot.* July 1931.

North Carolina Law Review. 9·108-10. *Tax Reform in North Carolina.* December 1930.

Oklahoma Municipal Review.—6 No 6:128-130 *Reducing Governmental Costs.* June 1932.

Oregon Voter.—*Are Intangibles Property?* April 18, 1931. *Intangibles Tax.* March 28, 1931. *Only 50% of Tax Paid by Realty.* April 18, 1931.

Public Dollar.—*Public Expenditures.* June-July 1931.

Public Management.—14 No. 1:11-2. *Taxes and Assessments.* January 1932.

Review of Reviews.—82:57-8. *A Battle over Taxes in Illinois.* November 1930. 84:86. *Canada's Sales Tax.* October 1931. 82:120-2. *How West Virginia Found New Revenue* October 1930. 85.25. *A Manufacturers' Tax for the States.* April 1932. 83:86-7. *A Postscript in the Sales Tax.* January 1931. 84:67-8. *Taxation in Hard Times.* August 1931.

Saturday Evening Post.—204 No. 23. *One State Cleans House.* January 2, 1932.

Tax Digest.—*Assessment Procedure.* April 1931. *Control of Public Expenditures.* August 1931. 8 No. 6: 193-6. *Effect of Taxation on Real Estate.* June 1930. 10 No. 3:76-9. *Public Finance and Taxation.* March 1932. *The Sales Tax.* February 1931. *Special Assessment Dangers.* July 1930. *State and Local Tax System of California.* 10 No. 6:195-9. June 1932. *What is a Good Budget?* November 1931.

Tax Magazine.—*Basic Principles Which Should Guide in Tax Legislation.* January 1931. *The Gross Sales Tax in Kentucky.* March-April 1932. *The Taxation of Intangible Property.* April 1931. 10 No. 6:211-5. *The Turnover or Sales Tax in France.* June 1932. *Unlimited Earnings and Tax Evasion.* November 1931. 10 No. 6:216-222. *Why Pay Property Taxes?* June 1932.

United States Daily.—*The Income Tax in South Carolina.* July 9, 1930. *Tax Reduction is Advocated on Realty in Iowa.* December 11, 1931. *Tax Reductions are Foreseen in Farm Property.* December 29, 1931. 7 No. 72:8. *Tax-Relief for Farmer by Levy on Intangible Property.* May 26, 1932.

Utah Taxpayer.—*Organized Effort—Its Accomplishment in Tax Control.* October 1931.

Woman's Journal.—*The High Cost of Inheriting.* September 1928.

World's Work.—60:30-1. *Hands Off Our Tax Laws.* March 1931.

SOCIALISM

An International Debate

Between Oxford (England) and Yale Universities

SOCIALISM

OXFORD UNIVERSITY VS. YALE UNIVERSITY

The Yale-Oxford Debate was held at Yale's Sterling Law Auditorium. The subject was stated, *Resolved: That Socialism offers no remedy for the present economic disorder.*

Oxford University was represented by A. J. Irvine and G. M. Wilson and Yale by F. Vinton Lindley and Eugene V Rostow. In the debate, both Affirmative and Negative sides included one Oxford and one Yale debater The Presiding Officer was Franklin Ferriss, 2d , who introduced the speakers.

These speeches were collected and contributed through the courtesy of Professor J. C. Adams of Yale University.

Introduction, Franklin Ferriss, 2d., Chairman

LADIES AND GENTLEMEN: I am tremendously pleased to see the Yale Sterling Law Auditorium full to its capacity. I think it is the first time in four years at Yale that I have witnessed such an event. I certainly agree with you all, and if I were to come to only one debate in the four years at Yale, I think it would be this one. We are very much honored to have the Oxford men with us this evening and I extend a cordial welcome to them. I cannot lean to one side or the other. The Oxford team feel they must say what they honestly feel, and consequently they are splitting with the Yale team and one Oxford man and one Yale man will take the Affirmative while the other two men will take the Negative side.

Each man, I understand, will speak about twenty minutes, and there ought to be no rebuttals. However, the men are willing to answer any questions anyone is willing to propose, and I will recognize people in the audience for that purpose.

Mr. Rostow and Mr. Wilson will uphold the Negative, and Mr. Lindley and Mr. Irvine will uphold the Affirmative. The subject is, *Resolved*: That Socialism offers no remedy for the present economic disorder.

First Affirmative, F. Vinton Lindley
Yale University

LADIES AND GENTLEMEN: I predict tragedy. We are rushing toward chaos. We are rushing toward destruction. I predict tragedy.

It is not the tragedy of economic collapse. It is the tragedy that for the first time in the history of debating, and in the history of the world two debating teams may come to complete and entire agreement. I am going to be, if I may, quite personal through this debate. Socialism is a fairly hopeless subject to discuss in the abstract. Gene Rostow, who sits there, and myself, for four years in college have eaten many meals together and have discussed this question so constantly that we have, alas, arrived disgustingly enough at complete agreement, informally if not before you; and after discussion the same thing was practically true this evening with the Englishmen at dinner. When more or less intelligent people get together and discuss subjects of this kind, it is apt to end in agreement.

We have with us tonight two gentlemen from a nation of globe-trotters, from the far-flung British Empire. We are delighted that they have been "flung" across the Atlantic Ocean to us!

The extent of our agreement, I think, is disgusting. That is the only word we can use. We are all agreed that there is present economic disorder. If I may read from a magazine, whose editor sits on my right, I think I can give you as good a summary as any there is of the situation: "With surprising community of judgment," he says, "the economists see America clearly in her dual position. As a business unit, first, whose internal arrangements for production and distribution as they exist are wasteful, self-destructive, incapable of sustained operation at an efficient level; as an international unit in the second place, turned creditor, and seeking nevertheless to maintain the tariff apparatus, which if unrevised must ultimately do away with American foreign trade. The world's monetary structure will fall, and in the phrase of Keyne's, 'destroy America with the curse of Midas.'"

I have not debated this subject as many times as these Englishmen but I have done so four times and it seems a little senseless to go into a long list of commonplace arguments against Socialism, because we all have complete knowledge of them. On both sides we agree that in America there is over-production and under-consumption, that the existence of business cycles is unfortunate, that tariffs should be gradually scaled down and that there is a great deal of unemployment.

The whole thing is pretty successfully summed up in an article in the November *New Outlook*, the only good article on "Technocracy" which I have read. "The rate of replacement of men by machines exceeds the rate of expansion of industry. You hear a good many plans these days for bringing about industrial recovery. Some so-called 'leaders' are talking about developing new industries without realizing Technology provides absorption in that line. Some are still speaking glibly about developing foreign markets, without knowing what they are talking about. To those who are presenting these plans, 'Technocracy,' a group of engineers which has been studying production and consumption for the last ten years, offers a few fundamental questions: 'Can we re-employ ever again under a price system all those of employment age to get production capacity?' 'Is recovery just around the corner with one to two years' supply of wheat, corn, copper, rubber, and other commodities in our warehouses?'"

It seems to me that the proper indictment against capitalist civilization has been made by "Technocracy," this group of engineers. It is very curious they should go out of their way to state that they do not think that Socialism is a remedy for these disorders. We are, nevertheless, I think, agreed once more on the general remedies for economic disorder. We all want more centralized control. We differ merely in degree—as to how much we want. We all want more planning; we all want more of a sense of social responsibility; we all want the rest of that which the intelligent Socialists mildly espouse.

There is one final tragedy in this tragic sequence I have been talking about; a tragic question that must have been in the minds of all of you as you came here tonight: "What *is* Socialism?" To fancify an American expression, I might Anglicize it by saying: "I'll be jolly well damned if I know!"

I have been studying for four years in Fabian Clubs, Liberal Clubs, in courses in Economics and Government and History and all the rest of it, and there is no agreement of any kind at all, as you all well know. Nevertheless, one has to get at some sort of definition of Socialism. The general description which is given in one of the "bibles" of the Yale Economics courses by Messrs. Fairchild, Furness and Buck is: "Socialism is a complex and many-sided movement." It nevertheless goes on to give some sort of definition in typical economic lingo. "Socialism is a program of reform which deprives private ownership of the means of production and competitive control of industry, and proposes a type of system in which productive capital will be owned collectively and economic activity will be controlled by authority."

Well, that is the typical school-boy Websterian definition. It is the definition I happen to know personally. Mr. Rostow does not agree with it. He thinks it is out-moded, old-fashioned. But, in order to arrive at some conception of what anything is, of any definition, of any kind, I think we have to take two points of view: First, the regular, Websterian type in italics, and then a general conception, and finally a cross between the two.

I should say the general conception of Socialism in America was one of unbounded revolution and complete Communism. How are we going to find a mean between these two? The only possible answer is, granting all these meanings, that Socialism is a sort of point of view. It is a state of mind. It is a personal philosophy, which includes all time and all existence. That is why this has been described, perhaps wrongly, in the papers, as a debate. It is really an expression of personal philosophy on the part of individuals.

I do not think it is a fair debating trick to attempt to foresee what your opponent is going to say, and in that respect I have an unfair advantage over Mr. Rostow, but he has an unfair advantage in speaking after me and in my not being able to rebut! Mr. Rostow will give you an excellent economic plan. I think I can say with surety beforehand that we shall agree with practically everything in that plan. I have read his economic plans before, and have been in hearty agreement with every single one of them. There is a type of general unfairness which comes out most clearly in arguments about religion. Somebody comes to you and says, "Are you religious?" and you say, "No"; and they say, "Do you believe in God?", and you say, "No"; and they say, "Well——," after a long period of argument, "——surely you believe that there is a certain amount of good in every one, don't you?", and you say, "Yes, I suppose there is"; and then they say, "Ah! you *are* religious!"

I think when you use a term, you have to use it in practically its extreme sense. I think when you speak of religion, you have to use it as meaning a belief in a God of some kind and a belief in some sort of church worship. It isn't fair to jump around in the argument, change your position all the time, the way people who argue for religion in that fashion do. And that, it seems to me, is exactly what most modern, intelligent Socialists are doing. And here we come upon a mild beginning disagreement. I am not going to indict Socialism in detail, because I think the arguments have been rehearsed too many times; because I think there is too general an agreement on what should be done to remedy economic difficulties.

My main disagreement would be that it is simply a mistake to call this Socialism. It is a gigantic mistake, because most people in America, as I pointed out, do not understand what Socialism means. This, too, is all part of the old debating paraphernalia. Why not have enlightened Capitalism instead of Socialism? Why not carry out mild reforms? Our opponents do not want the extreme of government ownership. We all want certain small fundamental improvements. Why not simply make them and not label them "Socialism," and then not drive people away from those changes by calling them Socialism?

A second, tiny point of disagreement would be that our opponents exaggerate the present evils. There is no point in carrying out this line of argument to great detail. The Englishmen have observed that while there is a great deal of talk about depression over here, the depression itself does not seem so terribly severe. The difference between us, then, appears to be a question of a difference in approach.

I like to approach these questions—and from what I learned of my partner, he does too—from a human rather than an economic point of view. In the last analysis all this originates in humanity, in the mind; it does not originate the other way around. Mr. Rostow is scientific, if you like, and I am psychological. He would vote for Norman Thomas more hastily than I would. I think Norman Thomas was unquestionably the most intelligent of the three candidates. Also, unquestionably, he is an idealist. We have seen a good deal of him at Yale, in connection with the Liberal Club and other activities. I think he and Reinold Niebuhr, second in command, have been conducting a sort of progressive abandonment of idealist thinking. First they were pacifists, and saw that was a pretty untenable position, and then they came, through various religious feelings, finally to Socialism, and now they are beginning to compromise more and more on Socialism.

I shall be accused, I am afraid, of being superficial, dilettante, emotional. If anything rests upon emotionality, I think it is Socialistic feeling. While Mr. Niebuhr was talking about unemployment here, to see what effect it would have on him, I asked from the audience whether it wouldn't be better to have the unemployed die and reduce the surplus population—an old phrase from Dickens which has been used a good many times. I don't believe that, but it had its effect.

He hit the ceiling. Pure emotion. Lost his temper completely.

I do not think our point of view is any more emotional than the Socialist's. Both sides agree Marxian Socialism is old-fashioned, and is not the solution. Both sides agree in general on the steps to be taken. Why on earth, then, call it Socialism? It is simply a psychological mistake.

I have brought out the arguments myself many times in this place against classical Socialism. I think it would be better to bring them out in somebody else's words for once. You will forgive me for reading so much—it is a school-boy trick that I have never done before—but I think in the last year of debating at Yale one may be happy to find out the things one has been saying for four years have been expressed far better by somebody else.

This is an entire chapter; it is not a long chapter, however, and I feel able to read it to you because although you might have read it at home, I do not think many of you would. It is from a book by a Yale Professor, a great figure around here, William Graham Sumner. The Socialists in this body here tonight are squirming in their seats because "he is old-fashioned." It is true; he is old-fashioned; he did not live among present economic problems. Nevertheless, his remarks on the subject are so trenchant that they strike at the root of classical Socialism. (Mr. Lindley here quoted Chapter 1 of Professor Sumner's book *What Social Classes Owe to Each Other*.)

The psychological approach of which Sumner speaks

is so obvious it might be well illustrated by a little incident which occurred tonight. We went down to meet the English debaters and did not have enough money to pay the taxi so we borrowed and said, "Oh, the Debating Society will pay." The State will pay; the State will do everything! It is an utter impossibility.

If Socialism is not the remedy, what is? I think the remedy is "man" or "men," not systems. A man like Sumner; put him into a position of power, and then let him do all the theorizing he wants to and make all the practical applications he would like to make. The solution is "man" and not systems. A man like Sumner, or possibly, or preferably, a coalition government of these four gentlemen here tonight!

First Negative, Eugene V. Rostow
Yale University

LADIES AND GENTLEMEN: As you noticed, Mr. Lindley and I came into this debate agreed to insult each other. I, for one, propose to avail myself of the opportunity. He has presented to you an elaborate, a charming, a plausible, but unfortunately an entirely irrelevant anthology of rosy theory. His speech is persuasive, his art laudable, his wit soothing—but his doctrine is shot through with a series of loose and misleading platitudes which refuse to be classified into order or coherence. . . . I wish I had brought a book along with which to confound Mr. Lindley!

There is a little volume, also by a distinguished Professor, Mr. Becker of Cornell, President of the

American Historical Association. In twenty pages he describes his concept of climates of opinion, and speaks of men being conditioned in certain lines—conditioned by the circumstances of their lives to refuse certain terms, certain words, certain ideas. Mr. Lindley has been conditioned to reject the word "Socialism." He finds it peculiarly, irresistibly abhorrent. Mr. Wilson and I do not find "Socialism" a peculiarly abhorrent word. And if that is to be the distinction on which this debate rests, we might as well call it off now. Mr. Lindley has been conditioned by Sumner and I by more contemporary Socialists, and we disagree.

We are all accustomed, both from Socialists and their enemies, to this pleasant and pointless speculation about justice, ideals, and mankind; general statements about honesty, workmen, and historical principles; sweeping generalizations about man, God, and society. The very word "Socialism" seems a license for the inexplicit and the inexact. Beating the bosom and proclaiming the glory of the word is thrilling drama for both sides. The advocates of Socialism and their opponents are both often romantic, and given overmuch to the vague and the emotional.

Socialism is, of course, a crusade, and a class movement. It is a religion, and a philosophy of history and a doctrine of social organization. It can make an appeal to ethics, morality, political principles, concepts of the virtuous, the true, and the good. Socialism is distorted by the frequency and the poverty of the popular appeals directed in its favor and in opposition to its policy. But if the emphasis on economic determinism which is constant in the Socialist literature means anything, it implies that the central point of all discussions of Socialism should be the economic program, the practical plan for immediate procedure which distinguishes the Socialist movement here and in England.

Let us then, in this discussion of Socialism and Capitalism, confine ourselves as exactly as possible to the evidence of experience, to what *is* in the world, not to what once was, what might have been, or what should be, ideally, some day. The exciting generalizations to which Socialists and non-Socialists are addicted are useful in debate, in the pulpit, and in politics, but they cannot be confirmed in experience and they are of little use in defining specific economic ends.

I am not going to attempt a brilliant emotional plea in the interests of a Socialist program for two excellent reasons: in the first place, 1 do not like to preach; in the second, you do not enjoy being preached to. Instead I shall limit this speech to the relationship of the Socialist policy to the industrial mess in which a non-Socialist world finds itself, to the concrete economics that make Socialism into a pertinent, a realistic, and a practicable program for sane resolution of the chaos which lies everywhere around us.

Accepting this limitation, one perceives that the simple, obvious definitions of Socialism and Capitalism correspond to nothing in the realm of experience. Neither the touching vision of Capitalism that the speaker from the conservative bench evoked, nor his red beast Socialism bears substantial reference to the facts of a contemporary world. Classic Capitalism ceased to exist long before tariffs and Reconstruction Finance Corporations, trusts and holding companies and Federal restrictions denied significance to the Capitalist boasts of rugged individualism and untrammeled economic initiative. The Socialism of easy formulæ, of nationalization, and bureaucracy, and equal income, and single-tax dissolves like so much fog when brought into contact with the actualities of a complicated economic system.

Confronting that system, one is impressed by two things: its contradictory formlessness and its collapse as an effective instrument for providing goods, services, and support to the society.

It is formless because it gives promise of being mechanized and efficient in its aspects as producer, but continues to be chaotic and disruptive as a means of distribution. It shows every sign of skill in the organization of individual business units, but has failed dismally to integrate and coördinate them upon a basis of stabilized growth. It has failed because there does not exist a background of security in which the technical developments of the engineers can work themselves out. It has failed to provide the balances of intelligent planning without which technical advances are a social menace, not a social aid.

Let us approach the problem of stabilization in a pragmatic manner. Let us consider in a practical way just what is required by the economy as it exists. Investigate the measures which are consistent with the actual need of the industrial order. Attempt to satisfy the requirements of a permanent, a stabilized, economic efficiency. To fulfill these concrete needs must be the primary obligation of any social program.

Any organism depending upon exact demands requires systematic provision of those demands; social systems as well as vertical trusts. Contemporary society consists essentially of large corporate units, which are advancing rapidly towards an all-inclusive balance of interlocking parts. They are based upon a variety of engineering developments, and are approaching a condition of technological equilibrium. Any society in 1932 must use factories and machines and corporate financing; must organize itself into moderately large units, deal with the problems of an essentially stable market.

The world in 1932 is a static world with a reasonably static population and a highly developed economic system whose interdependence demands a stable market. Heaven knows that the limits of production have not been approached. Natural resources remain to be exploited, inventions to be applied, the standard of life raised enormously in a hundred ways. But, in the nature of the productive system, that essential exploitation of resources cannot be free and unlimited in the tradition of the frontier, and the Jay Goulds, Fiskes, and Morgans to whom the dynamic growing frontier society gave full license. The cut-throat competition of the great days of an expanding Capitalism led to an efficient development of the procedures of production, but failed to provide for adequate distribution of profits, goods, and consumer purchasing power. To simplify the issue, then—the system of machines, factories, and trusts demands one basic condition for efficient operation: a wide, a permanent, and a prosperous consumer market. The equipment of Capitalism is already geared for production on a scale enormously higher than any yet known. There are inventions so revolutionary that their proprietors do not dare use them. There are means of eliminating the wastes of Capitalism and obvious steps towards rationalization of industry in coal, steel, wood-pulp, power and textiles here; and in coal, chemicals, and textiles in England. There are hundreds of minor steps which may be taken to eliminate minor sources of inefficiency. They are all corollary to the basic problem of revising our medieval and haphazard methods of distribution.

If one is to proceed with the development of natural resources, of industrial techniques, of national wealth, there must be an adequate and a permanently prosperous market for consumer goods. The problem of production cannot be solved if the problem of distribution is not solved with it, and all other phases of the economists' disputes—their jargon of capital goods and savings and cycles and all the rest of it—are to be grouped naturally around the basic equation of production and distribution.

To create and to guarantee a wide, a permanently increasing market for consumer goods is possible only if labor is given a higher proportionate return for its services, in the form of high real wages. It is possible only if that market is protected exactly as the industrial structure on which it depends and which, also in its turn depends on it, is protected. There must be parallel and integrated control of both classes of economic phenomena—the productive and the distributive. Industry must set about the basic problems of supplying existing markets and exploiting its natural and technological resources with the secure background of a stabilized market for its goods.

It follows from this primary condition in the economic world, this practical, empirical necessity for planning and coördination, that secondary steps in the shape of reforms in the speculative credit structure, in the procedures of farming, of industrial management, of rigid controls in a dozen relationships are imperative. They follow logically from the basic industrial necessity for balanced highly developed techniques of production with a prosperous and a permanently prosperous consumer market.

To achieve this equation of production and consumption, predicated by the nature of a machine economy, there must be added to the existing forms of society a mechanism of planning. The existing forms must be modified and realigned to fit into a more sensible and more efficient series of trusts, but that realignment will lose its only opportunity for permanence if the creation of policy is not given over increasingly to trained men. Lippmann's phrase is "planning through disinterested minds." It is a good phrase. The control of a highly mechanized industrial balance cannot be left to chance or to automatic law or to necessarily acquisitive business men. The fate of the worker and his adequate payment stand too basically at the foundation of all industrial progress to permit chance control for industry. The running of industry, all extraneous issues being neglected, is essentially an affair of experts. "Big questions of policy must indeed be decided in behalf of society as a whole, in the light of relevant expert advice," but actual administration is the expert's problem. It is essential to endow a group of experts with wide discretionary authority and to confine their functions to determination of directions and the exercise of general controls. The negative contribution of Socialism as such to policy is the guarantee of consistent general interest in the planning authority.

Tributary to this planning authority are the economic units, the trusts, in various forms, of various sizes, depending upon the industry and its conditions. In a practical analysis of business conditions then, two things are necessary: the creation of a planning authority, the center of disinterested technical control; the second, a recognition of the variety of forms which changes within this general unifying control of the economy will permit. There must be latitude in experiment, in procedure, in organization. Essential conformity to the rationale of planning, to the end of efficient stabilized industry, is the only constant. No single formula of public ownership can suffice. The basic fact is the equilibrium of planning which must underly the Socialist society.

If these are the conditions of efficient operation for any society that intends to use the mechanical tools which we inherit, what is their relationship to those curiously misleading words about which we have agreed to debate. What is Socialism in relation to this outline of "economic next-steps"?

Socialism is certainly not an easy concept of nationalism, or of little clerks and their government civil services, extended indefinitely into a gray and bureaucratic mist of unrelieved dullness. Socialism accepts the necessity of dealing with issues of organization in a realistic, even an opportunistic manner. It recognizes the trends toward collectivism which have revolutionized the Capitalistic world. It proposes to utilize and adapt its industrial development into a coherent structure of regularized growth. It proposes that the mechanism of control, the planning body, the center of an articulated economic structure, be in reality a disinterested and scientific group. This is in truth a Socialist nucleus; it is enough. Problems of nationalization, confiscation, private ownership itself, become relatively insignificant. Granted stringent control and realistic manipulation of the economy by trained men, Socialism—a stable social order in which economic security based on recognition for labor—is defined—Socialism is the closest public approximation of this trend in economic life and, even for liberals who agree with some points, is the inevitable title for this policy. It is not Communism because it predicates the use of existing forms. It is not Capitalism because it is set clearly against unrestrained private exploitation of wealth. Socialism is the policy for realists who breathe in the same collectivist climate of opinion. Socialism is planning: Socialism is the only permanent program for prosperity. Socialism, I should even go so far as to say, is the program for those recalcitrant and rationalizing liberals, Mr. Lindley and Mr. Irvine.

Second Affirmative, A. J. Irvine
Oxford University

LADIES AND GENTLEMEN: Let me first of all express to you the great pleasure which we of Oxford University feel in being able to come here and debate this question with Yale. Mr. Wilson and I are trying to get inside that exciting entity called "The American Mind." The addresses of Mr. Lindley and Mr. Rostow enlarge that field somewhat. I became, as I listened to them, more excited than ever about the future of the human race. Mr. Wilson and I are foreigners, of course. Coming from England, which you will see on the map behind me at the top left-hand corner, our only hope is that you will be able to understand the language we speak.

When I arrived in New York City they took me up to what I think was the thirtieth floor of my hotel, and I was overcome by grave apprehension of what I saw. I returned to the ground and went into a restaurant on Lexington Avenue. Because I was lonely, I entered into conversation with a girl who was serving me. I said to her, "You know, I have just arrived in America today; I have just come to your country," and she looked at me with astonishment, and said, "Well, I must say you speak English extraordinarily well." That was the kind of encouragement I wanted.

Now we have gathered here to discuss Socialism, and

of course the chief difficulty about Socialism is to know what it really means. I have listened to Mr. Rostow's lecture, and still—I don't want to be guilty of any discourtesy—still, to be honest, I do not quite know what he means by Socialism. As we are dealing with realities, we had better first of all try to agree about that. Quite clearly, it is not the Christian Socialism which excited England and America eighty years ago. The doctrines of Kingsley and Morris and even of Ruskin have undergone a sad eclipse. No one, I feel, pays them attention—not even sufficient attention.

The fact we have got to face in dealing with Socialism is surely that Karl Marx has won the day. For intelligent electors in the United States or in Great Britain in discussing Socialism there is only one final doctrine to be dealt with, and it is Marxism. Marxism has won the day, if you are dealing with realities, and there is about as much resemblance between Ruskin and Karl Marx as there is between—say, Cambridge and the stockyards in Chicago. Marxism is the enemy to which my colleague and I are opposed. It means, as I say, the virtual annulment of private property or private enterprise.

Now on the table which the Affirmative is using, along with other learned books, there is a book entitled *Elementary Economics*. To that book I have had recourse and it is on that basis that I make my plea. For I have listened to all the criticisms of private enterprise, and the Capitalist society, and I have listened to endless harrowing accounts of the depression, and I have never yet been able to discover any defect pointed out which was inherent in a system of private enterprise.

It is suggested on the one hand that there is no centralized organization in the present system; that there is no control; that too great free play is given to economic forces without proper regard being given for the consumer and producer and the wage earner. In other words, the claim is made by the Socialists, that they alone support what they call "planning" and they repeat the word in their sleep—"planning," "planning," "planning!"

Well, there is nothing whatsoever in a policy of economic planning which is incompatible with a system of private enterprise. Nothing whatsoever. You have in England already, I think, the germ of a central economic advisory council which will be able to influence government—observe, growing up within a Capitalist system of economics—an advisory council consisting of experts in their own field who have time to spend in making inquiry and investigation, and who, having done so, can convey their conclusions to the Executive and the Executive can act upon them. And if that isn't economic planning, I don't know what is! And you observe there an example of centralized planning growing up in what is admittedly a system of private enterprise.

All this endless talk about planning is not relevant so far as I can discover, to Socialism, at all. There is nothing incompatible in planning within a system of private enterprise.

Again, they stand up with all their talk about depression and point out the ghastly inequality of wealth. Well, we of the Affirmative recognize that is true. But that is not an evil inherent in a system of private enterprise. In most countries, in Europe and in America, taxation of inheritance and taxation of large incomes has already reached the point where the problems of inequality are being met.

You have witnessed in England before the War an extension of social legislation in the way of insurance and education at a time when the profits of industry and agriculture were already actually on the decline. I do not say Capitalists are actually on the decline. I do not say Capitalists are always altruistic. But falling profits have in this instance coincided with extensive social reforms. You had the two together; that's why it is so absurd for the other side to say that the philanthropy of the Capitalists is traceable only to the profits they are making.

Let me point out in this connection that wages in these countries where private enterprise has held sway have always been high or low in proportion to the calculated efficiency of the worker. And though we would all like to see a general rise in wages, we must admit the rectitude of a system which does at any rate pay wages in proportion to efficiency so far as that can be calculated. I can see nothing about inequality of wealth which is relevant only to Socialism.

They talk about international coöperation. And the best anyone can do is to consider their own history. International coöperation indeed! In 1914 the British

Labor Party, that gloomy body, abandoned its leader, Mr. Ramsay MacDonald, because he was opposed to the War. Mr MacDonald was driven into exile by these novel idealists who talk about technicological equilibrium—was that it?—driven out of the party by the British Socialists.

In France, Jaurés, one of the greatest Socialists who ever lived, and who a Socialist I was talking with recently thought was a medieval artist from the Abbey of Chuny-Jaurés, at the time he was assassinated in Paris, was well aware that he was deserted by the French Labor Party and French Socialists.

And in Germany, almost at the same time, the German Socialists were with surprising harmony—a harmony that has not always been so evident in other regards, passing the War Estimates. Well, that is the record of that Socialist Party!

I can see no hope there, frankly, of greater international coöperation, and I do complain about the persistent categories of the evils in the present system which are made to pass as arguments for Socialism. They are no more arguments for Socialism than they are for polygamy. The evils are there, we admit. Our claim is that they are not inherent in a system of private enterprise.

And, of course, perhaps I need hardly in such an august assembly as this put forward a humble but fundamental defense of private enterprise. It is that it gives full play to the initiative and the drive and ambition of the individual. It gives full play to these forces which in a hundred years, in spite of many errors and mistakes, have accomplished the miracle of the present industrial organization of Europe and America.

If a laborer says to himself, "I desire to become a leader of industry; I desire to influence my generation and plan out a new plant and develop new economic ideas"—if he says that as an individual, I do not see that it is due for him to face all the arsenals of Hell. I do not say that. I say he is displaying once again the great motive power which has created our present industrial system in a surprisingly short number of years; a system, which with all its defects is a standing monument to indicate what the human estate and human mind can do. And whether public committees could have accomplished the same thing, I greatly doubt. I do not like public committees. Æsthetically they are unattractive. Deplorably so. And intellectually they have not the worth of the normal individual saying what he thinks.

Consider the crises which have faced Great Britain since the War, and I do not believe in any one crisis a public committee could have dealt with the situation better and wiser than the private bankers and industrialists did.

In 1925 when we went back to the gold standard and embarked upon a policy of deflation, which has been since proved to be a mistake, I do not think a public committee would have done any better or any wiser. For this reason, to take a concrete example: At the time we were a huge creditor country, to whom was owed vast amounts of money in pounds sterling, and to devaluate at that time appeared on the face of it, taking the short view, the height of folly. Any kind of popularly controlled body, if it is really popularly controlled, is forced to take the short view; it cannot take the long view. It is always a temptation to adopt the course which in the public mind brings immediate apparent benefits, even if with the passage of years it is a policy which proves disastrous. The body which has any element of popular control cannot be expected to take the long view when questions arise in economic organization or fiscal policy.

My friend, Mr. Wilson, whom I know well—almost as well as Mr. Lindley knows Mr. Rostow, and Mr. Rostow knows Mr. Lindley—will probably mention to you—he always does—the subject of Russia, for he has been in Russia. Then, indeed, one is apparently well equipped to face the judgment of all eternity. And it so happens, and I am proud of it, that I also have been in Russia. Well, what did I discover there? I tried ever so hard to be an impartial observer. I ran away from guides who were trying to show me the right things. I tried to discover what it was really like, and I discovered a community of delightful but subservient people, about as remote in every characteristic from the American or Englishman as it is possible to imagine. Subservient, I say, and accustomed to control. And, of course, no liberty. The right to strike does not exist in Russia, and it does seem to me, especially in relation to Russia, that Socialism if it ever should be introduced into this country or England, would mean simply the annihilation of the political liberties which we have spent so long a time in trying to win. I know in England, dock laborers in Plymouth, where there is a measure of State Control, have less freedom of direct action than any other workers in the State, and I cannot understand how any transition can be made from the present state of society to a Socialistic state without such a measure of confiscation, such a measure of penalization of thrift and savings, as would constitute the annihilation of liberty. I cannot see how transition can be made without the reasonable rights of property being destroyed.

And it is all very well to talk about theory and point to Russia and say "I have been there." But we have, after all, on this globe examples of Socialism, not in theory but in fact. Mention Socialism and Socialistic control to any self-respecting Australian and see what he will say!

You can, if you will, look at England. England made the error of returning to power a Labor Government. It ran away; just ran away. Its leaders deserted it, or it deserted its leaders—it doesn't matter very much—it broke up, and Great Britain was forced off the gold standard and the Socialist party received such a blow as it will not very readily recover from, and rightly so. For during these two years the Socialist party sent to the British House of Commons complacent men, the prodigious extent of whose paunches was only equalled by the diminutive area of their minds. I do not wish to be merely flippant upon this thing, because it so happens it is a matter on which my optimistic colleague feels keenly, but it is the earnest opinion of myself and other men that the Labor Party was sending to the House of Commons men who, when they had a great chance, failed to take it. They did not truly and effectively represent the working class, and the rise of the Labor Party coincided with the cessation of social legislation. They divided on the smallest partisan matters. They had a great majority in the House of Commons willing to put through an Act which would nationalize the mining royalties, and transfer them to the State. It was a distinctly Socialistic measure and there was a majority of people, Liberals and Socialists, in the House to put it through. The Government failed to act. The Liberals urged them to deal with those matters, and the Government did nothing. It is such a pitiful record that I cannot be blamed for being a little skeptical about Socialistic idealism and Socialistic methods.

And then, finally, because Socialism—if we are going to discuss realities at all—is so inevitably connected with Marxism that we must realize it is a materialistic movement. In Europe that is undoubtedly so. A materialistic movement—a skeptical movement—and it is just that kind of movement which is least wanted at the present time. What are the characteristics of our present age? It is a big question, but we can agree upon it. There is an absence of any sense of loyalty and authority, and what is needed is just the opposite of what Socialism promises. What is needed, after all, fundamentally, is surely the spiritualization and intellectualization of the machine. What is wanted is some kind of authority, some kind of central belief which can inspire men to diligence and labor. Surely we all agree that what is wanted now by each one of us and by all is *leadership*. And if we want leadership there is only one direction in which we can look—we must get a *man*. If we want leadership, we must get a man—an individual given full scope to exercise his gifts. Socialism will not give it to us.

Second Negative, G. M. Wilson
Oxford University

LADIES AND GENTLEMAN: I should like to begin by agreeing with my friend, Mr. Irvine, in saying how glad we are to be here this evening. Owing to the fact that I am descended from one of the Pilgrim Fathers who had the misfortune to oversleep and miss the Mayflower, I feel considerably more at home in this country than Mr. Irvine apparently has done. In fact, I have actually been taken for an American.

There seems to be a most unfortunate tendency in this debate for the various sides to try to agree with each other. The Affirmative seems to be going out of its way to agree with what we are saying. Personally, after the speech which the first speaker delivered, in which he pointed out how much we agreed in what we were saying, I feel doubtful about the validity of our case. It is one of those cases where we have to be delivered from our friends, and I think part of the difficulty arises from the fact that Mr. Lindley appears to have spent his time studying Socialism in Liberal Clubs, of all places, instead of in Socialist Societies.

If he insists on going to Liberal Clubs in order to study Socialism, it *would* be doubtful what Socialism is. And I have something of a grudge against the way Mr. Irvine tried to treat this debate. He says that what he is discussing tonight is Karl Marx, and that what all intelligent electors in this country and Great Britain mean by Socialism is the theory of Karl Marx. Now I presume even a man who cannot pronounce Technocracy may still be intelligent, and I also assume that the audience here is at any rate moderately intelligent, and therefore I suggest that they have already found themselves as disgusted as I have when Mr. Irvine tries to disprove the Socialist theories of Karl Marx by reference to Labor Parties in Great Britain and Australia. They are two things that cannot be connected.

Take one example of it. He talked about internationalism, and the attitude of the Socialist parties in Europe in the beginning of the War, and said they all agreed with the policy of their countries. I wonder whether or not he is aware of the fact that the Third International was formed during the days of the War by the followers of Karl Marx in order to expound their doctrines against war? The Marxists in Europe were the only organized international body in Europe at that time who opposed the War, yet Mr. Irvine says that Marxism has no international ideals whatsoever.

Take again the question of Socialistic legislation by the Liberal Party in the pre-war days, and the fact that such legislation has declined in England since the rise of the Labor Party. Mr. Irvine omitted to mention the fact that we have today to pay two-fifths of the annual budget revenue in paying off the internal debt incurred during the Capitalist war.

Another curious fact is that the Liberal Government which was in power in 1910 relied for its support on the votes of sixty Labor members of the House of Commons, and the votes of sixty Irishmen, and in order to retain the votes of these Labor members they had to adopt the Socialistic legislation policy which was advocated and supported by the Socialist members. I am perfectly willing to grant that Mr. Lloyd George wanted that put through but it was put through in spite of the official leaders of the Liberal Party who did not want it. There you have an example of the fact that it was due to the Socialist party that sound legislation came about.

Another great difficulty of Mr. Irvine is that he agrees with practically all of the Socialist contentions —practically all of their economic policy in relation to the present depression, which, by the way, was not mentioned by the first speaker although it happens to come into the motion. And he said none of these things were really incompatible with Capitalism. He took as an example the Economic Advisory Council in England and he actually was able, through some physical feat or other, to mention that Economic Advisory Council without a glimmer of a smile. In England when it is mentioned, it raises hoots of mirthful laughter, purely from the fact that it is a body of whose opinions nobody takes any notice whatsoever and which everybody ignores completely at the present time.

What are we to think of this entire Advisory Body

without any powers of any sort as the instrument which will put through Socialism against the claims of thousands of angry, petulant shareholders?

Mr. Irvine failed to find any inherent difficulty with the Capitalist system. The real reason why such a system is a ghastly failure, and in fact positively indecent, is because it contains such a contradiction that no reasonable person could possibly accept it. You have the curious fact that industry is controlled by shareholders whose interest is to draw profits from it. You have on the other side, the workers in industry, and the cost of their labor—and the cost of labor of the workers in industry is regarded by the shareholders simply and purely as one of the costs of production, just like raw material or machinery or anything of that sort. Therefore, you have the constant tendency to reduce wages in order to reduce costs of production in order that profits may be increased. And so long as you have industry organized not in the interests of the workers or consumers but in the interests of the shareholders, you have a contradiction which you cannot get rid of.

Mr. Irvine suggested that wealth is becoming more and more equalized. I had the good fortune the other day to see the following figures published by Paul Blanchard in July of this year: In 1930, the wage loss in the United States was ten billions of dollars. During the same year, dividends in the United States increased by nine hundred million dollars. Mr. Irvine says that wealth is gradually being equalized! Here you have a plain, an obvious case—a plain example of what I said a moment ago. Total wages are steadily decreasing; the technical efficiency of industry is just as steadily increasing, and therefore productive capacity is ever growing faster. And you have ten billion dollars fewer with which to buy these goods. The shareholders' desire for profits acts like a boomerang which destroys first the workers and finally the shareholders. So long as Capital employs Labor as it does at present in the interests of Capital, that is bound to happen. The alternative is for Labor to employ Capital in the interests of Labor. *That is Socialism.*

I wish they would explain just how it all works out. I cannot see anything very dependable coming from a situation like the present and that is simply for the reason that capital has the largest importance at the present moment and aims in the first place at scarcity of goods and in the second place at cheapness of labor. Scarcity of goods and cheapness of labor—these are the Gods which Capitalism worships and it is for that reason that Capitalism has broken down at the present time, and is bound to break down in a similar way in the future.

Now neither of the speakers on the other side seems to be able to get a very clear impression of just what Socialism is. If they had conducted their studies in the proper quarters, they would have realized that this idea of schematic planning is the central point so far as the economic system of Socialism is concerned. In England, at any rate, that means that we want to have under democratic ownership and control what we consider to be the three essential services of the country:

First, the banks; second, the land; and third, power and transportation. And we want to do that because we must convert these services, and especially the banks, from the range of a narrow financial group into responsible instruments of national policy.

Let me take as an example of the narrow interests of a small financial group, the same example Mr. Irvine just mentioned as proving his case against Socialism. When England returned to the gold standard eight years ago, the people who advised the government to return to it were the bankers in London. The only people who have gained financially in England through that return to the gold standard have been the bankers of the City of London; and there you have a plain and obvious case that so long as the Government takes its instructions from the bankers, the bankers are going to profit to the detriment of the rest of the community.

And I suggest, if you have a community representative of industry and consumers and workers, that would not have been able to occur because the interests of the other sections of the community would have been taken into account.

The objects of the planned economy have been already stated by the first speaker on this side. The most important of them to my mind is that production and consumption may in some way be coördinated.

I came across a very delightful little item in the financial column of a London paper before I left England. It sums up the matter admirably. It was this: "The position of tea and petroleum is satisfactory, because there has been an appreciable shrinkage of supplies." There has been an appreciable shrinkage of supplies in tea and petroleum, so everything is going on fine! What sort of a system is that which we have got, when the less we have of these things—rubber, steel, wheat, cotton, tea and so on—the better everything is? And that at a time when millions of people are starving because they cannot get hold of these things! It is just as well to consider that in relation to what I said a few moments ago, about one of the Gods of Capitalism being scarcity of goods. The less and less there are of these things, the more and more certain private people make from their sale.

Let us take the other side, and suppose these things were democratically owned and controlled. Who, exactly, would lose when there is lots and lots of tea and petroleum, if the whole community owned that stuff? It seems to me perfectly plain and obvious that under democratic control the more we have of these things, the more the community would gain, and that is a condition we have not got at the present time. Therefore, increase in production of any sort whatsoever is a gain to a socialized community, while at the moment it stands as a dead loss.

In the second place we hope to be able, and in fact we shall be able, to cure unemployment by this coördinated system of economic planning, because treating labor as a cost of production, it is only natural to get rid of it at the first possible opportunity and increase the hours of labor.

It is estimated that the steel mills in Germany and the United States of America have a capacity far greater than is likely to be wanted by the whole world in the immediate future. Yet, what do we see? Competition of the most drastic sort, to increase hours of labor and cut wages. At the present time these mills are producing more than they know what to do with. Surely, the obvious thing to do under the circumstances, is to cut down the laborer's hours and produce less. And, at the time when it all belongs to the whole community, nobody will lose by that course being taken.

Technical improvements or rationalization benefit at the moment mainly the shareholders, and cause widespread unemployment. Socialism, by eliminating the shareholders, will make it possible for the full benefits of rationalization to be passed on to the consumer in the form of lower prices and to the worker in the form of shorter hours. It is the worker who should benefit from rationalization, not the owner.

In the third place, take this question of speculation which is largely responsible for what is happening in America at the present moment. Last year there was published in England the findings of the MacMillan Commission on Finance and Industry; published by a set of men who by no stretch of the imagination could be deemed to be Socialists, and they find that in the average year in England, fifty per cent of money invested on the Stock Market was lost in the space of two years. Here you have a fine structure, which has a few cracks in it which could be repaired, losing fifty per cent of the investors' money every year! By this planned economy we should be able to get the investors' money, at a fixed rate of interest, and put it into those industries where it is needed, and not necessarily those which happen to give the highest rates of return.

Mr. Irvine announced that I was going to speak about Russia—and then, after his own delightful way, he proceeded to speak about it himself. Since he has spoken about it, I shall speak about it also, and I would point out to him, and to you, that I am not going to discuss Communism, but the pure Socialism which is characteristic of her economic system. It is just as well to keep those two departments strictly apart, because the Socialism of her economic system can be completely isolated from the depression and terror which Mr. Irvine seemed to experience when he was there. He said they were living under a system which completely denied them any sort of liberty. It is true that that explanation is often given of the fact that there is no unemployment in Russia at the present time and that there is actually a shortage of labor. But the actual fact of the matter is that one of the greatest difficulties the Russian Government has to face at the present time is the constant shift of labor from one industry to another. They explain that on the basis of slave labor. How do they explain the fact that the Russian Government itself cannot check this drifting of labor from one part of the country to another? There is an actual shortage of labor.

The second fact is that during the last three years when production slowed up in every other place, it has gone on increasing in Soviet Russia.

In the third place, the standard of living has been

increasing during the last three years, although now, due to difficulties with agriculture, it may fail to maintain that standard during the coming winter; but that is recognized as more or less temporary.

There you have these three facts in a Socialist system—the one system in the world built under the Marxian system which Mr. Irvine deplores. No unemployment, increased production, and up to the present time at any rate, an increase in the standard of living. And in addition to those you have the fact that Russia—again the one Marxian State in the world—is the one State in the world which has proposed total disarmament on condition that other countries will do the same. Where does this cry of the "materialism" of Marxianism, about its being blatantly materialistic and not having internationalism, come in with Russia?

And again, Mr. Irvine talks about private enterprise; about initiative; about drive; and says they are notoriously absent from any sort of Socialism. Now, whether you agree with Russia or whether you do not, I do not think there are any people in this audience who will deny that whatever Russia lacks, she does not lack enterprise, initiative, and drive. And if the workers in that country have not got the liberty to strike, which they have in the other countries, they also lack the incentive to strike, in that they are producing for the benefit of themselves and not for the benefit of others.

If Mr. Irvine wants another example of how Socialism works out in practice, I would refer to a city out in Kansas, which is getting its gas and electricity under a municipally owned proposition, at just one-half the price it would cost for a private company to supply it and, in addition, there are no taxes in that city because they are being paid out of the receipts of the gas and electricity. Presumably, that is managed by some insignificant clerk who has somebody above him, and yet he seems to be able to perform the amazing feat of producing electricity and gas at just one-half the price charged by these enterprising individuals Mr. Irvine likes so much.

Then again, I might refer to the city of Milwaukee which I gather is the one socially controlled city in this country, and which is about the only city in the country which is in moderately healthy condition financially.

Mr. Lindley referred to the fact that what really matters in this connection is man and not systems, and I should be almost inclined to agree with him, but what I do maintain, very strongly indeed is this—That in order that those men may function properly and efficiently they want a system which helps and not a system which hinders them. At the present moment you have a system which gives encouragement to every sort of greed and rapacity they can properly put across. If Al Capone of Chicago retired from business early enough and gave enough money to founding libraries and educational institutions, and so on, he would become as honored and respected a member of this community as John D. Rockefeller or Andrew Carnegie.

That is my complaint against the system we have at the present time. So long as these men can get away with the accumulation of their wealth, they are honored and respected members of their community, and they are encouraged by the system. I admit, as in the case of some doctors, teachers, clergy and so on, there are people who can get away from the damning effects of the system under which they live and I am perfectly willing to admit that under a Socialist system which essentially encourages the virtues of a public and community service as against those of private interests—I admit that under such a system you will get cases like Andrew Carnegie and John D. Rockefeller. I admit there will be people more influenced, in its early years at any rate, by greed than by public service, but even so you have a system which encourages the social virtues that there may be in a man instead of the purely selfish and individualistic virtues. Therefore, I support Socialism, not only on the ground it is the only system that will properly work, but on the same ground as Mr. Lindley—it gives humanity a far better chance than under the system we have at the present time.

BIBLIOGRAPHY: SOCIALISM

Books

Berenberg, D. P.—*Socialist Fundamentals*. Rand Book Store. $1 bds. 50c.

Bibby, J.—*Capitalism, Socialism and Unemployment*. 1929. J Bibby and Sons, Ltd., King Edward St , Liverpool, Eng pa. 6d.

Brooks, J. G.—*Labor's Challenge to the Social Order*. 1920. Macmillan.

Cole, G. D. H.—*Economic tracts for the times*. 1932. Macmillan, N. Y. and London. $4. (12s. 6d.)

Cross, L. B.—*Essentials of Socialism*. 1912 Macmillan. $1.25

Ely, Richard T —*Socialism and Social Reform*. Crowell. $2.50.

Eucken, R. C.—*Socialism*. 1922. Scribner. $2.75.

Hamlin, S.—*Private Ownership or Socialism*. 1925. Dorrance. $2.
Hillquist, Morris.—*Present Day Socialism*. Rand Bk. Store. N. Y 1920. 25c.
Hillquist and Ryan.—*Socialism, Promise or Menace*. 1914. Macmillan. $2.
Hobson, John A.—*From Capitalism to Socialism*. 1932. Hogarth. pa. 1s.6d.
Hook, S.—*Towards the Understanding of Karl Marx*. 1933. Day. $2.50.
Laidler, H. W.—*Social Planning and a Socialist Program*. 1932. Falcon Press, Inc., 1451 Broadway, N. Y. $2.
LeRossignol, J. E—*What is Socialism?* 1921. Crowell. $2.
Paine, W. W.—*Menace of Socialism and How to Meet It*. 1932. Jarrold's. 1 shilling.
Richards, R.—*Socialism*. 1931. Pitman. 75c.
Roper, W. C.—*Problems of Pricing in a Socialist State*. 1931. Harvard Univ. Press. $1.25.
Seligman, E. R. A., Brockway, Nearing.—*Debate: Resolved, that Capitalism Offers More to the Workers of the World Than Socialism or Communism*. 1930. Rand Bk. Store, N. Y. 50c.
Shaw, G B.—*Essays in Fabian Socialism*. 1932. Constable. (Standard ed.) 6s.
Spargo, John and Arner, G. B.—*Elements of Socialism*. 1912. Macmillan. $2.10.
Thomas, Norman M.—*As I See It*. 1932. Macmillan. $2.
——*Socialist Cure for a Sick Society*. 1932. Day. pa. 25c.
—— *America's Way Out: A Program for Democracy*. 1931. Macmillan, N. Y. $2.50. London. 10s. 0d.
Where Society Stands To-day. 1933. Rich. 3s. 6d.
Withers, H.—*Case for Capitalism*. 1920. Dutton. $2.50.

PAMPHLETS

Berenberg, D. P.—*Socialism*. 1918. Rand Bk. Store. pa. 10c.
Chicago Daily News.—*Ramsay MacDonald Socialism*. pa. 10c. 15 N. Wells St., Chicago, Ill.
Fabian Society. London. *Some Essentials of Socialist Propaganda*. Cole. 1932. pa. 2d.
Hansford, C.—*Fallacies of Socialism*. Houghton Publishing Co. 1932. pa. 1s.

SOCIALISM

League for Industrial Democracy. New York. Blanchard, P.—
Technocracy and Socialism. 1933. pa. 5c. Laidler, H. W.—
Incentives Under Capitalism and Socialism. 1933. pa. 15c.
Laidler, H. W.—*New Capitalism and the Socialist.* 1931. pa.
10c. Laidler, H. W.—*Socialism of Our Times.*
New York Labor News—Peterson, A.—*Proletarian Democracy vs.
Dictatorship.* 1932. pa. 15c.
Socialist Party, The. Morris Hillquist—*Socialism Summed Up.* 50c.
Benson, A. L.—*Truth About Socialism.* pa. 25c.

MAGAZINES

American Economic Review.—19:1, March 1929. F. M. Taylor.
Guidance of Production in a Socialist State.
Annals of the American Academy.—149:12, May 1930. H. W. Laidler. *New Capitalism and the Socialist.* 162:6, July 1932. P.
Blanchard. *Socialistic and Capitalistic Planning.*
Canadian Forum.—12:405, August 1932. J. F. White. *Planned Production.* 13:92, December 1932. H. Martyn. *Marxism.* 13:130,
January 1933. L. Warshaw. *Reply to Martyn on Marxism.*
Christian Century.—48:1202, September 20, 1931. R. Niebuhr. *Crisis
in British Socialism.* 49:1271, October 19, 1932. P. Blanchard.
Socialism a Moral Solution. Discussion in 49:1350, 1476, November 2, 30, 1932. 50 456, April 5, 1933. L. Jones. *What did
Marx Really Mean?*
Commonweal.—17:123, November 30, 1932. G. Hirschfield. *American Socialism.* 17:272, January 4, 1933. S. Bigman. *A Reply
to American Socialism.*
Current History.—35:34, October 1931. R. Delson. *Attack on Socialism.* 37:141, November 1932. G. D. H. Cole. *Webbs:
Prophets of a New Order.* 37:691, March 1933. H. Laski
Marxism After Fifty Years.
Fortnightly Review.—131·148, 299, February, March 1929. R. M.
Banks. *Shifting Sands of Socialism.* 132.160, August 1929. R
Chance. *Socialism Looks Ahead.* 139:311, March 1933. J. Hallett. *Karl Marx, Fifty Years After.*
Journal of Political Economy.—39:713, December 1931. E. M Winslow. *Marxian, Liberal and Sociological Theories of Imperialism.*
Bibliography.
Living Age.—338:525, July 1, 1930. *How About Socialism: a Franco-*

British Debate. 341:388, January, 1932. J. Goebbets. *What Hitler Will Do.*
Nation.—135:82, July 27, 1932. A. Templar. *I Teach Socialism.*
National Republic.—18:12, February 1931. *Failure of Socialism.* 18:28, March 1931. W. S. Steele. *Aims of Four Movements: Analysis of Announced Objectives of Socialism, Communism, Internationalism and Pacifism.* 19.12, September 1931. *Anti-Nationalism and State Socialism.*
New Republic.—62:64, March 5, 1930. J. Dewey. *Capitalism or Public Socialism.* 66·236, April 15, 1931. Q. Howe. *Capitalism or Socialism.* 67:22, May 20, 1931. R. M. Lovett. *Review of America's Way Out by Norman Thomas.* 68:4, August 19, 1931. *Socialists as Conservatives.* 70:227, April 13, 1932. J. M. Keynes. *Dilemma of Modern Socialism.* 72:226, October 12, 1932. E. Wilson. *Marxist History.*
19th Century and After.—108:148, 318, August-September. S. L. Murray. *Socialism.* 112:327, September, 1932. A. L. Rowse. *Socialism and Mr. Keynes.*
North American Review.—234:292, October 1932. O. D. Tolischus. *Choice for America.*
Quarterly.—254:370, April 1930. A. Shadwell. *New Socialism.*
Quarterly Journal of Economics.—45:640, August 1931. E. S. Mason *St. Simonism and the Rationalization of Industry.*
Review of Reviews.—83:78, April 1931. E. Vandervelde. *Future of Socialism.*
Scribner's Magazine.—93:151, March 1933. M. Nomad. *Karl Marx, the Myth and the Man.*
World To-morrow.—13:66, February 1930. J. E. Edgerton. *Arguments Against Socialism.* 13:70, February 1930. N. Thomas. *Socialism Upheld.* 13:140, March 1930. J. F. Younger. *Christian Capitalism: a Reply to J. E. Edgerton.* 14:72, March 1931. N. Thomas. *Socialism, the Way Out for America.* 15:258, September 14, 1932. Kirby Page. *Socialism vs. Communism.* 15:443, November 9, 1932. A. F. Brockway. *British Pacifism and the Social Revolution.* 16:104, February 1, 1933. *Socialism's Four Year Plan.* 16:255, March 15, 1933. P. H. Douglas. *Karl Marx, the Prophet.* 16:323, April 5, 1933. Kirby Page. *Socialist Program for Deliverance.* 16:349, April 12, 1933. G. A. Coe. *Motives for a New Order.* 16:371, April 19, 1933. J. M. Murry. *What is a Statesman? Need for Socialist Statesmen.*

CANCELLATION OF WAR DEBTS
*Pacific Coast Pi Kappa Delta Province
Tournament Championship*

CANCELLATION OF WAR DEBTS

FRESNO STATE TEACHERS COLLEGE AFFIRMATIVE VS. UNIVERSITY OF SOUTHERN CALIFORNIA NEGATIVE

The Pacific Coast Province of Pi Kappa Delta held its second annual Invitational Tournament at the College of the Pacific, Stockton, California, March 23-24-25, 1933. All colleges west of the Rocky Mountains were invited to send debate teams and orators by the four Pi Kappa Delta Colleges in California which sponsored the meet. About twenty-five colleges and several Junior Colleges sent teams. Contests for men and women were separate and the Junior College debaters met Freshmen debaters from the four year colleges in a separate tournament.

In Women's Debate two Pi Kappa Delta colleges reached the finals, College of the Pacific and College of Puget Sound, the latter taking first honors. California Christian College won first in Oratory.

In the Junior College Meet, Glendale Junior College defeated Weber College of Ogden, Utah, in the finals.

In Men's Varsity, Fresno State College won both the Oratory and Debate, with the University of Southern California competing in the finals in Debate.

The Cancellation of War Debts was the Pi Kappa Delta National subject for the debate season of 1932-33 and was widely debated. The Question was stated, *Resolved: That the United States should agree to the Cancellation of the inter-allied war debts.*

The speeches in this debate were written out by the four contestants after the final contest, and submitted to the Editor of *Intercollegiate Debates* in behalf of the debaters by the coaches of the two colleges, Professor J. Fred McGrew of Fresno and Professor Alan Nichols of University of Southern California.

First Affirmative, Spurgeon Avakian
Fresno State Teachers College

LADIES AND GENTLEMEN: We are here this morning to discuss the inter-allied war debts that came into existence as a result of loans made to our allies during and immediately following the World War. These loans were made in the form of credits totaling eleven billions of dollars placed at the disposal of the borrowing nations in the Federal Reserve Banks in this country. These credits were used in buying food and war supplies from American producers.

Soon after the war, the United States concluded funding agreements with each of the debtor nations, with the total amount—principal and interest—to be repaid to the United States aggregating twenty-two billions of dollars. Up to the present time, about two billions of this amount have been paid, leaving some twenty billions still to be paid; and there remain approximately fifty-five years in which payment shall be made, which means that the average payment will exceed three hundred and fifty millions of dollars annually.

There can be no doubt that these loans were made in good faith and that they constitute just and legal debts; so we of the Affirmative, realizing that our time is limited, and wishing to deal with more important matters, are admitting at the outset that the debtor nations are morally obligated to pay the United States, if the United States asks to be paid. Furthermore, we are going to waive—without admitting, of course—the matter of whether or not the debtor nations are able to gather up enough wealth of one kind or another to make payment. Rather than spend our time on that matter, we are going to devote our attention to what we believe is a far more vital question. To our way of thinking, the fundamental issue in this debate—the answer to the war debt question—is found in the effect cancellation will have upon the United States; and it is our purpose to show you that the United States will be economically benefited by cancelling the war debts.

We realize, of course, that it seems strange that we should be telling you that payment will harm the creditor nation; possibly an illustration will clarify the problem. If you pay your groceryman five dollars that you owe him, the transfer of the five dollars from your pocket to his does not affect the total currency and credit and wealth of the nation; the labor and industry of the country are not affected by this purely domestic transaction. But when a payment on the war debts is made, there is a transfer across international borders; and the currency and credit and wealth, not only of the two nations, but of the whole world, is affected; and there is a reaction upon industry and labor. These war debt payments involve economic complications—and it is with these complications that we shall deal this morning.

Economists are in accord that there are but three basic methods by which international payments can be made. These are loans, gold, and goods and services. Payment by loans means that the debtor borrows from some other source to pay the creditor; but obviously this borrowing from one party to pay another is nothing more than a postponement of the actual payment to some later date, so let us pass on to the other two methods.

As I have told you, the debts still owed the United States approximate twenty billions of dollars. On the other hand, there is only about eleven billions of dollars worth of gold in the world; and over four billion of this amount is already in the United States. Thus, if the debtor nations used up all the gold outside of the United States, they would be able to pay us only a portion of the debt, which means that the bulk of the payment can be made only through a transfer of goods and services. But my colleague, Mr. Wiens, will show you that if we withdraw any appreciable amount of gold from the rest of the world in collecting the debts, the United States will be injured, since a nation can enjoy the maximum benefits of being on the gold standard only if the gold supply is evenly distributed throughout the important commercial nations of the world. Mr. Wiens will develop this point later on.

And now, in order to understand how payment in goods and services will affect the United States, let us see how international trade is carried on.

When an American exporter sends one hundred dollars worth of goods to some foreign country—say England—he creates in that country one hundred dollars worth of credit owned by himself. Conversely, when an English exporter sends one hundred dollars worth of goods to the United States, there is created in the United States one hundred dollars worth of credit owned by the English exporter. The two exporters are paid by what amounts to a trading of the credits which each owns in the other's country: the American exchanges the credits which he owns in England for the credits which the Englishman owns in the United States. The total amount of credit created abroad, and owned by Americans, is determined by the amount of goods and services which we sell to our foreign customers. The total amount of credit created in the United States, and owned by foreign exporters, is determined by the amount of goods and services which we buy, or import, from foreign producers. If we export more than we import, then we create a surplus of credits, owned by our exporters, in foreign countries. In such a case, if the owners of these surplus credits are to be paid, the foreign customers who have bought this export surplus must either send gold to the American exporter or pay him by borrowing from some other source.

On the other hand, if we import more than we export, then the surplus of credits is in this country, owned by foreign exporters. Here again, the balance is settled either in gold or in loans. While the balance fluctuates from year to year, these variations are self-correcting and self-adjusting, so that over a long period of years —and over the period of fifty-five years in which payment is to be made to the United States—we will export approximately as much as we import, we will sell about as much as we buy, and there will exist an even balance of trade—under the normal channels of trade.

But if any payment is to be made by this method,

then it will be necessary for us to continually import more than we export for the next fifty-five years; for the payment can be made only if there is created in the United States, and owned by foreign exporters, a surplus amount of credit over and above the amount of credit created abroad by our exporters. When there is a surplus of credits here—in other words, when we import more than we export—then the debtor nations can buy up these surplus credits with their own currency from the foreign exporters who own these credits in the United States, and then transfer the title of these credits to the United States government, which will now have received payment through credits created by an import surplus of goods and services. But remember, the payment can be made only if we import more than we export—and therein lies the detriment to American labor and industry.

If we collect the debts, it will mean that every year, for the next half a century. we will have to accept an import surplus, or unfavorable balance of trade, averaging three hundred and fifty millions of dollars and totaling twenty billions of dollars. If we collect the debts, it will mean that we will have to divert an average of three hundred and fifty million dollars of our annual purchasing power from buying the products of our own labor to buying the products of foreign labor and industry. Collection of the debts means that American industry will have to sacrifice three hundred and fifty millions of dollars of trade to foreign industry.

Now understand, we do not object to buying the goods of foreign industry; but we do object to buying more from them than we sell to them; for if we do collect the debts in this way, then we will throw out of work the number of American laborers necessary to produce three hundred and fifty millions of dollars worth of goods every year. And if we throw more men out of work, then we decrease their purchasing power, which will further decrease employment and drag us down deeper into the rut of industrial stagnation.

But to offset this drawback of collection, the Gentlemen of the Negative, if they run true to form, will tell you that Cancellation will raise taxes in this country. Of course, if we cancel, then it will be necessary for the United States treasury to collect a slightly larger amount of revenue each year. However, this does not mean that the rate of taxation will be raised.

The prosperity of the United States treasury is dependent directly on the prosperity of the nation's business. When business is healthy, there is a large amount of taxable property and taxable income, and the revenue of the treasury is correspondingly large. When business is depressed, there is less property and less income to tax, and the Treasury Department goes into the red. In other words, if Cancellation will stimulate business, the government will automatically collect more money—without raising the rate of taxation—because there will be a greater amount of taxable property and taxable incomes.

We of the Affirmative have shown you thus far that if the United States collects the war debts, American industry and American labor will be damaged for the next fifty-five years. We have shown you that if we collect the debts in goods—and all but a small portion cannot possibly be collected in any other way—we will throw our own men out of work. On that basis, we believe that the United States should cancel the inter-allied war debts.

First Negative, F. Clinton Jones
University of Southern California

LADIES AND GENTLEMEN: At the very outset, we wish to make it clear that the question debated this morning is one of complete and outright Cancellation. The Affirmative in this contest is obliged to offer proof that the inter-allied war debts should be completely cancelled, and unconditionally cancelled as well. No other stand, such as Cancellation with reservations, can be taken by the opposition in this debate if they wish to be successful in establishing their case.

Also, we would like to clear up the question of moral obligation in this argument. The Gentleman who just concluded his constructive speech told us that the Affirmative admits that the debtor nations are morally obligated to make payment to the United States, but that this is not essential or relevant to the discussion this morning. Now let me point out that any argument which tends to prove that the war debts should be cancelled is a valid argument in this debate, and also, that any argument which tends to show that these debts should not be cancelled is a valid argument in this contest as well. Now the Gentleman has admitted that the debtor countries are morally obliged to pay us the debts. We say, furthermore, that the United States is morally justified in demanding payment of these obligations, and that therefore they should not be cancelled.

Now in order to understand the moral aspects of the problem, it is necessary to review briefly the historical setting of these debts. During the decades prior to the outbreak of the war, economic rivalries and racial hatreds had been mounting throughout Europe. Germany, with a constantly expanding colonial empire and merchant marine, and a battle fleet second only to that of Great Britain, was challenging England's supremacy in the world market. France was brooding over 1870 and Alsace-Lorraine. Russia, thwarted in her war with Japan, sought an outlet to the open sea around Constantinople, and came into collision with ancient interests of England and Austria as well as the more recent German undertaking in the Bagdad railway. Italy was in alliance with the central powers, but not whole-heartedly, because Austria held the city of Fiume and other concessions which Italy wanted. This was the situation, a veritable powderhouse, when the assassination of Archduke Ferdinand of Austria touched it off in 1914. In the language of H. G. Wells: "All the great states of Europe before 1914 were suffering from the common disease of Imperialism, of aggressive nationalism, and drifting toward war."

And so the struggle for economic conquest began. But at the end of two and a half years it seemed that the best the Allies could hope for would be a draw. Throughout this period the German armies had maintained positions within fifty miles of Paris. Russia had been rolled back at the battle of Tannenberg and the revolution in the March of 1917, had eliminated her from the contest. The unrestricted submarine campaign of Germany during February, 1917, alone had sunk one hundred thirty-four ships, and the Allies for the first time faced the prospect of starvation. It was in this emergency that the United States entered the war, and there can be little doubt that we furnished the additional force necessary to insure the ultimate victory of the allied cause. Germany could never have been so completely crushed had it not been for the men, money, and supplies which we poured into the conflict. For proof of this we have the statement of none other than Marshal Foch, commander-in-chief of all the allied armies who, after the close of the war, stated: "The American people can feel justifiably proud for having brought to bear such powerful aid at the decisive moment of the war, and to have made victory possible by going straight into the conflict without hesitation and in accomplishing an end absolutely without parallel." So we stepped in and pulled the allied chestnuts out of the fire; and now let us see just how many chestnuts there turned out to be.

We fought the war on the basis of no annexations and no indemnities, future disarmament, and a war to end war. President Wilson went to Versailles with these objectives in mind—and what happened? Germany was absolutely stripped of her colonial possessions, her shipping interests, and great portions of her European territory. Great Britain received an aggregate area of over a million square miles and thirty-five million inhabitants. France got a total territory of over four hundred thousand square miles and ten million inhabitants. Italy received substantial territories in Southeastern Europe. It is clear that these huge gains through the Treaty of Versailles far surpass the amount of the war debts.

So we must remember that when the United States entered the struggle, about the best the allied cause could expect was a peace without victory. It was through our assistance that England, France, and Italy were able to so prostrate the Central Powers as to strip them completely of their territories and possessions. And yet these debtor nations are today asking that we cancel the loans. Why in reality, instead of cancelling the debts, they should pay us a bonus for helping them out.

Second, the United States is morally justified in demanding payment because these debts can in no way be considered as contributions to a common cause. France spent two hundred eighty-nine millions to pay off loans made privately before we entered the war—why shouldn't they pay back this amount? She spent one hundred eighty millions for public works—why shouldn't this be repaid? She used two hundred millions to purchase food after peace was declared and an additional twelve millions for French agriculture—why shouldn't these amounts be paid back? England spent three hundred twenty-five millions to pay a grain debt in Canada, two hundred sixty-one millions to support silver currency in India, and three hundred fifty-three more millions to redeem pawned British securities. If England could devote our loans to such purposes, why shouldn't she pay them back? And England and France together spend two billion six hundred eighty-three million dollars—one-fourth of the total borrowings—to support on the world market at high, artificial prices, the value of the franc and the pound sterling; why shouldn't this huge amount be repaid to us?

And now let us see what the United States was doing during this time. We paid cash to Great Britain for transporting our troops to France. If we paid her cash for such services, why shouldn't she pay us back the money she borrowed? We paid cash for British wool, jute, tin, and other materials used for war purposes. We paid for the privilege of landing our troops in French harbors. We recompensed France for the damage done in building military roads and railroads. We paid customs duties upon our war supplies carried into France. In all, we paid our allies over four billions of dollars in cash for goods and services utilized in the war. If we did all this, why shouldn't they repay us the dollars which they borrowed?

Third, we are morally obligated to the American citizens to demand payment, so that they will not be saddled with an unfair burden of twenty billions of dollars. Now the total amount of the war debt installments which remain to be paid under the funding agreements, approximates twenty billions. If they are paid, it means that we have the twenty billions of dollars in the United States; if they are cancelled, the twenty billions will stay in Europe. It is obvious that the American taxpayer will have to make up the loss if these debts are cancelled. But the evil effects of Cancellation do not stop there. If the American people must assume an additional tax burden of twenty billions, it means that they will have just that much less purchasing power with which to buy the products of American industry, and hence our industries will continue to suffer unfairly. Furthermore, relieve a burden of twenty billions from the debtor nations, and their industries will have that much less taxation to meet. This will lower their production costs and permit them to outsell our industries in the world market, and often in the American market itself. Hence an additional depression will be unfairly forced upon American industry and the American people.

In summarizing the Negative case thus far, then, we see that in 1914 the nations of Europe entered upon a war of economic imperialism. We see that in 1917 their situation was desperate, and it was only the assistance of the United States which enabled them to crush completely the Central Powers. We see that, as a result, the debtor nations stripped Germany of spoils valued far in excess of the war debts; and that, instead of demanding Cancellation, they should pay us a bonus for helping them out. We see that large portions of the loans were spent for purely domestic purposes having no relation to the conflict; and that while the United States was thus loaning them money, she was paying cash to France and England for all supplies and services. And finally, we see that if the debts are cancelled, the American people and the American industries will be saddled with an unfair burden of some twenty billion dollars. Based upon this evidence, we assert that the United States is morally justified in demanding payment, because we enabled the Allies to win the war and reap the spoils therefrom, because these debts can in no way be considered as contributions to a common cause, and because we are morally obligated to the American people to demand payment of the debts.

Second Affirmative, Henry W. Wiens
Fresno State Teachers College

LADIES AND GENTLEMEN: Although my colleague, Mr. Avakian, admitted at the outset of his speech that there is a just and legal obligation and also waived the question of whether Europe is able to pay, the Gentleman who just left the platform spent his whole time or most of it upon this irrelevant subject. He said that America is morally justified in demanding payment. Again we admit that but at the same time rule it out as irrelevant. We are not interested in whether Europe can or is morally obligated to pay, for certainly even the Gentlemen of the Negative would not maintain that we in the United States were morally obligated to accept payment if that hurt us.

Let me illustrate what I mean. Suppose Mr. Avakian is indebted to me and he is supposed to pay in goods—tomatoes, let us say. But I wait a while and find out these tomatoes are slightly aged and consequently would do me no good. In fact, since they might have a strong odor, it would not be to my best interest if Mr. Avakian dumped them into my backyard. Now certainly, Mr. Avakian would be morally obligated to pay me those tomatoes—that would be a just and legal obligation. And of course I would be morally justified in demanding such payment, but if I did, you would call me a fool.

Mr. Jones also tells us that the American taxpayer will have to bear this burden if the debts are cancelled. But my colleague already showed that if prosperity were restored to any appreciable degree, this problem would care for itself since the amount of revenue collected by the government depends directly upon the prosperity of the people. When the people are prosperous and there is much taxable property the government receives much more revenue than when the people are in a depression, even though the same tax-rate is used. Let me further illustrate this. In two years of this depression the annual income of our government fell off by over two and one-half billions of dollars, which is about seven times the size of the annual payments of the war debts. In other words, if we can show that prosperity will be restored by only one-seventh of what it has fallen off since 1928, then we will have shown that there need be no additional burden upon the taxpayer. Any increase in business above that will definitely lighten and not increase the burden of the so-called "over burdened American taxpayer."

In fact, Mr. Jones has really admitted that if there is a return to normal business conditions, then there would not be any additional tax burden. So the crux of this debate is: will Cancellation bring back prosperity? Perhaps we should rather say, can there be any return to prosperity without Cancellation?

Now my colleague already pointed out how the payment of these debts would necessitate an unfavorable balance of trade for the United States for the next fifty-five years and how this constituted an impediment in the way of business recovery. I will show how Cancellation will remove some other obstacles on the road to recovery.

It is generally admitted today that there can be no resumption of normal business activities unless there is an improvement in our international trade. Such is the opinion of President Roosevelt and ex-President Hoover and of our leading economists. About ten per cent of all our business is done during normal times for the world market and this constitutes the difference between prosperity and depression.

One of the chief impediments to international trade is the instability of foreign currencies, largely caused by the payment of these debts. During the past couple of years forty-five nations have left the gold standard and when a currency no longer has gold backing it inevitably fluctuates in value in relation to other currencies. For instance, the British Pound Sterling was at par worth $4.86 but it has depreciated to approximately $3.30. However, it does not stay there but is continually changing—one week it goes up three or four cents, the next it drops five cents in value. This is disastrous to international trade. An American exporting goods—wheat, let us say—never knows what he will get for it and the buyer doesn't know what he will have to pay. It's like buying cloth and measuring it with a rubber yard stick. Confidence in international trade has been shaken to such a degree that business has been seriously throttled. It is especially important to the American farmer since the majority of his products are exported in terms of the fluctuating Pound Sterling. It is ruinous to all international trade.

Do not misunderstand me, however. I do not say the payment of the war debts caused all these countries to go off the gold standard. The World War and the chaos resulting from it really did the damage and brought about the maldistribution of gold. But once the economic and financial strength of the world has been weakened, the burden of the war debts is sufficient to keep these currencies down. It is like a man who has been knocked out in a prize fight and then a burden is thrown upon him. He was not and probably could not have been crushed to the ground by the burden, but once he has been knocked down and weakened, he is unable to rise as long as the burden remains upon him.

Both payment in gold and goods tend to cause the currencies of the foreign countries to depreciate in value. If payment is to be made in gold, then it means that we will drain the gold from Europe as we have done in the past and a return to the gold standard is impossible. However, this also affects other nations not indebted to us. These European creditors of ours draw their gold supply from Oriental and South American countries. In turn our government drains it to America, causing permanent maldistribution of the gold supply. As a result of this process the United States already holds about four and one-half billions of the eleven billion dollars worth of gold bullion in the word.

Let me also illustrate how payment in goods tends to depreciate these currencies. You will remember that originally Great Britain had planned to make her December 15th payment to us by a triangular method of trade with Brazil, namely, by buying up her coffee credits in the United States amounting to ninety-five million dollars. But this necessitated the offering of British Pound Sterling upon the American money exchange market—in other words, buying American dollar exchanges with Pounds Sterling. When this policy was announced early in November, the Pound stood at $3.47. The mere prospect of having so many Pounds offered upon the money market made an immediate decline in their value. The Pound dropped to $3.30, to $3.20 and down until on November 27th, fully a half month before the payment would be made, it fell to the lowest point in its history, namely, $3.14½. Seeing this, the English government decided upon temporarily saving the situation by sending us gold from her already almost depleted supply.

Many Americans say, "Well, that's too bad, but why should we be interested?" The answer is apparent. Because of their depreciated currencies the cost of production in these countries has gone down and they can undersell us. For instance, I was recently near the Canadian boundary. They told me there, that if an American went across the border and threw an

American dollar on a Canadian counter, he got approximately $1.15 worth of goods, because the Canadian dollar has depreciated about fifteen per cent. It is quite apparent then that our customers will buy from these other countries where they can get more for their money. The Canadian dollar has depreciated only fifteen per cent but the British Pound has gone down about thirty per cent and the Japanese Yen fifty-five per cent. These countries can and do undersell us.

Here is an example. From 1931 to 1932, the year when these countries suspended the gold standard, the exports of American wheat fell off by one-third, a loss amounting to fifty million bushels of wheat exports. While this wheat was molding in American warehouses, Canadian exporters, due to depreciated costs of production, increased their wheat exports by one-third or about fifty million bushels. In other words, Canada simply took away our foreign wheat markets and brought unprecedented hardship to our wheat farmer. Now remember the same thing applies to cotton, lumber, canned fruits, raisins and other products. We say, cancel these debts, remove this obstacle and permit the American farmer to sell his produce.

Not only are the depreciated currencies ruining our foreign market, but they are demoralizing our domestic industries as well. They lower the cost of production abroad to such an extent that the foreign producers can jump over our tariff barriers and undersell us in our own markets. The Japanese, for instance, through their depreciated currency, can sell electric light bulbs at three dollars and twelve cents per hundred on the

American market while the General Electric Company cannot produce them for less than three dollars and seventy-two cents. In other words, the Japanese can produce them, ship them to the United States, pay the tariff duties, make a good profit and still sell them for fifty cents per hundred cheaper than the American manufacturer can even produce them. The *Literary Digest* makes an estimate—a thing which it seldom hazards doing, but when it does it is usually right—that through this method of underselling us, a million men have been put out of employment in the United States.

Let me remind you of one thing: these nations are not wilfully off the gold standard but have largely been kept off through these unnatural war obligations. Recently the Board of Directors of the Bank of England had a meeting and they voted almost unanimously that England should return to the gold standard whenever such a course is possible. We read in the January news-letter of the National City Bank bulletin, "All of the countries whose currencies are depreciated and fluctuating . . . are anxious for some constructive action to stabilize the exchanges, but there is no denying the fact that the war debt payments are everywhere regarded as a menace to all efforts of this kind." We find, therefore, all evidence indicating that these nations will return to their stabilized currencies if we will only make that possible through the Cancellation of the war debts.

To review, the collection of these debts is placing three big obstacles on the road to recovery: (1) the United States must have annually an unfavorable balance of trade of three hundred fifty million dollars for the next fifty-five years; (2) the fluctuations in foreign currencies throttle all international business; and (3) the depreciated foreign currencies are demoralizing both our foreign and domestic markets. We submit that if these impediments are removed, business will resume its normal activity. We, therefore, ask you to favor the proposition that the United States should agree to the Cancellation of the inter-allied war debts.

Second Negative, James K. Jacobs
University of Southern California

LADIES AND GENTLEMEN: Now the entire Affirmative case has been presented, and we find that the Gentlemen are interested entirely in the economics of the question. In fact, Mr. Wiens has told us, to quote his exact words: "We are interested primarily in the United States, and in whether or not it would hurt us to receive payment." Then the Gentlemen went on and attempted to show us that we would be harmed by payment; they told us that there are only three ways of paying these debts.

In the first place, they told us that they could pay if they received more loans from the United States, but they said that this method was, of course, undesirable. In the second place, they told us that the nations could not pay us in gold, because there wasn't enough gold in the world, and because gold payment would further depreciate Europe's currencies, and so this method of payment was invalid. In the third place, they declared that the only other method of payment was in goods, and that we would have to import more than we export, and that this certainly would be undesirable. In short they asserted that the only three methods of payment were loans, gold, and goods, and then they proceeded to tell us how none of these methods would work.

Well now, payment in loans certainly is undesirable. The Gentlemen are perfectly right and we most heartily agree with them. Secondly, there isn't enough gold in the world to pay the entire debt, so the Gentlemen are right again, and we agree with them. In the third place, payment in goods certainly would be harmful to the United States. The Gentlemen are right again, and here again we agree with them. But these are not the only methods of payment, Ladies and Gentlemen. What our opponents have done is simply this: Mr. Avakian has come out upon the platform and given us three methods of payment, and then he proceeded to tell us how each method was invalid; in other words, what he really did was to build up a Negative case, and then turn around and tear it down. In short, Mr. Avakian built up a straw man for himself, and then proceeded to knock it down. He might just as logically have argued that there were only two methods of payment: canary birds and goldfish; and that they couldn't pay in canary birds because they couldn't fly across the ocean, and they couldn't pay in goldfish because they couldn't swim that far. And so Mr. Jones and I have enjoyed refereeing the debate between Mr. Avakian and himself, and now we would like to have him debate us for a change.

Now then, as a matter of fact, the debtor nations can pay us without any of the evils which Mr. Avakian has suggested. Now the Gentleman has given you as proof of his statement that the nations can't pay, the fact that we have a favorable balance of trade. Well now, of course we have a favorable balance of trade, but that is not the point. The Gentlemen are only telling you half of the story by talking about the balance of trade, for the ability of a debtor nation to pay is not alone dependent upon the balance of trade as the Affirmative would have you believe. Now we should like to tell you the whole story.

The ability of a debtor nation to pay is dependent upon the balance of payments of that debtor, as is the ability of a creditor nation to receive. Now the balance of payments is composed of all the financial transactions between the nations and the United States. In other words, it includes such items as commodities, tourist expenditures, immigrant remittances, movements of capital, and so on. Now in order for a debtor nation to pay, she must have a favorable balance of international payments, while a creditor nation must have an unfavorable balance. With these facts in mind, let us examine the United States' Balance of Payments for the past several years. We have here Bulletin 803 of the United States Department of Commerce for 1931, giving the balance of international payments for the past ten years. Turning to page 77, we find that in 1931 we had an *unfavorable* balance of one hundred twenty-four millions, in 1930 an unfavorable balance of three hundred twenty-three millions,

1929 unfavorable one hundred seventeen millions, 1928 unfavorable three hundred twenty millions, and so on back through the years. Now let us look at the other side of the picture, the debtor nations.

On page 583 of the *World Almanac* of 1933 we find that in 1930 Great Britain, one of our two major debtors, had a *favorable* balance of payments amounting to twenty-eight million pounds; in 1929 a *favorable* balance of one hundred three million pounds, and so forth on back through the years, while *Moody's Index of Investments* states that the other debtors, France, Belgium, and Italy, have all had a *favorable* balance of payments for the past several years. So we find that in the first place, the United States has an *unfavorable* balance of payments, and the debtor nations have a *favorable* balance. In short, all of the conditions needed to pay these debts exist at the present time, and the nations can pay without the harm which the Affirmative has suggested. For example, the debts may be paid in this manner.

At the present time, the United States buys certain goods from Europe, and invests a certain amount in factories in Europe. In order to pay for these goods and factories now, we must secure dollar credits in Europe; briefly, we must transfer dollar credits from the United States to Europe. But if the nations pay us, we already have the credits in Europe to pay for these factories and goods which we already are buying regardless of the debt situation, so all we have to do is simply use our credits which are already over there instead of transferring more dollar credits from the

United States to Europe. In other words, we can be paid without loans, without gold, and without importing any more foreign goods than we are now receiving; that is, we can receive payments without any of the evils suggested by the Affirmative.

Now there is another perfectly good method of payment which also was overlooked by Mr. Avakian and Mr. Wiens in building their Negative case. This is the proposal of ex-President Hoover, President Roosevelt, and ex-Secretary of the Treasury Ogden Mills, a proposal sometimes known as the Hoover-Mills Plan. Under this plan, foreign currencies would be deposited in foreign banks to the credit of the United States to be used by American tourists, investors, merchants, and so on. For example, if Mr. Avakian were going to travel in England, instead of taking over American money, having it transferred, and spending it, he would buy notes from our government which would entitle him to use an equal amount of our credit which is already in Europe. So you see, we have given you definite statistics and facts showing you exactly how these debts *can* be paid without any subsequent evils.

But even if Mr. Jones and I had come out and admitted that the nations couldn't pay; even if we hadn't mentioned the Gentlemen's objections to payment, the Affirmative case would still fall for the following reasons. You will recall that the Affirmative admitted that we are debating complete and outright Cancellation. In other words, the opposition must prove that all of the debts should be cancelled in the near future. So if we can show you that *any* of this debt can be paid, the Affirmative case, since it must support complete Cancellation, will be invalid. Well now, as a matter of fact, Europe has already offered to make a two billion dollar cash payment, thus settling for a dime on the dollar. She has admitted she can pay, she can transfer, she will pay, and we can receive. Now if Mr. Jones and I hadn't even given you any method of paying the whole debt as we did; even if we hadn't touched upon the point, the Affirmative case in supporting complete Cancellation would still be invalid until they proved very definitely why we should not receive the cash payment of two billion dollars that has been offered and that can admittedly be paid without harm. Until the Affirmative proves just exactly why we should not accept the two billion dollars in the face of a huge treasury deficit, their case for complete Cancellation will not be substantiated, and we await evidence that the two billions should be refused.

Furthermore, even if we hadn't given any method of payment and had also neglected the cash payment, the debts should not be cancelled just as long as there is a chance that the nations might be able to pay some day and that we might be able to receive. . . . Just that long we should not cancel the debts. In other words, if we had admitted that the debts could not possibly be paid today, the debts *still* should not be cancelled, because we have no way of telling that at some future date conditions would not be favorable to payment. For instance, we may have a war with Japan sometime and need materials from Europe; conditions may be such that we will need gold and services; or, far more probable, trade balances may be reversed. At least we must all admit the possibility, and just as long as this possibility remains, we should not cancel the debts for we are just throwing away twenty billions of dollars.

Instead, we could have an indefinite moratorium on all principal and interest until such time as they could pay. In this way we would at least have a good chance of repayment, and in the meantime satisfy the Affirmative by giving them all the so-called benefits they have claimed for Cancellation, and by removing the asserted evils of collection. So, even if we disregarded the definite methods of payment we have given you, and the two billion dollar cash payment, the Affirmative has still not proved its case until it shows exactly how Cancellation is preferable to this indefinite moratorium. We await the Affirmative's proof on this point.

In conclusion we have shown you that the United States has an unfavorable balance of payments and the debtors have a favorable balance, thus allowing payment without any of the Affirmative's asserted evils which they brought out in answer to their own model of what the well made Negative case should be. We have shown how we could be paid under the Hoover-Mills proposal. We have shown that the Affirmative has not substantiated its case until it proves exactly why we should not accept the two billions of cash payment already offered. And finally we have demonstrated that until the Gentlemen prove why Cancellation is preferable to an indefinite moratorium, they have not fully upheld the Affirmative burden of complete and outright Cancellation.

First Negative Rebuttal, F. Clinton Jones
University of Southern California

LADIES AND GENTLEMEN: Now let us take up the arguments presented by Mr. Avakian and Mr. Wiens, and see just where and how they have been met by the Negative case, or how they fall invalid when analyzed.

Mr. Avakian in his constructive argument, took up in detail three methods by which the debts might be paid, and showed you how each of these three was undesirable or impracticable. And then Mr. Jacobs, my colleague, in answering his speech, showed you that we need not accept loans, gold, or goods as the only methods of payment. As he told you, of course to continue the policy of loaning Europe money with which to pay is a foolish and undesirable plan; of course there is not enough gold in the world with which to pay; and of course payment in goods would flood our markets with cheap foreign products, and bring further disaster to American industry.

But then my colleague went on to show you that there are other ways by which the debts may be paid without these detriments suggested by the Affirmative. He presented you with the figures of the United States Department of Commerce, showing that the United States has had an unfavorable balance of international payments for the past ten years, that is, she yearly owes Europe more then Europe owes her, and that therefore, the debtor nations already have the credits with which to make the debt installments. Then he offered the Hoover-Mills proposal for payment, whereby foreign currencies could be deposited in foreign banks to the credit of the United States, and could be drawn upon by American tourists, or used to satisfy business transactions in the debtor nations, thus forming another means by which the war debt obligations could be met. Following that, Mr. Jacobs pointed out that the debtor nations had already offered to make a lump sum payment of two billion dollars to the United States, and that we certainly should not cancel the debts when they had made such an offer, which shows that they must be able to pay. Thus we see that there are several ways that may be used in paying the war debts, and therefore the arguments of Mr. Avakian fail to establish his point that the transfer problem cannot be solved.

Mr. Wiens then came upon the platform and proceeded to answer my constructive argument by declaring that the main consideration in this contest is that of economic laws, and that my argument proving we are morally justified in demanding payment is not a valid or relevant point in this debate. Now if the judges will examine their ballots they will find a sentence in the instructions reading: "It is the duty of the two teams in the debate to meet each other's arguments, and they have performed their duties when they have done so." Now we of the Negative brought forth the argument that the United States is morally justified in demanding payment of the war debts. This is an argument against Cancellation, and it is the duty of the Affirmative to meet this argument, according to the judge's instructions. But the Gentlemen of the

Opposition have failed to do so, and therefore our first issue still stands. Of course we have to meet the Affirmative points, but that is no reason why we cannot bring up Negative arguments as well.

To continue in meeting the Affirmative's arguments, now, we find that Mr. Wiens painted for us a picture of a world of unstable and depreciated currencies. He told us that due to instability of foreign currencies, confidence was being lost; that American tariff walls were being evaded through depreciated currencies; that payments in gold were aiding instability. He said, "If we can remove the impediments of unstable currencies, depreciated currencies, we can revive our world trade. The war debts act as a burden; remove them, and world trade will increase." Now this whole argument is based on the false assumption that the war debts constitute some huge colossus which is completely disrupting world trade. In 1929 world trade aggregated sixty-eight billions; in 1930, some fifty-five billions; in 1931, thirty-nine billions. The foreign trade of the United States in 1930 amounted to four billions. Now the annual war debt installments amount to only about two hundred fifty millions. Thus the Gentlemen tell us that the war debts, not even a drop in the bucket in comparison with our foreign trade, or world trade, if cancelled, will bring back a great increase in world trade. Obviously, the war debts are too small a part of that trade to make any material difference, and therefore, the second Affirmative argument is found invalid upon examination. We have taken up the arguments of the Affirmative, one by one, and shown you that they are unsound in this debate.

First Affirmative Rebuttal, Henry W. Wiens
Fresno State Teachers College

LADIES AND GENTLEMEN: The Gentlemen of the Negative tell us that these war debts constitute but a very small part of all our international trade and thus could not affect our international commerce to any appreciable degree. If they are really so small, we are surprised that the Negative is so vehemently opposed to cancelling them. However, we will admit that relatively they are pretty small, but even at that they do have a vital effect upon our international and domestic trade. Most of you have read lumberjack stories. While logs were floated down a river, they would occasionally jam. It was often found that the whole jam was caused by two or three insignificant logs in key positions which got stuck. When they were removed the whole mass would float down the river again. Another illustration. You remember the Battle of Thermopylæ in which a handful of Spartans held back a whole army. Why? Because they were in a narrow pass—a key position. Even so the war debts constitute but a small item of the total international trade, but they are obstacles in key positions on the road to recovery. If you remove these obstacles you make possible a return to normal business activity.

Now it seems that the Gentlemen of the Negative have taken it upon themselves to instruct the judges how to vote in this contest. We, however, have no instructions for the judges—we believe they have enough intelligence of their own to take care of that.

Furthermore, the Gentlemen from Southern California told us we have set up three straw men and then proceeded to knock them down. In other words, they assert there are other methods of payment besides loans, gold, and goods and services, but let us examine these methods of payment and see how they would affect the United States.

Their first method is through the crossing off of surplus credits which these nations have with us. They told you that figures on Page 77 of Bulletin 808 issued by the Department of Commerce show that the United States has had an unfavorable balance of trade with these debtors ever since 1921. We wish to direct your attention to the fact that considering all visible and invisible items of trade, the United States actually had a favorable balance of trade in all these years. Moulton and Pasvolski in their book on the war debts say that in eight years of this period we had a favorable balance amounting to four billion dollars. It was only through the tremendously large private loans made by Americans to these nations which make those figures which they quoted appear as if we had an unfavorable balance of trade. And so, if our debtors paid us through this method, namely, by crossing off surplus credits, they would actually be paying by making further loans from us, which would, of course, be harmful.

Now let us consider their second proposal, the Hoover-Mills method. Through this means, although the Negative has not fully explained it, these nations would create credits in their countries for our use at some future time. That's rather indefinite. But even this must be paid in gold, goods or services. Now if this money is kept in their countries for some future use, they must either pay interest upon the debt or compound the interest. If they pay interest, it must be paid in gold, goods or services. And if they compound it—well, I guess you all know that compound interest will kill anything in time. Perhaps you have heard of the fact that if a penny had been deposited at four per cent interest at the birth of Christ, the compound interest would today amount to a lump of gold several times the size of this world. So, the Hoover-Mills method of payment means that the principal plus interest must be paid in gold, goods or services.

Finally, they tell us that if all other methods fail, then we should not cancel because we might need the money or goods in some future emergency such as a war with Japan or a disaster. It seems the Negative is going to be sitting around waiting for a national disaster. Remember, however, that if our debtors kept this money the same problem of how to pay the interest or compound it would arise as it would under the Hoover-Mills method of payment and this would defeat their whole plan. It would inevitably lead to the payment of gold, goods or services. Furthermore, by using such an argument they have virtually admitted that their other methods would not work and that they are suggesting this as a means of last resort.

Since there is no method of payment which would

not be harmful to the United States and since Cancellation would remove some of the obstacles in the way of recovery, we ask you to agree with us that the United States should cancel these debts.

Second Negative Rebuttal, James K. Jacobs
University of Southern California

LADIES AND GENTLEMEN: Mr. Jones and I have taken the major contentions of the Affirmative in this debate and have shown you that they cannot be considered valid arguments in favor of Cancellation. Now let us consider the Negative's case in the light of the attacks which the Gentlemen have made upon it.

In the first place, you will remember that Mr. Jones' first point was that these debtor nations are morally obligated to pay us. Then Mr. Avakian came upon the scene and said, to quote him exactly: "We wish to admit that they are morally and legally obligated to pay; whether they are or not is entirely irrelevant in this debate." Well, Mr. Jones already has told you that just because the Affirmative does not wish to discuss the moral issue is no logical reason why it is not a valid point in opposition to Cancellation. Obviously, any argument tending to show that the debts should not be cancelled is a perfectly sound point until the Gentlemen of the Affirmative answer it, and Mr. Wiens and Mr. Avakian cannot refute it simply by telling us that they aren't interested and that they admit it. Consequently, this point still stands unrefuted in favor of the Negative.

In the second place, Mr. Jones showed you that Cancellation would transfer a burden of twenty billions of dollars to the American taxpayer. In answer to this point, the first Gentleman said: "Of course we will lose twenty billion dollars, but if Cancellation will remove the impediments of trade recovery, there need be no increase in taxes." *If* Cancellation will remove the impediments of trade recovery! You see, Ladies and Gentlemen, the Affirmative answer to this point is based entirely on the word "*if*." Now when we cancel, we lose the twenty billions, as Mr. Jones has told you. There is no "if" about this. But how do we *know* that foreign trade will increase suddenly if we cancel the debts? Of this we have no assurance, and as a matter of fact, all of the evidence tends to prove that the result will be the very opposite. For this we have the very best of precedents. In 1932, the year following the Hoover moratorium, which virtually amounted to a one year Cancellation, our foreign trade, instead of increasing as the Affirmative contend it would, actually decreased three hundred twenty-five million dollars. Europe, instead of using the money we had released to purchase our goods, immediately rushed over to Russia, the cut-rate store of Europe, and used our money to buy Russian goods.

Now we *know* we are going to lose twenty billions if we cancel; the Affirmative has admitted this. Since we *know* we will lose this amount, we must likewise *know* that we will gain the amount back in increased trade profits if the Gentlemen's claim of a benefit is to be valid. And so, the fact remains, admitted by the

Affirmative, that Cancellation will impose a twenty billion dollar burden on the American taxpayer.

In the third place, I showed you that the debtor nations have a favorable balance of payments and that the United States has an unfavorable one, so that the nations already have at their disposal the credits with which to pay us, so that we could receive without any harm. The Gentlemen have answered this point by saying that we have "told them something vague about the balance of payments," and that Moulton and Pasvolsky say that we have a favorable balance of trade. Well of course we have a favorable balance of *trade;* the Gentlemen are only considering one-half of the story and are leaving out the invisible items such as tourist expenditures, immigrant remittances, interest payments, etc. When we include these items, we have an unfavorable balance of *payments,* and this is what we must consider, not merely one item, trade. So we see that this fact that the debtors can pay has not been touched and hence still stands in this debate.

Then I showed you another feasible means of payment, namely the Hoover-Mills proposal. The gentlemen have totally ignored the point, and so this method also stands untouched by the Affirmative speakers.

In the fifth place, you will recall that I pointed out that the European nations already have agreed to settle by paying us two billion dollars in cash, and that in order to establish complete Cancellation, the Affirmative would have to show why we should not receive this payment. Mr. Wiens answered this fact by informing us that our arguments were becoming weaker, but while he was telling us that this was a weak point, he overlooked refuting it; in fact, he failed to say anything else about it. So this payment of two billion dollars still stands valid in this debate, a challenge to the Affirmative to prove why we shouldn't accept it.

Finally, we pointed out that even if we hadn't given any feasible methods of payment, just as long as there is ever a chance of payment, we should have an indefinite moratorium in lieu of Cancellation. All Mr. Wiens said about this point was that we would "have to prove that we will have prosperity some day." Well now, obviously, Ladies and Gentlemen, if the speakers on the other side insist that Cancellation is preferable to this indefinite moratorium, it is their duty to show that we will never have prosperity, not that we *will* have it. Besides, we pointed out emergencies in which we could be paid, such as wars, floods, or changed balances of trade, depleted gold reserves, etc. So the Gentlemen have not yet proved wherein Cancellation is preferable to the indefinite moratorium, and the Affirmative must show us exactly wherein Cancellation is preferable to the indefinite moratorium.

So we find that the moral argument has been admitted; we find that the Gentlemen's only answer to the twenty billion dollar burden, which they admitted, was based upon an "if"; we find that the two methods of payment which we have advanced have not been answered; the Gentlemen have not yet told us why we should not receive the two billion dollars which already has been offered, and please remember that they *must* show this in meeting the burden of *complete* Cancellation. Finally, they have not shown wherein Cancellation is preferable to an indefinite moratorium, a proposal which also stands as a challenge to Mr. Avakian. So we have taken the Affirmative case point by point, and the Negative case has been reset point by point; and these now stand as a challenge to Mr. Avakian to answer them.

Second Affirmative Rebuttal, Spurgeon Avakian
Fresno State Teachers College

LADIES AND GENTLEMEN: If you will not be bored by further reference to Department of Commerce Bulletin No. 803, I would like to correct the statements made by the Gentleman who just left the floor. The figures to which he has referred on page 77 making a balance of international payments against the United States deal with loans and investments; and we do not see why he has mentioned them, since he has admitted his opposition to payment through loans.

However, on Page 76, which is just opposite Page 77, are given the balances of trade for the United States for every year since 1922. The table shows a favorable balance of trade for each of the years from 1922 to 1931. The totals given represent all of the visible and invisible items which enter into the balance of trade; and, if the Gentlemen will follow me in their copy of the bulletin, I will read to you the amount of the favorable balance for each year in order, starting with 1922: 557 million, 208 million, 802 million, 513 million, 205 million, 588 million, 658 million, 277 million, 713 million, 257 million. Now how can the Gentlemen conclude from this bulletin that the United States has had an unfavorable balance of trade during any of these years or an unfavorable balance of international payments when that is accomplished only by including our loans to Europe?

You will remember that Mr. Jacobs told you that "of course, payment through loans will hurt us," and "of course, payment through gold will hurt us," and "of course, payment through goods will hurt us." He then proposed the Hoover-Mills plan, with which I shall deal in just a moment.

Since he has so emphatically made all these statements, then all that remains for us to show is that the debts can be paid only in these three ways which he has admitted are injurious to the United States. All of the economists in the world—with the possible exception of the Gentlemen of the Negative—are agreed that, basically, there are but three methods of payment. These are, as we have said, loans, gold, and goods and services.

Now let us consider the Hoover-Mills plan and see just where it leads us. This plan would allow the debtor nations to pay us by establishing credits in their own countries and placing these credits at the disposal of the United States Government. As Mr. Wiens has pointed out already, if we are to collect interest on these debts, we can do so only by shipping either gold or goods into this country—but the Gentlemen have admitted that payment in either gold or goods will be harmful to the United States.

Furthermore, if we are to use these credits, the only thing we can do with them is to use them in buying goods in the foreign countries—but this is payment in goods, a thing which the Gentlemen have admitted to be detrimental to the United States.

Mr. Jacobs has suggested that the United States government sell these credits to American tourists who travel abroad. Let us see what this would mean. At the present time, the expenditures which our tourists make abroad are recorded on the balance sheet of international trade as an invisible import into the United States. Remember that over a long period of years, our exports and imports have to balance each other. If our tourists use these credits, then they will no longer meet their expenses by buying up international exchange; which is just another way of saying that tourist expenditures will no longer be recorded as one of our invisible imports. In other words, this plan would extract one of the items from the import side of our trade balance.

But when we decrease the import side of the ledger by pulling out one of the items, then one of two things must happen: either we must increase our imports among the other import items, or we must decrease our exports, so that the trade balance will be even again. If we decrease our exports, then we injure our own industry by curtailing trade; if we increase our imports along other lines, then we have received payment in goods. No matter whether you decrease exports or increase imports, the payment is made through an import surplus of goods—a thing which we have shown, *and the Gentlemen have admitted,* to be detrimental to the United States.

Thus we see that the Hoover-Mills plan reduces itself to nothing more than a payment in goods. And since the Gentlemen of the Negative have so definitely and emphatically agreed that payment in goods will harm us, we submit that the United States should cancel the debts.

Now we have disposed of all the Negative arguments advanced in this debate with the exception of the point made by Mr. Jones that these nations are morally obligated to pay the United States. Mr. Jones saw fit to spend seven minutes in proving this, despite the fact that we had admitted the point before the debate was two minutes old. Obviously, even though we may be morally justified in demanding payment, we should not collect the debts if we can gain more by cancelling them.

Thus, we of the Affirmative, having shown you that collection will injure our own industry and labor, and having pointed out that Cancellation will remove one of the important barriers impeding the stabilization of world currencies and the revival of world trade, believe, not because we are philanthropists, not because we wish to bestow charity upon Europe, but because enlightened self-interest demands it, and because the United States will gain by it, that the war debts should be cancelled.

BIBLIOGRAPHY: CANCELLATION OF WAR DEBTS

Books

Chew, Oswald.—*The Stroke of the Moment.* 1928. Lippincott. $3.
Dexter, P. and Sedgwick, J. R —*War Debts.* Macmillan. $1.50
Gerould, J T. and Turnbull, L. S. (Comp.).—*Selected Articles on Inter-allied Debts and Revision of the Debt Settlements.* 1928. H. W. Wilson. $2.40.
Johnson, J. E. (Comp.).—*Cancellation of the Allied Debt.* 1922. H. W. Wilson. (Reference Shelf.) pa. 75c.
Kuczynski, R. R.—*American Loans to Germany.* 1927. Brookings Institute. $3.
League of Nations.—*Statistical Year Book.* 1931-32. Geneva. 1932. World Peace Foundation. $3.
Lloyd George, David.—*The Truth About Reparations and War Debts.* Doubleday. $1.50.
Moulton, H. G. and Pasvolsky, L.—*War Debts and World Prosperity.* 1932. Brookings Institute. Century Co.
Nichols, E R. (Editor).—*Intercollegiate Debates.* Vol. 13. Noble and Noble, N. Y. 1932. (Oxford Harvard Debate.)
Phelps, E. M —*University Debates Annual.* 1929-30. H. W. Wilson, N. Y. (Debate on Foreign Debts and the Tariff, p. 11.)
Phillips, A.—*Economic Aspects of Reparations and Interallied Debts.* 1930. Stechert. pa. $1.80.
Taylor, Horace.—*Good Business and the War Debts.* 1932. Columbia University Press. pa. 25c.
World's Almanac. 1932. 1933.
U. S. Dept. of Commerce. *Trade Information Bulletin No. 803.* Supt. of Documents, Washington, D. C. (Gov't Printing Office.) pa. 10c.

Magazines and Periodicals

Catholic World —135:620, August 1932. *Echoes of Lausanne Conference.*
Christian Century.—49:800, July 20, 1932. *Will America Cooperate?* 49:1057, August 31, 1932. *Prices and Debts*
Commonwealth. - 16:261, July 6, 1932. *Whose Bill Is It?* 16:265, 16:319, July 27, 1932. *War Debts in a New Stage.* 16:361, August 10, 1932.

CANCELLATION OF WAR DEBTS 163

Contemporary Review.—141:791, June 1932. *United States and the Real Problem.* 142·1113, July 1932. *Chain of Debts.*
Foreign Affairs.—10:529, July 1932 *Great Depression.* 10:688, July 1932. *American Interests at Lausanne.* 11·146, October 1932. *Balance Sheet of the War Debts.*
Fortnightly Review —138:137, August 1932. *Turn of the Tide*
Literary Digest.—114:5, July 2, 1932. 114·3, July 23, 1932. 114:7, July 30, 1932.
Living Age.—343:186, October 1932. *Tory to Yank.*
Nation.—135:68, July 27, 1932. *President Warns Europe* 135:48, July 20, 1932. *Settlement of Lausanne.*
National Republic.—20:12, June 1932. *Cancellation or Chaos.* 20:10, August 1932.
New Republic —71:247, July 20, 1932. *End of Reparations.* 71·273, July 27, 1932. *Franco-British Accord*
North American Review.—234:327, October 1932. *Can Europe Pay Us?*
Review of Reviews.—86:21, August 1932. *Lausanne and Debts to America.*
Saturday Evening Post.—204.23ff., June 25, 1932. *What Europe Wants.* 205.20, July 16, 1932. *The Way Back.* 205.20, August 6, 1932. *Repudiation or Disarmament.* 205:22, August 13, 1932. *Whose Capacity to Pay?* 205:20, September 10, 1932. *No Blanket Settlement.*
World Tomorrow.—15·222, August 1932. *Is It Now Our Move?* 15:273, September 21, 1932. *As Brailsford Sees It.*
Yale Review.—22:78, September 1932. *American Stake in the War Debts.*

WAR DEBTS
Delta Sigma Rho Public Discussion Contest

WAR DEBTS

THE DELTA SIGMA RHO PUBLIC DISCUSSION CONTEST

The public discussion contest is an interesting combination of the debate and the contest in extemporaneous speaking. It differs from the usual extemporaneous speaking contest in that all of the speakers discuss the same topic. Since the topic is known for some weeks in advance, there is opportunity for study of the problem and a more careful preparation of the speeches. The fact that all speaking is on the same topic also makes possible some testing of the speaker's ability to adapt his arguments to those made by the preceding speakers.

This contest differs from the debate in that, instead of taking the Affirmative or the Negative of a motion, each speaker is free to take any position in which he believes. Thus, a discussion team of three speakers may have representatives of as many differing points of view.

The originators of this contest are not attempting to supplant the debate. Rather, they are attempting to reproduce the mass-meeting stage in the development of public opinion before sides have been taken and definite measures have been proposed. The debate stage naturally comes later when the group is trying to decide upon some course of action. Then it is necessary to frame a definite proposal, present its merits and demerits, and have it adopted or rejected by the group.

The following contest rules may be of interest. Teams consist of three speakers. Each speaker has seven minutes in which to state his position and argue for its adoption and three minutes which he may use to refute some opposing argument or to restate his position. The speaking order for the first speeches is decided by lot just before the discussion begins. The three-minute speeches may be made whenever the speaker wishes and can get the floor. The chairman attempts to focus the attention of the audience on the problem itself.

At the conclusion of the hour members of the audience often join in an informal discussion.

The judges for the contest are asked to rate the speakers from first to sixth on the basis of their general effectiveness. If it is desired to eliminate teams, rather than individuals, the team having the low point score remains in the competition. In the Delta Sigma Rho tournament, the speakers receiving first, second, and third places in each discussion are retained and constitute a team for the next round of speeches. The six speakers who appear in the contest here reported, were chosen as the finalists in a tournament in which there were thirty entries.

The judges' decision gave first place to Mr. Wirtz of Beloit; second to Mr. Kluss of the University of Iowa and third to Mr. Hanson of Carleton College.

First Speaker, Mr. Hanson
Carleton College

LADIES AND GENTLEMEN: We may safely assume, I believe, that any audience which has shown sufficient interest to come knows quite well the fundamental facts; but just to renew our minds briefly let us consider the origin of this problem. While the United States was in the war we sent to Europe about ten billion dollars in food, ammunition, and clothing, and in return the warring nations gave us a promissory note to repay at five per cent interest. Payments were made very satisfactorily until we came to the present world wide depression. Now payments are so difficult that European Governments have called for reconsideration of the entire problem. We do not believe cancellation of the war debts will bring back prosperity, as the chairman has suggested it might. But I believe that, regardless of whether Europe is in prosperity or depression, or regardless of the condition, the United States is bound to lose more money by collection of the war debts than she gains by the face value of payments. Allow me to illustrate in the fashion of Mr. Æsop.

On the island of Borneo is a tropical stream, on one side of which is a wooded area in which live the orang-outangs, the wisest of all the animal kingdom. On the other side of the stream are rolling hills in which live the rhinoceroses, and in the stream which flows down the center we have the hippopotami. Now, at one time the rhinoceroses declared war on the hippopotami because one of their princesses had been killed. The rhinoceroses began running short of ammunition and clothing and went over to the orang-outangs and said, "Won't you send us over some supplies," and the orang-outangs gladly consented upon this one condition, that all loans be repaid in cocoanuts, their medium of exchange. The war was soon over and the rhinoceroses began to look around for cocoanuts. To their embarrassment they discovered that all the cocoanuts on their side had been destroyed by the war, and the remainder were in the land of the orang-outangs. So they organized foraging parties to go across the river and take cocoanuts and use them in payment of their debts. Unfortunately, the orang-outangs, being the wisest animals on earth, built a high stone wall to protect those cocoanuts. Can you imagine a more agonizing situation than being forced to pay ten thousand cocoanuts to the other side when virtually all the cocoanuts are over there already, protected by a high stone wall? Fortunately, the orang-outangs, realizing those cocoanuts could not be paid, and valuing the friendship of the rhinoceroses, cancelled the war debts.

The United States today is a tribe of orang-outangs troubled with the collection of ten billion cocoanuts. We went to the debtor countries to state specifically that all debts must be repaid in gold, which is our medium of exchange. Each of our European debtor nations, except France, finding it did not have the gold with which to meet the payments, organized a policy of foreign trade. But the United States, not lacking in the cleverness of the orang-outangs, has built a high tariff wall to protect our gold, so we have placed Europe in the impossible position of having to pay ten billion dollars in gold to the United States, while practically all the gold is over here already and can not be got without doing economic harm to the United States.

Great Britain is our largest debtor nation. She is off the gold standard and yet is required to pay the United States one hundred million dollars in gold every six months for sixty-two years. To get that gold Great Britain has adopted two abnormal policies. First, she has tried to create a favorable balance of trade with the United States by refusing to buy American products and forcing us to buy British products. In 1920 Great Britain was buying one-fifth of our surplus, today she buys less than one-tenth. Thus, in attempting to get the gold Great Britain is depriving us of our foreign markets. The foreign producer has cut his prices and is selling through the Smoot-Hawley tariff bill. This is throwing American men out of employment.

Nor is Great Britain's influence upon foreign trade

the only injury to the United States. We find when she could not get enough gold, she started selling her silver reserves to the French Government. Thus by selling and by flooding the silver market Great Britain was forcing down foreign prices on wheat and cotton, to mention two American products. The American farmer has to cut his prices in order to meet foreign competition, and the United States suffers again.

We have only to look at a recent issue of the *Business Week* which estimated the United States is losing one dollar for every ten cents collected. You throw up your hands and say, "That is obviously exaggerated," but we find upon consulting statements of such economists as T. E. Gregory of Cambridge, Norman Angell of London, and H. G. Hjalmar Schacht of Berlin, these losses are three or four times the size of the payments on the war debts. Mark Twain affords an illustration of the utter folly of demanding the impossible by telling the story of two darky boys who tied a donkey's tail to a fence post and then held a carrot out to see the donkey wince when he pulled his tail. With all due respect to the United States and the ordinary horse sense of the American people, it seems to me we have tied our tail to a fence post and are jumping impatiently at a twenty billion dollar carrot in Europe. And I should say not a single carrot of it is 24-karat material.

In conclusion, Shylock demonstrated that you can not take a pound of flesh without taking some of the life blood along with it. Our experience with the war debts has shown we cannot take gold from Europe without sacrificing some of the life blood correlated with throwing men out of employment, depriving us of our foreign markets, and lowering the prices of our products. The logical step is to follow the example of the orang-outangs and cancel the war debts.

Second Speaker, Mr. Elmer
Northwestern University

LADIES AND GENTLEMEN: With a certain brusqueness and with an old Roman contempt for the superfluous, I am coming right to the subject matter at hand and say I am a cancellationist, and if you like, upward and onward forever cancellationist!

When a person of ordinary intelligence comes face to face with the problem of war debts he find a confusing scene. In the first place he find facts which are complicated in themselves. In many cases they are contradictory. He find these facts of such complex nature that their implications are not often obvious and they do not float lightly on life like ducks on a pond. He finds there has been shot through the whole scheme of war debts, sordid motives and purposes which are obviously not for the common good. What does he do? I would recommend to him, if I saw him in that ordeal, that it would be the best thing for him to step boldly onto the scene, plant his legs widely apart and ask, What can you tell me that is not disagreed upon by competent authorities? In other words, what debated subject is concerned with the war debts that is not debatable?

And if he asked that question seriously I think there is one answer that must be given first of all, because it has behind it the weight of all authorities who have studied the problem. That answer is: If these debts are paid they must be paid in the form either of goods or of services, and mostly in the former. That then is given to him as something not disputable. After he has the fact he wants to go and ask certain questions which bump into him and demand answering. Among those questions are, Can they be paid? Can the war debts be paid? Should they be paid? If they can and should be paid, what would be the effect if they were paid? I propose to consider a possible answer that might be given to him to show what would happen if these war debts could be paid and to try to show that it would be detrimental to the creditor nation to receive them.

In adopting my suggestion I say with unashamed simplicity it is a naïve attitude, the attitude of the old proverb, "Join the naïvians and see the world." The only way you can get anywhere is, as I said before, to have your feet planted solidly on the ground and consider the problems which are not disputable. We find in examining world trade much complex material.

When I first tried to find out how world trade acted in order to find out whether or not it would be detrimental for the creditor nation to receive these goods, I sat down and read volumes and excerpts from volumes, and made very little progress. Then I went to a gentleman who was formerly foreign representative of the American Express. He is a real kind of gentleman, a fine old fellow that smokes a pipe and sits in a chair and does everything an old man does when he grows old gracefully. I said to him, "Can you tell me how foreign trade works?" "Well," he said, "I don't know what they teach you over at school, and I don't know what the textbooks say, but I can tell you how it actually works." He used this example: "Here is a single English exporter who wants to ship goods to the United States. How does he do it? He receives orders and ships goods over here. We'll assume that he ships one thousand dollars worth of goods. That one thousand dollars is deposited to his account in a New York bank. He, in turn, can sell this credit to an English importer who wants to buy goods from us. Now, if an Englishman wants to buy one thousand dollars of cotton or wheat he does so by buying credits in the New York bank and applying them on the purchase of cotton or wheat. You can readily see that trade moves in healthy circulation, which finds an affinity in the whirling wheels of every factory on both sides of the big pond. That is how it works without the artificial atmosphere or the artificial injecting of the war debts into the whole scheme of world trade.

"When you get war debts, here is the situation. This English exporter ships over one thousand dollars worth of goods and he gets credit in the New York bank. What does he do with his credit? Instead of selling to an English importer who would buy goods from us, he sells his credit to the English Government to apply on war debts."

I must confess a light dawned upon me. The whole

thing seemed absurdly simple for so much speculation, and I saw therein an explanation to my questions. It answers among other things the problem of whether or not we should cut down war debts and collect as much as we can, because it is a simple fact even if you do cut them down, every dollar you collect which is used to pay off the war debt is not a dollar which can be used to buy goods from us. Here is another thing that may not be minimized in importance: our export trade may not be considered an insignificant factor of the world trade picture. If you were to ask me today what, in my opinion, constitutes the greatest single phenomenon of the industrial depression, I would be bold enough to say those unprecedented means of production and equally unprecedented limited means of consumption. There is only one solution—I am again being naïve—to get rid of over-production. How are we going to do that? By demanding that we use every dollar which an Englishman gives in return for goods he buys from us? It will never happen that way, obviously. What we have to do is to sell our goods for the dollar he wants to pay. Now we are producing in this country eight hundred million bushels of wheat every year. Domestic consumption is six hundred million. We have two hundred million bushels of wheat that we must get rid of or glut the market. The only way we can do that is to remember the truth of that statement which I wish could be emblazoned across the sky so that every politician could see it, and that is: A dollar used for payment of war debts is not a dollar that can be used to buy goods from us.

Third Speaker, Mr. Vogel
University of North Dakota

LADIES AND GENTLEMEN: The gentlemen have set forth their proposition for the cancellation of war notes in a very business-like manner. In doing that it has seemed to me very unlike the European nations. There has been a lot of agitation for the cancellation of the war debts during the last three or four years. Most of this has come from Europe. It has always seemed to me that the European nations in asking for the cancellation of the war debts, have gone at this business in the wrong way. They have said to the Americans, "Well, the debts were not owed after all. We fought your battles for you. The war was fought in common cause," and American taxpayers and American citizens remember that during the war fifty thousand American lives were lost over there. They remember that forty-two billion dollars of American money was spent during that war. But Europe goes on and says, "You loaned us the money, but the money was spent in your country and you got profits from that money." The American people remember that during the war six billion dollars of American money was spent in European nations and European nations asked exorbitant prices for their products. European nations go further and say, "You are bound to cancel the war debts because of the Hoover Moratorium." But the American people remember that when the Hoover Moratorium was declared, the Senate of the United States, in sanctioning that moratorium, specifically told the European nations that the United States would not agree to outright cancellation of the war debts.

The European nations have set forth these arguments, arguments which today appear illogical, arguments which the American people have answered. These arguments have created lots of animosity and hatred toward Europe; and Europe in turn has hated America. I sometimes wish the European nations might have been like the first two Speakers tonight and set forth the proposition in a business-like manner that should appeal to the taxpayers, and say, "It is better business to cancel war debts; it is good economics to cancel war debts." It is the thing to do, and to understand that we must remember that something of great economic importance happened in 1914 and up to 1920.

Between 1914 and 1920 the United States was changed from a debtor nation to a creditor nation. During those six years the United States was changed from a nation which had been paying out five hundred million dollars every year to a nation which was to receive twenty-two billion dollars in the form of war notes. And not only that. At the same time, America was maintaining a favorable balance of trade. Imagine that economically! Here were these nations shipping gold to the United States in payment for the war debts. On the other hand here were these nations shipping gold to the United States to make up the unfavorable balance of trade in favor of the United States. Obviously such a situation cannot go on economically. The European nations have tried to pay, they have paid in part, but they cannot go on doing that indefinitely.

Just as soon as the American taxpayer, just as soon as the American people realize that America cannot be a creditor nation and at the same time have a favorable balance of trade, just that soon the American people will say, we are willing to cancel the war debts. Therefore these alternatives are up to the American people. Either we are to become a creditor nation and have an unfavorable balance of trade or we are to become a debtor nation and have a favorable balance of trade. That is the proposition up before the American people today. For my part I say it is far better economically, it is far better from a business standpoint for the American people to cancel those war notes, to give those war notes back to Europe and maintain the favorable balance of trade by keeping American manufacturing men working in this country, by keeping American laboring men working in this country, and by selling our goods to Europe. Under the situation today we find America is trying to sell to Europe and Europe will not buy.

The first speaker told you that England, as far as buying products from the United States is concerned, finds that its buying power has dropped off from one-fifth to one-tenth. France last week erected more tariff barriers against the United States.

We are finding out it is a pretty hard proposition to sell to someone who owes you money. If you don't believe that, try it yourself. Go down the street and meet a man who owes you five dollars and try to sell him something and increase that debt. It is a lot easier to go to a man to whom you owe money and sell him something and thereby have something cut away from the debt you owe him. And so I say, in consideration of these economic facts, the American people should cancel the war notes; the American people should take the view that they should maintain a favorable balance of trade and at the same time be a debtor nation.

Fourth Speaker, Mr. Bury
University of Wyoming

LADIES AND GENTLEMEN: In opening my part in this question of war debts I want to say how very glad I am that we are discussing this question and not debating it. If this had been a debate it would probably have been stated, *"Resolved;* that America should cancel the war debts." Now, as a theoretical proposition it may be all very well that we should cancel the war debts. But, when something must be done between now and June 15, and that something can't be done as a practical matter, it makes very little difference whether we should do it or not. In this discussion I am going to consider American public opinion and American politics as facts. In a debate we would not be allowed to do that. They would tell us we were discussing this question in order to form public opinion, but I believe that public opinion and politics do have to be considered just as much facts as, for example, the capacity of Germany to pay. Recently in my college work I circulated a questionnaire and one of the questions was, Do you believe that war debts should be cancelled? The answer was decidedly, No. American public opinion is set against the cancellation of war debts.

The present war debt set-up then is very briefly this. Germany can't pay. Various economists' studies prove that quite conclusively. The preceding speakers have elaborated on that contention. Germany can't pay. The Allies won't pay unless Germany pays, and America won't cancel. Public opinion in the United States being what it is and American politics being what it is, America can't cancel the war debts. Politics and public opinion being what they are, America is just as powerless to cancel war debts as is an unarmed individual or an armless individual to throw a stone.

There are two alternatives. We can repudiate the war debts or we can extend them. We can extend the debts until such time as Germany can pay, or we can extend the debts until such time as American public opinion would shift. There is that possibility, until such time as we can cancel. After all, today, the time of depression, is a very poor time to judge the capacity of Germany to pay. We know in 1824, over one hundred years ago, Mexico borrowed six million pounds from Great Britain. In those days six million pounds was a lot of money and meant a great deal more than it does now. For forty years Mexico paid scarcely a dime upon those English bonds. They were adjusted and refunded and extended until finally, in 1864, forty years after the debt was contracted, Mexico paid her bonds. As a result of that experience English investors are still hoping that the confederate bonds contracted and defaulted around the time of the Civil War may yet be paid, and according to a recent writer, if conditions in the southern states should pick up in the next half century, English investors may yet see their hopes realized. Mexico could not pay for forty years. She was a new country just getting set up. She had a small population. Like Germany in recent years, she had a war, a war with the United States in which one-half of her richest territory, California included, was torn away from her. She couldn't pay her war debts then. She was as helpless to pay them as Germany is today. But other things happened in that forty years. The Civil War took place in the United States. It smiled on Mexico. Mexico profited by the Civil War in the United States just as America profited by the World War, and finally she was enabled to pay her debts.

If we are ever to have a world in which nations harmonize, contracts must be made just as binding and inviolable as contracts between you and me in private life. In private life if an individual defaults for a short time in his contracts, we allow him to take a bankruptcy. His debts are cancelled and he is given a new start in life. However, a nation can scarcely be compared to a man. A nation goes on for hundreds of years. Its affairs fluctuate and vary. There may be a condition of prosperity, a condition of depression.

Today is a very poor time in which to judge the capacity of Germany to pay. In 1914 we were a nation with an unfavorable trade balance. We could not foresee the World War. We could not foresee that we would have a favorable trade balance with all the gold in the United States, that there would be no possibility of Germany and the Allies paying their debts. Just a few years ago we could not see the present depression. We refund Germany's debts on the basis of inflated prices and a depression comes along and turns the tables on our refunding work. It is hard to say just what economic international factors may happen within a few years to change the capacity of the Allies and Germany to pay. Debts should be extended until such time as debts can be paid, or until such time as American public opinion can shift to the point where debts can be cancelled. That is, as I see it, the only solution —extension.

Refutation, Mr. Elmer
Northwestern University

LADIES AND GENTLEMEN: The gentleman who has just spoken to you raised a very interesting point that I think should be dealt with and considered whether or not it was a sound condition. I believe it is within the province of a discussion of this kind to say it is a factor whether or not the debtor nations will pay. Now, ordinarily in a debate or discussing a proposition of this kind we say that does not matter, we are arguing whether or not they should pay. But in any communication between the governments or in the councils which the President holds, that is a problem: whether or not the debtor nations *will* pay.

Mr. Bury, in elaborating that point, said that public opinion in the United States is definitely against the cancellation of war debts. How did he prove that? He quoted to us. He said, "We have conducted a research among the housewives of America and they have been," I think he said, "overwhelmingly in favor of collecting the war debts." Now, it seems to me that if any group of housewives could get any unanimity on a question of this sort, that if the allied housewives of America would ever move in a solid block behind some gesture involving international trade, I would be inclined to decide that they were wrong. Because, after all, they bring to this problem—and I have tried in my first speech to show you some of the complexities that arise out of it—they strike boldly and bring to it their experience with the milk man in bickerings over the amount of cream that is consumed. In other words, they have taken the dangerous attitude towards the whole affair of the man who says, "I loaned you ten dollars last week, now, hang you, pay it." But we can show you the situation is not analogous at all. The real solution is, "I loaned you ten dollars last week, and it is going to hurt me a lot to receive that ten dollars, I don't want it." That would be a closer analogy, if there were ever any such thing.

His premise, of course, is valid. That should be considered but not in the light he means. I noticed especially his point. I think that the whole thing centers down to approximately this, that the war debts should be extended until such time as public opinion will finally assent to cancellation. But is that the solution? If you had a nation of people who were desperately united against an action which you firmly believed was the right thing, is the correct policy for you to sit back and calmly wait until they are educated? There has not been a book written on democracy in the last one hundred fifty years that has not ended with that theory. Or should you try to convince them that they are wrong and that it would be actually to their detriment to receive these war debts?

It has been the experience of political questions that the minority is almost always wrong, but, at the same time, that any progress is made by the enlightened few. Therefore, the solution is not to collect the debts —I mean reduce them and collect them when public opinion is molded—but to convince the men enough to swing over to our side and see the thing carried through because it would be desirable to cancel the debts.

Fifth Speaker, Mr. Wirtz
Beloit College

LADIES AND GENTLEMEN: We have heard some comments on the matter of questionnaires. If the keynote of this discussion is informality, I would like to ask how many of this audience are in favor of cancellation. I am going to ask all those opposed to cancellation to raise their hands. I compliment you on your bravery. Now, I want to see the hands of those in favor of cancellation. I want to compliment you on agreeing with me. That is my position. I compliment you on your intelligence. But, presuming on my intelligence, I am going to address my remarks to you goats on the opposite side of the fence from my sheep pasture. I would like to sell my idea to you.

I am trying to diagnose your trouble as one of two

things, either a bad case of misunderstanding peritonitis, or of "ununderstanding" hallucinations. Those are heavy terms. Let us cut out the last, either misunderstanding of the situation or "ununderstanding" of it. Briefly, I mean this. I am afraid if it is misunderstanding, you have been called Shylocks until you are becoming so impregnated with anti-European attitude that you have lost your perspective. They have been telling you, you do not have to cancel. You fought in the European war; you know these debts should be paid. And the Republicans have built up that anti-continental attitude until your sense of judgment is distorted. That is what I would call misunderstanding, but I do not believe that is the principle that may cause the flush in your face. I am afraid it is "ununderstanding." You do not understand the situation. The second speaker, I think it was, told you that these debts cannot be paid; that the European nations cannot pay them. I did not understand that at all until I started to investigate, and I doubt if you realize the fact that European nations are not in position to pay. I think a good deal harder to understand is the fact that the United States is not in position to accept payment. That seems absolutely foolish. I am sure it is not although I know every magazine I pick up tells me that is the very situation. It is a paradoxical situation when the housewives are opposed to cancellation, and all magazines are in favor of it, and all senators are opposed to cancellation, and the President will not even consider the proposition!

You cannot realize that the economic welfare of the

world is so interdependent between the nations today that our business cannot prosper until England and France prosper. I cannot fathom it, myself. My point is this—the question is so complex that the man in the street cannot understand it and neither can the Congressmen.

I have one little proposition I would like to throw out to you to see what the rest of you think about it. You have read of this plan of Mr. Levinson, Chicago business man whom you might know as the originator of the Kellogg-Briand pact. His plan briefly is this: to correlate the cancellation of these debts and reduction of international armaments. I cannot go into that in detail but the proposition is this. We say to France, "You owe us two hundred million dollars this year. We will cancel that, cross it off and reduce our armaments two hundred million dollars if you in turn will reduce your armaments two hundred million dollars." The result is a saving to France of two hundred million dollars in debts and a reduction of two hundred million dollars in armaments. The saving to us is two hundred million dollars we will not have to spend on armaments, so our position remains the same and France benefits. It sounds like snake oil and I am afraid it is Utopian. I think it will not work out, but theoretically it is a good plan.

I think the United States should be ashamed of itself for taking no position of leadership in this matter. I think all we need to start the disarmament ball rolling is some kind of a lever and we have that lever in our hands if we will use it. We can solve the international economic situation and at the same time take a forward step in the matter of international coöperation and peace.

Now, I present to you that President Roosevelt's biggest problem is debunking and disinfecting American public opinion. If we will extend our perspectives beyond the limits of our own noses, we may get somewhere. If we stop consulting our emotions and our rights and turn to our interests and see where they lie, we may find a solution to this whole situation.

Sixth Speaker, Mr. Kluss
University of Iowa

LADIES AND GENTLEMEN: It seems we are involved in a discussion of a subject, which, with all of its ramifications, is something far beyond the comprehension of the average individual. I am sure I do not understand it, and a good many of these men who profess intelligence on the question do not understand it as thoroughly as they seem. It seems to me these people who are saying war debts should be cancelled because they cannot be paid should have some thesis by which they prove that assertion.

I have tried to study the subject a little and it seems there is a definite, logical way that the reason Europe cannot pay can be explained so that everyone can understand it. Before we go into this very intricate explanation, let us consider this fact. We do not want to deal with the ideals of the situation. We want to deal with the realities. There are people who say if

Europe should cut down her armaments she could pay the United States, or if Europe should make certain budgetary reductions she could pay the United States. Instead of dealing with the things that should be done, or with whether or not they should be done, I feel it would be better if we temporarily would project ourselves into the realm of reality; take the facts as we see them; discuss them in simple terms that everybody can understand; and then draw our own conclusions.

Now, it would be absurd for anybody to stand before an audience and assert that Europe with her vast resources, with her energetic people, her manufacturing industries, could not pay a sum approximating ten billion dollars a year. If Europe were to pay the entire debt tomorrow it might cause considerable distress, but we cannot argue that Europe does not have the ability to pay that. I am going to use a very unfortunate term which I feel may be disputed by some of you when I say Europe does not have the capacity to pay that. What do I mean by capacity as distinguished from ability? Let us project ourselves into another Utopian realm and assume that each of us has a ten dollar bill in his pocket, and each a debt of ten dollars to be paid. Certainly no one can dispute our ability to pay that debt because here is a ten dollar bill and there is a like amount we owe, so we have the ability to pay. Now, assume we have to live for the next two weeks—board, room, clothing and other expenses are going to cost us approximately ten dollars. Now, what is our capacity to pay that debt? The sheer necessities of life cannot be purchased and still render us able to pay a cent toward the debt we owe. That is what I mean by the capacity of anybody, whether it be an individual, a nation, or a corporation, to pay a debt. It depends upon the excess of your income over your outgo.

Now, in dealing with that capacity there are two means by which the debt might be paid. The United States says, "We will accept payment only in gold," and economists warn that we will pay in goods and services eventually. Everything will reduce to that. Let us consider gold. Again we come back to economics. What is gold anyway? We have heard it called the life blood of a nation; we have heard it called cocoanuts and various other things during this discussion. But, in reality, it is just a material thing in which people have an unlimited amount of confidence. What part does this gold play in a nation's entire monetary and financial system? I think the best illustration of the nation's financial system is an inverted pyramid. Let us assume this pyramid is turned upside down and at the peak on which the pyramid is resting is a gold reserve. Following up as the pyramid expands is currency, and beyond that is credit, the checks we use, and so on. It seems everybody abhors the word "inflation." We call it reflation. We do anything so that the people will not feel we are inflating currency, and certainly Europe has an innate abhorrence of the term. But what is inflation? It is issuing more currency on this little piece of gold until your inverted pyramid becomes top heavy and begins to wobble and eventually crashes on one side. The point is this. If Europe pays in gold, she is going to subtract from that base upon which the pyramid is resting. So what is the difference whether Europe issues more currency or whether she subtracts from that pyramid as to whether or not it is going to be top heavy and crash? That is the predicament of Europe. All I can say is this, economists and men acquainted with the subject assert that Europe has expanded credit facilities far beyond the ability of the gold reserve. France has developed enormous credit facilities throughout Europe, and subtracting from that is going to imperil the value of that credit, so Europe feels she has not the capacity to pay in gold.

Now, the other medium, goods and services. Europe has seen during the past ten years what has happened to Germany. Let us again go back to the old ten dollar analogy. We have ten dollars in our pocket. Let us assume each year for the last ten years we had subtracted one dollar and given it to another individual for nothing in exchange. Eventually our resources would be exhausted, if we had no more than those ten dollars. That is what happened to Germany. The other nations have seen what happened when she began pouring her resources, coal and chemicals into allied nations. It resulted in complete exhaustion and economic collapse for the German nation, so the Germans will not pay in services because they realize they cannot. Now, realizing the fact that they have not the capacity, they tell the rest of the world, especially the United States, "We will not pay." The United States says, "I am going to collect." France defaulted and we did not collect.

These people who advocate anti-cancellation have

WAR DEBTS 191

not as yet given us any concrete way by which the war debts can be paid. So I contend that unless they can give us some definite medium by which they can be paid that we should cancel the war debts.

Refutation, Mr. Bury
University of Wyoming

LADIES AND GENTLEMEN: I find myself in the very delicate position of defending the American housewife, and on top of that I am going to bring relativity into the matter! Let us consider this matter of public opinion. The Gentleman, who objected to my contention that public opinion and politics should be considered as just as much of a fact as Germany's capacity to pay, argued that we should be trying to form public opinion here, but, Ladies and Gentlemen, this war debts question is something which must be settled before June 15. We cannot change public opinion in America. It might be desirable. True, housewives probably do not know what they are talking about, but that fact of what the housewife thinks exists and our Congress is not going to cancel war debts so long as the American public, the American housewife if you like, says, No.

Now, this matter of relativity. The other speakers in this discussion take this war debts question at the present time. They look at it in sort of a cross section. They say, Germany can't pay now. All right, let's cancel. What would happen if I was your debtor, in bed, on crutches, broke? I could not pay my debts.

Would you cancel them or would you wait until my legs or limbs or lungs or whatever it was that was wrong mended themselves and I could meet my obligations? I believe you would do the latter. I mentioned Mexico. They contracted their debts in 1824. They were extended and adjusted and defaulted and one thing and another until 1864, forty years later, when the debts were paid.

These international problems are something which cannot be considered as a cross section, they must be considered in relativity. Bring the time element in. We cannot tell what is going to happen in the world in the next few years. There may be a war between Russia and Japan. Then Germany would profit as Mexico profited by the Civil War, and America by the World War. Germany could pay her debts in that condition.

Refutation, Mr. Hanson
Carleton College

LADIES AND GENTLEMEN: We started out this discussion this afternoon with considerable monkey business, but we would like to get down to the plain facts of the case. It is unfortunate, as the preceding speaker has said, that only one out of the six of us defends even a partial payment or an eventual payment of war debts, so the only thing for the rest of us to do is to contrast ourselves with him and I am sure you will pardon me for making reference to his statement.

He says we are only considering a cross section of the present area when we say we want war debts cancelled, that we must consider a longer period of history, consider possible changes in the economic situation. We know as far back as the Phœnicians the law of supply and demand and many other economic laws were in effect. Obviously, if the laws of supply and demand are in permanent effect and according to the laws of supply and demand or any other law we are going to lose more by collecting than we can gain by the face value of the payments, we would not try to collect any of them for we lose money.

What I should like to do is consider an historical prospectus of this problem. I should like to take as an example Germany in 1871. You remember Germany tried to collect one billion dollars indemnity from France in that year. Of course, indemnity is not contracted in the same way as war debts, but nevertheless we have two parallel countries trying to collect from another country a large sum of money in time of peace to pay for expense in time of war. During 1880 and 1890 and thereabouts war authorities were saying, "Germany has proven to the world that you can have a war and make a profit because they collected one billion dollars after fighting six weeks." But the facts were not brought out until 1910, when Sir Norman Angell, eminent British economist, published a book called *The Great Illusion* and showed that for every dollar Germany collected on her indemnity she lost two dollars in foreign trade and had to spend a third dollar on her army—a three dollar loss for every dollar gained. It sounds like the balance of the farm board today and we certainly would not want the international finances of the United States in the same category with the farm board financial status.

Now, since I am nearing the end of my time I should like to reiterate—since we cannot hope for a payment without losing more money than we can gain by the face value, the logical step is to cancel the war debts.

Refutation, Mr. Vogel
University of North Dakota

LADIES AND GENTLEMEN: The speaker who advocated suspension of payment took into consideration the attitude of the American people and the opinion of the American housewife. I wonder in advocating his plan for suspension of payment if he did not also take into consideration the opinion of the European nations. I believe in this discussion thus far we are assuming as the third gentleman pointed out, that the European nations are willing to pay for the war debt. I believe the contrary is true.

We know last December 15, many of these nations defaulted in payment and so when we talk about war debts I think we are assuming those war debts are of real value as far as the American people are concerned. I can say in the past they have not been of value because no gold has been transferred to the United States. I was very much interested in a proposition set forth by one of the gentlemen in the discussion who advocated another method of payment, whereby the European nations were to pay for the war notes by an agreement to disarm, such an agreement to be consideration for the giving up of the war notes. I think it is a fine idea. I think it is an ideal way to deal with the war debts, for not only would it be a forward step to peace, not only lift the burden of taxation from the backs of the American people and European people, but at the same time take the money spent in armaments and release it for domestic and foreign trade. It is a fine idea but I believe it is just a bit Utopian. I do not believe it is going to work. We look at Europe today and find France watching Germany like a hawk; we find the threat of the Hohenzollerns coming back; we find Mussolini in Italy, and in the far east we see Japan carrying on a warless war in China. In the light of these circumstances with these European nations, and Japan armed, and Japan not owing the United States a cent, we have no reason to believe Japan would come under the plan. If they did not, probably the rest of the nations would not. I say much as the idea is right, much as it would solve economic difficulties connected with the war debts, it is not practical.

Refutation, Mr. Wirtz
Beloit College

LADIES AND GENTLEMEN: I have been interested in these requests that we consider these matters from a political standpoint. I think we have to and I would like to pursue that political line a little more deeply. Where does the start of all this political sentiment against cancellation begin? I propose it started in the election of 1921 when the Republicans swept into power on a platform whose plank was stirring up a sentiment against coöperation with European nations. Wilson was defeated upon that. The Republicans played upon the emotions of the American people to develop that pathetic anti-continental attitude and since then the Republicans have felt obligated to defend those principles upon which they were swept into power. You cannot possibly get Congress today to go on record as being in favor of cancellation. They are afraid to do it because the principles of their party make it impossible. That is the reason the United States has failed to take a position in world peace. They conjured up these goblins and were forced to deal with them.

I propose to you this ridiculous situation. Somebody is going to jump on me hand and foot but I am in favor of default right now for the reason that I think it is the only possible solution of this problem. Congress is not going to change its mind, and you are not going to be able to educate the housewives and you are not going to be able to get Europe to pay. If they default, Congress will be forced to take a new position and until they default they cannot possibly take a new position. You are going to tell me a default will generate a lot of hatred, but we might as well make up our minds to accept that hatred. We have stepped in quicksand and cannot get out of it. The sooner they actually default the sooner this matter comes to a head, and the sooner we will be able to find some solution. When we stop discussing this problem in terms of "should" and "could" and "would" and start discussing it in terms of actual "won't," we will find a solution.

Refutation, Mr. Kluss
University of Iowa

LADIES AND GENTLEMEN: One time this afternoon some of us were referred to as goats. Now, I don't think that was meant in a derogatory sense, just in a discriminatory way to distinguish us who favored anti-cancellation. I raised my hand with the cancellationists but at the same time I was going to place myself in the position of the goat. I have the greatest respect for these people who feel war debts should be paid. They are typically Americans and justly so. I am going to try to answer questions that came into my mind as one of those who thought war debts should not be cancelled. I stood up here and said Europe cannot pay and we cannot collect and as one who favored payment I said, doesn't it seem absurd we should cancel because they cannot pay? As individuals we can go into court and secure redress if an individual does not pay a debt.

My only reply to that would be this: Those nations have said they will not pay because they cannot. That is the reason they won't. How are you going about collecting? You insist upon payment. No economist, no authority in the world has given you any method of payment. How are you going to do it? Probably they will make no reply. I sat there for one minute wondering what the reply might be. You could take the army and navy to Europe and demand payment. No, you say, the losses would be too severe, and too great. That is the way I feel about it. Then you might come back with this. I am an American taxpayer. If Europe does not pay I will have to, and you must give me some remedy. The only way I can see is, if I can show you any way you might possibly benefit, probably you will accept my argument. This is the way I would go about it.

Today everyone wants money—the currency of America—in banks. It is a theory that money in a bank will result in ten times that much credit. During the last several years we have lost three billion dollars in banks and at the same time our National income has decreased thirty billion dollars. Assume that Europe would leave two hundred fifty million in gold in that country every year. Two hundred fifty million multiplied by ten would mean two billion five hundred million in actual credit. Credit means that the purchasing power of the people of Europe would be increased to two billion five hundred million dollars. Again we revert to authorities and say for the last ten years America has secured forty per cent of Europe's purchasing power. That seems tremendous but the statistical abstracts in the *Statesman's Year Book* support that. Assume we secured forty per cent of Europe's income, one billion of American commodities being purchased, it would put men back to work, start the wheels of industry turning, and bring back the thirty billion dollars lost in the last few years. It seems to me America would profit regardless, if we did lose that two hundred fifty million dollars.

Closing Remarks, Chairman

LADIES AND GENTLEMEN: I think all of you will agree if a speech is boiled down it isn't nearly so dry. I am going to boil my speech down. I think confession, as most psychologists admit, is good for the soul, but possibly bad for one's standing in the community. I am going to make a little confession. I feel, for myself and practically every person here in this assembly, we must admit there has been a lot of fruitful discussion of this topic here today. There have been at least suggestions of many sound and scientific plans and policies which might be worked out for the successful readjustment of this debt problem. We cannot hope for too much in an hour's time but I believe what has been accomplished has been very notable.

I think most of us will agree with the Editor of the *Columbus Democrat* who recently, referring to the propaganda that had been circulated on both sides of a question, said something like this, speaking editorially of this problem of war debts. "It has recently come to the notice of the editor of this paper that one of the fastidious newly-weds of this town kneads bread with her gloves on. This incident may seem somewhat peculiar but there are others equally strange. For example, the Editor of this paper needs bread with his gloves on, he needs bread with his pants on, and he needs bread with his hat on, but unless some of the subscribers to this paper pay me up, he is going to need bread without a dog-gone thing on, and Wisconsin is no Garden of Eden in the winter time."

I am sure every one will say Wisconsin is no Garden of Eden in the summer to say nothing of the winter and judging by the expression of you folks from Wyoming and Pittsburgh I am sure you will agree with the Editor of the *Columbus Democrat* who made those remarks that this particular piece of humor is in no way pertinent in so far as European debts are concerned. He says, however, that most of the senatorial objections and most of the discussions and editorials have been equally impertinent and it is for that reason it is necessary for the people of America who are informed upon this particular problem to get together in just such discussions as this and try to arrive at a sane and scientific understanding of the issue involved.

THE AMERICAN LEGION SHOULD BE CONDEMNED
A Discussion of the Bonus

THE AMERICAN LEGION SHOULD BE CONDEMNED

PRINCETON UNIVERSITY AFFIRMATIVE VS. UNIVERSITY OF GEORGIA NEGATIVE

The presence in the United States of such a large body of voting citizens united for a common political purpose, whether or not that is the ostensible purpose stated in their constitution, has aroused considerable comment and much unfavorable opinion, especially since the agitation for the Bonus payment began, and the Bonus Expeditionary Force marched on Washington and encamped within the city limits of the National Capital until forcibly ejected.

The debate on this subject presented here is one between Princeton and the University of Georgia held in the historic Whig Hall on the Princeton Campus, and is one of the debates held by Georgia while on a debate trip which included in addition to Princeton University the following: Columbia University, New York University, Swarthmore College, and the University of North Carolina.

The Question was stated, *Resolved: That the American Legion should be condemned.* Princeton upheld the Affirmative and Georgia the Negative. The decision went to the Affirmative. Mr. W. J. Montgomery, debate manager at Princeton, presided.

The speeches were assembled by Professor George G. Connelly, Director of Debate at the University of Georgia, and contributed by him to this Volume.

First Affirmative, Noel Hemmendinger
Princeton University

LADIES AND GENTLEMEN: There are two American Legions. One is what it purports to be, what it might be, and what, if it has any right of existence at all, it ought to be. The other is what it is. Let us first consider the ideal American Legion.

The ideal American Legion is a spontaneous organization of overseas veterans, banded together for the purpose of preserving the comradeship and ideals of the American Forces in the World War. Nothing I can say is half so expressive as the preamble to the Legion Constitution, which despite a tendency to rhetorical catch-phrases of indefinite meaning, is none the less an admirable declaration: "For God and country we associate ourselves together for the following purposes: to uphold and defend the Constitution of the United States of America; to maintain law and order; to foster and perpetuate a one hundred per cent Americanism; to preserve the memories and incidents of our association in the great war; to inculcate a sense of individual obligation to the community, state, and nation; to combat the autocracy of both the classes and the masses; to make right the master of might; to promote peace and good will on earth; to safeguard and transmit to posterity the principles of justice, freedom and democracy; to consecrate and sanctify our comradeship by our devotion to mutual helpfulness." The addition to this of part of Article II of the constitution makes the picture complete: "The American Legion shall be absolutely non-political, and shall not be used for the dissemination of partisan principles nor for the promotion of the candidacy of any persons seeking public office or preferment." An organization faithful to this spirit and these principles would deserve our hearty approval.

Unfortunately that organization does not exist. For the real American Legion, about one-third of whose members, according to General Butler, saw shell fire, is a million dollar chartered corporation, with a large efficient permanent business organization, its emblem division, its film division, and its publishing corporation, and with branches in every section of the country. The real American Legion is far from spontaneous. It was fathered by prominent men, with contributions of money by various corporations, all of whom were concerned about the possible radicalism of returned soldiers and desired to lead them in paths of conservatism. Having such a huge overhead in its permanent organization, the real Legion is dependent on large membership and is continually exerting its efforts in that direction. A bond salesman could learn from an American Legion organizer. The real American Legion represents, with its million members, between a fourth and a fifth of our veterans of the World War.

There are three activities that the man on the street associates with the American Legion. They are, in the order in which he would probably think of them: raiding the treasury, holding conventions, and red-baiting. Red-baiting, the means which the Legion has adopted for "safe-guarding and transmitting to posterity the principles of justice, freedom and democracy," is one of the things I want to talk about. Of how the legionnaires "maintain law and order" at their conventions little needs be said. The treasury raids, which the man in the street is not mistaken in considering their outstanding activity, will be described by my colleague.

With whatever energy survives its annual convention and bonus grab, the American Legion is accustomed to act as the self-appointed guardian of Americanism. Of course, being a patriotic organization, the Legion has a prior right to the definition of Americanism over ministers and college professors, and other ignoramuses, who, since they probably never fought for their country, have no way of knowing what their country stands for.

The Legion creed is not based on the principles of Americanism; Americanism is that which agrees with the Legion's creed. I don't mean by the Legion creed that fine-sounding statement I read a while ago. That's just the preamble to their constitution. No, the Legion creed, were it in black and white, would go something like this: "Anyone who believes in disarmament, who believes that any American institutions could be changed for the better, or is associated with people who believe these things, is a Red or a Pink and takes his orders from Moscow." That sounds like exaggeration. Let's have some details. Organizations branded as dangerous by the Legion are: the Foreign Policy Association, the National Council for the Prevention of War, the Woman's International League for Peace and Freedom—to say nothing of the American Civil Liberties Union and the Federal Council of Churches. Subversive persons are Carrie Chapman Catt, James Harvey Robinson, John Dewey, Stephen S. Wise and John Haynes Holmes, to single out a few. Here's how Legionnaires practice their convictions. Frederick J. Libby, a gentle-spoken Quaker who heads the National

Council for the Prevention of War, once a Congregational minister, and a Red Cross worker during the war, has been prevented by the Legion from speaking in many cities, by a campaign of lies and defamations. Mrs. Lucia Ames Mead, a gray-haired worker for peace, especially through the agency of a league of nations, scheduled a speaking tour through the South. The Legion forced cancellation of three of her engagements. Sherwood Eddy, a nationally known Y.M.C.A. worker, has often been prevented from speaking by the Legion. The attempt by the Los Angeles Legion to prevent the visit of that vicious pacifist Albert Einstein, aroused much amusement. A Legion speaker said he didn't think much of the theory of relativity, but he did know that Einstein was a propagandist against the best interests of the country.

Rampant Legionnaire patriotism has not stopped short of our schools. After many attempts, often successful, to get schools to discard such inadequate texts as those by David Muzzey, Albert Bushnell Hart and William West, the Legion decided to write its own textbook. School children who read it have no doubt a glorious conception of the country they live in. The only question is whether they can recognize it! With a fine insight into fundamentals, twelve pages are devoted to the Mexican War, one to American literature and one to Economic History.

It wouldn't matter much if members of the Legion were content with making fools of themselves. A little comedy does no harm. But we do think it is a pretty bad state of affairs when an organization that supposedly represents America's war veterans, can wage a continual and rather effective campaign against some of the nation's finest leaders. The Legion has not always used peaceful methods, either, in its curtailment of constitutional guarantees. In Wilkes-Barre an armed group of Legionnaires forcibly broke up a meeting where Lenin's memory was being honored. At Centralia, Washington, parading Legionnaires were fired upon, rioting and bloodshed ensued, and several labor leaders were railroaded to jail by a court admittedly packed by Legionnaires.

Every beneficent action that the Legion has ever performed is not sufficient to offset the acts of criminal intolerance I have mentioned, and yet they are a small part of its activities. You have seen how it upholds and defends the Constitution, and safeguards the principles of justice, freedom, and democracy in domestic affairs. Now let us see how the Legion promotes peace and good will on earth.

The American Legion promotes peace and good will by a campaign of war-preparedness that is sometimes frankly pro-war, and by an anti-foreign policy which threatens international friendship. The Legion, it is true, no longer prevents concerts by Fritz Kreisler or bans German opera, but it still conducts a campaign for the expulsion of aliens which makes Secretary of Labor Doak appear a liberal. I do not know whether the Legion still insists that every alien in this country who did not fight in the war should be deported, but in 1923 it demanded that all immigration should be prohibited, and it is still an advocate of drastic curtailment of immigration. The Legion's attitude has aroused much resentment abroad, and if, early in the last decade, the Legion had had to fight another war against Japan, it would have been largely the result of its own efforts.

We do not doubt that members of the Legion are sincere in their desire that this country should be preeminent in military strength, and, being more tolerant than the Legion, we acknowledge their right to an opinion on the subject. But we do insist that that opinion is not worth two cents, and that the Legion's attempt to force it on the country is inimical to the country's welfare. The Legion not only is not especially qualified to determine our policy in respect to war, but is emotionally unfit to judge on the subject. The counsels on war of men who had hate and fear drilled into them, who became inured to bloodshed and murder, who were taught to consider war inevitable and even desirable, should be shunned rather than sought. In view of which, and of the large number of worthy ex-service men who hold aloof from the Legion, we believe no more confidence can be reposed in the Legion's opinion on war than in the paranoiac's on the subject of his delusion.

This is the organization which maintains at Washington the most efficient lobby, probably, that that haven of lobbyists knows—a lobby whose head estimates he has written between fifteen hundred and two thousand bills, originating in the Legion, no small number of which have been passed by Congress. Of course, the Legion is a non-political organization, and so all these bills are introduced for non-partisan and patriotic motives. They are chiefly of two kinds. The most important one of those two kinds will be discussed by my colleague. The other relates to national defense and preparedness. Disregarding the many drives of the Legion lobby which have failed, I shall mention just a few of its accomplishments in the field of legislation. The Legion has fathered a plan for universal draft in wartime by which there would be immediately delivered to the government not only man power for fighting, but all the Capital and Labor of the nation. That bill was passed, minus the Capital and Labor provision. The Legion has prevented a cut in the number of reserve officers, and a decrease in the appropriation for rifle matches. When Congress declined to increase the appropriations for Citizens' Military Training Camps, the Legion, by a campaign of propaganda, procured so many applications that Congress was forced to act. The Legion has consistently opposed every attempt to abolish the Reserve Officers Training Corps, or make it optional where it is compulsory. The Legion has been a continual big navy advocate, and has deplored with huge lament every disarmament move or suspension of naval construction. A bill designed to outlaw poison gas, in accord with our treaty obligations, was killed by the Legion. It did not bother the Legion that their lobbyists who blocked that bill also received a salary from the chemical manufacturers' lobby. Theodore Burton's resolution to prohibit the exportation of munitions or implements of war was likewise killed, on the ground that our arms manufacturers had to keep their hand in.

To those of us who believe that the path to peace lies along the road of increased international understanding, making possible armament reduction, these activities are most highly reprehensible. To those who believe that preparedness prevents war, despite the lesson of history that preparedness for war and the martial spirit invariably cause war, they may be praiseworthy. In any case, whatever our convictions, no intelligent person can fail to condemn a powerful organization of a million voters, which uses every method known to paid persuaders, and holds a club over the head of every Congressman to defeat him if he does not vote its way, in order to force through Congress measures which it happens to favor. No matter for what purpose such an organization acted, it would be a dangerous threat to the integrity of our democratic institutions. In this case it is a far more serious threat because it is acting for purposes which millions of responsible people believe contrary to the national welfare.

Gentlemen, the American Legion should be condemned because it has been false to its ideals—because it has declared itself a non-political organization, and for its ends has done everything possible in a political way except to ally itself with a political party. It should be condemned because it has sworn to uphold the Constitution and has trampled it underfoot. It should be condemned because it has sworn to maintain law and order and has indulged in drunken riots. It should be condemned because it has sworn to foster a one hundred per cent Americanism and has fostered a narrow-minded chauvinism. It should be condemned because it has sworn to combat the autocracy of the classes and is itself a glaring example of class domination, compelling class legislation. It should be condemned because it has sworn to make right the master of might, and has acted with strong-arm methods in utter defiance of law. It should be condemned because it has sworn to promote peace and good will, and has promoted a bigoted nationalism provocative of international hatred. The American Legion should be condemned because it has sworn to safeguard the principles of justice, freedom, and democracy and has done more to undermine them than any organized body in the history of the American nation.

First Negative, M. S. Hodgson
University of Georgia

LADIES AND GENTLEMEN: We feel that there is so much that public discussion has left in the background, that we shall attempt to show you the constructive side of the Legion, its good works which are quietly and unobtrusively done.

I shall read the Preamble to the Constitution of the American Legion, "For God and Country, we associate ourselves together for the following purposes:

"To uphold and defend the Constitution of the United States of America, to maintain law and order; to foster and perpetuate a one hundred per cent

Americanism; to preserve the memories and incidents of our association in the Great War; to inculcate a sense of individual obligation to the community, state, and nation; to combat the autocracy of both the classes and the masses; to make right the master of might; to promote peace and good will on earth; to safeguard and transmit to posterity the principles of justice, freedom, and democracy; to consecrate and sanctify our comradeship by our devotion to mutual helpfulness."

I shall also quote two excerpts from the Second Article of the Constitution: "The American Legion is a civilian organization" and "The American Legion shall be absolutely non-political and shall not be used for the dissemination of partisan principles nor for the promotion of the candidacy of any person seeking publice office or preferment."

Now, I'll take the most important parts of this preamble which points out the purposes and aims of the organization and attempt to show you that the Legion has lived up to its ideals and has been of great benefit to this country.

"To maintain law and order." In a vast number of cases, in times of trouble and disaster, the American Legion has organized for the purpose of keeping law and order until the proper authorities had arrived. When such times arrive, a call is sounded and the Legionnaires gather, ready to meet any crisis.

You people in New Jersey cannot appreciate the necessity for some organized force working for law and order in certain emergencies. In small communities we do not have the necessary protection that can be called forth. For instance, in floods and other catastrophes, the Legion is a God-send to the small unorganized community, and fills a real need.

"To foster and perpetuate a one hundred per cent Americanism." Their campaign of propaganda to combat Socialism and Communism through the public schools has been criticized as snooping interference and as Un-American. However, it is in accord with the general principles laid down by our Government to promote Americanism in educating the coming generation as regards democracy. There is no use denying that the Communists and Socialists have their propaganda; yet for some strange reason the so-called Liberals put up a great cry as soon as one of our patriotic organizations sees fit to teach Americanism. Their fight to combat the spread of Communistic and Socialistic propaganda in the public schools, is part of their desire to have a government in which neither the masses nor the classes will have control. They want a government in which both the lower and upper classes have a hand. This desire comes under that part of their purpose, "To combat the autocracy of both the classes and the masses."

Then the education of immigrants who come to this country forms an important phase of their Americanism work. They also advocated legislation for the quicker naturalization and citizenship for those immigrants who fought in the war, attributing their patriotism as shown by their fighting for our country.

"To promote peace and good will on earth and to make right the master of might." I should like to discuss this purpose under three headings. First, their plan of Home defense. The men composing the Legion have all been through this last Great War, and they, more than any other group of men, are desirous of peace. Their conception is that peace is maintained by the upkeep of an adequate Home Defense. There is nothing in the record which justifies the much talked of criticism of the Legion that they are a group of war lords. What they seek is simply an adequate national defense. This is nothing new or radical. Every active and well-informed organization is advocating the same preparedness program as a guarantee of world peace. And you people here in the East should be particularly interested and quick to agree with the Legion, since you would be the first and greatest sufferers in case of foreign invasion. They do not mean that every nation should go armed to the teeth, but merely that we should have forces that can be mobilized and be made ready for action in a short length of time. Every nation would then have a healthy respect for every other nation and would be rather hesitant about trying to overcome it by war.

Second, the plan the Legion presented to the War Policies Commission. Under this proposed plan, universal conscription would be practiced, with no immunities allowed. Every man, woman, and child would be subject to draft, to do whatever he was needed for. Every corporation, in fact, all industry, all transportation facilities would be conscripted for the common cause. Under a plan of this kind, no one would be safe in thinking he could escape being drafted, and no one could possibly make any financial gain from the war. With personal freedom and the making of profit absolutely removed from the realm of possibility, the desire for war would be minimized to the lowest degree. This very program calling for the conscription of private wealth and industry for the public good proves that the Legion is not dogmatically opposed to Socialism as its critics would have us believe. It is broad enough to take one of its principles and use it when the ultimate end is world peace.

Third, the relation of the Legion with Fidac, which is an organization of the veterans of every nation which participated in the war. By their association with this organization, by the erection abroad of monuments to celebrate our deeds and theirs, by sending yearly groups of Legionnaires to visit these countries, the Legion is helping tremendously in creating a universal attitude of peace. By a recent act of the Legion, the relations we have with this international group are being spread among the school children of the country, thus instilling in them the idea of world peace. The very existence of this organization, founded for the purposes of maintaining peace, is another indication that the Legion is not the belligerent group of war lords that their critics have made them out to be.

The last point I want to discuss with you is their Welfare Work. The Legion has an Endowment Fund of practically five million dollars. This fund was raised by subscription in the Legion for the purpose of use in welfare work. The interest from this fund amounts to a little over two hundred thousand dollars a year and is divided equally between their National Rehabilitation Work and their Child Welfare Work.

The National Rehabilitation Committee sits in Washington. It has probably carried on one of the most important services of the Legion these past few years. Veterans who feel that they have received an injustice in the matter of compensations and pensions, bring their pleas and complaints to this committee which has a tremendous staff to handle such matters. Money recoveries to the extent of seven million five hundred thousand dollars were made during the past year, which figure exceeds that of the preceding year by about one million dollars. Then, too, the cases of disabled and needy veterans who either have not needed help before or who just were not able to get it before, are brought to the attention of this committee and given prompt service. This Rehabilitation Work acts as a go-between for the veterans and their just dues.

The Child Welfare program also comes under this Endowment Fund. The object of this Child Welfare work is that of training good citizens. To do this, they strive to keep the family ties intact, to help fathers and mothers in their work of raising children, and to afford them the pleasure of securing and enjoying the normal necessities of life. This work is carried on separately in each state, which in turn is in one of five districts, which report to the National Welfare office. These state agents investigate worthy cases in order to determine who shall receive aid from the Endowment Fund. This organization is a member of the Child

Welfare League of America and coöperates with them in every possible way.

The care of the widows and orphans of the veterans is a part of the creation of individual obligation to the community. During the first six months of 1932, forty-three thousand dollars was spent in caring for orphans of veterans. This was done through the National Organization and there is no way of estimating how much was spent through the local posts individually.

Then through their Unemployment Commission, much valuable work has been done in securing and creating jobs for the unemployed. During the Fall and Winter of 1930 and the year 1931, over two hundred thousand people were employed through the efforts of the Legion. Thousands of others were helped through the individual efforts of the Legionnaires. If every one of us could apply ourselves with the same interest and enthusiasm, how much sooner would this present economic situation grow brighter and easier to bear?

Now this review of how the Legion has lived up to its principles as expressed in its constitution may seem a bit prosaic to my Opponents. The recitation of its constructive program may seem a bit elementary. But we feel it is a worthwhile program well-executed by the Legion, and far more important for discussion purposes than a squabble over the bonus question.

Second Affirmative, Arthur Northwood, Jr.
Princeton University

LADIES AND GENTLEMEN: The American Legion is to be condemned for its hypocrisy, its conventions, its bigoted conservatism, and its militaristic attitude. These facts my colleague has already clearly shown to you. I wish to prove that the American Legion deserves our condemnation because of its stand on the bonus, and allied issues.

The American soldier was not badly treated in comparison with the soldiers of other countries or with the men back home. He received thirty dollars a month salary. The French infantryman received one dollar and fifty cents. The American got food, clothing, and shelter worth two dollars a day, giving him a real wage of ninety dollars a month, whereas the average worker here received only eighty-nine dollars a month. The soldier's physical, mental, and moral needs were taken care of as well as conditions would permit. So we ask, "Why is the Legion raising a row about the debt this country owes the veterans?"

It must be admitted that the pension tradition has always been strong in this country, but just because an unholy tradition is strong, it does not mean that we should not fight back with every ounce of energy that we have, and that we shouldn't condemn every organization that is trying to have these scandals recur.

In 1917 Congress did everything in its power to take care of the soldiers, and to prevent a recurrence of the scandals. It inaugurated a War Risk Insurance Plan, which made it possible for all the soldiers to insure their lives for ten thousand dollars on a very liberal basis, so liberal in fact that this plan alone has already cost the government nine hundred twenty-four million dollars. Provisions of this act said that the government would see that adequate care was taken of the families of veterans. It did so, at a cost so far of two hundred ninety-eight million dollars.

When the soldiers returned from France they were each given sixty dollars, and if they had been hurt, generous care was provided for them in the form of pensions, hospitals, and vocational training. This treatment of the soldiers was bountiful enough, and most of the army thought so at the time. Then, the American Legion was formed, with avowedly patriotic, non-political, unselfish aims. But if its attitude ever was that way, it soon changed, for its members almost immediately started a policy of grabbing what they could get. As early as 1920 their speaker, Manuel, boasted that in one year they had "extracted" from Congress—*extracted,* the word is theirs, not mine—I use it to show their attitude; in one year they had extracted from Congress more than had the Civil War Veterans in thirty years.

I have shown thus far that the American soldier was treated generously. By a quotation we have seen that the attitude of the American Legion practically from the start, was to grab all it could get. To aid in the grabbing, the Legion built up one of the most powerful lobbies in existence. In the next few minutes I would like to show you what this lobby has accomplished in six different fields; in other words, I will give you the various accomplishments of the Legion, and the various counts upon which it is to be condemned.

Soon after its inception, the Legion started a drive which culminated in 1924 in the passage of the Adjusted Service Compensation Act, a pension in disguise. This act was passed over the President's veto, who said at the time, "We must either stop this bill, or reverse our theory of patriotism." His words have proved true, but we did not stop the bill. This bill states that the government owes each veteran a dollar or a dollar and a quarter a day more for his services than he has already received; takes the figure which these calculations give, adds to it interest on the basis of a twenty-year endowment plan, and gives the veteran a certificate with the final figure on it which certificate the government promises to redeem in 1945. Its efforts to get this bill passed to give the veterans an undeserved pension constitute *Count One* against the Legion. Its recent demand that these certificates should be immediately redeemed for their face value, giving each veteran forty-five cents on the dollar, unaccrued interest, is *Count Two*.

With the passage of this bill in 1924 as a starter the Legion has gone from glory unto glory. It has been so successful in its efforts that it is no longer a question of what the country will do with the veterans, but what the veterans will do with the country!

Having seen why the veterans are to be condemned for their stand in the realm of the pensions themselves, let us turn to another field, the one known as the "medical racket."

The government assumed responsibility for, and took care of veterans who got sick after the war, when it could be presumed that the sickness was caused by war service. But this presumption was stretched so far that in 1924, Congress threw open the government hospitals to any veteran who was sick for any cause whatsoever, except wilful misconduct. The attitude of the Legion on this bill is somewhat questionable, but at least it did not oppose its passage. Last year more than half of the admissions to veterans' hospitals were for causes absolutely unrelated to the war. The veteran is given his traveling expenses, and two dollars and sixty-five cents a day while he is in the hospital. For these provisions, the American Legion is responsible. To show how far veterans are taking advantage of the government for free treatment, it need only be stated that while our war casualties were one-eighth those of Great Britain, we have three times as many men under treatment as she has. Yet the Legion is clamoring for more free service, more hospitals! It is now supporting a bill in Congress for the outlay of twelve million dollars for these. General Hines, head of the Veterans Bureau, has said that this hospitalization service alone will eventually cost the government one hundred forty million dollars a year. Do you wonder that this is called a racket? The Legion's present aim is to have the clause removed from the statute books which keeps veterans from our hospitals who are suffering on account of wilful misconduct. I suppose so that a larger percentage of its law-abiding members will be able to use the hospital facilities.

Now, let us turn to a third field in which the Legion has been active—getting big pensions for Retired Emergency Officers. The Legion fought for eight years to have this undemocratic, unjust, bill passed, fought against the opposition of such organizations as the Veterans of Foreign Wars and the Private Soldiers' Legion. The bill provided that an Emergency Army officer, whose service might consist of ten months at a desk at Washington, should receive seventy-five per cent of his salary upon retirement, if he could show thirty per cent disability which it might be presumed had been caused by the war. Under this law, a certain man who enlisted thirteen days before the Armistice, and who went back to civil life in 1922 with no wound, injury, or disease, is now drawing one hundred eighty-seven dollars and fifty cents a month as a retirement fee, at the same time that he receives nine thousand dollars a year as a counsel for the Veterans Administration. Under this act the government is now paying eleven million dollars a year.

I have not the time to go into the disability allowances, which the Legion put through Congress in 1930, which permit a man whose sole service to his country was spending five weeks at government expense in Camp Dix to draw twelve dollars a month from the government because he has a cold in his head.

The American Legion has been equally successful in its efforts to get its members into government jobs. Whereas, the passing grade in the Civil Service Examination is seventy per cent for the ordinary citizen, for the veteran it is sixty per cent. And once a veteran has passed, he must be given preferment over all the others. There is an instance recorded of where one hundred and forty-four people were taking examinations for three posts. Everyone passed, some with marks in the high nineties, except three veterans who were in the sixties, a flunking grade for ordinary people. But veterans are not ordinary people, and so these three also passed and it was they who received the jobs. The disastrous effects of this arrangement upon our Civil Service is apparent. The American Legion claims, and must be given, the responsibility for this.

We have now finished condemning the Legion on specific counts. They are: *first,* pushing through the Adjusted Service Compensation; *second,* demanding full payment now of something that does not come due till 1945; *third,* forcing the building of government hospitals, and trying to have the laws so liberalized that the government would become the greatest treater of venereal diseases in the world; *fourth,* forcing the government to give to Emergency Officers fees far out of proportion to their services; *fifth,* making it possible for soldiers to secure disability allowances for peacetime injuries; *sixth,* disrupting our Civil Service System. For all of these activities, the Legion is to be condemned.

Now, I should like to have you investigate with me the present condition of the Legion. If its members are poor, if they have been unable to fit themselves back into civil life, perhaps there is some excuse for the policy of grab. But are they poor? I will go to their own magazine, *The American Legion Monthly,* for my answer. It records that the salary of the average Legionnaire is three thousand four hundred twelve dollars a year. We all know that the average citizen makes less than one thousand dollars. Now if these are facts, and they are, what is the excuse for the Legion's policy of taxing the latter group to aid the former? There is none. It is bald-faced robbery. It can't even be excused as a reward for patriotism, for less than half of the veterans ever fought for their country. Yet at a time when every penny counts, this class is taking twenty-five per cent of the government income, nine hundred twenty-eight million dollars. Does not the organization which is responsible for this travesty on justice deserve our condemnation?

Let us compare our policy toward our veterans with that of other nations. We find that we have been extremely liberal. France, who had eleven times as many casualties as we had, is paying benefits to one hundred and fifty thousand fewer men. Other nations give pensions only to those who did some real fighting. The United States gives pensions to those who received free board in our army camps, and ran no risk, other than falling off trolley cars and contracting social diseases.

Great Britain pays five hundred twenty dollars a year for disability. The United States pays up to two thousand four hundred dollars.

Foreign countries had thirty-four million men under arms, a good many of whom fought for the duration of the war, four and a quarter years. The United States had five million men mobilized, half of whom never fought at all, and the other half did not fight more than six months. Yet the United States paid in the past year in pensions, fifty million dollars more than all the other countries put together. In view of these figures, can anyone doubt that the policy of the United States has been so liberal to the veterans that it has absolutely disregarded the rights of the other citizens of this country?

Now, let us see how these Legion-made laws work out in practice. Are they fair or just? First, we must consider the ex-soldier, who, in a fit of drunkenness, falls down and breaks his leg. He may obtain care at government expense, and then get a pension of twelve to forty dollars a month, even though his service consisted of three months of fresh air at Camp Upton.

If he has a pain in his stomach, he can go to the nearest veteran's hospital at government expense, draw his pension and an extra allowance of two dollars and sixty-five cents a day while undergoing observation, and then, discharged as cured, collect from the government for his fare home.

A widow who lost her only son and support on the battlefield gets twenty dollars a month. The man whose sole service to his country was to catch mumps at Camp Spartanburg gets twenty-five dollars.

Among those who are receiving anywhere up to one hundred fifty dollars a month as full retirement, because they have a thirty per cent disability, are professional athletes, police captains in New York City, and business men with a regular salary of four thousand to ten thousand dollars a year.

A retired Emergency Captain can get one hundred fifty dollars a month. A dead Emergency Captain's widow who has to support a child gets forty dollars. You see, the Legion is so busy grabbing for the undeserving living, that it has forgotten the deserving dead.

I have tried to show you that our soldiers were generously treated during the war, that the Legion from the very first had the policy of grab, that this policy worked out unfairly in six specific fields, that our country in comparison with other countries has been more than lavish with its veterans, that the present condition of the veterans does not warrant their receiving such a share of the national income as they are getting, and, finally, that the laws which they have enacted are manifestly unjust.

I close with a word to the future. Under the existing laws the veterans will soon be costing the country three billion dollars a year. Yet the Legion is clamoring for more. Is it not the duty of every citizen to oppose this organized minority? Should not every honest man fight it with all his energy and condemn it with all his force?

Second Negative, Aaron Hardy Ulm
University of Georgia

LADIES AND GENTLEMEN: If you are going to condemn the American Legion on the grounds offered by the Gentlemen of the Opposition, you could never deny being violent iconoclasts. They have eloquently demanded that we condemn the Legion for what any large organization may always be criticized, and in doing so, they have unconsciously demanded that nearly every institution which we possess be likewise condemned. Now, I do not think that we are going to remodel the entire system of life in this world, not tonight at least, and yet to abolish the American Legion on the charges supported by the Gentlemen of Princeton would entail quite similar procedure.

Let us start where every reasonable discussion should start, at the beginning, and ask the question: Was there really any need for such an organization as the American Legion? Possibly such a need is not recognized by many of my audience tonight, but it was recognized and emphasized by the leaders of the army in France and the administration of that day, headed by no other than your own Woodrow Wilson. In fact, the original idea of this association of veterans was proposed and developed by these men, for they, having history to convince them, readily realized that returning soldiers are much less dangerous when they are organized in patriotic groups. They had the records of Hannibal, of Cæsar, of Cromwell, to urge them in this decision.

But in late wars it has been customary for veterans to form themselves into some kind of political party, and until the American Legion was formed, not one of these groups has much considered the welfare of the country. Nearly in our own time we have the disgusting spectacle of the Grand Army of the Republic, which fifty years ago was practically running the entire government. Four men went to the White House elected by the G.A.R., and more than half of the National Legislature owed their seats to the support of these ex-soldiers. Why in Washington in those days, the citizens spoke of the Capitol as the old soldiers' home. There you have an example of the power which these men in the Legion might exercise if they were not restricted by the principles of their organization. You accuse them of selfishness. Here I offer you the possibility of what they might do if they did not have a purer interest in this nation than the opposition has described.

Furthermore, the Legion, unlike the G.A.R., has never purposely tried to make raids on the Treasury under the claim of patriotism. The entire subject of the bonus originated in the platforms of campaigning congressmen. These demagogues encouraged the veterans to ask for the payment of their compensation certificates, and, finally, such men as Congressman Patman of Texas urged them to march on the Capital. Thousands of veterans swarmed to Washington when the House passed the bonus this summer. The Legion realized that this was a false hope and tried to discourage these men. What happened when they arrived in the city at the behest of their congressmen? They were in the midst of exercising their constitutional right of assembly and petition, and possibly that of pursuing happiness when they were driven from the city by the regular army at the command of President Hoover. Only when their comrades had been outraged in this fashion did the Legion enter the picture. Every past convention of the Legion had defeated motion for payment of the bonus, and only after they were incensed against the administration by the brutal action at Washington, did the Legion declare for immediate payment.

They tell us the Legion is begging and is trying to force the American people to pay for what has been described as their patriotism. That is false. The Legion is simply asking that the soldiers who were in the late army be paid for what they lost while defending this nation. World War veterans have actually received less than any of the veterans of American wars. The opposition may quote large figures in dollars, but no mention is made of the enormous tracts of land which were given to Revolutionary, Mexican, and Civil War veterans. Why, I have an ancestor, of whom I am justly proud, who fought in the war against England and was given as a reward six hundred acres of land in the state of Georgia. You might not think so, but it was worth something.

Everyone in this country during the last war could ask for and get just about any salary he desired, while the men in the army were being paid one dollar per day, of which they actually got one half. Why is it, then, that these people who have had their share of the profits, refuse the ex-soldiers a bit of money which would increase their wages to about two dollars a day for the time they spent in service?

Thus you are not paying a man because he risked his life, and if you were it would be rather cheap payment, but you are compensating him for the loss he sustained while making the world safe for democracy, and to you smug Americans that must be a valuable service.

Possibly you may say that the Legion is making an exorbitant demand when they know that the United States is nearly bankrupt. How strange it is, then, that the Reconstruction Finance Corporation can easily distribute millions of dollars to defunct railroads and shaky banks all over the country. Speculator Dawes can get ninety million dollars for his bank a few days after he resigns as president of the Reconstruction Finance Corporation, but veteran John Smith can't get the few hundred dollars which the government actually owes to him for services rendered.

Then there is the argument that the government has been very generous to the veterans by lending them half the value of their certificates. To you it might seem to be a gallant concession, but in practice it was an excellent business transaction, and on it the government profited to the extent of twenty million dollars. And, furthermore, the interest is so arranged, that by the time the payment of the balance is due, the balance will hardly exist. That is, if the certificates are permitted to run their agreed time the government will practically escape ever paying them.

Probably the chief objection to the Legion is the mistaken idea that it is opposed to liberalism. Now, from my own investigations I can assure you that the Legion as a unit has no enmity for Socialists or even Communists as political groups, but it does fight against, and for this it deserves commendation, the subversive tendencies of these parties. And how could you condemn them for this action. Why, according to all election predictions the citizens of this nation are almost thoroughly opposed to any radical change in the government. Most of the audience tonight feel exactly the same way. Now, isn't patriotism the support of your nation's accepted customs and government? Consequently, are you going to denounce the Legion for patriotism?

Gentlemen, you have heard a great deal about how dangerous this large organization of young men is; that it is a menace with its great potential strength. Now this may be good propaganda to frighten taxpayers with, but it is readily discounted by a few facts. Whatever power has been thrust into the hands of the Legion by congressmen, greedy for the Legion vote, has been most conservatively used.

Has this so-called powerful lobby of the Legion in Washington been pictured to you in its true circumstances? Lobbies in Washington cover two complete pages in the 'phone book; nearly every organization of any importance at all maintains one there, for as a matter of fact, it is the only way minority groups can be represented under our system of legislation. Now, if the Navy League, The Manufacturers Association, The American Federation of Labor, and hundreds of others are to have this privilege, shall we refuse it to the Legion? Don't condemn the Legion for this, condemn the nation.

I am afraid that the opposition has made the common mistake of accusing the Legion of many things which are really faults of veterans in general, not the American Legion. Of course, it is a convenient thing for critics to point to the Legion as a target for abuse of all veteran activities which have not met with their approval. There may be graft in pensions, rehabilitation, and bonus payments, but none of this has been sought for, or encouraged by the Legion. Why the fact is, Gentlemen, that the Legion maintains in Washington an investigating bureau simply for the purpose of preventing fraud, and to see to it that none but the deserving get aid from the government.

I do not propose tonight to white-wash the American Legion, nor do I think such action is at all necessary. The truth is that the Legion is a decent group of typical American young men, and if you are going to condemn them, you must at the same time condemn the entire population of America, which is a large order. There is only one way to judge the Legion, and that is by contrasting it with veteran organizations of other wars. When it is put to that test, I think it shall always receive a favorable verdict.

You all told them back in 1918 that they were the flower of the nation. Have they so sunk beneath you in fourteen years that you are to rise up now in an holier than thou manner and condemn them?

First Negative Rebuttal, Morton Hodgson, Jr.
University of Georgia

LADIES AND GENTLEMEN: The first speaker for the Affirmative has probably overcome you with a maze of inconsistencies and dogmatic assertions; his flow of oratory was superb; but his facts I must point out to you as being of little value in proving that the American Legion as an organization should be condemned as having been more of a bad influence than a good.

He admits that the Legion and its purposes are good but tries to show you that the real Legion is a sinister, underhand organization composed of blackguards and thieves, just after which I spent fifteen minutes of your valuable time showing how the Legion in every particular has actually, concretely, and fully lived up to its many fine aims. He has thrown his opinions out as the final word to be had on these rather important questions of the day, supporting these opinions of his by facts of wrong-doing in isolated cases, quite possible to be found among so many men.

The Legion is blamed for drunken behavior at conventions, for brow-beating gray-headed old ladies working for promotion of peace, for preventing old men with different views from speaking publicly, for advocating wars with anyone and everyone, for making the United States an almshouse for all its pauper citizens, and for being an all-round bad-boy organization. Most of these charges are self-evidently childish; the others are easily answered. The Legion gets credit for much that it is not responsible for as an organization; for instance, the Legion was blamed for the Bonus Expeditionary Force march on Washington. As a matter of fact, there were only a few Legionnaires in the group. The Legion voted against the bonus in every national convention until after the outrageous treatment accorded the few Legionnaires in Washington infuriated most of its members. The Legion gets the blame for any action of veterans when according to my Opponent's figures the chances are five to one it is not a Legionnaire.

In every large organization there is bound to be a certain low element. This low element with many other veterans and spongers is responsible for the bad reputation given to Legion conventions.

If the Legion is so all powerful, why doesn't it carry into effect some of its terrible intolerances? In spite of one feeble protest against Einstein, I notice that he came into the country and was welcomed most heartily. Why isn't every school made to use Legion books and have its children taught about the terrible Reds? I have attended rather representative grammar schools and high schools, and I do not recall a single instance of having been taught anti-socialism.

My Opponent says in one place that not one-third of the Legionnaires saw action and then again wants to know how this great body of men inured to bloodshed and murder are competent to judge of peace? If these seven hundred thousand men in the Legion did not fight, I ask you how should they be acquainted with the horrors of war? And should not the opinions of this large number of middle-aged men who saw the other war through, backed by some of our country's ablest statement and finest brains, be accorded more attention and respect than those of my Opponent?

The plan of universal conscription which he so heartily condemned as being advocated by the Legion, in the opinion of quite a number of learned men, would be the cause for the abolition of all war if adopted by every nation in the world. As I have tried before to show you, no one is going to have the slightest desire for war if he knows that he will be drafted for some hard service, no matter what his age or station in life. The forwarding of this plan is in reality one of the finest services rendered by the Legion. When the evidence is weighed, for or against the Legion, we find the balance tipping in favor of the Legion. Of course, it is not perfect in many respects and we are not attempting to prove it is so, but the Negative does contend that in view of the fact that all the good works of the Legion outweigh its bad effects, the Legion should not be condemned as a bad influence on the United States as a nation.

First Affirmative Rebuttal, Noel Hemmendinger
Princeton University

LADIES AND GENTLEMEN: The picture of the American Legion which the Gentleman of the Negative who spoke first has painted is a very pleasant one. He has taken at face value the purposes of the Legion as expressed in the preamble to its constitution, and has portrayed an organization prepared to maintain law and order in times of emergencies and to combat subversive radicalism; an organization supporting adequate national defense and encouraging the idea of world peace; an organization aiding its members through rehabilitation and welfare work. The only trouble with this organization presented in such a favorable light is that it does not exist. As I showed in my previous speech, there is a wide gap between the ideal and the real American Legion. Some of the activities, which have been so eloquently described are performed by the Legion, but they are either social functions of value only to the Legion, or they are acts with an ulterior motive contrary to the interests of the American people.

You will note that the Gentlemen of the Negative gave few or no specific examples of public services performed by the Legion. They spoke in the same agreeable generalities used in the preamble to the Legion constitution, and they were grievously misled by them. The Legion is not to be judged by fine-sounding declarations of purpose; it is to be judged by its acts, and we have already told you how in reality it has violated both in letter and in spirit its most fundamental principles. We ask you to consider not what the American Legion says it is, which is the Legion described by the Negative, but what the Legion really is. You cannot then fail to condemn it, for the American Legion is condemned by its own acts.

Let us consider the examples of public service advanced by the Negative in behalf of the Legion. They have said that the Legion maintains law and order, and is a valuable reserve in such disasters as flood and fire. Perhaps so, and yet the Legion does no more in this regard than should be expected of all public-spirited citizens whether affiliated with any organization or not. It remains to be shown that particular credit should be given the Legion on this score, but there is much on this score to its discredit. As we have shown, the Legion has frequently indulged, as an organization, in drunken rioting and criminal violence. When the balance sheet is added up, the Legion has done more to destroy law and order than to maintain it.

The Negative has lauded the Legion for its patriotic propaganda against radicalism. They gave us no specific examples, whereas we have cited cases, and can cite many more, in which the Legion has acted with vicious intolerance and has denied by both violent and underhand means the right of free speech to some of our country's finest leaders. The Legion has condemned itself by elevating its own bigoted views to the rank of sacred dogma.

The Negative has praised the Legion, in the same breath, for its policy of war preparedness and for its work for world peace, entirely ignoring the fact that such a policy of preparedness as advocated by the Legion has never, in the history of the world, led to anything but war. The fact is that these ex-soldiers are militarists with no breadth of vision, who use the political strength of their numbers to force on the nation a militarism which now costs dearly in money and may in the future cost dearly in lives. The Legion's peace activities can be discovered only under a microscope; like its other noble purposes they consist only in words and conflict with the actual deeds of the Legion.

The first speaker of the Negative discussed the work of the Legion's Rehabilitation Committee with much naiveté. Veterans who think they have been unjustly treated in the matter of compensation, he said, come to this committee, which made recoveries in the past year to the extent of seven million five hundred thousand dollars. Precisely what we complain of! The Federal Government has the proper channels for the adjustment of veterans' claims. The American Legion has set up a powerful political organization which loots the American Treasury of many millions a year, and the Negative say it should be commended for it!

You see, Gentlemen, that the activities of the Legion suggested as being praiseworthy are actually either negligible or reprehensible, while on the other hand the American Legion, by its violence, its intolerance, its militarism, and its greed has forfeited the confidence of all thoughtful Americans.

Second Negative Rebuttal, A. H. Ulm
University of Georgia

LADIES AND GENTLEMEN: If what has been said by these Princeton speakers is as truthful as it is vehement, I must confess that to defend the American Legion would be a foolish way to waste time. I am afraid, though, that their remarks have been tempered more with the rashness of crusading reformers than with the discretion of just investigators. I trust that I shall be able to convince you of the frequent inaccuracy and also the not infrequent fallacy of their many pleas for condemnation of the Legion.

Throughout their argument, despite repeated denial, the mistake of confusing the actions of veterans in general with those of the organized American Legion has composed the large part of their case against the party on trial. Furthermore, they have been more or less inclined to attribute the sins of the government to the Legion. We must, you know, most carefully distinguish between the abuses for which the Legion is responsible and the abuses for which the government in Washington is responsible. Only by law can public monies be dispensed, and if they are dispensed wastefully, which I do not altogether admit in the case of war veterans, then the responsibility for such misuse devolves upon the legislators, and through them, upon their supporters, the people.

Now if these two Gentlemen of Princeton will condemn the latter for their consummate bigotry and selfishness, why then I shall be most glad to join them in concerted denunciation. But when they lay the blame for this waste on the door-step of the Legion, I am afraid I shall be forced to seek more honest company.

The second speaker has remarked on the fashion in which returning soldiers were so generously cared for in the form of pensions, hospitals, and vocational training. In that one statement is contained the essence of the entire veteran question. To a man who goes to war, and doubly so to a man who is forced to go to war, the citizens of the nation owe a debt which is enormous, and so what curious reason might they have for expecting the cost of veterans to be low?

The kind Gentleman who spoke last for Princeton has concisely indicted the Legion on two bonus counts. First their success in getting the bill passed, and second their demand for immediate payment of these certificates. I think it has been economically proved that the incidental sum, which these notes represent, is justly owing to all men who were in the army as compensation for their actual time. As to the second charge, I can think of no better way to practically inflate the currency than by paying these notes immediately. If farmers, bankers, and crooked city corporations are getting their share of the pork-barrel, why deny this truly deserving group their well-earned portion?

Constantly the Opposition has drawn our attention to isolated examples of rather startling conditions which have developed as a result of the actions of the Legion. Do these Gentlemen expect all veteran legislation to be infallible? Simply because abuses have occurred in scattered instances, there exists no justification for condemning the entire principle or the entire result. Possibly a few indolent plutocrats are drawing government pensions, but what reason have we for saying that that unfortunate result was the seeking of the Legion. I say it most positively is not!

The Legion has been denounced tonight on the amazing charge that it has persistently striven for increased hospital facilities and more liberal treatment of veterans. Of course this is expensive but will anyone for a moment declare that any expenditure by a government in the cause of the health of any of its subjects is a bad practice? If, as the second speaker has mentioned, the United States government is to become the "world's greatest treater of venereal diseases," may we not boast with pride that we have taken a great forward step in the path of progress? And if the Legion is responsible for this therapeutic expansion, does not that indebt us all to this altruistic organization, which seeks the suppression of one of life's greatest horrors?

Some rather startling facts have been thrown at you concerning the great wealth of the average Legionnaire. I happened to be in Washington during the disastrous bonus conflict last summer, and what I saw of veterans would never lead me to the conclusions of the Opposition. I saw men living in hovels not fit for my dog, and eating food which I am definitely certain I would never risk on myself, let along my dog.

Gentlemen, thank you for the kind reception you have afforded myself and my colleague tonight, and in closing, let me ask you to accept these facts openly and calmly, and not to permit yourselves to be carried away by the anger and impetuosity which seems to be in the air tonight.

Second Affirmative Rebuttal, Arthur Northwood, Jr.
Princeton University

LADIES AND GENTLEMEN: The Negative has praised the Legion because it is, they say, trying to build up an adequate national defense, and to prepare the country for war. We do not necessarily condemn them for this. What we do condemn them for is their blocking of every constructive effort for world peace. They do not even give those whose views differ from their own a chance to speak on the subject.

The Negative has said that the government has treated the veterans in a niggardly fashion. Allow me to repeat to you some figures that I gave in my original speech. All the other countries engaged in the war had thirty-four million men fighting, some of them for the whole time, four and a quarter years. The United States had only five million men under arms, half of whom never fought at all, and the other half for not more than six months. Yet the United States is paying in pensions fifty million dollars more than all the other countries put together. Is not our policy more than generous?

I feel that our Opponents are doing a grave injustice to the memory of Woodrow Wilson when they say that he was one who oppressed liberalism. Wilson delighted to be called an enlightened liberal. Particularly is their assertion untrue in the light of the fact that John Haynes Holmes, one of those whom the Legion opposes, spoke in the Princeton Chapel last Sunday.

Our Opponents have said that the government was doing nothing for the soldiers in setting up the War Risk Insurance Plan, for insurance is a regular business. That's just the point. This insurance was not; its terms were so liberal that the government has already lost nine hundred twenty-four million dollars in it.

Our Opponents have sought to excuse the Legion on the grounds that abuses have occurred before, and that they are occurring now in other fields. I fail to see their reasoning here. Merely because an evil has been, and is, prevalent, there exists no reason why we should condone it. On the contrary, the more widespread an abuse is, the more is it the duty of every citizen to rise up and condemn that abuse. But our Opponents have gone farther. Admitting that the pension scandals connected with the history of the G.A.R. have been terrible, they have asserted that the Legion is lily-white in comparison. I doubt that, for the G.A.R., in its whole history, succeeded in getting only seven billion dollars, while the American Legion has already filched five billions from the government. Is there any course left to us but to condemn this organization?

One of our Opponents asserted that what I said applied to veterans in general, rather than to the Legion. I resent that, for most of my remarks were directed explicitly against the Legion. With your permission, I shall read a summary of my speech to prove this. I said that we should condemn the American Legion because it had pushed through the Adjusted Service Compensation Act; because it demands the full payment now of something that does not fall due until 1945; because it has forced the building of government hospitals, and has tried to have the laws so modified that the United States shall become the greatest treater of venereal diseases in the world; because it is responsible for the government giving Emergency Officers retirement fees far out of proportion to their services; because it has secured for veterans disability allowances for peace-time injuries; and finally, because it has disrupted our Civil Service system. For all of these things the American Legion is responsible, and it has very often secured these things against the opposition of other veterans. I am convinced that it is the American Legion that is to be condemned.

Furthermore, if there were any doubt on the matter, the Legion lobby would soon dispel it, for it claims credit for all of this legislation. It is proud of what it has done. It boasts that it is the most powerful lobby in Washington. And I don't see how it can be excused merely because other lobbies exist. Our Opponent, when he mentioned the Anti-Saloon League Lobby, condemned it. Let him in like manner condemn the Legion Lobby. And then let him condemn the Legion, which is responsible for this lobby.

Our Opponents have said that after all, the Legion is not very important in our national life. President Hoover thought it was so important that he made a special trip to Detroit just to speak to it.

It has been asserted that veterans received nothing in this recent loan on their Adjusted Service Certificates. Well, if they did not deserve it in the first place, I do not see that they have any complaint coming.

Ladies and Gentlemen, we have shown the American Legion to be both chauvinistic and unpatriotic, we have shown it to be bigoted and selfish. I think that you will agree with us that it is to be condemned.

BIBLIOGRAPHY: AMERICAN LEGION SHOULD BE CONDEMNED

Books

Minton, R. Brulingame.—*Peace Veterans.* 1932.

Moody, H. G.—*Meet the King.* Winwick Co., 240 W. 40th St., N. Y. C. 1931.

White, W. C. and Walters, W. W.—*The Whole Story of the Bonus Army.* Day. 1933.

Hapgood, Norman.—*Professional Patriots.* Boni and Liveright. 1927.

American Legion National Headquarters, Indianapolis, Indiana. Will furnish the following material: *The American Legion, Its Ideals, Accomplishments, and Purposes.* May 1931. Same. October 1932. *The National Constitution and By-Laws of the American Legion. Proceedings of Conventions. Pamphlets on Educational and Welfare Activities. Speakers' Information Service. A Plan to Perpetuate Peace. Americanism Handbook.*

Magazines and Periodicals

American City.—25:505, December 1921. *American Legion Serves the Community.* 32.160-61, February 1925. *Civic Activities of American Legion Posts.*

American Legion Monthly.—July 1927. Rupert Hughes. *Letter to the American Legion Monthly* 19:414, April 1930. *Free Speech in Khaki.*

American Mercury.—13:169, February 1928. O. L. Warr. *The Heroes Union.*

Christian Century.—47:1418, November 19, 1930. Hankins. *American Legion Conventions.* 48:1234-60, October 7, 1931. Hutchinson. *Drunk with Sight of Power.* 49:1159-61, September 28, 1932. *Legion Raid.* 49:1212, October 5, 1932. H. N. Dukes. *Why Blame the Legion?* 50:380, March 22, 1933. *Final Test for the Legion.*

Collier's Weekly.—89:10-11, June 11, 1932. Davenport. *But the Dead Don't Vote.*

Congressional Digest.—11:266, November 1932. Stevens. *Legislative Aims of the American Legion.*

Forum.—85:257-65. May 1931 Duffield. *American Legion in Politics.* 86:29-32, July 1931. H. Fish. *In Defense of the Legion.*

Independent.—November 12, 1927. V. S Yarros. *Making Patriotism Hum in Darkest Chicago.*

Literary Digest.—95·5-7, October 1, 1927. *Legion's Conscription Program.*

Nation.—113:703-4, December 14, 1921. H. R. Warren *American Legion: A Defense.* 124:414, April 20, 1927. *Free Speech and the Legion.* 131:469-71, October 29, 1930. Gordon. *Legion Takes Boston.* 132:170, February 8, 1931. *Bonus Raid.* 136:287-9, March 15, 1932. Angell. *American Legion Versus America.*

National Congress of Social Workers.—1926:151-4. J. W. Garby. *American Legion's Program for Child Welfare.*

Nature.—12:374, December 1928. *Legion Shrine. Wild Game Refuge in Wisconsin.*

New Outlook.—161:7, October 1932. A. Roosevelt. *Enemy Within the Gate.*

New Republic.—66:30, February 25, 1931. *Mercenaries of Patriotism.* 68:221-2, October 14, 1931. *Lesson of the Legion.*

Outlook (See also New Outlook).—138:364-5, November 5, 1924. J. A. Drain. *American Legion in Years to Come.* 144:401-2, November 24, 1926. H. P. Savage. *American Legion's Program for 1926-7.* 157:323, March 4, 1931. *Bonus Record.*

Playground.—221:22-3. April 1928. *Cooperating with the American Legion.*

Scribner's Magazine.—90:174-81, August 1931. Duffield. *Legion Prepares for War.*

Survey.—62·254-5, May 15, 1929. R. D. Moot. *American Legion as City Planner.*

World To-morrow.—15:292, September 28, 1932. *Give Us This Day Our Bonus.*

GOVERNMENT CONTROL OF THE BANKING SYSTEM

A Mid-West Conference Debate

GOVERNMENT CONTROL OF THE BANKING SYSTEM

BELOIT COLLEGE AFFIRMATIVE VS. MARQUETTE UNIVERSITY NEGATIVE

The Mid-West Conference Colleges chose Federal Regulation of Banks for their subject during the 1932-33 debating season, and thus without prophecy and foreknowledge, gave their member colleges a most unusual experience—debating a public question which came to a boiling point during the debate season with the National Bank Holiday.

The present debate was held just a few days before President Roosevelt took things in hand and declared the National Bank Holiday. The question was stated, *Resolved: That all banking functions should be regulated by the Federal Government with deposits guaranteed.*

The present debate was not a decision contest but partakes of that style as both colleges represented engaged in numerous decision as well as non-decision debates on this subject during the course of the season This discussion is of unusual value because of the current and continued interest in the subject since nothing has been done up to the time of going to press to settle this giant problem, and the Senate hearings in the Morgan Bank Inquiry are still echoing about us.

The speeches were collected and submitted to this Volume by Professor G. F. Rassweiler of Beloit College, Director of Debate.

First Affirmative, John S. Nash
Beloit College

LADIES AND GENTLEMEN: Before proceeding with the Affirmative case I should like to clarify the question. *First,* we waive the constitutionality of the question. *Second,* by the term "all banking functions" we mean all those functions necessary for the operation of a commercial or savings bank. *Third,* by the word "regulate" we take our definition from the Standard Dictionary which defines it as follows, "to dispose, order, or govern by rule or system." *Fourth,* by the "Federal Government" we mean any authorized agent of the government such as the Federal Reserve Board. *Fifth,* by "deposits guaranteed" we mean a complete reimbursement to the depositor for losses due to bank failures.

This question is of supreme importance at this time for the newspapers are full of accounts of bank failures, which we individually feel either directly or indirectly. President Hoover, in his message to Congress declared that banking reform is imperative, and Henry Ford says that it is so necessary that he who shows us the way will make his name immortal.

Let me summarize the present situation with a few pertinent statistics. In the past twelve years ten thousand four hundred eighty-four banks have failed with a loss to depositors of nearly five billion dollars. There were nearly six times as many state banks failed as national banks, and more than sixty-five per cent of the closed banks were capitalized at less than twenty-five thousand dollars. Eighty per cent of the failures were in towns of a population of five thousand or less. This clearly indicates that the weakness of the system is in the small state banks. Further statistics show that from January 30, to September 30, 1932, there were seven hundred seventy-eight failures in the Federal

Reserve System. This amounted to ten and three tenths per cent of the number of banks in the system with a loss of four and two tenths per cent of the deposits that were in the Federal Reserve Banks. In contrast with this we find that three thousand eight hundred ninety-eight non-member banks have failed during the same period. This is twenty-two and two tenths per cent of all the non-member banks, with a loss of deposits of six and eight tenths per cent. In other words the non-member banks are nearly twice as bad as the Federal Reserve Banks in both of these respects.

We find that currency has been hoarded until it was estimated in excess of one and one-half billions of dollars according to figures of July 1932. And in case any of you think that the depression is the sole cause of bank failures, let me remind you that four hundred ninety-one banks failed in the year 1928.

It is interesting to note that during the same period of twelve years that there was only one failure in Canada, none in England, and none in France. This proves conclusively that it is not impossible to correct our banking system.

Many more such appalling figures could be given, but in general we have found the following "public enemies" in our system.

1. The lack of a central organization which can force through a definite reconstruction program.

2. Dangerous competition between member and non-member banks, which impairs the operation of the Federal Reserve System.

3. Many under-capitalized and poorly directed country banks which are contributing many bank failures.

4. Our Dollar is unstable—not in mint value, but in buying power. Economists tell us that this is due to insufficient control of credit.

5. The inability to expand credit at times when it is most needed.

6. The lack of ability to liquidate quickly in times of a crisis. This is due to a lack of rigid control of bank investments.

7. The loss of millions of dollars of depositors' money at a time when it is most needed, and the consequent limitation of buying power.

8. The inability to keep the faith and confidence of the public.

With these weaknesses in mind we, of the Affirmative, have formulated a plan which we believe will do much in the direction of the curtailment of these pathological conditions.

We further contend that the Negative must show that there will be a worse situation under our system than at present, or else they must develop a new plan which they can prove is superior to ours. It is the duty of the Negative to do more than just wrangle about detailed points of our plan. We ask them what they intend to do.

We have based our argument on this logical syllogism. "It is the duty of the government to protect the property and lives of its citizens, and therefore to protect their deposits. Our plan will protect the depositors. Therefore, it is the duty of the government to adopt our plan." It is, therefore, only necessary for us to show that our plan will protect the depositors, which we shall do during the course of the debate this evening.

Our plan, in general, is to extend the Federal Reserve System downward and outward so as to include all banks, and to so enhance the regulation of these banks that failure will be reduced to a minimum. Further we would guarantee all deposits which should become tied up through failures. Note that this plan is very similar to the Glass-Steagall bill now before Congress, except that we would make it compulsory for all banks to enter the system.

Our plan more specifically is composed of four parts.

First, we would legislate to force all banks into the Federal Reserve System. This was the original idea of Senator Glass and other originators of the Act. Now our Federal Reserve System is merely a compromise plan. This factor in our plan would have very definite advantages.

It would give us a central organization which could put through a definite reconstruction program. This corrects "public enemy" number one.

It would do away with the dangerous competition between member and non-member banks, of which Eugene Meyer, a member of the Federal Reserve Board, says, "It should be recognized that effective supervision of banking in this country has been seriously hampered by the competition between member and non-member banks, and that the establishment of a unified system of banking under national supervision is essential to fundamental banking reform." Thus we see that "public enemy" number two has been conquered.

We can in no wise consider a plan which reduces the number of banking systems in this country from forty-nine to one, dangerous or radical. It is a plan which is recommended by the Federal Reserve Board, countless economists, and many bankers including Thomas Lamont, Number One Morgan Partner, who says, "No thorough-going banking reform can be brought about until two vital changes have been accomplished. First, we must have all commercial banks under the Federal Reserve System. Second, we must establish sensible provisions for regional branch banking."

This brings me to the *second* step in our plan. We would bring the smaller banks under the wing of the larger and more ably-directed banks by means of branch banking. Mr. Lamont goes on to say that it is his opinion that "almost all of the bank failures in Chicago could have been averted with branch banking."

This eliminates the small banking unit with its insufficient capital ("public enemy" number three). We have already noted that sixty-five per cent of the bank failures in the last twelve years were in this class. With small banks as they now are, competition is so strong that the profits for all of them are minimized and as a consequence they are encouraged to make unsafe investments in the hope of greater profits. Another weakness that will be eliminated by our system is that the smaller banks will be able to have a greater distribution to their investment, and they can take long-time paper without the fear of not being able to liquidate. As you all know this is the basis of the Canadian system which has proved so successful. Ogden Mills, the Secretary of the Treasury, and also the Comptroller of the Currency are firmly in favor of branch banking.

Thirdly, after we have all the banks in the system, and we have eliminated the small banking unit by bringing it under the wing of the larger banks, we would set up a stricter system of control of the member banks. We would force the banks to keep a certain per cent of their investments in that type of highly liquid paper which the Central Banks may rediscount. As our system now operates the banks have this privilege, but few of them keep in a position where they can take advantage of this privilege. Besides forcing the banks to keep a definite per cent of this highly liquid paper we would have closer supervision of all bank investments. This stricter supervision will keep the bank in a better condition. They will be able to liquidate when necessary, expand credit when necessary, and this will in turn be a material aid in keeping our dollar more stabilized. Thus we have conquered "public enemies" numbers four, five, and six.

This factor of our plan will insure safety in the case of a run on the bank. It will increase the confidence of the public in the banking system, and it will check unwise investments made to gain a larger rate of interest.

And finally, after we have all the banks under the

system, eliminated the small banking unit, and added stricter supervision to the member banks, we would add as an additional factor the guaranteeing of deposits. We believe that this is essential to the regaining of public confidence in our banks.

To do this we would set up a fund from the franchise taxes and the profit of the system. Don't you think it better to pay for losses in advance by means of this fund than to have the same cost borne by depositors at a time when we can little afford to have their buying power taken away from them?

Don't you think we have a plan here that is at least better than the lack of plan which we now have? Don't you think it will strengthen our banking system and regain the confidence of the public? This plan is not new. It is one which has the favorable opinion of many of the nation's leaders in this field. In conclusion let me quote from the "Sooner or Later" column of *The Business Weekly* which says, "Congress should immediately amend the Reserve Act to compel all banks of deposit to become members of the Federal Reserve System, and set up in the system a deposit fund for the protection of the depositors. This is a step without which confidence in our banking system cannot be completely restored and continuously maintained."

First Negative, Donald W. Gleason
Marquette University

LADIES AND GENTLEMEN: I am very sincere when I state at the outset that Marquette University is pleased to have the opportunity to present its version of this important question of banking, a subject which is so intimately related with the lives of all people. The occasion tonight is even more pleasant for us, because it is Beloit College that furnishes the opposition.

While, therefore, we engage in this controversy this evening with a most friendly attitude toward our Opponents, the first speaker for the Affirmative has made so many unusual remarks, that we are forced to disagree with our worthy Opponents from the very beginning. He declared somewhat strikingly "that the Negative tonight must uphold the present mess in our banking system, or they must propose a counter plan, and we would like to know what the Negative intends to do." When Mr. Nash was thus mistaking the true function of a Negative team, I was reminded of a certain prisoner who had committed a very serious offense and who was sentenced to be hanged. A few days before the hanging was to take place, the prisoner approached the warden and said: "Warden, I would like to have a little exercise." The warden somewhat amazed at the request answered: "Well, my good man, just what kind of exercise would you like to have?" And said the prisoner in reply, "I'd like to skip the rope." Apparently, the Affirmative tonight would like very much to skip the burden of proving the proposition by calling on the Negative to prove a counter proposition.

Ladies and Gentlemen, we intend to do but one thing tonight, namely, to show that the Affirmative proposal cannot be substantiated upon the fundamental issues which it involves, and that it is such an impracticable theory that it is dangerous and unwise seriously to consider its adoption. More than this the Negative need not do in any debate. We want it to be distinctly understood that the Affirmative has the burden of proof, and we do not intend to permit them to skip that burden by creating in any manner the impression that the Negative is under an obligation to present a solution for the ills of our banking system. However, I suppose the worthy opposition will now harp long and loud throughout this debate that our answer to their assertion of the Negative duty was very weak; they may even attempt to capitalize on the answer by suggesting to you that the Negative cannot produce a better plan. To forestall such an attitude it has just occurred to me that our closing speaker, Mr. Hansen, is a man of many moods and inclined to be very charitable, and he may even present several plans that would be better than that of the Affirmative, but I repeat that should he do so, it will be the result of his disposition and will not in any sense be done with a feeling of obligation.

Not only has Beloit's opening speaker misconstrued the duty of the Negative team in this debate, but his analysis of the question indicates that the Affirmative has misinterpreted their own burden so badly that up to this point they have not debated the question. The Affirmative case begins with the argument that the present banking system is defective; they point with alarm to the great number of banks that have failed in recent years; next, they listed about eight causes for the failures, and then they present a remedy. I could not write down all of the eight causes as Mr. Nash recited them, but here are a few of them: *First*, a lack of central organization in our banking system—*Second*, the competition between member and non-member banks of the Federal Reserve System—*Third*, too many rural, small banks, and so on. What was the remedy proposed for these alleged defects? First, the placing of all banks under the Federal Reserve System. Second, the establishment of regional banks. Third, the further development of branch banking. What do you notice, Ladies and Gentlemen, about each one of these remedies? You should note this—that every single one of these proposed remedies is a remedy for some part of the *organization* of our present banking structure, and that not one of them has anything at all to do with the *functions* of a bank. In that very essential regard, the Affirmative case is entirely beside the point. Our question tonight deals with the regulation of the *functions* of a bank, not with *organization* of banks. The Affirmative is supposed to argue a particular method of regulating banking functions—and what are the functions? The chief function of a bank is to receive money from depositors, retaining their money with interest. But the Affirmative case does not touch that function at all; instead, they tell you too many of our banks were under-capitalized—but is it a *function* of a bank to be capitalized at any amount? That is a defect in *organization* of banks. Their whole plan, to place banks in the Federal Reserve System, to establish regional banks, to promote branch banking,

—in every detail the plan is a remedy for *organization* of banks, a plan that does nothing in the way of regulating banking functions, and, therefore, the Affirmative is in the embarrassing position of having debated before their home audience on the wrong question. We challenge the Affirmative to show that banking functions are not now properly regulated, and to explain how they propose to regulate those functions so as to come within the bounds of our proposition.

Another general criticism of the Affirmative case thus far, is that the analysis of the question as given by Mr. Nash was not complete. Let us, therefore, examine the wording of the question to determine in more detail the exact issues of this controversy and to show more clearly what the Affirmative must prove tonight in order to establish its case.

The proposition is worded as follows, *"Resolved: that the Federal Government should regulate all banking functions, and guarantee deposits."* You will note, therefore that there are three distinct parts to the question:—first, *Federal Regulation;* second, *"of all banking functions";* and third, *guarantee of deposits.*

Let us now consider the first issue, "Should we have Federal Regulation." That issue really means should we have Federal Regulation of state banks, for our national banks are already regulated by the Federal government. It is therefore the burden of the Affirmative to prove that state regulation is directly responsible for the defects; that there is a direct causal connection between the defects and the system of state regulation; for without such proof, they cannot arrive at the conclusion that state regulation should be abolished; and it must then be shown that Federal Regulation of state banks will not be possessed of the same evils.

The Affirmative condemns the present system chiefly because a great number of state banks have failed. We are sensible enough on the Negative to admit that banks have failed, but what the Affirmative must show is that those banks failed because they were under state regulation, and until that be shown, any further mention of bank failures by the Affirmative is immaterial.

How about these failures? What did cause them? Do you think for one moment that it was the state that caused all these banks to fail? According to the first speaker's very own argument, some of our banks failed because they were unable to keep the faith of the public, but is that the fault of the state? No system of regulation, no division of government could prevent the distrust of banks that has grown among the masses during the past few years, for some people were frightened by newspaper accounts, some depositors were victims of the pessimism of their friends and neighbors, and as a result a certain fear and loss of confidence was created. Rumors that certain banks were going to fail have recently been widely circulated, creating more fear, and the result would have a telling effect on the resources of any bank. The whole spirit of uneasiness often produced a run on various banks, as was experienced in Green Bay, Milwaukee, and Chicago within the last year. The point is, that many banks were forced to close their doors, not because of state regulation, but because of idle rumor, fear, and loss of confidence. State regulation did not cause that feeling of distrust. It was caused in great part by the dishonesty of a few bankers and their unlawful practices. Two large banks were closed within the last year, and in each case the status of the bank was jeopardized by the unlawful practices of the president and cashier respectively. Both men, prominent as bankers for years, were recently convicted in Milwaukee and are now at Leavenworth. In each city, the depositors suffered and lost their confidence as a result. In the city of Milwaukee, the president of another bank was recently sentenced to Waupun for unlawful banking practices; the trial of another banker in the same city is now pending, and depositors there also suffered and lost confidence. No system of regulation is responsible for the weakness of the human flesh and yet the Affirmative condemns state regulation because banks have failed, including banks that failed through weaknesses in the human element.

An even greater number of our banks failed because of the severe adverse economic conditions. There has been a world-wide depression for forty-one months and our banks have not been immune to its effects. A bank is not a large stately edifice, located on a busy street corner, whose principal function it is to have uniformed attendants to direct customers to the proper window. In its broad aspects, a bank is the mechanism for the distribution of the products of the world, and its proper functioning in that capacity is just as essential to our economic well-being as the physical transportation of goods. As soon as there is a break-down in our money-credit system, there is inevitably an interference with the normal production and distribution of goods. It is a maxim of banking that the strength of any bank depends on the value of its securities. Our banks were caught in the tide of the depression just as you and I were caught; the value of their securities was lowered, beyond all reasonable expectation. Their financial stability was shattered just as the financial status of the individual was broken. Naturally, some of the banks could not withstand the intensity and duration of the economic upheaval and were consequently forced to close their doors. State regulation cannot be blamed for the depression; no agency of government could have reasonably been expected to foresee this particular disorder; yet the Affirmative propose to abolish state regulation because banks have failed, including those which were caused by the disrupting of our economic structure.

I have purposely refrained from plunging into statistics on the causes of bank failures, because statistics are often boring and unreliable, and have wished to base my argument upon matter that has been part of the general thought and observation of every member of the audience. But I do have some authentic statistical evidence, which I desire to present because it contains such a strong challenge to the Affirmative case. The record of annual bank failures shows that from January 1, 1929 until August 31, 1932, eight hundred thirty-nine national banks failed. In other words, for a period of forty-four months, twenty national banks failed every month; twenty banks failed every month under Federal regulation, yet the Affirmative proposes to cure our banking ills by placing all banks under Federal regulation. Now the challenge is this—the Affirmative must do one of three things; *First,* admit that their system is defective, in that banks also failed under Federal regulation; or *second,* admit that my argument is correct, namely, that it is not the system of regulation that causes banks to fail, but certain extraneous matters such as dishonesty in bankers, loss of confidence by depositors, the economic depression, and so on. Such an admission would be a declaration that they cannot prove the first issue. Or *third,* they must offer some other explanation for these national bank failures. We demand that the Affirmative answer this challenge to the record of Federal regulation—and until it is answered it stands as prima facie evidence that banks fail under both systems of regulation, which admits that state regulation is not to blame, and which means that the Affirmative cannot establish the first of the three basic issues in this discussion.

It has been my intention, Ladies and Gentlemen, to establish that the Negative does not have the burden of proving a counter plan; that the Affirmative has misconstrued the question in proposing remedies for the *organization* of banks rather than for the *functions* of banking; that the proposition involves three basic issues, and that as to the first, "should we have Federal regulation?", the Affirmative proposal cannot be sup-

CONTROL OF THE BANKING SYSTEM 267

ported since it cannot be shown that state regulation is directly responsible for the evils of the system.

Second Affirmative, John Martin
Beloit College

LADIES AND GENTLEMEN: The Negative has said among other things that we must show that state regulation has been defective, and I wish to do this before I go any further. In 1929 there were in the United States 7530 national banks. From January 1930 to September 1932 there were 778 Federal Reserve banks that failed. About ten and three tenths per cent of the total number of national banks. At the same time there were 17,580 non-national banks or state banks of which 3898 failed or twenty-two and two tenths per cent which was more than twice the proportion of those that failed in the National system. At the same time there was deposited in the national banks $19,500,000,000.00. During this same period in this Federal Reserve system there were tied up deposits to the amount of $783,800,000.00 or about four and two tenths per cent of the total of deposits, while in the state banks at the same time there were $34,500,000,000.00 of which amount $2,356,248,000.00 was tied up or about six and eight tenths per cent which is more than half again as much in proportion tied up in the state banks as in the national banks. So this distinctly shows that state has been defective in comparison to Federal regulation.

The Negative speaker also went on to say that since

some state banks are well regulated there is no point in bringing them all under the system. In other words he wishes us to go right on letting these banks fail, causing suffering and hardship to all persons concerned, until they all have failed, because until that time there will be some of them that are well regulated and have not failed. Now I do not, and I am sure that you do not believe that this is good sense for would it not be better to put this group of state regulated banks into the National system which we have just shown to be better, rather than let a great many go on failing just because a few are better regulated? This is especially true since there will be no hardship imposed on the better regulated banks because they would have high standards anyway.

As has been pointed out by the first Affirmative speaker, one of the basic faults in our present economic system is the instability of the American dollar. We thought for a while the technocrats had solved this problem by the simple method of doing away with the dollar. But it seems the plan of the technocrats has to be put into working order and we won't be able to live under it for a time at least. In the meantime I believe that we had better try to get along with the dollar.

I say, "get along with the dollar," but I do not mean to go ambling along letting this most important measure of value fluctuate up and down in the manner it does at the present time. We are very careful to keep all other forms of measurements correct—we put the standard yardstick in a glass case, and throw a man in jail for selling wheat from a different sized basket, and so on. Yet our dollar which measures almost all kinds of commodities is allowed to fluctuate over two hundred per cent in just a few years. Let us take two examples to show just what I mean by changing the dollar.

Suppose that you had purchased a piece of land in 1918, and were going to pay for this land with wheat—using wheat as an average commodity. The first year you paid four hundred bushels of wheat; the second the same, and so on. But, although you were paying four hundred bushels a year, the bushel basket was being made larger and larger, until in 1929 it was just two and one-half times as large as it had been when you started making your payments. In other words you were paying one thousand bushels according to the 1918 standard under which you made the contract. The standard of value had expanded two hundred and fifty per cent. Unbelievable. Yet this is just what happened to the most important standard of value, the dollar, during this period.

Or to take the case of a man who was not a debtor, but a thrifty man with one hundred dollars who in 1896 decided to follow the approved method of saving and put his money in a savings bank at three and one-half per cent interest. In 1918 this thrifty individual withdrew his money and found to his great delight that it had grown to three hundred dollars. That was fine until he went to spend the money and then he found that over an average list of commodities his three hundred dollars would only buy what seventy-five dollars would have bought when he deposited the money. He had lost money by putting it in the bank—and the bank hadn't closed. Our standard bushel basket for all commodities had changed size.

These examples show how the buying power of the dollar varies, but to impress upon you the seriousness of the situation let me quote from the booklet *Honest Money* by the American Farm Bureau Federation:

"The effect of the deflation since 1929 has been the increase of public and private debts in this country (in terms of commodities) by eighty billion dollars. On the present price level, when we have paid off our debts on the basis of what those debts were worth in terms of commodities in 1926, we shall still have eighty billions more to pay. Even the most avaricious loan shark never dreamed of legalized robbery in such terms as that."

For all practical purposes this is the same thing as the wildcat currency which we had at one period in our history but which was controlled for contractual payments by regulating the amount issued. But it is just as important that we stabilize the dollar in terms of those commodities which we can use. Economists are declaring this with increasing emphasis. For instance the Special Banking Commission of the Chamber of Commerce of the United States says:

"Our objective should be first of all to raise prices a long way above the present level and then to maintain them at the level thus reached with as much stability as can be managed. We recommend that this objective be accepted as the guiding aim of the monetary policy of this country."

And from another country, England, we hear that the Industrial report of the British Liberal party contains this statement:

"A steady healthy development of trade requires, as an indispensable condition, the utmost stability in the purchasing power of money."

As we have seen the currency of this country has been stabilized, but when we realize that money in this form takes care of only about ten per cent of our business transactions we realize that this control has very little effect. The money that takes care of the other ninety per cent of the business is what we are concerned with—this is credit money: money created when a person deposits cash in a bank, and the bank makes a loan to another person by giving him a checking account, using the cash just as a reserve. This person pays another person by check and that check is deposited in another bank where it serves as the basis of more credit. This expansion of credit goes on until it is theoretically possible to expand it about ten times the volume of actual cash.

Now the banks control this credit expansion and they can make money dear or cheap according to the amount they contract or expand credit. This is generally a result of raising or lowering the discount rates. It is now generally recognized that the boom market was partly caused by the low discount rate which allowed speculation to get too big a start and then nothing could check it.

It then follows that the banking system could largely

stabilize our monetary system by regulating credit on a scientific basis. That is all banks acting as a unity could do this—no individual bank can get away from the profit motive which in many cases does not run parallel to the best interests of the country. This was recognized by those who drafted our Federal Reserve system for there was a clause in the bill as adopted by the House of Representatives in 1913 directing the Federal Reserve System to use its powers to stabilize the purchasing power of money. Though this was eliminated in the Senate, it is becoming increasingly evident that something of this kind must be done. There are several ways the dollar may be stabilized, but they all depend on the unity of the banking system because an increase and decrease of the discount rate is essential to control the value of the dollar. This unity and power we propose in our extension of the Federal Reserve system.

We do not claim that this would revive a dead business world, but we do say it will control live and going business activity. The benefits of the plan toward reviving business will be taken up by another speaker. Not only do we say this but let me read what some authorities on the subject say.

Owen D. Young says in regard to the policy of the Federal Reserve System:

"It desires to contribute to the stabilization of purchasing power of our money."

A. C. Whitaker in the *American Economic Review*

(March 1930) makes various proposals for change in the Federal Reserve System. One is;

"That the statute be made to declare the stabilization of commodity prices to be a leading or perhaps the chief objective of the Federal Reserve policy."

Lastly we have some legislative action in this direction in the Goldsborough bill:

"The Goldsborough bill passed by the House in May, 1932, would make it the duty of the Federal Reserve banks and the Treasury to undertake the policy of restoring the level of wholesale commodity prices to the 1921-1929 average; and after such result had been accomplished, to maintain a stable price level thereafter."

In summary let me point out that we have seen that we do not allow other measures of value to fluctuate and there is no reason why we should make an exception to the most important one—the dollar. This can be controlled by a definite policy to that end on the part of a unified banking system, and we propose such a system. Notice further that we rest this policy of control of the dollar for the protection of the people's property on a three legged stool, any one leg of which may have little utility in holding up the policy. But, when we take the three—all banks in the system, strict regulation, and guarantee of deposits—we have a firm and sound foundation.

Second Negative, Ernest O. Eisenberg
Marquette University

LADIES AND GENTLEMEN: It is most regrettable that one of the modern requisites of debate technique seems to consist of the practice of putting one's audience to sleep before the first twenty minutes of speaking are completed. As I gaze about this room and notice with what tremendous effort you are struggling to maintain an air of alertness, my heart wells with sympathy for you. And yet I am quite sure that you did not come here merely for the purpose of being put to sleep. There are so many more congenial methods of conducing slumber, that it is at once obvious that you came here for some other purpose. Frankly, this is no ordinary debate question. True, it has its baffling array of statistics; well, all debate questions have their statistics. As a matter of fact, what would a debate speech be like if it did not have statistics? And yet, this question involves much more than the mere recitation of facts and the facile flow of words. Upon a correct understanding of the issues involved in this debate, upon a correct solution of the problems presented herein, depends your own future existence. Your own presence in this University one year from this day will be determined largely by the action the people of the United States take as to the safe-guarding of their economic interests.

Our friends of the Opposition advocate as a remedy for our modern ills the plan of Federal Regulation of banking functions with a guaranty of deposits. In seeking to convince you of the feasibility and desirability of their proposal, our worthy Opponents have assumed a tremendous burden of proof. In the first place, they must show you that Federal Regulation is the only possible solution. They must absolutely convince you of the fact that regulation by the states is hopeless, that there can possibly be no means by which state regulation can be improved. The first speaker of the Negative, in opening our case this evening has established without any question of doubt the fact that although state regulation is not perfect at the present, there is no reason why it cannot be improved to a point where it would possess all the advantages of Federal Regulation without any of the disadvantages of Federal Regulation. It is the contention of the Negative that the defects in state regulation are not inherent in the system. True, state regulatory bodies in certain parts of the country may have been lax; state laws may have been unwise; but we wish to remind you that where model state banking regulations have been enacted, competent commissions have given to the public a protection which has been as adequate and complete as that offered by the Federal Government.

Then, in the second place, the Affirmative must show you that it is desirable and practical for the Federal Government to regulate the functions of banking. At this time, we think it wise to draw the distinction between banking organization and banking functions. By the organization of banking is meant the structural form of banking, such as its capitalization, its operation as a unit, or its operation as a member of a chain system. For example, laws providing that banks must have a capital fund of fifty thousand dollars, laws providing that banks cannot be organized except where necessary to the best interests of the community, laws prohibiting the organization of chains of banks—these are all laws pertaining to the *organization* of banking. On the other hand, it is well recognized that the *functions* of banking consist of the business of taking in money in the form of deposits and of giving it out in the form of loans. Federal Regulation of banking functions would therefore consist of a regulation of the very business of the bank. Federal agents and inspectors would have supreme authority over the advisability of certain loans and extensions of credit. We submit this question for your consideration: is it to the best interests of a community to have an experienced banker lend money to the people he knows and trusts, or to have those loans checked and regulated by some distant official in Washington? The plan the Affirmative proposes, if logically carried out, would of necessity mean a financial dictatorship such as America has never had, and such as America will never want to have. If the government is to regulate banking functions so completely, why not have complete government ownership and control of banks? And if the government is not to have control over the banks, why should the government be forced to guarantee the deposits which may be jeopardized by factors beyond its scope of supervision? Bluntly speaking, the Affirmative is caught between the horns of a dilemma from which there is no escape.

Finally, in the third place, the Affirmative must show you that it is desirable and practical for the Federal Government to guarantee the deposits of all American banks. And, because this question in the debate lends itself so readily and so easily to attack, I shall devote the remainder of my time in disclosing to you the impossibility and the undesirability of guaranteeing bank deposits. As the Opposition has already pointed out to you, guaranty of bank deposits by the Federal Government would consist in the building up of a huge insurance fund wherewith the government would recompense the depositors of insolvent banking institutions. We base our criticism of this plan upon three grounds, the first of which is that the sum required for this fund would be so large as to be impossible. According to statistics quoted you earlier in this debate by our Opponents, according to statistics furnished by the Federal Reserve Board, more than 10,000 banks with deposits of over $5,000,000,000 involved, have closed their doors since 1920; and in the past two and one-half years more than 5,000 banks with deposits totalling more than $3,000,000,000 have crashed down in the collapse of our general economic structure. Were the Federal Government to attempt to guarantee these deposits, to pay out dollar for dollar the amount of money involved, we should have to build up a guaranty fund of not $100,000,000, nor even $500,000,000, but actually of more than $2,500,000,000. This is but elementary insurance. In times such as these, when our local governments are breaking down, when our Federal Government faces the hugest deficit in its history, is it at all sound or feasible to suggest that to this added burden we take $2,500,000,000 and say, "Here is something more you can pay for"?

Further, we wish to add that this guaranty fund must essentially consist of a cash or gold fund. You cannot insure deposits unless you have a fund of insurance money. And if you have money, you must have a gold security behind that money. The Affirmative may suggest that we guarantee deposits with a credit structure. But let me point this out to you: if you guarantee deposits by credit you are directly inflating the American dollar in a most pernicious and objectionable manner. For example, let us say that 1,000 banks with $1,000,000,000 deposits close. The government has guaranteed the deposits, but it lacks a fund wherewith it can pay out $1,000,000,000. Consequently, under the credit system it will issue $1,000,000,000 of notes on the credit of the government and deliver these notes to the depositors. What has actually happened is that the government has inflated its money. It has gone to the printing presses and has caused money to be printed without any gold backing. Germany tried this in 1923, and the mark crashed down to the disappearing point. Every nation which has tried the policy of inflation has learned to rue the day when it set the printing presses whirring. Such men as Bernard Baruch, New York financier, and Senator Glass, one of the foremost banking authorities in America, denounce the very thought of inflation. Yet, a guaranty of bank deposits based upon the credit of the government can mean nothing else but inflation.

On the other hand, if you try to build up a gold reserve, you must come to the understanding that there is only $5,500,000,000 of gold in the United States. Remove $2,500,000,000 from this total and you destroy the credit structure of the nation. The Affirmative speaks of the dangers of hoarding. The formation of this insurance fund would be wholesale hoarding on a scale never before attempted in the United States, and I assure you, never again to be attempted. Further, remember that this huge gold sum will lie idle. It is capable of earning at six per cent interest a year, approximately $150,000,000 a year. With this sum lying idle for a period of ten years, the net loss to the United States at compound interest would exceed $1,500,000,000. To summarize then, guaranty of deposits would require the setting up of an enormous fund. It is impossible to guarantee deposits without this fund, since any other system would lead to inflation; yet the maintenance of this fund would destroy the economic fabric of our nation, and cause greater loss to the nation than the present total of bank failures.

The second ground upon which we attack this plan is that such a plan will remove every incentive for honest and careful banking. With the government providing a guaranty of deposits, shrewd and unethical bankers will find an opportunity to speculate with dangerous risks, since if they lose, their depositors will be safeguarded. To quote Representative McFadden, former Chairman of the House Banking and Currency Committee, speaking in Congress, May 25, 1932:

"The establishment of a guaranty fund is not going to stop bank failures. If anything it will encourage through irresponsible management more bank failures. This is going to permit promoters and schemers to buy up banks and to use them because the deposits will be insured."

Representative Hull of Illinois, speaking on the same day in Congress, has this to say about the plan:

"When you guarantee bank deposits by law, you immediately penalize the honest and conservative bankers for the mistakes made by bankers who are not conservative, and even at times reckless in their negotiations."

Thus, the plan of the Affirmative, instead of encouraging a system of safe and prudent banking, will actually tend to lower the standards we already have.

Finally, we oppose the guaranty of deposits, because the actual experience of eight states has shown this plan to be disastrous in practical operation. You know, we in America are fortunate in our system of government. We have forty-eight states acting as forty-eight laboratories in which we can conduct our various sociological and economic experiments. By the results of these experiments the nation can gradually improve its system of government. Well, to state the matter briefly, eight states adopted this guaranty plan for deposits. Everyone of these eight states repealed the plan, and for this reason:

In Oklahoma, the plan resulted in a deficit of $8,000,000. In Kansas, the plan resulted in a deficit of $7,000,000; in Mississippi, of $4,000,000; in North Dakota of $14,000,000; in Texas of $16,000,000; in

Nebraska of $20,000,000; and in South Dakota of the grand total of $32,000,000. Washington adopted the plan, but repealed it immediately upon the failure of the Scandinavian American Bank.

Thus according to Representative McFadden, speaking in the House of Congress, May 25, 1932, this plan which was adopted so gloriously in eight states, was repealed in one after another, as the total of losses soared and soared until these states are faced with a total deficit of more than $100,000,000. The rest of the states can thank their lucky stars that they did not join in this gay procession. And yet, our friends of the Opposition advocate this plan as the salvation for American banking. If you go into a laboratory and place a mixture into a test tube, and the test tube explodes, and you place the mixture in another test tube, and that also explodes, and you then place the mixture into a third, a fourth, a fifth, a sixth, a seventh and an eighth, and they all explode, you begin to understand that there is something wrong with the mixture. Similarly we say that there is something wrong with guaranty of deposits. It can't possibly work; it doesn't work; and it never will work. Consequently, in conclusion, I will say that because of these three reasons, *first*, the impracticability of building up a fund large enough, *second*, the increased inefficiency of banking under it, and *third*, its failure wherever tried, guaranty of bank deposits should not be adopted by the United States Government.

Third Affirmative, John K. Strong
Beloit College

LADIES AND GENTLEMEN: Two negroes were having an altercation, and one, growing angry, pulled a razor and slashed at the throat of the other, who laughed uproariously and cried, "Well, Sambo, I guess dat's the first time you evah missed." "Missed?" chuckled Sambo, "missed? Shake yo-self, Henry, shake yo-self."

Now we've been playing the rôle of Sambo, and Henry across the table there hasn't realized what has happened. Our Opponents have been decapitated, and they don't know it yet! For look—we have shown them that the state banks, in fair weather and foul, have had a record about twice as bad as that of the National banks. We have exposed the defects of the present dual banking system which in spite of the transcendent faith of our Opponents has brought American life into this present morass. And we have also proposed a plan that would remedy, with major effectiveness, the evils of the present situation. And what do our opponents do but take a wide detour around this unshakable case that fulfills our obligation as Affirmative, and begin to peck at us on matters inconsequential or unrelated to the subject for debate.

They have rung all the changes on a brain-tantalizer which they call *Organization* versus *Function*. In this it is apparent that they have fallen prey to a common philosophical error. It will be distasteful to you, Ladies and Gentlemen, for me to enter the metaphysi-

CONTROL OF THE BANKING SYSTEM 283

cal realm, and resurrect Descartes and Leibnitz; let it suffice to say that all matter is meaningless unless it has organization; and it is the organization of an institution that determines and controls its function. A cat does not function like a carburetor because it is not organized on that principle. And every speck of control over *Function* is to be found in *Organization.* Therefore the only way that we may effectively control the functions of banks is to control their larger organization.

Still ignoring the Affirmative case, the Gentlemen of the Opposition have presented us with an ultimatum. We must show three things, they declare, and the first of these is that regulation by the states is hopeless. Upon my soul, do we have to *prove* this to them? Do I have to present to you conclusive proof that there *is* a depression, and that the breakdown of state regulation has contributed enormously to the severity of the disorder? I do not have to defend this point—it shouts its truth through the blinds of ten thousand closed bank buildings.

We are told in the second place that we must prove that regulation by the government is practical. All right: (*a*) We have tried everything, including state control and private initiative, until we now jingle pennies instead of dollars in our pockets, and until one-third of Beloit's families are receiving County aid. From the record of the government in contrast with private enterprise, there is much to be hoped for in complete Government Regulation of our wildcat banking. (*b*) The eight defects of our present banking system, enumerated, by Mr. Nash and so studiously avoided by the Negative, are all defects which are remediable to a significant degree by inclusive membership in the Federal Reserve System, whose *Organization* and therefore whose *Functions* are controlled by the government. (c) With Government Regulation will come the elimination of other causes of bank failure mentioned by Mr. Gleason of the Negative. Distrust of banks, uneasiness concerning deposits, dishonesty of bankers—these will become negligible when the National Government manages the entire banking system. Even a fourth cause (d) of failure also mentioned, the general breakdown of the money-credit system, will be removed since, as Mr. Martin has shown, the Federal Reserve System does, in the words of Owen D. Young, "contribute to the stabilization of the purchasing power of our money."

And the third challenge that has been flung at us this evening is to show that the guaranty of bank deposits is practical and desirable. Let us look more closely at some of Mr. Eisenberg's statements about this. (a) He says that the fund required is too large. But let us see what Senator Glass, foremost banking expert in the country, has to say. In the Glass-Steagall bill now before Congress, he would establish a Federal Liquidating Board consisting of the Secretary of the Treasury, Comptroller of the Currency, and three appointees of the President. They are to administer a deposit guarantee fund of not more than five hundred million dollars, one-fourth of which has already been obtained, to be raised by (1) treasury subscription to the amount of franchise payments, (2) levy upon surplus account of each Federal Reserve bank, (3) assessment upon member and participating non-member banks in proportion to their deposits, and (4) borrowings from the Reconstruction Finance Corporation. Senator Glass says that it can be done! Equally as powerful an argument is the fact that an estimated amount of one billion six hundred million dollars is being hoarded today because of people's fear of losing their bank deposits. The establishing of a guaranty fund of five hundred million dollars would be of inestimable aid in returning to active turnover this huge amount of money. Moreover Canada has guaranty of bank deposits. Does she find it to be too expensive?

(*b*) Mr Eisenberg also has declared that the guaranty of bank deposits would eliminate good banking. How can he be sure? It never has been tried long enough for anyone to tell what the results in that particular line will be! And yet I think that we may lean a big question-mark against this Negative argument by demonstrating by analogy what effect such a scheme might have upon the tender art of banking. In England in 1925 a Workmen's Compensation Act was put through by the British Labor Party providing compensation for injuries received in pursuit of work. Not deposits, but welfare was protected. Did this encourage sloppier work or more careless attention to the use of dangerous machinery? Well, all over England, Safety Campaigns were put on; industrial workers and employers were informed of the implications of this social legislation, and as a result, the number of industrial accidents dropped off appreciably the following months. If anything, the guaranty of bank deposits, placing a real obligation to the government on the shoulders of our bankers, ought to create a sounder kind of banking. Canada has guaranty of deposits; does it eliminate good banking there?

(c) The third reason presented as to why guaranty of bank deposits is neither practical nor desirable is that eight states have tried it and failed. Yes, and failed dismally. In proposing this argument, the Gentleman of the Opposition shows, I fear me, only a rouge-deep apprehension of the conditions of these State fiascos. He knows that they failed, but does not ask why. Let me tell you why they failed, for I find in their mistakes the most powerful argument for national guaranty.

They failed in the first place because they violated basic principles of insurance in not extending the risk over an area large enough to include a diversity of economic and industrial interests. You would think a company crazy that sold all its hail insurance in only one county. But these eight states were too ignorant to realize that actually they were making a similar error. For they were all Mississippi basin states, agricultural, and in the time of agricultural disaster, the banks in this area were all equally hard hit, and none could absorb the strain. The plan we have proposed is national in scope, tending to distribute sectional strains over the whole of the United States, in accordance with sound insurance principles.

In the second place, these states failed because they

guaranteed something impossible under the present banking system;—and please notice that I said the *present* system. You stockholders in the Second National Bank downtown know that your bank would not guarantee the financial stability of Fairbanks-Morse and Company unless your bank had a large measure of control over the financial policy of that company. Yet this is precisely what the states did. Even though our banks have proved themselves incapable of practicing sound banking under the present law of private initiative, these states guaranteed bank deposits *without the assurance that their banks would remain solvent.* Is it any wonder that those states found the discharge of their guaranty obligations to be so onerous as to cause the abandonment of the scheme? The guaranty of bank deposits must be founded upon a National Federal Regulation that will force all banks into policies and practices that will strengthen the financial world. And as you will remember, this is one of the foremost tenets of the plan we proposed.

A third reason also might be added: because the guaranty was based upon narrow state areas, the fund had to be raised by taxing the state banks. To avoid this objectionable tax the state banks tended to go National, thus throwing the whole burden of the guaranty fund upon the banks with too small capitalization to become Federal Reserve members. Obviously these few weak banks could not support the strain. A unified National scheme, with an equal distribution of obligation is necessary if guaranteeing deposits is to work, and as you know, this is one of the stipulations of our plan. And I might just throw in the fact that Canada has a National plan of guaranteed deposits that has functioned successfully since its inception.

But we are not satisfied merely with annihilating their counter-arguments—we offer you proof of several benefits that will result from the functioning of such a plan as we propose. The first and most obvious benefit that will result is that of absolute safety of deposits. Four billion two hundred and twenty-seven million dollars are lost or tied up by bank failures of the past ten years—an amount so enormous that it is almost impossible to comprehend. If every minute from the birth of Christ one dollar and fifty cents had been dropped into the ocean, this loss by today would be four hundred and twenty-five million dollars *less* than the loss caused by the failure of our banks. Of course a rather large percentage of this has eventually been returned, but only after causing uncertainty, untold suffering and misery, and economic maladjustment.

Not only will there be no money lost, but also there will come a peace of mind and public confidence that long has been a significant lack in our American life. Once we are sure that we can lose no money in our banks, we will be glad to coöperate with them in putting the dollar back to work along with our citizens. This is the greatest need, says Roger Babson, that of increasing the velocity of our money turn-over. The one billion six hundred million dollars of hoarded money would return to circulation and aid greatly in stabilizing industry. But all this will happen only when public confidence is created by a policy of guaranteed deposits.

I would invite your attention to only one more of a number of benefits, namely, that our plan would remove the major cause for bank failures. The University of Chicago professors several weeks ago in their Sunday afternoon radio round table agreed that most of the bank failures were precipitated by drains in the time of economic duress or psychological uneasiness. The Michigan moratorium of several days ago was the necessary climax of a series of disastrous runs. It is possible that if the situation continues as at present, there may be a national moratorium that will become the first step in the adoption of the very plan we are proposing to you this evening. When men and women know for certain that they cannot lose their money, the disaster of bank failures may in large measure be averted.

In summary, we have presented our case and have met the three requirements of the Negative, to show that state regulation has failed, that Government Regulation would be desirable, and that the guaranty of deposits would be practical. As regards the latter, I have shown that with a system of guaranty we will lose no more money, will support and stabilize business, and will check disastrous runs on our banks. Therefore, we submit to you our plan of guaranteed deposits, functioning within an inclusive Federal Reserve System, as the solution of our present problem.

Third Negative, Robert W. Hansen
Marquette University

LADIES AND GENTLEMEN: The preceding speaker returned to Biblical times to secure a basis for computing certain statistics. Possibly, it was his so doing that reminded us of the Biblical parable of the wheat and the tares, in which, you will remember, the master said to the servant, ". . . and in the time of the harvest I will say to the reapers, Gather up first the tares, and bind them in bundles to burn them; but gather the wheat into my barn." It is in somewhat this spirit of selection and discrimination that we propose to analyze the case of the Opposition separating the wheat from the tares, the relevant from the irrelevant.

Great emphasis has been placed upon the fact that while in former days checks came back marked, "No funds," nowadays they return marked, "No bank." Yet can banking institutions stand unmoved in the midst of commercial and economic wreckage? This very speech is punctuated by the detonations of crashing industrial enterprises. This nation has had over a decade of agricultural paralysis; it has been four long years since the last paper profits went west in the covered wagon of margin calls. If banks fail, the fault lies not in our banking structure, but in the economic system of the country. If banks fail, it is because the economic communities in which they are located are failing. Much has also been said about branch banking, a very interesting question; much can be said in favor of and against branch banking, but all such arguments are entirely irrelevant as far as the question of Federal Regulation of banking functions and Federal Guaranty of bank deposits is concerned. Remove the legislative barriers to branch banking and the unit banker will go for a one-way journey reminiscent of a Windy City's gangster's last ride. Whether such branch banking would be desirable is a separate debate question, and, therefore, feeling that the issue raised is irrelevant to the question under discussion we resist with firm resolution the temptation to wander into the by-path of branch banking.

However much we might extend the list of sins of commission of our Affirmative brethren, we feel that the sin of omission of which they are guilty is far more grievous. The question puts upon them the burden of arguing in favor of Federal Regulation of banking functions. What are the functions of a bank? In our humble opinion they consist quite largely of accepting deposits and making loans. No bank performs a more important function than that of extending credit to certain enterprises and individuals; the problem of what enterprises are going to be given loans is all-important to the continued existence of the bank. Yet the plan of the Affirmative provides for no effective regulation of these actual operations of a bank.

To this they counter that they will control the organization, permitting the organization to control the functions. This is certainly Government Regulation of banking organization, but it is a remarkably indirect method of regulating banking functions. To illustrate: if we had been debating Governmental Regulation of public utilities some few years back, it would have been the Affirmative's position that the control exercised would be to tell the Insulls and the Byllesbys that they might have branch companies, that they were to have a certain minimum capitalization, that they were to be subject to no state restrictions. This might be controlling the organization but it would hardly be regarded as control of the functions of the utility. We now realize regulation implies the government's determining what rate the utility may charge, what standard of service they shall render; or, in other words, effective control over the actual operation of the utility. Without such active control, it can hardly be said that the functions of any enterprise are being Governmentally Regulated.

We might remark, however, that there is one fundamental disagreement between the two teams upon this platform this evening. It seems to be the Affirmative's viewpoint that banks are failing because there is not sufficient Federal Regulation and Federal guaranty of bank deposits. And yet, in the forty-four months following January 1st, 1929, eight hundred thirty-nine national banks, operating under the very system which the Affirmative lauds so highly, failed. Twenty national banks, many of them located in larger cities and strongly financed, closed their doors each month. In every state which has attempted guaranty of bank deposits, despite the fact that the resources of the state were pitted behind the banking institutions, banks failed and deficits accumulated. It is the opinion of the Negative that in these and other cases the credit institutions have failed because the economic communities from which they draw their strength and permanence also failed. Thus it is that when the bottom dropped out of the Florida real estate boom, even the chain banks located in that sector were forced to the wall; thus it is that so many small rural banks, with their eggs resting in the basket of farm prosperity, have failed because farmers remained impoverished and farming remained a not especially lucrative form of endeavor. The cases where defalcating cashiers and embezzling bank presidents ruin banks are comparatively rare. No banker goes into ecstasies of delight nor sings rhapsodies of joy when the banking commissioner tacks the sign "Closed" upon his bank entrance. It is to the banker's interest, aside from any altruistic motives of community service, to keep the bank functioning. If the bank does fail, it usually fails because of outside circumstances over which the banker has no control.

It is then the considered opinion of the Negative that the instability of American banks can be attributed to the instability of the entire American economic structure. And, as we view it, the problem is not to attempt to build a stronger banking system; it is to build a substructure of sound agricultural and industrial prosperity. With such substructure the present banking system will prove more than adequate to meet the tests of stability and flexibility; without such foundation no banking system can be devised that will be able to stand upon the shifting sands of business chaos. We do not come as a Moses leading a depression-weary world to a land of plenty. We intend merely to indicate the direction in which the nation must travel and the mode of attack the nation must adopt.

Some means must be found to stabilize our economic system. Ability to produce must not be permitted to outrun ability to consume. Some method of teaming productive capacity and power to consume in double harness must be devised. It is possible that, if the so-called Roosevelt agricultural domestic allotment plan proves feasible, it might be given a wider application. Perhaps some more stringent form of social control along the lines of economic planning as suggested by Stuart Chase or of industrial coördination as suggested by Gerard Swope and other industrial leaders will have to be adopted. Quite possibly minimum wage legislation and restriction of the hours of labor for both men and women will be utilized to increase the purchasing power of the ultimate consumers. There may be differences as to the choice of method; possibly we can return to this platform to discuss the comparative advantages and disadvantages of the various plans for remodeling our economic structure. However for the present our general position remains clear; it is that in a coal mining section where for thirty years the miners have averaged but nine months employment per year and in agricultural regions where the market price of farm commodities does not pay for the costs of producing them; in such sections, no banking institutions can expect to carry on a profitable or long continued business. And the problem is not to bulwark the banks but to rebuild the economic community.

If we might consider these periodic economic crises as surging, seething torrents sweeping down upon a countryside, causing untold damage, and shattering all dikes and engulfing all buildings, then it seems to be the Affirmative position that we should build taller buildings and higher structures. But we have learned that when the freshets come, no building can withstand their fury. And so the Negative proposes that we go up into the headwaters of the river and there, where the floods are starting, build the reservoirs of a planned production and plant the forests of more equitably distributed purchasing power, so that we may check these floods before they begin. It has been our sad experience that once the flood has started no institution, industrial or commercial, can long withstand its fury.

First Negative Rebuttal, Donald W. Gleason
Marquette University

LADIES AND GENTLEMEN: In my constructive speech, I indicated that the first issue involved in this proposition was—"Should we have Federal Regulation"?, and that to substantiate that issue the Affirmative would have to prove that the defects in the banking system were due to state regulation. I hope that the stenographer heard me say that, for apparently the Affirmative did not. The Affirmative has utterly failed to show that any one defect was directly due to the system of regulation. If there were three more speakers on the Affirmative side, they would remind us of the "secret six" of Chicago fame, for they label the defects of banking as being "public enemies," and their secrecy lies in the fact that they prove nothing relevant about what produced these so-called public enemies.

You have heard from the lips of the Affirmative speakers, that today we have too many small, rural, under-capitalized banks; but if that is true then greater capitalization is the remedy and not the abolition of state regulation. Banks are organized with a certain capitalization and if the amount thereof has proved too small, then we have discovered a defect in the organization of banks, which does not prove anything for the Affirmative except that the argument is immaterial to the issue. They told you further that the American dollar is unstable, and that our banks are not able to extend credit at a time when it is most needed, but if those factors were intended by the Affirmative to be pertinent to our discussion, then they should have shown that state regulation of banking functions was responsible for their existence. If you have heard the Affirmative take any single defect of banking and say in regard to it "now this defect is directly due to state regulation and, therefore, state regulation has failed" —I repeat, Ladies and Gentlemen, if you have heard the Affirmative say that, then we of the Negative are the "deaf trio" and the Gentlemen from Beloit are not the "secret six." It is our contention that the Affirmative has failed to prove the necessary elements to win the first issue.

The second basic issue in this debate is "Should Federal Regulation be extended to *all banking functions*" and as to this issue the Affirmative proceeded on the bald assumption that our state governments are incapable of regulating *any banking function*. In none of their three speeches can we find as much as an illustration to prove that a state cannot regulate the functions of a bank, to say nothing of the fact that their case lacks any mention of why the Federal Government must step in to regulate *all functions*. The Affirmative ignores the fact that many of our state banks, familiar with the problems within the particular state have experienced twenty and thirty years of successful bank management. The equipment, efficient organization, and careful personal attention given by most of our state banks to banking problems has constituted a very satisfactory service.

According to the *Banker's Magazine* for September, 1932, of the total number of all banks in existence during the year 1931, only ten per cent failed. Despite the dishonesty of some bankers, despite the loss of confidence and even despite the depression, ninety per cent of our banks in 1931 remained in existence and bore testimony to the fact that our states can and do successfully regulate banking functions, but the boys from Beloit seize upon the ten per cent that failed and then hasten to the conclusion that no state can regulate bank functions.

If I have a draft issued by a Milwaukee bank, I may present it to a bank in Beloit for collection. The Beloit bank accepts the draft on deposit for collection, but only in the capacity as my agent. All that is required of the Beloit bank is that it send the draft to Milwaukee; in other words, it need only make use of the mails.

But the Affirmative case assumes that the Beloit bank is unable to perform that function because it is under state regulation, whereas in fact, it has successfully handled such transactions for many years. When the Affirmative recommends that the Federal Government regulate all banking functions, they in effect say to you that your bank in Beloit cannot receive your money or retain it for you at interest, that it cannot collect your drafts, give you investment advice, or provide a checking account service for you, while you know from experience that your bank has done all these things for you ever since you became part of the commercial world. We believe, not only that the Affirmative has failed to prove that our states cannot regulate bank functions, but that it is absurd to even attempt to do so, and that consequently, they have lost the second issue.

"Shall the Federal Government guarantee deposits" is the final issue this evening. Mr. Eisenberg, our second speaker, has shown that such a proposal is unwise, impossible, that it has already failed in eight states, and will further deal with the issue in his rebuttal, since my time is about spent.

In closing I want to raise an important inquiry. The Affirmative supposedly condemns state regulation; they would replace it with Federal Regulation. I presume that the idea is that Federal Regulation would be so much better. (Presumed, because not shown by Affirmative.) But in that case, why does the Affirmative contend that the Federal Government should also guarantee deposits? If Federal Regulation is to mark an advance in our banking system, why must deposits be guaranteed? To the Negative your double proposal is contradictory; the guaranty clause seems to be an implied admission that Federal Regulation alone will not be sufficient. I submit the question to our Opponents but I do so with shaken confidence that it will be answered, for as yet the Affirmative has refused to tell us why the eight hundred thirty-nine national banks failed. Gentlemen, shall we assume that it is because so many national banks fail under Federal Regulation that you want to guarantee deposits?

First Affirmative Rebuttal, John S. Nash
Beloit College

LADIES AND GENTLEMEN: At the outset of this debate the Affirmative took the position that the Negative must either uphold the present situation or else present a plan which they can prove to be a better one. The Negative denied this and said that if they gave a plan it was from choice and not from necessity. The Affirmative of the question as stated implies that there are more benefits to be derived from having the government regulate banking functions than under the present situation. The Negative therefore, implies that there will be less benefits, and as yet they have only given you a hatful of reasons why they think that the Affirmative plan will not work. But they have not shown you that there will be more harm than good done by our plan, and until they can point with proof at the items of our proposal and say, "These would make the present mess worse," we maintain our position.

Now let us examine this plan which they have presented. They would stabilize the whole economic structure, and thus the banking structure would necessarily be made stronger. Now we believe strongly in stabilizing the whole economic structure, but what a hypothetical plan it is that supposes that we can do this without a complete overturning of our present economic order. It will be absolutely impossible to do this unless we start with smaller units. Our plan is really a component part of making the whole structure more stable. It is impossible to have business unless we have a banking system that can take care of the demands of it. We contend that the Negative have presented a metaphysical thing which in no wise can be used as a substitute plan for the one which we have presented this evening.

The Negative, this evening, have neither presented a substitute plan nor have they proven the results of our plan to be worse than the present situation, and so we claim that our position has been untouched.

Now the Negative have further contended that we must show that the state banks are the cause of our present crisis or else there is no justification for turning the banks over to the Federal Government. We have shown that the record of the state banks is twice as bad as the Federal Reserve Banks both in regard to the proportion of bank failures and to the percentage of the deposits lost. Our main fight, however, is not with the state bank as such, as it is against having forty-nine systems instead of one central system. We have already shown the dangerous and unfair competition which exists between member and non-member banks.

The second speaker for the Negative attempted to show you how impossible it would be to establish a fund for the guaranteeing of deposits. With mathematical precision he showed that it would demand a cash fund of three or four billions of dollars. If the Gentleman had spent more time reading the papers instead of on his mathematics he would find that it is not only possible, but that it is being done—and not at the sacrifice of having billions of dollars tied up either. Canada is guaranteeing deposits very successfully. As a matter of fact the Glass-Steagall bill now before Congress provides that when the fund reaches $500,000,000 they will refund money to the banks.

We have been accused of arguing against ourselves as we propose a sound banking plan, and then feeling that it isn't so sound after all, we decide to guarantee deposits. They ask us why we include this. There are two reasons. Superficially we include it because it is in the question. But there is a much more real reason. We feel that without guaranteed deposits we cannot establish confidence in the banking system. This item in itself reduces failures for it reduces the danger of runs on banks. We note that Canada, although it has had only one failure in the last twelve years, guarantees deposits. Further the cost of guaranteeing will be reduced to a negligible amount as the number of bank failures is minimized.

In regard to the failures in the eight states which the Negative made so much of, let me remind you that there is a lot of difference between state and Federal action. We notice that all the states that adopted this plan were agricultural states, and the investments were local instead of being spread over the whole nation. It would be analogous to an insurance company insuring against a hail storm in a local area. Further, the state guarantee system did not include National banks, and so, as the system weakened the stronger banks that were able to, withdrew and became nationalized and left the small, weak banks to support the system, which of course was impossible.

In conclusion then, we have presented a plan which the Negative have not proven worse than the present system, nor have they themselves produced an adequate substitute plan. They have wasted your time and ours by merely wrangling about minor points. We have presented this plan, and we have shown definitely how it will meet the pathological conditions which are in our present system. We have included guaranteeing of deposits and we have proven to you that this is not only easily possible and now successfully in operation in Canada, but we have shown that it is necessary to restore the confidence and faith of the public in our banking structure.

Second Negative Rebuttal, Ernest O. Eisenberg
Marquette University

LADIES AND GENTLEMEN: Our worthy Opponents have seen fit to wax philosophical in this debate. In fact they have taken the famous French philosopher Descartes and have embraced him in their arms. May I add, that their entire case is built upon a process of reasoning which is typical of Descartes. If you will remember, Descartes achieved fame because of one simple sentence, namely, "I think; therefore I am." The fallacy in this statement should be quite obvious to you, for what Descartes actually said was this: "*I am* thinking; therefore *I am*." Similarly the Affirmative states: "The Federal Government should regulate banking functions with a guaranty of deposits. Therefore the Federal Government should regulate banking functions with a guaranty of deposits." It may be pertinent to point out to you at this time, that thus far in the debate the Affirmative has failed to show you, *first* that state regulation cannot cope with the present problem; *second*, that the Federal Government can actually regulate the functions of banking; and *third*, that the Federal Government can practically guarantee deposits. We want more than mere assumptions; we demand proof!

It is characteristic of the Affirmative that throughout this debate they have failed to attack fundamentals, and have concerned themselves only with the superficial manifestations of what is really a deep rooted problem. Bank failure is not due so much to methods of regulation, as to the failure of the economic communities supporting the banks. Yet the Affirmative contends that regulation will prevent failure, without first proving to you that regulation will prevent failure of the economic communities supporting the banks. In a similar manner, they have proceeded throughout their entire second speech to prove to you that the lack of stabilization of the dollar is a cause for bank failure, and that through their plan for relief, they will stabilize the dollar.

This matter of stabilizing the dollar, however, cannot be so simply explained away. As a matter of fact, just why is your dollar worth more today than it was in 1928; and why was the dollar in 1928 worth less than it was in 1913? Simply for this reason: the relative value of the dollar depends upon the ratio between consuming power and producing power. We have had no tie up, no connection between our producing power and our purchasing power. The plan proposed by the Affirmative errs in that it neglects to make any provision for the financing of consumption. The reason why banks fail to lend money today, is not due to the fact that the banks have no money, but rather due to the fact that business men are afraid to borrow money, since if they do manufacture goods they will have no market for those goods.

Throughout this debate the Affirmative has refused to recognize the ultimate problem involved, namely the problem of the collapse of the American credit structure due to the failure of purchasing power of the public to keep up with producing power. The third speaker for the Negative, Mr. Hansen, has shown you in his speech that the proper method of curing this evil is by the plan proposed by President Roosevelt, namely the farm allotment plan. Use the principles outlined in this plan in every other phase of economic activity, use the principles of scientific planning in our national economy, balance consuming power and purchasing power, and the problem of bank failures together with the problem of the fluctuating dollar will disappear.

The failure to recognize the fundamental nature of the problem on the part of the Affirmative, naturally causes our worthy Opponents to suggest to you methods of reform which will not bear close scrutiny. For example they propose to stabilize the dollar by increasing or decreasing the rediscount rate of the Federal Reserve Structure. May we remind you that though the Federal Reserve Board repeatedly increased the rediscount rate in 1929, it failed to check the stockmarket boom; and may we point out to you once more that in spite of a fifty per cent reduction in the rediscount rate this year, the credit situation has not been eased. Why has this method failed? The Affirmative rightly claims that its failure is due to the fact that there is too much money outside the Federal Reserve System; they err, however, when they state that under their plan this money would be controlled by the Federal Reserve Board. All that they would embrace would be the banks now outside the system; they could do nothing to control the investments of large industrial corporations with millions of dollars of cash assets; they could not control investment trusts; they could not control building and loan societies; they could not control huge private pools of professional lenders and stock market speculators; in short, they could control but a fraction of the nation's credit. We say, on the other hand, regulate production and purchasing power; strike at the root of the evil, and not at its most prominent branches. Further, we should like to remind you that under the proposal of the Affirmative, nothing is done to extend credit to the consumer. As long as there are fifteen million men unemployed in America; as long as the farmer is destitute; so long will our factories remain closed. If people cannot buy, the industrialists cannot manufacture. The plan of the Affirmative in no way seeks to remedy this problem, which is perhaps the most vital of all.

Therefore to summarize the weaknesses of the Affirmative's case:

1. They have pointed out as "public enemy" Number One the lack of central organization. We have shown you that two-fifths of the bank failures occurred within the Federal Reserve System.
2. They have shown as "public enemy" Number Two competition between member and nonmember banks. We have shown you that this competition will continue between member banks.
3. They have given as "public enemy" Number Three the failure of rural banks. We have shown you that rural banks failed because of the rural depression. In no way have they pointed out how they would safeguard rural banks under their plan.

4. They have offered as "public enemy" Number Four the instability of the dollar. We have shown you that this instability is due to basic economic conditions which would not be altered by the plan they propose.
5. They have asserted as "public enemy" Number Five the inability to expand credit. Yet their plan would in no way expand credit to the consumer who needs credit the most.
6. They have indicated as "public enemy" Number Six the inability of banks to liquidate. This weakness is due to the loss of confidence of people in the business structure of the country, and can in no way be affected by a plan of regulation or guaranty.
7. They have proposed as "public enemy" Number Seven the reduction of buying power. However, they could not prove to you that under their plan buying power would be expanded. We, on the other hand, have continuously advocated a better control of the ratio between purchasing power and producing power.
8. And finally they have tendered as "public enemy" Number Eight the inability of the banks to keep the faith of the public. My friends, the public has not lost its faith in the banks so much as it has lost its faith in the business structure of the entire nation. We propose to put that business structure on a permanently sound basis.

Therefore in conclusion, I should like to state this: our banking system is comparable to a train speeding along the country. At a certain place that train must cross a bridge. Economic disturbances however, like a torrent beyond the control of the engineer of the train, have demolished the bridge. The Affirmative does not propose that we rebuild the bridge; our Opponents do not wish to dam back the waters; all they advocate as relief is that we regulate the speed of the train, and guarantee that if the first train falls over the bridge, we shall have a second train ready to proceed, and likewise to fall over the bridge.

Second Affirmative Rebuttal, John Martin
Beloit College

LADIES AND GENTLEMEN: I certainly feel pretty badly about that first speech of mine; for after having spent ten minutes expounding the necessity of a stable dollar for a sound economic development of our country, Mr. Hansen stated that we were building on a foundation of shifting sands and that we should "dam the torrent at the headwaters" in order to have a sound economic development. This is just exactly what I was proposing, only I tried to put a very definite plan before you as to how this could be done rather than sluffing off this subject with a figure of speech and vague references to boards and commissions. The point is, we maintain that the banking system is a part and in fact a very important part of the basis of our economic system and anything that is done must be done with an eye to and a help from the banks.

And as to the point about whether we are regulating

Function or *Organization,* I think that you students will take it just as lightly as they did Mr. Strong's allusion to a like subject of discussion between the Platonic and Aristotelian schools. As we have said before, organization and function are so interwoven that nothing can be done to one without affecting the other. As far as that goes I believe that our control of the volume of loans by means of the discount rate is a very direct means of regulation of banking functions.

We have shown how the change in the discount rate precipitated the stock crash and fixing the discount rate is certainly a banking function. This shows how necessary it is to regulate banking functions that we may avoid another such crash, and in regulating the discount rate as we propose we would certainly be regulating banking functions.

On the subject of loans there is one point that is very obvious that might bear repeating. I refer to competition between member banks. The Negative say that under our plan competition would still be carried on between the banks even if they all became national banks. We admit this, but it will not be that unfair and demoralizing competition that now exists under our dual system, for it will be competition under the same rules, instead of competition against banks operating under lower standards thus bringing about lower standards for all banks. It is like organizing kids' gangs into football teams—they still fight with each other but in an organized way and the sticks and bricks are discarded in favor of more favorable competition.

And, lastly, I wish to touch on another of the Negative's analogies. He referred to the fact that the state failures were like putting chemical mixtures in one test tube after another and watching them break. Then he inferred that the Nation was just another test tube and another failure would result. We have pointed out that in the Nation we have a chance for diversification, and, hence, weakness in one part of the country would not ruin the whole system. We say that with the Nation we do not have just another test tube which will break with the mixing of the elements, but we have a strong pyrex beaker which will easily stand the strain and a successful reaction is the result.

Mr. Hansen maintains that what we need is a general readjustment of commercial and industrial conditions, but even if we could find a perfect and all-inclusive society stabilizer, we still maintain that it would not be the solution for our banking problem. Ten thousand four hundred eighty-four banks have failed in the last ten years in America, in times of both prosperity and depression. And yet in Canada, where the same conditions have prevailed, there has been only one bank failure! During the same years and under the same economic conditions, Canadian banks have remained firm and sound, while American banks have failed on every side. The difference is not in the economic substructure but in the banking system! The Canadian banks are Government Regulated, and have guaranteed deposits.

Third Negative Rebuttal, Robert W. Hansen
Marquette University

LADIES AND GENTLEMEN: Two darkies were slowly making their way up a dimly lighted stairway when their boss asked them, "Boys, what you-all doin' here?" And Sambo answered, "Boss, we done been carryin' dis heah trunk up dese stairs." "Ah," but the boss answered, "Where is de trunk?" "Rastus," Sambo mournfully informed his partner, "we done forgot de trunk." It is in somewhat the position of having forgotten the trunk that the Affirmative team has placed itself. They have rather completely ignored the burden placed upon their shoulders of arguing in favor of Governmental Regulation of banking functions. And when they remark that control of *Organization* means control of *Function,* we mention the fact that if one set out to control the functions of a saloon, and merely regulated the organization by placing larger brass rails under the well worn shoes of the customers and hanging larger curtains in the window, you might be controlling the structure, the form, the organization, but you would not be controlling the activities or the functions.

The importance of the distinction cannot be over-emphasized. Some time ago a Milwaukee bank failed, and in the closing there was involved the nine dollar deposit which represented a sizeable portion of your humble servant's private fortune. So I have a keen personal interest in the activities and reason for failure of this particular bank. It failed because of unfortunate investments. It invested in real estate, and real estate values fell; it dabbled in South American bonds, than which there was no more perilous pastime. Its directors were no lineal descendants of Midas; whatever they touched turned out to be considerably less valuable than gold and less valuable than they had anticipated. It is, then, the contention of the Negative that when the Opposition exercises no control whatsoever over the investments of this bank or over the types of investment that other banks may make, they do not sufficiently regulate banking functions. It might also be again remarked that they certainly encourage slipshod banking by allowing the banker to make the choice and having the government underwrite his losses. Uncle Sam has often played the similar rôle of wet nurse to various businesses, but never with distinction. And so, we ask the Opponents, "Why all the talk about regulating banking functions when your plan does not include regulation of such functions?"

As to the strenuously maintained argument that unifying banks would control industrial stability by controlling credit, we might remark that although the National City Bank bulletin for January, 1933, mentions "further reduction of interest rates, already unprecedently low to almost the vanishing point," the effect upon the business structure of these additional credit facilities is not noticeably apparent. As a matter of principle it would appear the tail of credit could hardly wag the dog of industry. The banks and the manufactures may have credit; but the consumers have no purchasing power. And even if the manufacturers might secure greatly increased credit, they could not sell the products which they might produce with this additional credit. The problem in this nation is not that of securing credit for business men, it is the problem of securing purchasing power for the masses of the people in the land.

And when we asked the Opposition, in regard to the guaranty of deposits feature of their plan, where they would get the money and how they would avoid harmful effects upon the business of the nation involved in withdrawing so much gold from the channels of trade, their only answer was the rather naïve remark, "Guaranty is in the question, and we will have to debate it." We certainly offer them our heartfelt sympathy, but we can hardly grant them exemptions from their burdens. And so we tell them that if they do not build up a fund, every bank liquidation in time of stress will put an additional strain upon the remaining solvent financial institutions. And if they do propose to build up a fund, we ask them, "Where do you propose to get the money?" and "How do you propose to avoid the almost inevitable repercussions upon the credit system of the land involved in withdrawing billions of dollars of gold from active circulation in the channels of trade?" Their answer will be rather belated, of course, but that is better than no answer.

Newspaper dispatches tell of the two hundred mile battlefront between warring Chinese and Japanese troops. In the not quite as extended battlefront and hardly as bitterly contested struggle between the two teams this evening, we conceive it to be the duty of the Affirmative to shell every vantage point, to wage the war all along the line of battle, to establish every ultimate issuable fact. We conceive it to be the privilege of the Negative commanders to mass their argumentative battalions anywhere along the battlefront. This we have done. We have had one intrenched battalion training its guns on regulation of banking functions; what does it mean, what does it involve, what benefits will it bring. This conflict was rendered a bit unsatisfactory by the fact that we could not ascertain the nationality or even existence of the Affirmative troops. We placed one flank of our army opposing guaranty of bank deposits, pointing out the record of failure of such systems, pointing out the impossibility and inadvisability of building up a great gold reserve fund. The Opposition guns were also strangely silent in this sector. Finally, we made one counter attack at the very heart of the Affirmative position when we maintained that the problem in this country was not that of building larger banks but that of building stronger economic communities, feeling that banks are strong or weak dependent upon whether the economic communities in which such banks are located are strong or weak. This is the position of our respective troops at the present time, and we yield this war-torn platform to the Affirmative who will attempt, we suppose, to dislodge our troops with a barrage of argument and fusillade of criticism.

Third Affirmative Rebuttal, John K. Strong
Beloit College

LADIES AND GENTLEMEN: In order to give validity to his arguments the third Negative speaker turned to scriptural sources. There is a verse of scripture, however, in Second Kings, I believe, that may be very happily applied to the debate this evening. A paraphrase would read something like this: "And a great and strong wind rent the mountains and brake in pieces before the Truth; but the Truth was not in the wind: and after the wind an earthquake; but the Truth was not in the earthquake: and after the earthquake a fire; but the Truth was not in the fire: and after the fire, a still small voice, which was the voice of Truth." Ladies and Gentlemen, while you and I have been entertained this evening with roaratorical contests, the states of this union are having moratorical contests that are profoundly influencing the life and interests of the American people. And still the Gentlemen of the Negative blare that if we will have faith in our present system everything will be lovely some day. Wise was that writer who said, "But the Truth was not in the wind."

The still small voice has spoken this evening, but the deaf have not profited therefrom. The Negative has left the Affirmative case, as progressively established, almost completely untouched. It has executed several admirable circumlocutions around it, as if it were a briar-patch rather than just an ordinary bush. We have shown you that the dual, state-national banking system is the major evil of the present system. Mr.

Nash proved this, Mr. Martin supplemented it, and the present speaker gold-leafed it. And still they say to us—"First, you must prove that state regulation has failed."

With urbane boldness they continue to tell us, directly to our faces that we must also prove that Governmental Regulation is desirable and practical! If they had not been worrying so much they might have heard Mr. Nash give you the eight defects of the present banking system—later very kindly supplemented by Mr. Gleason—and show you how in each case a remedy would be effected through membership in the Federal Reserve System. They would also have heard Mr. Martin tell you about the opportunities in government control for the stabilization of the purchasing power of our money. Even I took the occasion to reiterate all these points in my constructive speech, but I noted at the time that the Negative was in a strained huddle.

There has been, I will admit, the semblance of a debate upon the proposition of guaranteed deposits, but we have shown you, in answer to Mr. Eisenberg's charges, that the fund would not be too large, that it would not eliminate good banking, and that the eight states failed because they didn't try it on a national scale. We further cited several outstanding benefits that would result, not one of which was even sniffed at by the Negative.

These three points then, seem to have been the center of this debate, but it is equally interesting to notice that this center is well within the bounds of the Affirmative's case. Only two minor matters remain. One of these is that Lilliputian matter of *Organization* versus *Function*. Although I recognize that you of the audience understood my answer the first time, let me briefly reiterate it. *Form* always determines Function, and Function is possible only through the medium of, and in conformity with, Form. Hence it is absolutely necessary to control the Form in order to control the Function. Now the three Functions of banks are to make investments and loans, support the credit structure, receive and return deposits. And the Federal Reserve System through its *Organization* controls these very *Functions!*

And just one more word—as regards the Negative plan which Mr. Hansen so charitably proposed. From Plato's *Republic* through Bacon's *New Atlantis* down to Scott's *Technocracy,* Ladies and Gentlemen, mankind has been striving toward this Utopian goal. And like these visionaries of old, our friends of the Negative have seen the Perfect State, but have forgotten to consider the component elements that first must attain perfection. They see the complete tapestry, but have no eye for the thousand threads that must be perfectly coördinated. Their mistake is a good case of the error that the medieval *Nominalists* made,—that of thinking the universal-general to be more real than the immediate-particular. This splendid society envisioned by the Opposition will undoubtedly come some day, but only when men and women forget the larger pattern and work with the individual and component parts of society. And one of the first steps we must take in this direction is the very thing that we have so consistently upheld this evening and which the Negative has as consistently opposed—the *stabilization of our banking structure.*

Some of you no doubt are acquainted with the *Peterkin Papers,* whose delightful philosophy has whiled away many a rainy day. In one of them is recorded the story of how Elizabeth-Eliza made a cup of coffee, but put salt in by mistake. The whole family assembled around that tea-cup, and one by one made suggestions as to what would remedy the situation. One suggested putting in a dash of baking soda, another would add some capsicum. A third tried a quarter of a spoon of cream of tartar, and Elizabeth-Eliza finally pulled out the drug-chest, none of the contents of which make the coffee taste as it should. In despair Elizabeth-Eliza finally telephoned the Lady from Philadelphia, who, after being introduced to the trouble, suggested that another cup of coffee be made. And the family gave three cheers and carried out the advice successfully. The Gentlemen of the Negative have been telling us this evening that our present situation must not be changed, and that we can doctor it up, and drug it so that perhaps it will operate soundly in the future. But we are tired of such Elizabeth-Eliza tactics, as no doubt you are, and we propose to create an entirely new cup of coffee, as it were, a national banking system on the lines of the present Federal Reserve Plan that will guarantee to the people of America the financial integrity of their banks. This we most thoroughly believe in, and this we recommend to your most earnest support.

BIBLIOGRAPHY: CONTROL OF BANKS

BOOKS

Aggar.—*Organized Banking.*
Conant.—*History of Modern Banks of Issue.*
——— *Principles of Money and Banking. Vol. 2 Regulation of Banking and State Interference with Banking.*
Bradford.—*Federal Regulation of Banking.* Reference Shelf. 1933. Wilson.
Dowrie.—*American Monetary and Banking Policies.* Chapters: 1. The Nature of Monetary and Banking Policies. 2. Policies Relating to the Banking Structure. 3. Policies of Internal Management. 4. Public Regulation of Banking. 5. Stabilization Problem.
Hodgson —*Federal Control of Banking.*
Holdsworth.—*Money and Banking.* Chapters: 8. Banking. 10. Functions of the Bank. 11. The National Banking System. 12. Administration. 13. Deposits. 21. Defects of National Banking System.
Harris.—*Practical Banking.* Chapters: 1. What is a Bank. 2. The Stockholders. 15. National Banks. 16. National Bank Notes. 19. Crises in the United States. 20. The Federal Reserve Bank.
Encyclopedias on Banking.—*The Americana. Britannica. New International. Encyclopedia of the Social Sciences. Dictionary of Political Sciences. Encyclopedia of American Government.*
Kilburne.—*Reports of the Comptroller of the Currency.*
Kniffen.—*The Business Man and His Bank.* Chapters: 1, 2, 16, 23, 24, 25.
Rodkey.—*The Banking Process.*
Scott.—*Banking.*
Westerfield.—*Banking Principles and Practice.* Chapters: 6. Bank Operations and Functions. 7. Protection of Bank Note Holders. 8. Protection of Depositors. 9. Reserves for Protection of Bank Credit. 11. Classification and Function of Banks.
Willit.—*Selected Articles on Chain, Group and Branch Banking.*

Magazines

American Economic Review.—March 1932. *Bank Failures.*
American Federationist—April 1932. *Branch Banks.* May 1932. *Branch Banking.* July 1932. *Federal Reserve System.* August 1932. *Branch Banking.*
American Bankers Monthly. May 1932.
American Mercury. September 1932. *Relief for Bankers.*
Annals of the American Academy. November 1932. *Banking and Credit.*
Business Week.—September 23, 1931. December 16, 1931. February 24, 1932. *Sooner or Later.* March 23, 1932. *Bank Reorganization.* March 30, 1932. *Glass Bill.* April 13, 1932. *Federal Reserve Asks for Unified System.* April 20, 1932. *Glass Bill.* October 12, 1932; December 21, 28, 1932; January 4, 1933.
Collier's Weekly.—April 16, 1932. *Something to Bank on.* October 1932. *Plight of the Farmer.*
Congressional Digest.—February 1932. *Revision of Bank Laws.* March and April 1933.
Current History.—May 1932.
Forum.—December 1931. August 1931. July 1932. *What Happened to DuBois.* May 1933. *Danger of State Banking.*
Harper's.—January 1932. *Banker's Bankrupt World* April 1932. *Confidence, Credit, Cash.* January 1933. *Why Canadian Banks Don't Fail.* February 1933. *Inside the R F.C.*
Journal of Political Economy.—June 1932.
Living Age.—December 1931.
Literary Digest—December 12, 1931. *One Hundred Per Cent Liquid Bank.* January 2, 1932. *Guaranteed Deposits.* August 1932. *How Uncle Sam Will Fix His Mortgages.* April 9, 1932. *Glass Bill.* February 27, 1932. *Deflation and Undeflation.* March 26, 1932. *"U.S." Guarantees Bank Deposits.*
Nation—November 1931. *Guaranteed Deposits.* April 13, 1932. *What Shall We Do with Our Banks?* August 24, 1932. *Editorial. Dismal Record of Bank Failures.*
New Republic.—July 1932. *Not on the Ticker Tape.*
Outlook.—July 22, 1932 *Failure of Bank Guarantee Plans.*
Popular Science.—June 1932. *Millions Now Behind Banks.*
Quarterly Journal of Economics.—February 1932. *Branch Banking in California.*

CONTROL OF THE BANKING SYSTEM 321

Redbook Magazine.—June 1931   Article by Walter Lippmann.
Review of Reviews.—September 1931. February 1932. *Insurance Against Bank Failures* December 1932. *The Strength of Our Banking System.* January 1933. *Urgent Need of Bank Reform.* May 1933. *Failure of State Banking.*
Saturday Evening Post.—October 17, 1931; July 11, 1931; August 8, 1931; May 7, 1932. *Safer Banking.* July 2, 9, 16, 1932.
World Tomorrow.—September 1931.
World's Work.—October 1931. December 1931.

NEWSPAPERS

New York Times.—August 29, 1932. p. 24, c. 1. *Branch Banking.* August 8, 1932. p. 2, c. 6. *District Bank Plan.* August 9, 1932. p. 21, c. 1. *Dr. Gries Explains.* August 26, 1932. p. 3, c. 3. *J. Bain Sentenced.* August 25, 1932. p. 40, c. 3. *McDonald and Senator Glass on Insuring Against Loss.* June 26, 1932. Sec. 4, p. 1, c. 1. *Recommendations by United States Chamber of Commerce.* June 11, 1932. p. 21, c. 8. *Senator Cheney Tells Plans for Central Banks.* June 26, 1932. p. 27, c. 4. *F. McWhirter Attacks Plan for Unified System, National Conference Approves.* May 9, 1932. p. 27, c. 2. *C. B. Axford Attacks Branch Banking Provision.* May 10, 1932. p. 32, c. 1. *Senator Glass Defends Plan of Branch Banking.* May 20, 1932. p. 4, c. 4. *H. I. Harriman Defends Plan.* May 20, 1932. p. 33, c. 1. *Maryland Bankers Endorse Glass Bill.* May 21, 1932. p. 21, c. 7. *H. A. Wheeler Against Branch Banking.* April 24, 1932. p. 16, c. 1. *G. W. Norris Advocates Branch Banking.* April 6, 1932. p. 23, c. 1. *Federal Reserve System Reports Legal Bar to One System.* April 15, 1932. p. 1, c. 3. *E. Meyer Advocates National System.* March 17, 1932. p. 36, c. 1. *H. W. Beers Assails Combinations.* March 8, 1932. p. 16, c. 2. *Representative Steagall Offers Bill to Guarantee Deposits.* March 9, 1932. p. 29, c. 7. March 31, 1932. p. 36, c. 3. *Representative Steagall.* March 18, 1932. p. 1, c. 8. *Glass Bill. Text of,* p. 16, c. 1. March 22, 1932. p. 2, c. 5. March 24. p. 1, c. 5. March 25. p 27, c. 8. *Hearings on Glass Bill.*
United States Daily.—December 12, 1932.

LIMITATION OF WEALTH
Ohio Conference Debate

LIMITATION OF WEALTH

COLLEGE OF WOOSTER AFFIRMATIVE AND NEGATIVE

The Ohio Conference colleges chose during the 1932-33 debate season to discuss a most unusual and interesting proposition inspired of course by the depression and by the problem of maintaining buying power in this country. The question was stated, *Resolved: That no individual in the United States should be permitted to receive as a gift or inheritance more than fifty thousand dollars during lifetime, or to receive as income more than fifty thousand dollars a year.*

The question as stated was selected in September 1932, by a group of colleges meeting in conference at the City Club, Cleveland, Ohio. Representatives from the following colleges were present: Ohio Wesleyan, Western Reserve, Allegheny College, Oberlin College, and College of Wooster. These colleges have been associated together for a number of years and maintain perhaps one of the oldest organizations for debate and oratory in the country. Other questions are debated in addition to the one chosen annually for this conference, but this is usually their main varsity proposition.

This question proved to be very popular and was chosen by several colleges not in the above organization The College of Wooster held about twenty open forum debates on this subject before clubs and organizations in the vicinity of Wooster, Ohio. The debates were well attended ranging from thirty to three hundred and fifty in the audience Open forum discussions following the debates lasted from thirty minutes to two hours.

The debate as given here is representative of the open forum debates held by the College of Wooster as contributions to community discussion. The speeches were prepared by the debaters and collected by Professor Emerson W. Miller, Director of Debate at the College of Wooster, who contributed them to this Volume.

First Affirmative, Adeline Heisner
College of Wooster

LADIES AND GENTLEMEN: American economic life faces increasing complexities. As usual when problems become particularly pressing, many prescriptions for cure are brought forth by well-meaning individuals. We are to consider in this discussion the advisability of limiting incomes to $50,000 a year and gifts and inheritances to $50,000 during lifetime.

Our foremost economists tell us that what we lack today is mass purchasing power. Until we place enough money in the hands of the worker to enable him to buy back what he produces, depressions will be inevitable. Mass producing power has been developed; mass-producing wealth has been accumulated; but all these facilities for greater production do not spell progress until we supply a means of distributing our wealth.

One of the most startling discoveries about our present condition is the fact that there is a definite class making more money than ever before. Although our business activity has decreased fifty per cent and wages sixty per cent and many of our schools and libraries have been forced to close, interest charges have risen thirty-five per cent. The Standard Oil Company of New Jersey for example, had as their average annual dividend payments from 1921-32, $190,000,000. In the last three years, during the most severe depression our country has ever faced, their dividend payments have increased to $230,000,000.

When we turn our eyes in the other direction we discover a most pertinent contrast. The average income in 1912 was $1500 a year while the average debt was $3,000. Today the average income is the same while the average debt has about doubled itself. Again we feel strongly that the problem we face is one of distribution.

Upon further inspection of the situation we face today we find that the most outstanding difficulty contributing to this lack of mass purchasing power is the fact that twelve millions of men are unemployed. Many more have accepted salary cuts or are only employed part of the time. With every day, these men are being confronted with more disheartening conditions. They are burdened with debts; banks restrict withdrawals. We have learned with the bitterness of actual experience that mass production without mass purchasing power can only give us the ghastly contrast of ragged bread lines on one side of our streets and unmarketable surpluses of both food and clothing on the other side.

In this connection I am reminded of a cartoon I saw in a recent issue of the *Business Week*. The cartoonist had pictured Old Man Depression as a well cleaner. He was fishing such malodorous things as the Kreuger affair from the depths of the well which was labelled "American Business." John Citizen, in the background, was remarking that it certainly smelled bad, but if the Old Fellow hadn't come along we might still be drinking the stuff from the well.

It is quite certain that the depression has focused our attention upon our economic order and has made us ask ourselves, "What is wrong?" There is another condition, however, that makes the spectre of the army of the unemployed even more disturbing and paradoxical. We find that when we look at the other extreme of our society we see a decided contrast to these who are so lacking in the necessary purchasing power. Here are those who have incomes which exceed their spending power. The concentration of wealth at the top strata of our society is made evident when we discover that ten per cent of the people in this country control sixty-six and two-thirds per cent of the wealth. Only one thing do these two groups have in common—both are idle. We have at the bottom twelve million idle poor suffering for the mere necessities of life and at the top we have the idle rich. This great concentration of wealth is in the hands of 10,799 men who earn more than $50,000 a year.

From the income tax returns for 1929 we can see that there are five hundred individual yearly incomes in this country exceeding $1,000,000. In fact, thirty-six of these incomes exceed $5,000,000. In other terms there is an aggregate income for five hundred and four persons of $1,470,000,000,000. We discover that C. E. Mitchell, Chairman of the Board of the National City Bank, managed to bestow on himself the tidy sum of $3,500,000 as a bonus; at the same time he adequately provided for some of his relatives to the tune of several more millions.

The opportunity to make unlimited profits has not only brought about this maladjustment between our idle poor and our idle rich but it has been responsible for much of the graft, bribery, and dishonesty in business. Notice the Penn Road Corporation. They sold shares at 15 to their employees and, today, when the whole thing is exposed, we find the shares selling at one and one-quarter, and a receivership has been asked for. Small holders are the ones who suffer in deals such as this. The same thing occurs frequently. It happened in the Van Sweringen interests through the Allegheny Holding Company. The Insull interests as well as Kreugers brought the same effects to these small holders.

Unlimited profits have invited men to use every means to gain control over huge sums of money and, in gaining this control, the small consumers were crushed. Morris Llewellyn Cooke, the hydro-electric engineer says we pay $1,000,000 a day too much for electricity. In Ontario, where the utility is under government control, the housewife pays $3.40 on the average for her monthly electricity bill. Just across the line, in New York, where public utilities are privately controlled for profit, the housewife pays $11.15 for the same amount of electricity.

This great contrast in our economic order, between the idle rich and the idle poor, is constantly being aggravated by unlimited profits. Our need is for some means of bringing these two extremes of our society into greater equality, placing the surplus idle capital in the hands of the masses to enable them to buy back the things they produce. Why do we advocate the limiting of incomes and inheritances as a means of bringing this adjustment?

First of all, because this plan is not radical, not extreme. It is a sane, sensible step carrying us forward in our program of social legislation. Such a plan will perform one of its greatest services in preventing more radical measures. Norman Thomas, for instance, would have a family dole system; Kirby Page would limit incomes to $20,000; far too many Communists in our country see Communism as the only way out.

One is not a calamity howler when he says that unless some such sane, moderate measure is adopted very soon, a greater evil is sure to result. We cannot close our eyes to the fact that the people of this country are desperate. Though we may feel ourselves immune from such things as a revolution, we have no assurance that people will placidly watch their children starve while they see five hundred individuals receiving million dollar incomes annually. America has learned that hunger knows no holiday. When many of the farmers of Ohio band together and prevent the foreclosure of mortgages again and again with a sort of grim determination; when hunger marches are a thing of daily occurrence; when seven thousand women parade the streets of Springfield, Illinois, to depict the suffering of the coal miners in that state; when Wisconsin has relentless milk dumping and Iowa has farm products picketed, we cannot consider our country a barren rack for the seeds of revolution. Desperation in the hearts of millions of unemployed is very fertile soil for such an occurrence.

Thus we see that the limitation of incomes, gifts and inheritances is not only a live question but it is also one that strikes directly at the heart of our present difficulty —maladjustment of wealth. We do not claim that such a measure is a cure-all, a panacea. Rather we say it is a sane, sensible measure that provides one means of bringing about an essential distribution of wealth that we must have.

First Negative, Marguerite Garber
College of Wooster

LADIES AND GENTLEMEN: "Many are out of work; gold is scarce; the laborer gets nothing while he who does not work reaps all the profits; the whole land is turned upsidedown; the end of civilization is drawing near." This sounds like Miss Heisner's description of present conditions, doesn't it? But this is a translation of an Egyptian papyrus over forty centuries old. These people just couldn't see how the world could wobble along any longer; yet here we are nearly five thousand years later. The Egyptians had a name for these conditions—the equivalent of our word depression. And to think that we lay the whole blame for past and present depressions on our capitalistic system which is only one hundred fifty years old; on the system which allows freedom of enterprise and the accumulation of wealth!

In reality there is no agreement among authorities on the cause or causes of our sad state of affairs today. For every man who blames large fortunes there is another who blames the World War, another, reparations, another, the tariffs, and so on ad infinitum, including everything and everybody from prohibition to Senator Huey Long. The International Chamber of Commerce which met in Paris to discuss the depression named twelve causes. All but two of these were of an international nature such as the gold standard, credit, and reparations. Mr. Hoover's committee of five hundred men who have been studying conditions all over the United States for three years reported on January first 1933 that the causes of a great many of our ills, especially of the widespread unemployment which the Affirmative rightly bewails, is not large fortunes; it is technological development. We can readily understand this if we notice on every side the examples of men replaced by machines. A railroad switching device puts one hundred sixty-eight men out of work in one yard, a razor blade machine fills the places of five hundred men; a certain rayon factory in New Jersey runs twenty-four hours a day without the help of a single hand.

Miss Heisner is right: cures are just as numerous as causes—another deplorable sort of overproduction. What reason have we to believe that this is not just another prescription proposed by some well-meaning individual? Remember, the partisans of this plan do not promise anyone any income. They reason, thus, "If we limit incomes to $50,000 the surplus must go somewhere and therefore, it will go down to those without incomes."

We of the Negative maintain that the plan is not desirable because: it would inhibit the progress dependent on a surplus of capital and on risk, it would neither meet immediate needs nor form a sound policy for the future, and it would prevent the adoption of a more fundamental measure.

Thus far in the case we have been told a single reason why this plan should be accepted: it is not extreme. On this point a great many doubts crowd into my mind. Would men stand by and watch themselves be dispossessed without a murmur? Could this measure be put into effect without a class war such as Russia's? Even if the government *could* gain control over incomes and inheritances, *should* it have this control? Does the government's past record in business warrant the addition of this great power? Just consider for a moment, the Farm Board, the Federal Shipping Board, and war control of the railroads, then decide the advisability of such a step. However, I shall not tarry on these questions. My main contention is that breaking up of pools of wealth would cut down production and halt our progress. I will let you judge whether a measure which would do this is extreme.

Let us glance back over the progress which we have made in the last few decades. For the sake of fairness we must examine the benefits as well as the evils arising from large fortunes. In times of stress we are too prone to see only the flaws in anything and most of all in our economic system. Now our progress in America has always been a point of pride, and rightly so. The underlying cause of this progress is what? Professor Taussig, of Harvard, in his book, *Principles of Economics* says that it is the very thing which the Affirmative wants to destroy—the concentration of wealth.

"The plain facts must be faced," says Mr. Taussig, "that without marked inequalities in earnings and possessions the material progress in the modern world would not have taken place." He also adds, "There is no clear indication that this condition of progress can be dispensed with in the future." Thus we see that accumulations of wealth are indispensable unless we want to stagnate. Accumulations of wealth are indispensable unless we want even our common conveniences taken away. Because money is concentrated in the hands of a few we can ride on the train for 3.6 cents a mile, make a telephone call for a nickel; because money has been concentrated we have the radio, airplane, refrigerator, telegraph, electric lights; because money has been concentrated we have enough automobiles that very person in the United States could go riding at once. Mass production has meant just what it says—production for the masses. Our common workers now enjoy conveniences which kings couldn't have one hundred years ago. Mr. Rockefeller a few years ago said, "I am harnessed to a cart in which the people ride; whether I like it or not, I must work for the race." If a man makes a profit for himself he must serve others. For example, when Andrew Carnegie started in the steel business iron rails for the new railroad tracks cost $130 per ton. He built up a company so large and efficient that he was able to bring the price of rails down to $22 per ton. Think of the greater number of roads that could be built and lands opened up for development when the price of transportation was brought within the reach of the common man. This is one instance of what big fortunes mean to you and me, and why we do not want them destroyed. There are provinces in China more fertile in land and resources than any in the United States yet there has been no one to build railroads or low cost systems of transportation. For hundreds of years the standard of civilization in these provinces has been stationary. In the United States the railroad is a good example of an attack on surplus savings too. Guy Morrison Walker tells us in *Defense of Wealth* that we are paying fifty per cent more than formerly for poorer service because the government destroyed the surplus savings. As soon as this happened it became impossible to get new capital to invest in the roads.

We have scores of products brought within the reach of the common man by the concentration of wealth. The price of kerosene has been reduced from 30¢ to 10¢ a gallon; of sugar from 20¢ to 4¢ or 5¢ a pound, of gas from $2.50 to $1.00 per thousand cubic feet, and of electricity from 25¢ to 8¢ per kilowatt and as low as 2¢ if used in large quantities. If incomes are limited production and progress will be limited for two reasons: Risks will not be taken and industry will be decentralized. An abundance of wealth is necessary before a man will take a risk for the chances are three to one against him. Under the new plan capital, if not driven out of the country, would go into safe and tax-exempt government bonds. The development of most of our large companies such as Henry Ford's has been the result of the foresight and direction of one or a few men. Can you imagine how the companies would be run if one hundred thousand or so stockholders had equal rights in determining the policies? Liberal leaders, even Norman Thomas, admit that production would probably decrease if accumulations of wealth were broken up. Kirby Page, one of the Affirmative's own authorities, estimates that there are scarcely enough of the necessities of life produced now to go around if equally divided. Would limiting incomes and diminishing production then help solve today's problems? Instead of having breadlines on one side of the street and storehouses of grain on the other we would have breadlines on both sides.

Something must be done and done now. I think the major part of the last speech was spent in impressing that upon our minds. But what does this plan offer to the twelve million people who are starving right now? A whole year would have to pass before we could get much money through the functioning of this plan, for how can we know a man's income in less time than that? He might make $85,000 in the first nine months of the year and lose $35,000 in the last three months. We fear if the men are so near starvation now they would not be here to appreciate the plan.

If the plan were once adopted what would be the results? We have in France a glaring example of the effects of such a scheme. In 1799 the French Directorate decided to take a large percentage of the big incomes. Even before they actually took any money the people were panic-stricken; the mere imminence of the plan caused fraudulent bankruptcies, a standstill in the circulation of money and in business, and a lowering of the standard of living. Imagine all that added to the present depression burden.

We want to remind you we are not laboring under the delusion that the present system is perfect. But we are not talking in terms of perfections; we are talking in terms of comparatives, and we believe the present system would not be improved by trying to graft on it something entirely contrary to its principles. Since its very beginning our nation has been called the "land of the free," and it has made incomparable progress under this principle. Do we want to block this progress as well as blot out the significance of our proud name by limitation at every turn, by binding the individual hand and foot? We believe with Hartley Withers that "individual freedom, initiative, and enterprise have been the life blood of our race and of our nation. If we throw away this heritage because we think that regulation and regimentation will serve us better, we shall do a bad day's work for ourselves and for human progress."

Second Affirmative, R. A. McBane
College of Wooster

LADIES AND GENTLEMEN: Miss Garber has pointed out to you that there are many causes of our present social chaos. That is true. There are many causes. Behind each of these causes, however, we find one fundamental motive—selfishness. Why was the World War fought? We of the Affirmative believe that the fundamental reason was a selfish desire for advancement. Why do we have high tariffs? Is it to protect the workingman or to enable those few owning and controlling our major industries to make more profits? We believe that if it is designed to protect the working man it has failed—miserably. Who is it that furnishes the money for our lobbies for high tariffs? It is the few who profit from those same high tariffs. In short we feel that in striking at excessive profits, gifts, and inheritances we are striking at the fundamental cause of our present economic crisis. We feel that our proposition dealing directly with the cause is, therefore, a more fundamental remedy than any other so far proposed. Miss Heisner has shown you the differences between the top and the bottom of our economic organization and has pointed out the connection that high incomes have with the low position occupied by the great masses at the present time. I shall, therefore, try to demonstrate that this inequality of wealth is morally wrong—that it has no just place in our society.

Let us examine a few of the men who have had incomes of over $50,000.00 a year and see just how they have acquired them. Starting with Jay Gould and coming down to the present time we find always the same basic story—a keen, hard headed young man starting out in business for himself, gaining the confidence of his associates, the confidence of the public, performing perhaps a real service; then having obtained a position for himself, seeing a possibility to advance himself economically by sacrificing his friends, his honor, or the public for the almighty dollar, this same young man gives everything to advance himself. To become more specific let us examine a few of these cases. How did Jay Gould attain his position? Several biographies have been written on Gould but through them all we find a few singular facts standing out. Throughout his entire life he never hesitated to sacrifice the welfare of those opposed to him, to sacrifice those innocent investors who had no quarrel with him. In his attempt to corner the gold market you will remember that he did not let even John Drew, his partner in many previous coups, know his plans. On Black Friday he permitted his best friend and business associate to lose his entire fortune. Here is an example of a man sacrificing everything in order to advance his own personal interests. Yes, it is true that he later took care of Drew, but it is also just as true that he never took a thought for the thousands of others whose entire fortunes had been swept away. We may turn to John D. Rockefeller and his speculation in oil. There also we find a man building a mighty corporation— establishing a mighty business on the destruction of others.

When we read of the ancient Kings of Egypt forcing the slaves to build vast pyramids we condemn them. The pyramids are mighty but they were built at a tremendous cost in human suffering. We appreciate the system of Roman laws established throughout the old world but when we look at the cost in human lives we doubt the efficacy of the establishment of the system. The cathedrals of Europe are magnificent. They are among the wonders of the world but think back to the existence endured by the serfs, think of the excessive taxation forced upon them, of the many times the laborers had not enough to eat. Are the cathedrals worth the price that was paid for them? Today history is repeating itself. We have many fine Carnegie libraries being built, fine hospitals being built, art galleries being established, museums being founded, philanthropists giving money for schools or charities and yet we are paying for them even as the Egyptians and the Europeans paid for their culture. Our contention is that we are paying too high a price. Too long have we kept our left hands from knowing what our right hands are doing. And then we try to reëstablish our ideals with gifts to charitable institutions. What good is it to have hospitals to heal the sick when we build them with money needed by the employees of the donor in order to live? We have hospitals to save but at the cost of destroying many others. What are fine music halls to feed the æsthetic soul when we deny millions of the right to earn sufficient to feed their stomachs? Carnegie's name is known throughout the world. He has done much to advance culture among selected groups yet this advance has been made at the cost of much suffering on the part of his employees. Consider Henry Ford for a moment. He has done much to advance transportation. Yet whenever his costs of production must be cut down it is not the large owners of stock that bear the loss. When the plant closes down to install new machinery, it is not the stockholder that suffers, rather it is the man working in the factory producing cars that bear the name of Ford. When railroads have to cut expenses in order that they may continue to operate it is not the white collar man at the top that takes the slash but rather it is the man working on the section gang. In the tobacco industry we all hear the name of Duke and remember the philanthropic bequests of Mr. Duke but let us not forget the thousands of men and women that worked long hours in the factory that Mr. Duke might acquire and accumulate this money. When next you buy a suit and remark how wonderful it is that you can buy a suit for so little and still enable the manufacturer to make a profit, remember the textile worker that earns scarcely enough to make a living. When you go to the Five and Ten cent store for some little trinket do not praise Mr. Woolworth for enabling us to buy at such a low price until you think of the thousands of girls working for a few dollars a week in his stores. Thousands of girls are not sure that they can make the pay check last long enough to pay their room rent and to pay for the food they must have. It is true that I have painted a black picture, but the facts themselves are very black. These men, giving their thousands to charities and philanthropies, have robbed their employees of millions of dollars —millions of dollars needed for food, for shelter and the other necessities of life. The gain of the few has been made at the expense of and by the suffering of the many. It is interesting to note that on the income tax blank there are two columns—one for earned income up to $30,000.00 a year and the other a column for unearned income over that figure. The government evidently believes that $30,000.00 is all that a man can really earn in one year. Have any of the men we have been considering been so much better than the ordinary individual? I think you will agree with me when I say that these huge incomes have not been earned.

For a moment let us consider inheritances and gifts. A good many years ago the Astors bought Manhattan Island for something like $24.00. As the years slipped by, New York grew. Manhattan became valuable. Nothing the Astors had done had increased the value of the land but nevertheless they received the income. From this fortune they have been able to pass to each succeeding generation a very large inheritance. They have been able to pass unearned wealth to their sons and daughters when millions lack the price of a meal. Or let us look at the House of Morgan, International Bankers. Although many of our men have had to withdraw all of their wealth from the banks still the House of Morgan goes maching on, marching on with the control of twenty-seven per cent of our corporate wealth. These are only a few of the examples I could bring up to disprove the gross statement that our present system is desirable or just. Time does not permit me to continue much longer.

In summing up what I have been saying I can merely point out that in practically all cases of concentration of wealth, it has been secured as a result of the crushing out of the personalities of the masses in the benefit of the few. This we contend is morally and socially wrong.

Second Negative, Don H. McMillen
College of Wooster

LADIES AND GENTLEMEN: Mr. McBane has attacked our problem from the standpoint that inequality of wealth is morally wrong and that it has no just place in our society. He has attempted to prove this contention from several different standpoints. First, he has attacked the low wages that many people receive in contrast with the large incomes that others receive. But my Opponent, seemingly forgetful of the fact that there are many implications to adopting such a plan of limitation, insists that since Jay Gould, Carnegie, Ford and a few others have or have had incomes in excess of $50,000, while many others receive much less than this sum, that all incomes should have this arbitrary limit placed upon them.

Next he attacks the problem from the standpoint of the inequalities of inheritance. An absolute limitation will destroy all incentive for accumulating a sum larger than that which may be passed on to one's children. This, as we have already seen, will mean a great decrease in productive capital. Without productive capital increased purchasing power won't be worth a continental to anyone.

The first speaker, Miss Heisner, has explained to us that conditions at the present time are bad and that this proposed measure is not an extreme one. They have told us that our need is increased purchasing power; yet what evidence have they presented to show that their plan will provide it?

I am going to uphold the Negative with the contention that the adoption of this plan will, in the long-run, cause social disruption; our last speaker, Mr. Wallace, will present some measures which are more fundamental and basic, since they are in harmony with present social trends. I believe that limitation will cause social disruption because: it will result in a loss of taxes to the government and in a limitation of philanthropies; it will result in widespread evasions, and, if the government were to get the income, it would disrupt the security market.

Before this debate is over the Affirmative may tell us that with the adoption of this plan the government will receive a greatly increased income because of the incomes and inheritances over $50,000 that will be confiscated. This may all work very well the first year since the incomes will already have been earned but will it work out so nicely after the first year? Will the large income receivers willingly turn over all incomes in excess of $50,000 to the state or will they see to it that their incomes do not exceed that amount? You see we are faced with a dilemma and we shall first consider the more likely way out.

Here are some of the disrupting effects of this plan. The government now gets approximately $800,000,000 from taxes on income over $50,000 each year. If no one permits his income to exceed this amount the government will not get anything in taxes from this source. State and federal inheritance taxes amount to $100,-000,000 per year. This revenue will also be lost. We must not forget that the government will also lose this source for obtaining any revenue whatsoever in the future. No longer will it be possible to tax incomes over $50,000 as a source of revenue to help balance the budget. These implications are terrific!

Furthermore, because of philanthropic enterprise we, the masses of people, enjoy such things as hospitals, colleges, libraries, museums, research foundations, scholarships and fellowships, as well as a host of other things; the Rockefeller Foundation, Carnegie Libraries, the Hart Schafner and Marx Foundation. These many benefits have been ours to use largely because a few men have had incomes greater than $50,000. Last year more than $2,000,000,000 were expended on just such enterprises. What is the relevancy of this information? Just this—without unlimited incomes and large fortunes we would not have these things or else the state would have to provide them. It would be an *added* expense to the state of $2,000,000,000 each year. This is a sum as large as that demanded by the bonus marchers last year; and we were told by our gubernatorial representative that the payment of this sum would wreck the whole financial structure of our government.

You have probably all heard the expression "money talks"; and you know what it means. Here we will have a loss to our government of $900,000,000 in taxes and an increased burden on the state of $2,000,000,000 because of philanthropies. This makes a total of $2,900,000,000 combined with the loss of a possible source of increased revenue from any incomes over $50,000.

You have not heard the whole story yet; besides this potential burden for the taxpayer we had an accumulated deficit in the national budget of $3,247,000,000 in 1932. This plan would increase the deficit by eighty-nine and three-tenths per cent; at the same time we are told that balancing the budget is an absolute necessity, a prerequisite to recovery. Our hard pressed legislators will be even more sorely pressed to balance the budget and find a source for the necessary revenue, yet the Affirmative say that this is not an extreme measure.

That we may not be thought to be unfair we must also consider the possibility that the government may get a continued revenue from incomes and inheritances over $50,000. It will be utterly impossible to transfer the confiscated values to the government in the form of money. The only alternative will be to give the government property and to give it stocks and bonds. The turning over of property outright would mean the worst kind of Socialism, and it would not stop with natural resources or key industries. It would mean the turning over of every conceivable sort of industry and property. Is our government *prepared* to administer every sort of property that it might be called on to administer? If the government were paid in stocks and bonds the large quantities of them offered for sale would mean untold disruption of the security market with the accompanying evils of falling security prices and market panic. Is the inevitable disruption worth the risk for such an uncertain result? Is any plan morally right which threatens such disrupting effects as this one promises?

Another obstacle in the way of adopting this plan is the fact that there will inevitably be evasions. It is not inconceivable, is it, that small gifts could be made over a period of time without detection? We have no machinery to enforce a law prohibiting it; any machinery that would perform the task with even a moderate degree of success would require hundreds of additional employees, some of whom would no doubt be susceptible to bribes.

Another means of evasion is the sale of property or securities for a nominal sum; that is, selling them for a price far below the actual value. Let me remind you, too, that this measure of evasion would be absolutely legal according to the proposition in question. Let me refer you to a specific instance of this sort of evasion. Charles E. Mitchell, recent chairman of the Board of Directors of the National City Bank of New York, sold thousands of dollars worth of stock to his relatives for only a few dollars. Mr. Mitchell's reason of course was to *evade* the income tax and yet keep *control* over the money. The low selling price meant that he sold the stock at a loss which would be subtracted from his total income when considered for taxing purposes. We might also cite the example of a New York stenographer whose attorney employer assisted a client to find sufficient exemptions to make his income tax less than the stenographer's.

It would also be possible to evade the law by forming a corporation to receive your income. In this way it would not be an individual income and therefore not taxable according to the proposed measure. There are illegal evasions even now while we have a comparatively light income tax. What will happen if this tax is made so heavy as to prohibit all income over $50,000? An Associated Press dispatch of February 28th, 1933, says that Andrew W. Mellon, recent Secretary of the Treasury, along with two former officials of the Internal Revenue Bureau, was sued for $220,000,000 for conniving with officials of foreign steamship companies to evade just income taxes.

Let us review briefly what has been presented thus far on both sides of this debate. Miss Heisner opened the discussion for the Affirmative by presenting evidence leading to the conclusion that our problem today is to place purchasing power in the hands of the masses. She told us that although their proposition is neither a panacea nor a cure-all that their contention is that its adoption will provide this needed purchasing power. She upheld this contention with the argument that the plan is not extreme. Mr. McBane continued for the Affirmative, contending that inequality of wealth is morally wrong and has no just place in our society.

Thus far our Opponents have not shown us how this purchasing power will trickle down to the masses, nor have they assured us that our purchasing power would not be materially reduced. This is a question that can't be passed by without due consideration.

On the Negative side Miss Garber has presented a defense of the concentration of wealth, showing that progress is dependent on unlimited income; she has shown us that we have an immediate necessity to meet and that the Affirmative proposition will not meet this necessity. I have argued against the measure because of the long-run effect that it will have in causing social disruption. Mr. Wallace, the last speaker for the Negative, will present some measures which will be in accord with our present trends in social legislation.

The Negative is basing its case on three main contentions; that the proposed measure cannot be immediately effective, that the long-run effect would be very undesirable, and, that more effective and basic measures are available.

Third Affirmative, Roy McCorkel
College of Wooster

LADIES AND GENTLEMEN: Am I merely generalizing in a vague way when I say that nearly everywhere extremes in life are checked? We are forced, if we are wise, to limit the amount we eat, the amount we drink, the time spent in sleep, the number of times' we go to the theatre, and now in our industrial system we have limited the number of hours a man can work. Why is this so? Isn't it because moderation is sensible in all things. And isn't it true that if we don't have a system of limitation, we always have a group of people who take advantage of their opportunities to exploit, and who abuse the privileges that they do have? What I am trying to say, in other words, is that without limitation on the number of hours a man can work, we have some employers who would expect their laborers to work sixteen and twenty hours a day. I can't see why this same principle of limitation should not apply to the amount of money a man can earn or pass on. This limitation should be particularly appropriate when we are only trying to curb the extremes and the absurdities of the arbitrary number of 10,799 men at the top of our financial scale who are making annual incomes in excess of fifty thousand dollars, or those who have accumulated tremendous sums of money to be passed on to their friends or progeny.

The Negative speaker who preceded me has said the Negative case is based on three main contentions. First Miss Garber says our proposal cannot be immediately effective. However, in her speech she admitted the possibility of the government being able to collect considerable money the first year. Furthermore, she should remember that the debate is primarily concerned with the great principle of limiting wealth by governmental legislation, and that the congressional act necessary to make the proposition a law is to be waived for the present.

The second contention was that "the long run effect would be very undesirable." Mr. McMillen based his contention on three main arguments. He says in the first place that our resolution will result in a great loss of revenue to the government, and in a decrease in the many philanthropies which we now have. Well, to be sure anyone can see that if you take away great amounts of wealth from the people who own and control it today, you are undoubtedly losing revenue from that particular source, or from the particular men who have and control taxable wealth in excess of fifty thousand dollars today. But the Opposition must remember that it is not our plan to destroy this wealth. It is our plan to redistribute it. We are merely taking it away from the group that already has far too much to benefit either themselves or society. Regardless of where the money above fifty thousand dollars goes, it can be taxed at that source. True we may have to change our tax rate and our tax system; but I would rather pay a tax on fifteen hundred dollars that I have earned than be denied the privilege of earning it. That is certainly better than to have someone else have it (those in the higher income brackets) just to insure the government an adequate revenue. As for philanthropies—suffice it to say that we of the Affirmative wonder whether, if to have philanthropies, we must submit to our present injustices to labor, to our present inequality, maldistribution of wealth, and super-privileges. We wonder whether these gifts are worth the human suffering that their donors force on society. It may be that we could still have much philanthropy by generous people who would be making more moderate incomes.

Mr. McMillen says the long-run effects of our proposal would be undesirable in the second place because it would result in widespread legal and illegal evasions. But the income tax law has worked pretty well even though there has been some evasion. There has been some evasion in connection with every law which has ever been passed; but does that condemn the law against stealing or murder? No! If this great principle is fundamentally right, we can find a way to make the thing work in practice.

The third argument against our proposal was that it would lead to a disruption of the securities market. Rather humorous, I would say. Especially so when, only last week, the stock exchange had to close its doors, and when the government had to step in to save our banking system. And our proposal is not in effect now. The truth is that the present system of super-privilege and ownership and control by the few has been the admitted cause of the recent chaos and disruption in our securities market and in our financial institutions generally; so that our plan doesn't have to lead to disruption, our present system has already brought us there.

I propose to show the temporary and lasting effects of our proposal. May I say that even if our resolution would not help the men at the bottom of the social scale (if that is conceivable) the measure would still be justifiable; because, as Mr. McBane has pointed out, as well as Miss Heisner, when there is only so much wealth to be had, it is unfair and unjust that one per cent of the people should own and control thirty-three per cent of the total, and especially when wealth means privilege and power.

What are some of the temporary and permanent effects of our proposal? The power industry in this country is dominated by five or six major corporations. Each of these corporations is controlled by a few men who are mainly interested in making money in large amounts. According to Stephen Rausenbush, the

American public is paying one million dollars a day more than it should for electric power. Morris Llewellyn Cooke has estimated that domestic power rates in the United States are approximately one hundred per cent too high. When we consider that the basic things that the great masses of people need:—power, steel, coal, telephones, railroads, banks—are controlled by a few men who are permitted to make money in unlimited quantities, we begin to see why we have the abuses of our present system. The great masses of consumers in this country are being exploited because the basic things that they need are in the control of the few who are in the business to make profits, excessive profits, as is exemplified by the exaggerated rates they charge for their products, the way they under-pay their help, and the disproportion in the amount that goes to dividends and high salaries.

We are maintaining that if you take away the opportunity for a man to accumulate and pass on unlimited amount of wealth, there will be no incentive to charge exhorbitant power rates, or to exploit to the present degree the employees and consumers. Because, what is the point in charging excessive prices for products, and of paying extremely low wages if you are not permitted to keep the money above a specified limit that you gain thereby? If this resolution, then, means that electric light rates, coal bills, and the others are going to cost the consuming public less, if it means that there will be less incentive to exploit the workers, then we think that the resolution will benefit the masses both now and in the future.

If you ask me how our plan of limitation is going to work in detail, I cannot tell you. But I do know that if our plan is adopted, wealth will be more equally distributed, and I know that Senator Norris, Dr. Henry Pratt Fairchild, Kirby Page, Norman Thomas, and even President Roosevelt are strongly in favor of a re-distribution of wealth. Moreover, I know that the ownership and control of immense fortunes brings about an unjust, selfish, monetary control over the great masses of our citizenry. I know that the desire for unlimited fortunes manifests itself in the greedy exploitation of the many by the few who own. I am also confident that fifty thousand dollars is an ample income, a worthy monetary incentive, and that there is comparatively little danger of our business progress suffering because we lack private capital. Germany is ahead of us in transportation facilities. She has developed the Deisel Electric train with a running speed of ninety-five miles per hour and without the aid of private capital.

We are not expecting that our plan will cure the world's ills. But for the above mentioned reasons we do feel that the plan will help present conditions, and that it will curb the abuses of the present system. We have tried to show that concentration of wealth is the significant factor in our present economic debacle. We believe that consuming power is the crying need. The justice of our resolution, and the injustice of present day gifts, inheritances, and incomes have also been emphasized. I have tried to show that our plan would take away the selfish, unjust, monetary control from the super-privileged class.

Third Negative, Eugene H. Wallace
College of Wooster

LADIES AND GENTLEMEN: As the Opposition has unfolded its case here this evening, I have been reminded time and again of that old fable called, I believe, "Belling the Cat." As I remember, the mice were suffering from the depredations of a cat and decided in high council that the solution to their problem would be in putting a bell on the cat so that they might be warned of his approach. The plan sounded great; it met with almost unanimous approval. Some kill-joy, however, asked how the bell would be tied on. That is like the Affirmative's proposal to limit incomes in order to solve the mystery of the missing purchasing power: it sounds fine in theory; the benefits to be derived from it are glorious to consider; but will the plan work? Is it based upon a valid assumption?

It is all very well for Mr. McBane and Mr. McCorkel to tell you that large incomes are unjustifiable and should be limited, but in considering their method of so limiting incomes, the matter of practicability cannot be excluded. Of course Mr. McCorkel cannot draw a blueprint of his plan; but neither can he waive the argument aside so easily as he has attempted to. The Negative has gone into some detail to show how the system would inevitably result in a loss of revenue to the government, a loss of the philanthropic enterprises which comprise so large a part of our life, and wholesale evasion which would almost negate the scheme altogether. The Affirmative's beautiful theory has been murdered by a gang of brutal facts. This plan is not practicable.

Nor is it based upon a sound premise. In reply to Mr. McMillen's argument that the government would lose $900,000,000 in revenue from taxes, Mr. McCorkel says, "We are not destroying wealth; we are merely re-distributing it." He assumes that surplus wealth may be sliced off the top and thrust in at the bottom, and even presumes that he will get some of it. "I would gladly pay a tax on an income of $1500 if I could get it, as I can't today," he remarks. Well now, I admire Mr. McCorkel's altruism, but I condemn his economics. Won't we destroy wealth? Isn't "wealth" merely "value"? It isn't, you see, actual bank notes and coin. For instance, statistics indicate that in 1929 our national wealth was four hundred billion dollars. In 1933 it is estimated at two hundred billion. What happened to the missing two hundred billion? Was it burned; lost; destroyed? No; evaluation of property merely fell off. Now take away these big fortunes that operate industry and create more wealth, and what do you do? Instead of re-distributing anything, you merely make it impossible for additional wealth to be created. You really have nothing to play with under this proposal except value, and you can't divide that up and pass it around. You are destroying actual value or wealth which is working, and are putting nothing in its place. Mr. McCorkel never would get his $1500 if he had his way in this matter. If you are in any doubt as to the truth of this statement of mine in regard to the nature of wealth, just look at the money in circulation today: nine billions of it. However, there are forty-four billion in Federal Reserve credit. Our economic society is conducted on a credit basis, not upon a cash basis. No, I am afraid that while the idealism of the Affirmative is greatly to be commended, their fundamental premise must be highly condemned.

Accordingly, you see, the assumption upon which this plan is based is unsound. In addition to that its use would be extremely impractical. Not only that, but we do have a very definite need for big incomes, as Miss Garber pointed out not long ago. Our critical economic status calls for a remedy, but certainly this plan is not what we are looking for.

Our attention has been too easily turned in the wrong direction. We see great wealth in one place and little wealth in another, and we think we can solve everything by simply evening things up. But that is not the point of attack. The fact that credit is the basic and fundamental thing in our economic society indicates the proper place upon which to focus our attention in endeavoring to escape from this chaotic condition which Miss Heisner has so ably pictured.

Let us see if our hope does not lie in credit. Industry depends for its operation upon credit. When credit is easily obtained, industry booms, and production increases rapidly to a point where over-production results and surpluses are created. Then men are laid off, production declines or stops altogether, prices fall, and deflation ensues which carries us into a depression such as this current one. That is in brief outline the business cycle. On the one side of the norm you have abnormal prosperity, and on the other, abnormal slumps. The result is the chaos which gives cause for this debate. Now is it not logical to suppose that if business activity were to be stabilized at normal, we would have a very desirable economic order? It would not be perfect, of course, but what is perfect? Very well then, since business depends on credit, and our deplorable economic conditions depend on business, why not remedy conditions by controlling credit?

The approach of the Negative, therefore, to the solution of this problem would be through the Federal Reserve System. Today that organization embraces more than one-third of the banking institutions of the nation and over three-fourths of the resources of the country. It exercises a large measure of control, accordingly, over credit. We propose that the Federal Reserve system be given complete control of credit by compelling all banks to come into the system; by increasing and extending the powers of the various Reserve boards so that they might touch very definitely upon each bank's supply of credit; and making more sensitive each bank's contact with each individual industry in its community. What you have done then is to centralize the control of credit in the hands of the Federal Reserve System. By doing that you have made it possible to regulate the supply of credit—its increase or diminution—and have accordingly succeeded in controlling business activity.

We have data available today which indicates when expansion should take place; that is, when a boom is coming and when a depression is in sight. The trouble is that with decentralized control, the warning signals are not heeded. By centralizing control, all the numerous signs of a coming boom period could be the dictators of policy and the boom could be avoided. So too with the depression which inevitably follows this artificial inflation of value.

In line with such a policy as this would be such social legislation as old age pensions, abolition of child labor, unemployment insurance, minimum wage laws, the thirty-hour week, et cetera. All these measures will protect the worker while control of credit will do much to abolish the need for protection.

This course has been the trend of action since 1890. Not action which would disrupt the whole order of our lives; not action which would destroy the fundamental precepts upon which this nation is founded—precepts of freedom, and individuality; not foolish and untried theories; but rather sound, rational, logical action; action which has constantly raised our standard of living; action which has brought us to a point man never dared hope to reach; albeit, action which has not been complete. This step to control credit and regulate business activity is the next step in a very definite trend which we are following.

Well, where do we stand now in this debate? The Affirmative has told you that because we have this terrible condition upon our hands, something must be done. We agree. They have told you that huge fortunes and incomes are unjustifiable and unfair. They have insisted that the existence of such incomes and fortunes results in monetary control by a few men.

On the other hand, you have the Negative's contention that progress depends upon large incomes; that this proposal to limit incomes would be of no immediate value in alleviating conditions; that it would be decidedly detrimental in that it would mean a loss in revenues and philanthropies; and finally, and most important of all, that the whole case of the Affirmative is based upon a false assumption—the assumption that wealth is money and could be handled as such. In addition to demonstrating the fallacy of the limitation proposal, the Negative has also indicated the proper course of action, control of credit.

The Negative feels that the Affirmative is right in saying that something must be done. But we cannot agree that the plan proposed is sound, logical, desirable, or basic. It cannot work; its premise is invalid. We propose, therefore, that we do not disrupt the social organization which has undeniably brought us so far along the road of progress; but rather that we act rationally and logically in carrying out the trends of the times.

Affirmative Rebuttal, Adeline Heisner
College of Wooster

LADIES AND GENTLEMEN: Mr. Wallace claims that you have witnessed a brutal murder here tonight—a murder of a beautiful theory by a gang of brutal facts! Strangely enough the theory seems to be feeling new signs of life, in fact before I finish I hope to have it quite revived—a lusty, hardy theory. The Affirmative believes that it takes more than some technical objections and opposition in the form of counter propositions to kill our plan for limiting wealth.

You see both sides of this debate are really quite altruistic. We all realize the immediate and pressing need for some definite economic reform; we all are agreed that the millions of people who are suffering privation, tonight, must be given relief. The Affirmative is quite willing to agree with Mr. Wallace that a control of our credit system might be a very helpful measure; we are quite willing to approve of all the social legislation he has suggested—old age pensions, minimum wage laws, unemployment insurance, the six-hour day and the five-day week. Why, Ladies and Gentlemen, I doubt very seriously if we could even work up a debate over these issues. But we are not here to debate the advisability of these measures; we are here to try to find out if limiting incomes is a just, sane and practicable measure that will help to redistribute wealth. We have not claimed that our plan is a miracle-worker, a cure-all; we claim that it is one measure that strikes at the deepest root of our economic distress—the unlimited privilege and the consequent power of individuals who secure vast sums of unearned wealth by fair or foul means, while millions lack the necessities of life. Maldistribution of wealth and lack of purchasing power are the brutal facts that we must correlate. Perhaps the most brutal fact with which to reply to Mr. Wallace's speech is that we are debating limitation of incomes, gifts and inheritances, *not* credit control. I have nothing to say against his proposition; it is not my responsibility to show that credit control is not advisable, in fact I know very little about credit control and have no intention of dealing with the subject now; too much time has already been spent on this irrelevant matter.

I was particularly interested in the last speech, in the statement: "the whole Affirmative case is founded on a false premise—the premise that wealth is money and could be handled as such." In an earlier part of the same speech we were told that our national wealth had decreased two hundred billion dollars between 1929 and 1933. I resent the accusation made against the Affirmative case in suggesting that we do not understand the difference between wealth and money. Of course the national money values fluctuate; perhaps they will fluctuate when our plan is put into work but the $50,000 limitation is not rigid; it is merely a convenient figure settled upon to make the discussion definite. Limitation can be made flexible and correlated with the fluctuations in values. National wealth is in land, cattle, tangible possessions—not in money, securities, stocks and bonds.

Mr. Wallace pleads with you to endorse only those plans which are compatible with the "fundamental precepts upon which this nation is founded, precepts of freedom and individuality." That is a most commendable plea, my friends. We add our voice to that of Mr. Wallace in asking you for respect for individuality. There is a great distinction between individuality and selfish individualism. How much individuality and freedom do the oppressed coal miners in the southern part of our state have? Can they demand decent wages even when they are offered part time work? There is no freedom when definite class oppression such as this exists.

It seems to me this question is a matter of ratios. Shall 10,799 men be free—perfectly free—to get as much as they can, in any way that they can at the expense of millions of others? The Affirmative has tried to show you that a great maldistribution of wealth exists in this country today, that the unlimited profits system leads to social abuse, great suffering and injustices; that the limitation of incomes, gifts and inheritances to $50,000 is a sane, moderate plan which will strike at this root problem—the need for a more even distribution of wealth.

BIBLIOGRAPHY: LIMITATION OF WEALTH

Books

Adams, James Truslow.—*The Epic of America.*
Brown, H. G.—*Economics of Taxation.* 1924.
Chase, Stuart.—*A New Deal.*
Corey, Lewis.—*House of Morgan.* G. H. Watt, N. Y. 1930.
Douglass, Paul H.—*The Coming of a New Party.*
Faulkner, H. U.—*American Economic History.* 1932.
Flynn, John T.—*Graft in Business.* Vanguard Press. 1931.
Foster and Catchings.—*Money.* Houghton, Mifflin. 1923.
Hamilton and May.—*The Control of Wages.* 1923.
Hansen.—*Economic Stabilization of an Unbalanced World.* 1932.
Hobson, J A.—*Economics and Ethics.* D. C. Heath. 1929.
——— *Taxation in the New State.* 1919.
Lutz, H L.—*Public Finance.* 1930.

Minnigerode, Meade.—*Jay Gould.* Putnam's, N. Y. and London. 1927.
Patterson, E. M.—*The World's Economic Dilemma.* 1930.
Peck, H. W.—*Taxation and Welfare.* 1925.
Shulz.—*Taxation of Inheritances.* 1926.
Statistical Abstract of the United States. Supt. of Documents, Government Printing Office. 1932.
Taussig.—*Principles of Economics.* Chapter 51. 1921.
Walker, G. M.—*A Defense of Wealth.*
Warshaw, Robert I.—*Jay Gould.* Greenberg, N. Y. 1928.
World Almanac, The.—1933. *Income Tax Reports.* N Y. World.

Magazines

Annals of the American Academy.—January 1933. Sumner H. Slichter. *The Immediate Unemployment Problem.* 1933. L. C. Walker. *The Share-the-Work Movement.*
Atlantic Monthly.—December 1932. G. W. Anderson. *Our Railroads.*
Business Week.—January 13, 1932. *European Real Wages*
Christian Century.—47:1210-12. October 8, 1930. L. F. Wood. *Pauperizing the Rich.* 47:1385-6. November 12, 1930. H. F. Ward. *Stagger Incomes Instead of Wages.*
Commonweal—July 5, 1932. *Distribution of Income.* August 17, 1932. *That Rugged Individualism.*
Current History.—October 1932. E. Gruening. *Power as a Campaign Issue.* February 1933. R. W. Robey. *The Outlook for Recovery.*
Journal of Commerce.—United States Department of Commerce. *Survey of Current Business.*
Literary Digest.—May 24, 1930. *Tale of Two Income Taxes.*
Monthly Labor Review.—April 1927.
Nation, The.—November 21, 1929. *The Ideal Income.* 134:339-40, March 23, 1932. M. S. Stewart. *How to Tax the Rich.*
Ohio State Journal.—February 28, 1933. *Mellon One of Trio Named in Tax Case.*
Review of Reviews.—July 1931. *Wealth Rises to the Top.* September 1932. *All Quiet on the Yankee Front.*
Saturday Evening Post.—July 16, 1932. F. Britten Austin. *Soak the Rich.*
World Tomorrow.—August 1932. *Why Not Income and Wealth Also?* February 8, 1933.

NEWSPAPERS

Christian Science Monitor.—February 6, 1933. *European Labor Conference.*

New York Times—February 8, 1933. *Smith Urges Public Works Dictator.* February 26, 1933. *Senate Currency Committee Stock Market Investigation Looks to the Masses for Economic Aid. Governor Lehman's Message on Minimum Wage Laws.*

JAPAN'S POLICY IN MANCHURIA
A Radio Debate

JAPAN'S POLICY IN MANCHURIA
BUCKNELL UNIVERSITY AFFIRMATIVE AND NEGATIVE

The following debate on Japan's Policy in Manchuria is one between two men's teams of Bucknell University, Lewisburg, Pennsylvania. The debate as printed here was given over the University radio station WJBU. During the regular season Bucknell teams took trips through the New England states, through Ohio, and through New Jersey and Eastern Pennsylvania. Teams from ten states were met in Lewisburg. Among the season's opponents were the University of Pennsylvania, Bates, Rutgers, Davidson, Fordham, Colby, Bowdoin, Boston University, Colgate, Ohio Wesleyan, Washington and Jefferson, and Denison.

Bucknell is one of the few Eastern co-educational universities that conducts an extensive debate program for women. This year a women's team made a trip through Indiana, Missouri, Oklahoma, and North Texas for a series of ten debates.

The 1933 Bucknell teams discussed four subjects, with the *Cancellation of War Debts* the featured proposition. The present discussion, *Resolved: That Japan's policy in Manchuria is justified*, would, in all probability, have been the outstanding debate topic of the year, because of its international importance, had not changing economic and political conditions in Europe and the United States brought other subjects hurriedly into prominence.

Speeches for the debate herein printed were collected and contributed by Professor Arthur L. Brandon, Director of Debating at Bucknell University.

First Affirmative, Harald E. Kenseth
Bucknell University

LADIES AND GENTLEMEN: We shall attempt to show you tonight why Japan's policy in Manchuria is justifiable. Manchuria, as you all know, lies north of China proper and consists of the four provinces of Liaoning, Kirin, Heliungkiang, and Jehol. The Japanese classify this territory as North and South Manchuria and Eastern Inner Mongolia. Manchuria was an independent state until the Manchus conquered China in 1644, displaced the Ming dynasty, set up the Ching or Manchu dynasty, and ruled China until the Republic was established in 1911. From the time of the Manchu conquest, Manchuria has never been more than nominally a part of China although it has been accorded the same color on the maps of our geographies as China proper.

The Japanese policy which has provoked this discussion began with the military intervention in Manchuria by the Japanese in September, 1931, and includes the establishment of the new state of Manchukuo. This policy has resulted in the substitution of a free, independent, and stable government capable of discharging its international obligations in the place of the confusion, chaos, Communism, and feudalism which characterized the régime of the Manchu war lords. Japan has been condemned by the world for aggressions against the sovereignty of China, and for jeopardizing the peace of the world. We believe that this condemnation is unjust, and is based largely on inflammatory misinformation and anti-Japanese propaganda spread by the press throughout the world. We believe that Japan stands condemned before she has been proven guilty, a condition which is contrary to the practice of all the great courts of justice in the world.

Furthermore, we feel that the nations of the world by their inactivity, have given tacit consent to the Japanese policy and that the League of Nations' report concerning this policy, which was prejudicial to Japan, was used merely as a sedative to quiet the feelings of the people of the world which had been aroused by the sensational betrayal of facts by the press. It is for these reasons, then, that we believe the time has come for the nations openly to adjudge Japan's policy to be justifiable. We of the Affirmative wish to enter our plea for the overt approbation of the policy of Japan on the grounds that it was dictated by the law of self-preservation, and that it will redound to the benefit of all the world, including China.

The law of self-preservation dictated the Japanese policy, because Japan is economically dependent on Manchuria. According to the Lytton or League of Nations' report, Japan's population stood at 65,000,000 in 1930 and was expanding at the rate of 900,000 yearly. Her population per square mile of arable land was 2,774, the densest in the world, and in order to support this huge and expanding population it was necessary for Japan to industrialize on a large scale. With such a rate of population increase it will be necessary for her to industrialize still further in the future. The correlaries of this increased industrialization are well stated by the Lytton report which says:

"If Japan is to find employment for her increasing population through the process of further industrialization, the development of her export trade and foreign markets capable of absorbing increasing amounts of her goods becomes more and more essential. Such markets would at the same time serve as a source of supply of raw materials and of foodstuffs."

Where, may we ask, was Japan to find a market and source of raw materials that would be unrestricted in time of peace and war? She had no colonies. In fact, all the land available for colonization had long since been acquired by such capitalistic nations as Great Britain, France, and the United States. Was it not natural, then, for Japan to seek special interests in the richest source of raw materials and most potential market in the Far East, Manchuria, which lay in her own back yard? Shall we penalize Japan because she awoke to her needs after ours had been sated? Is not such a condemnation doubly unjust since her policy is not that of colonization like Great Britain's and France's? Would we ask Great Britain to give up her colonies because she acquired them by force? We feel that the time has come for us to look upon Japan in the same light as we look upon the island kingdom of Great Britain, whose case closely parallels that of Japan's. Like Japan, England could not long survive unless she had an unrestricted flow of raw materials and ever open markets in her associated commonwealths. We cannot conceive of Englishmen starving through the loss of their colonies. Neither should we forget the fact that the Japanese will starve unless they are able to maintain a special position in Manchuria.

Japan needs this special position in Manchuria also because she must defend her economic interests there with military force. She is constantly threatened by

Soviet Russia, but since the problem of the Red advance is not only a problem for Japan but for the whole world, I shall leave that part of this discussion for my colleague to emphasize. Let us not forget, however, that it is necessary for Japan to have strategic military bases in Manchuria to protect her economic interests and her life.

Japan secured such a position in Manchuria fairly. By the Portsmouth treaty after the Russo-Japanese War, (a war in which Japan preserved the integrity of China), by the famous 1915 agreements, and by various later treaties certain rights were given to her, rights which she has held for years. These rights, which gave a major share of the exploitation of Manchuria to Japan, include the South Manchurian Railway running through central Manchuria to the sea, together with the right to administer the railway zone, to station guard troops there, and to exploit contingent coal and iron mines. There was also an agreement made by China not to build parallel railroads. Japan was also to have the first chance at investing money in Manchuria. She secured by lease the ports of Port Arthur and Dairen which have become great trade centers. She has the right of extra-territoriality or the privilege of having court jurisdiction over her nationals in China. Because of the rapid development attendant upon these secured privileges, Japan has over a million nationals in Manchuria, more than any other nation except China; she has invested seventy-three per cent of all the money invested in Manchuria; and she handles fifty per cent of the Manchurian trade.

The present Japanese policy was inaugurated in self-defense because of the infringement of these rights which were vital to Japan's very life. Chang Tso Lin, Manchurian general, is definitely known to have had an anti-foreign attitude in the last years of his life. He built a railroad parallel to the South Manchurian Railway in order to ruin the Japanese enterprise, although China had agreed not to build such a road. Moreover, he took over roads under joint control of Japanese and Chinese and integrated them with his system, meanwhile working the far-eastern plan whereby he and all his officials got their cut on all freight shipped over its lines. The fact that Chang Tso Lin declared himself independent of the Central Government of China, and fought that government, shows that the government officials were powerless to make him abide by the treaties they had made. Moreover, the Koreans, subject to all kinds of mistreatment in China, were not permitted to lease land in Manchuria although they were expressly given this right by treaty. Further treaty violations came with the demands for the return of Port Arthur and Dairen, and the demand that Japan withdraw her guard troops from the railway zone. Added to this infringement of rights was the boycott instituted against Japanese goods by the Chinese people—an act which is of itself often a cause of war. Thus the direct assaults on the Japanese positions around September 1931 served only to set off the hair-trigger relationship which existed because of these widespread treaty violations. Japan at last awoke to the fact that she could no longer sit back and watch these aggressions on her special position in Manchuria and save her life. She therefore intervened.

The policy of intervention is legally justifiable according to International Law which states that: "Independence may be defined as the right of a state to manage all its affairs whether internal or external without the control from other states." No nation has the right, then, to challenge Japan's action. Moreover, the law states, "the most important of the fundamental rights of a state is that of existence which involves self-preservation and defense" and "the right of self-preservation includes the right to preserve the integrity and inviolability of its territory," and further "that intervention for the sake of self-preservation is a fundamental right which takes precedence over all systems of positive law and custom." It can readily be seen then that Japan is fighting for her very existence, and that she has been subjected to direct aggressions against her. I have cited International Law to show that her policy is legally justifiable. This right of self-preservation is more fundamental than any peace pact she may have been party to because of membership in the League of Nations. Moreover, lest the Negative ask "what about China's independence," let me say that, even if China were a sovereign nation, the policy of Japan would still be legally justifiable, for the law states "that the right of self-preservation is even more sacred than the duty of respecting the independence of others."

You may agree to the legal justifiability of Japan's action and still wonder why it was not possible for an amicable settlement to have been made. The fact is that China is no longer a sovereign nation. Sovereignty implies, besides the possession of land and population, that a nation has a stable government and that this government has the power to impose its will on its people. The hope expressed in the second article of the Nine Power Pact that China would put her house in order has not been realized. It was China that made this pact a scrap of paper by her ineptitude. No one will deny that in recent years she has lacked a stable government. In fact she was so politically disunited that while the Central or Nanking government claimed to be in power, the Soviets were controlling outer Mongolia, the Communists were in control of three western provinces, the Canton government was law unto itself, and war lords ruled various provinces, including Manchuria. Thus China could not boast any central government. The futility of arbitrating with such a political topsy-turvydom is evident.

Moreover, as I have said, sovereignty implies the power of a state to impose its will upon its people. Political disunion in China made any such power impossible. The fact that the Central Government could not impose its will on the people is shown by the aggressions against the Japanese position legally granted by the central government, by the widespread anti-foreign acts in China and Manchuria, and by the attacks on the persons and property of foreign nationals. Great Britain was forced to intervene in China to protect her nationals in 1927. In fact, China is a backward nation suffering from the blights of Communism, hatred of foreigners, and chaotic and corrupt government. It would be foolish for us to believe that any such pseudo-state was a sovereign nation, or one capable of arbitrating the present controversy with Japan and then abiding by the decisions of such a settlement.

I have shown that Japan's needs justified the acquisition of her special position in Manchuria, and that her defense of this position is justified by the dicta of International Law. Therefore, we favor Japan's policy in Manchuria.

First Negative, Samuel Barker
Bucknell University

LADIES AND GENTLEMEN: "When there is a fire in a jewelry shop the neighbors cannot be expected to refrain from helping themselves," is an old Japanese saying which seems to be especially applicable to the present policy which is being pursued by the Nipponese government in Manchuria. According to the first speaker for the Affirmative, Japan is justified in using force because she can use the products of Manchuria. In other words, *need* is a justification for robbery.

Since 1894, when the first Sino-Japanese difficulties arose, Japanese publicists have attempted to justify Japan's policy on the grounds that possession of Manchuria was necessary for economic and military reasons. The preceding speaker has substantially followed these lines, although he has overlooked the fact that China has her needs too. We may well pause at this moment and ask, what about the national existence of China, the national defense of China, and the economic requirements of China?

The claim of China over Manchuria has been undisputed for nearly 300 years. On July 13, 1928, Sir Austin Chamberlain declared that England considered Manchuria a part of China, while on May 21 of the same year Frank B. Kellogg, then Secretary of State, said: "As far as the United States is concerned, Manchuria is essentially Chinese." In 1922 Manchuria was definitely recognized as part of China at the Washington Conference and has always been so considered by the League of Nations. So we see that not only China but also the rest of the world recognizes China's claim to Manchuria.

Since the establishment of the Ching dynasty, Chinese people have been peacefully colonizing Manchuria. Today ninety-seven per cent of the people in Manchuria are Chinese. Moreover, the language and customs of the Manchus and Chinese are identical, while inter-marriage has established similar traditions for all.

Although Japan claims that she needs strategic military bases in Manchuria, we cannot overlook the fact that Manchuria is China's outpost against penetration from the North and from the East. Chinese history proves conclusively that her security depends upon a protected northern boundary. Japan's recent advance to the Great Wall is in itself sufficient proof of the importance to China of a well protected northern frontier.

The first speaker has emphasized the economic needs of Japan, yet the fact that Manchuria is of vital economic importance to China does not enter into his survey. Over 500,000 Chinese annually settle in Manchuria, while approximately the same number of Chinese outside of Manchuria depend upon her for seasonal employment. China, as well as Japan, needs coal, iron, and food for her crowded population.

Let us analyze the case advanced by the Affirmative thus far. They maintain that Japan needs the resources of Manchuria; and they say that this need justifies Japanese aggression. I have pointed out that Manchuria is an integral part of China, and that China also needs Manchuria. Shall Manchuria go to Japan merely because she is more powerful? The entire justification of Japan's policy is based upon the fact that she needs Manchuria. Well, so does China, and what is more important, Manchuria belongs to China.

The opening speaker for the Opposition has told you that Japan has special interests in Manchuria which she secured as a result of certain treaties, notably the Protocol of 1905 and the 1915 agreements. At the same time he has told you that China is no longer a sovereign state. Yet he asserts that the reason Japan has invaded China is that these treaty rights are not being carried out. If China is not a sovereign state, how can Japan have a treaty with her? However, let us waive this question for the time and look into the actual making of these "treaties."

China has never recognized the existence of the 1905 Protocols. She maintains that the provisions referred to in the agreement were discussed at the Conference, but were never sanctioned by any Chinese government

The statement made by C. Walter Young, after a study of the controversy, is highly illuminating:

"It is conspicuous that where the treaty and additional agreements of 1905 appear in the official Japanese Foreign Treaty collections there is no version, either in French, Japanese or Chinese, or any language, of such 'Protocols.'"

And so we see that as far as this treaty is concerned, Japan is attempting to enforce a document which she herself introduced and which was never accepted by the nation upon which she is attempting to enforce it.

The 1915 agreements have also been mentioned. Let us see just what these famed twenty-one demands included. *First*, they asked for railroad mining, and concession rights in Shantung. *Second*, they asked for an extension to ninety-nine years of the leases of Port Arthur, Dairen, the Southern Manchurian railroad, the management and control of the Kiren-Changchun railroad, and other exclusive railroad and mining rights, and priority in investments. All these leases were unconditionally renewable. Japan could extend the life of the leases indefinitely although China opposed such action. *Third*, they demanded the control of China's main source of iron and coal. *Fourth*, they demanded special concessions on the coast of China. And *finally*, they demanded that China should have Japanese police and that China should employ Japanese advisors in financial, political, and military affairs. Only five months previous to these demands, the Premier of Japan had made the following statement:

"Japan has no ulterior motive, no desire to secure more territory, no thought of depriving China or other people of anything which they now possess."

Let us briefly examine the situation as it then existed throughout the world. The rest of the world was at war; the 1905 Portsmouth "rights" would expire in 1923. Japan had no particular justification for making the Demands. China had done nothing against Japan; there had been no grievances and no quarrel. Well aware of the unjust action which she was taking, Japan demanded secrecy of China and attempted to keep the world uninformed as to the content and character of the Demands. China has never accepted responsibility for this treaty which was forced upon her by the Japanese military machine.

Under the guise of so-called treaties Japan has invaded China and has struck at the very heart of her sovereignty. Immediately after the capture of Mukden, a Japanese mayor was appointed. The Mukden Telegraph office is now controlled by Japanese as is the Chinese Post Office. The Bank of The Three Eastern Provinces, the official organ of the former Chinese adminstration, was taken over by the Japanese military officials. The Pen-Chi Hu Coal Mine, previously a Sino-Japanese enterprise, was forcibly taken by the Japanese; while the Mukden Electric Light Company constructed and operated by the Chinese, was likewise confiscated. At Shanghai, the Japanese destroyed the huge printing presses which were used to write the textbooks for the Chinese schools. And so we might enumerate endless similar actions, all done to "protect Japanese special interests."

The first speaker for the Affirmative has claimed that the Chinese government is not sovereign because it cannot prevent lawlessness in Manchuria; however, he evades the fact that the Japanese army is creating bandits rather than establishing order. The farmers who are driven off the land are compelled to resort to robbery in order to survive. The cruelty of the Japanese soldiers in Manchuria is well illustrated by the following incident related by Stanley K. Hornbeck:

"Here (Changli), as a result of a quarrel between a soldier of the Japanese railway guard and a Chinese fruit-vender, the former refusing to pay the latter for wares he was consuming, Japanese guards set upon and killed five Chinese policemen. The investigation which followed show that the Japanese were clearly the aggressors and had acted with wanton brutality."

The Japanese established an independent state in Manchukuo by threatening the Chinese officials. Sherwood Eddy, in his report of the Japanese invasion of Manchuria, points out that several prominent Chinese leaders were approached by Japanese officials who attempted to force them to establish a new government. Some Chinese statesmen have yielded to this use of force and are now being referred to as advocates of the new régime.

Briefly, then, here is the situation: Japan claims that she has certain special treaty rights in China; China contends that the treaties are illegal and refuses to be governed by their provisions. We have attempted to show you the Chinese position; our Opponents are giving you the Japanese angle. However, regardless of which party is right in the treaty controversies, our contention is that armed force is not a justifiable method of settling this dispute.

Naturally during an international crisis, the statesmen of the conflicting countries are prone to write "air tight" cases in justification of their individual states. We have seen that this is especially true in regard to both China and Japan. Now it is our purpose to attempt to get above this dogmatic attitude and to try to discuss this matter upon the fundamental issues of the case.

We have two nations each demanding a certain section of land. Both countries need the province for economic and military positions. One country has an undisputed priority right to the contested area, while the other country—more powerful—claims a special position as a result of certain treaties. These treaties are contested by one of the parties and the second party is attempting to set herself up as a judge in a dispute in which she herself is involved. It is not only Japan's action that is on trial, it is the well-known policy of imperialism and exploitation that is at stake in this dispute!

We do not believe that it is our duty to settle these controversies at this time. What treaties are valid and what treaties have been violated are questions which must be settled by an impartial international body. But we contend that the use of force by Japan to settle these disputes is unjust and unfair to China.

In conclusion, let me remind you of our contentions this evening. *First,* we believe that Manchuria is an integral part of the Chinese empire and belongs to China. *Second,* we feel that the Japanese invasion of China to enforce treaties which she alone claims are legal, strikes at the very heart of China's sovereignty, and is unjust to any sovereign country.

Second Affirmative, Franklin H. Cook
Bucknell University

LADIES AND GENTLEMEN: Let us pause a moment to analyze the statements of the previous speaker. His argument rested upon two main contentions: *first,* the invasion of Manchuria by Japan is detrimental to the interests of China; and *second,* Japan's claims to a "special position" in Manchuria conflict with China's sovereign rights and policies. The first point the speaker of the Negative attempted to substantiate by claiming that Manchuria for nearly 300 years has been recognized as a part of China. Replying to this argument we contend that the only relationship between China and Manchuria has been that incurred through alliance. Previous to 1644, Manchuria was an independent state; then when the Manchus conquered China, China became a part of the Manchurian empire; Manchuria did not become a part of the Chinese empire. Until 1912 Manchuria always had an emperor independent of China. For purposes of safety and defense he found it to his convenience to enter into alliances with China. However, in 1912 Emperor Pu

Yi of Manchuria was dethroned by Feng, the leader of the Chinese Revolution. Since that date independent war-lords have ruled Manchuria, at times asserting their independence from China, at times, for strength, making alliances with the national government of China and the northern Chinese war lords. On the basis of these flimsy alliances China claims sovereignty over Manchuria. Now, Japan has returned to the deposed emperor of the Manchus, Pu Yi, his state, freed from the influences of the Nanking government.

The Negative speaker has supported his argument further, concerning the detrimental effect to China of Japan's policy in Manchuria by contending that the Chinese colonists have emigrated to Manchuria, and that Manchuria is of vital economic importance to China. The first point we refute by simply stating that it is an invalid argument; for, if we should pursue the same line of reasoning we should have to argue that Southeastern Pennsylvania should belong to Germany because of the predominance of inhabitants who possess German blood in their veins; the second assertion, regarding the economic importance of Manchuria to China, which our Opponent stressed so heavily, we refute by stating that the economic stability of Manchuria is more important to an industrial Japan than to an agricultural China which at present has only fifteen per cent of its tillable land under cultivation, and that, in the future, Chinese economic relations with Manchuria will not be restrained but should grow greater each year because of the stability of the Manchukuo state.

At this time, in order to advance the Affirmative case further, we shall defer answering the preceding speaker's second point, that Japan's claims to a "special position" in Manchuria conflict with China's sovereign rights and policies. This point we shall answer in rebuttal.

Briefly, for a moment, let me summarize the Affirmative case as it now stands: *first,* we have shown by legal precedent that self-defensive intervention is recognized by all international tribunals; *then,* we have shown that Japan *is* fighting self-defensively in Manchuria. No international tribunal may order a nation to commit suicide; no power is restrained from entering a foreign country to protect its nationals; no nation in the world today can question Japan's right to enter Manchuria as a defensive measure against Russia. England has her lowland countries of Belgium and the Netherlands to protect her from Europe; she has her Gibraltar, Egypt, and Palestine to protect India. France has her Little Entente. The United States has her Cuba, Puerto Rico, Haiti, Santo Domingo, Panama, and the *Monroe Doctrine* to protect her. Japan has no protection against Russia; Manchukuo will serve as an *independent* "buffer" state. On anyone of the aforementioned grounds, which were established in the opening speech and which I have repeated here for emphasis, Japan's policy in Manchuria is legally justifiable.

However, now that we have established that the present policy of Japan in Manchuria is beneficial to Japan, let us see the results of this action upon the rest of the world and especially upon China and Manchuria. From a brief survey of the Japanese policy we note that Japan's action will save the Far East from Communism, that the establishment of a stable government in Manchuria will mean a resumption of the open-door policy in that state, and finally, that world peace will be enhanced by friendly relations between Manchuria and Japan.

Japan has entered Manchuria to keep Russia out. Japan fears Russia as a nation, but she fears her more because of the close relationship between the Third International and the Soviet. Japan has been alarmed at the rapid strides of Communism throughout the East. The weak, disorganized governments of China have been toys in the hands of Moscow. With the sanction of the Chinese governments, Communism has spread throughout China. Authorities now agree that half of China is Communistic. Outer Mongolia, a Chinese province, in area larger than Manchuria, has become unofficially part of the United States of Soviet Russia. Chinese are forbidden within its borders. Russian officials administer its government; Russian officers train its army; Russian engineers run Russian railways to the Chinese borders; Russian schools teach Chinese students the lessons of Communism, and then send them into China and Manchuria to boycott the foreigner, destroy foreign capitalistic interests, and to demolish Chinese civilization by pillage and slaughter. The Chinese officials who have realized the dangers of Communism have been too weak to check the rapid spread of the Red Menace. A few sporadic raids have been the only measures taken by the fighting war lords to check the impending danger. For the last five years Japan has seen Chinese war lords fighting in all parts of chaotic China for the spoils of a corrupt government, entirely oblivious of the powder magazine which the Communists have been placing directly beneath their feet. Realizing that it would be dangerous if she waited two years until the two big Siberian steel mills had been completed, and faced with the actual fact that the Trans-Siberian railway had been double-tracked, Japan decided that to act now was the only means by which she could protect herself from being embroiled in a world conflict with Russia within the next five years. Japan has acted, and from the world point of view she has acted wisely, for if she can check Communism she can save the Far East from a Communistic Revolution. The other nations of the world should applaud Japan for fighting their battles for them; but they are too engrossed with tariffs, with war debts, and with the depression to realize the true status of affairs in the Far East. Like the Chinese generals they have failed to heed the warning against the Red Menace as pointed out by such Far Eastern authorities as Sherwood Eddy, George Sokolsky, and G. B. Rea.

Japan, if she can maintain her position in Manchuria, constitutes an effectual barrier to the spread of Communism. But her presence in Manchuria means more than that to the inhabitants of that state and to the foreign nations having relations with her. To the inhabitants Japan gives a stable government—a government free from bandits, from Communists, from war lords, from corrupt officials.

These are replaced by free schools, free clinics, hospitals, and a unified government supported by an efficient police force. A stable Manchuria means prosperity and freedom from danger to the Soya bean farmer. But further, the well-being of the Manchurians means the well-being of the 500,000 Chinese and the millions of Japanese dependent upon these farmers for their livelihood. Previous to Japan's entrance into Manchuria the government in control of Manchuria had violated the open-door policy, which was sought so eagerly by the nations of the world in the Nine Power Pact of 1922. Japan's entrance into Manchuria has re-established the open-door policy, giving to every nation, England, France, the United States, Germany, all the nations of the world, as well as China and Japan the right to participate in the trade which naturally results from a prosperous nation, a prosperous Manchuria.

We have been considering the effects of Japan's policy upon the world generally. First, we have seen that Japan's penetration into Manchuria constitutes an obstacle to a Communistic Revolution in the East; second, we have noted the economic benefits of the establishment of a stable government in Manchuria. Now let us regard from a different point of view the benefits of Japan's action to the world, especially to England and the United States. Because of the pressure of an increasing population, Japan for the last decade has been a threat to the peace of the world. Ten years ago because of the population pressure in Japan the United States and Japan almost had war. Since 1924 conditions in Japan have not improved; they have become more acute. Japan, in the past kept from the United States, from the English domains, from China, and from Manchuria, had to have an outlet somewhere for her increasing population. Instead of turning her face to the West she turned to the East and made a place for herself in the "reservoir," Manchuria. Previous to the establishment of Manchukuo, Manchuria was closed to the Japanese; now they may emigrate to that nation freely or if they do not wish to settle in it they may have access to the raw materials of its vast domain, which as an industrial state will help Japan to support her huge population at home. The establishment of friendly relations between Japan and Manchukuo means that the threat of a future war with Japan has been removed from the minds of English and American statesmen. Peace has been re-established in the East, for in Manchuria Japan has found an outlet for her excess population.

In conclusion, let us review Japan's position in Manchuria. First, we see that she is fighting self-defensively for her economic self-preservation as a national state, for the protection of her nationals, and for the prevention of Russian encroachment. Self-defense is the primary law of nature; it is the primary law of International Law. Self-defensive action is always justifiable. We have seen that Japan's policy in Manchuria is beneficial to Japan. Let us summarize the benefits of Japan's policy to the other nations of the world. First, Japan is fighting the world's fight against Communism, and the world will benefit from the Japanese barrier erected against Communism. Second, the establishment of a stable government in Manchuria benefits not only that state but also the nations having trade relations with Manchukuo. Finally, the overflow of the Japanese population into Manchuria removes the threat of Japan, fighting under population pressure, to the peace of the world. Therefore, Japan's policy in Manchuria is justifiable.

Second Negative, Robert N. Cook
Bucknell University

LADIES AND GENTLEMEN: We have been told that Japan is the hero in a great drama which is now being enacted. The first speaker of the Affirmative tried to separate Manchuria from China. We of the Negative cannot agree with such an interpretation of history. My colleague has shown that Manchuria is an integral part of China, inhabited by ninety-seven per cent Chinese and recognized by the nations of the world as part of the territory of China, having similar customs, language, and traditions. Only our opponents and Japan contend that Manchuria and China are two separate and distinct nations. The burden of proof rests upon the Affirmative to establish the fact that China and Manchuria, or should I say Manchukuo, are separate states.

Then with typical Japanese logic, our opponents tried to prove that Japan is fighting in self-defense, and for the benefit of the world. We believe that the best way to help China form a stable government is not by taking part of her territory and disrupting her social, economic, and political life, but by coöperating with her in arbitration conferences. Japan has refused to arbitrate when China was willing to do so. We believe that the method of settlement used by Japan, *force,* is not only detrimental to China, but also to the peace and welfare of the nations of the world. Japan has violated the Covenant of the League of Nations, the Nine Power Pact, and the Kellogg Peace Pact. These pacts or treaties were established to protect the peace and welfare of the nations of the world. Any power which acts in such a manner as to violate any or all of these treaties is a menace to world peace. Such a power is Japan. Japan signed the Covenant of the League of Nations, which provides in Article X "The Members of the League undertake to respect and preserve as against external aggression the territorial integrity and existing political independence of all members of the League. In case of any such aggression, the Council shall advise upon the means by which this obligation shall be fulfilled." China is also a member of the League of Nations, and is safe-guarded by treaty against aggression. The League recognized and continues to recognize China as a sovereign, independent state whose territorial rights, which include Manchuria, should not be violated. The invasion of Chinese territory by the Japanese military forces is an offense against China and against all members of the League.

Also, Japan has broken the Nine Power Pact, a pact

signed in 1922 by the nine leading nations in the Pacific —the United States, Great Britain, France, Belgium, Italy, The Netherlands, Portugal, and Japan. Article 1 reads:

"The contracting powers, other than China, agree:

1. "To respect the sovereignty, the independency, and the territorial and administrative integrity of China;

2. "To provide the fullest and most unembarrassed opportunity to China to develop and maintain for herself an effective and stable Government;

3. "To use their influence for the purpose of effectually establishing and maintaining the principle of equal opportunity for the commerce and industry of all nations throughout the territory of China;

4. "To refrain from taking advantage of conditions in China in order to seek special rights or privileges which would abridge the rights of subjects or citizens of friendly States, and from countenancing action inimical to the security of such States."

This last provision which prohibits the securing of special privileges in China was placed in the treaty because Japan had demanded special rights in China. Today Japan bases her action upon certain special privileges which she claims in Manchuria although such rights are denied to her by the treaty of 1922 which established the *open door policy* for China.

In 1928 Japan signed the Kellogg Peace Pact, which reads:

Article I

"The High Contracting Parties solemnly declare in the names of their respective peoples that they condemn recourse to war for the solution of international controversies, and renounce it as an instrument of national policy in their relations with one another.

ARTICLE II

"The High Contracting Parties agree that the settlement or solution of all disputes or conflicts of whatever origin they may be, which may arise among them, shall never be sought except by pacific means."

Fifty-six nations signed this pact renouncing war. The aggressive policy of Japan in Manchuria is an offense against practically every nation in the world, and a threat to world peace.

We admit that every nation has the right to protect itself against aggression or destruction; but we deny that Japan is fighting a defensive war. According to International Law and practice a nation may legally defend itself only when it has been attacked or when there is a threat of immediate, impending, irreparable injury and for these purposes alone. Japan was not attacked by the Chinese forces; neither was she threatened with immediate and irreparable damage. The Chinese sentries on duty at Mukden carried dummy guns so that they could not fire, thus giving the Japanese an excuse to take Manchuria. Unfortunately, on the night of September 18, 1931, some one, no one knows who, dynamited the South Manchurian Railway. About a foot of track was blown out at ten o'clock at night, but the train crossed the damaged track and arrived unharmed and on time at the station. However, the Japanese soldiers had reported to Japanese headquarters that the South Manchurian Railway had been dynamited; Japanese headquarters immediately put into execution a well-planned attack upon the Chinese garrisons in Manchuria. Many garrisons were taken with practically no resistance being given by the Chinese, because they had been commanded not to resist, thus provoking hostilities.

The Japanese people had been aroused by inflammatory propaganda against the Chinese spread through the Japanese newspapers and through the use of handbills. The use of military force on September 18, 1931, was entirely unwarranted. Such action did not prove who bombed the railway, nor was it necessary to protect Japanese nationals against a threatening danger. The incident was a subject for arbitration, not war.

The Japanese military organization is like a certain Captain Moir who owned a piece of property in a small community. He first warned the people of the neighborhood not to trespass on his property. When they did not obey his command, he seized his gun and killed a young man. The Captain was tried for murder, convicted, and hanged. The moral of this case in criminal law is that no person should assume the power of enforcing his imagined rights. Captain Moir should have called a policeman; Japan should have appealed to the League of Nations, a qualified and proper tribunal to settle international disputes to determine who dynamited the railway.

The League of Nations appointed the Lytton Commission, a committee of neutrals, to investigate and to study the Japanese invasion of Manchuria. Japan was willing at that time to have such a committee study the facts of the case. However, when the Lytton Commission reported against Japan, the Japanese protested, claiming that they alone were competent to decide whether they had acted in self-defense. Permit me to read a statement made by the then Secretary of State, Mr. Frank B. Kellogg, in connection with the Kellogg Peace Pact: "Every nation is free at all times and regardless of treaty provisions to defend its territory from attack or invasion, and it alone is competent to decide whether circumstances require recourse to war in self-defense. If it has a good case the world will applaud and not condemn its action." The Japanese statesmen have often quoted this same statement, but they always forget to add the last sentence,—*"If it has a good case the world will applaud and not condemn its action."* This statement means that each nation has the power to act in what it considers self-defense, but the action will be judged by the world through the proper tribunal, being praised if just, condemned if unjust. The Council of the League of Nations, a proper tribunal, considered the action of Japan in Manchuria and condemned it.

Japan has been condemned by the world for her policy in Manchuria because she is fighting a war of aggression. When a nation uses military power to force upon another nation her demands, that nation is pursuing a policy of aggression. Japan maintained her troops in Manchuria, and has continued to invade not only Manchuria but also China beyond the Great Wall, while she was negotiating with the Chinese government.

The League of Nations demanded that Japan withdraw her troops from Chinese territory so that negotiations might be conducted in a fair manner. Although the Japanese representative assured the Council of the League that the Japanese troops were being withdrawn within the zone of the South Manchurian Railway, the cable dispatches from Manchuria stated that the Japanese military force was extending its control over Manchuria, taking new towns every day. To the world it seemed that the Japanese war lords were out of the control of the civil government of Japan. Throughout this debate our Opponents have been telling us that China is disunited, because the central government could not control the action of the Chinese generals. They forget that the only difference between a Chinese and a Japanese war lord is that the Japanese generals are better equipped.

Ladies and Gentlemen, is it necessary for a nation to take Chinese railroads, to seize Chinese banks, to operate Chinese utilities, to collect Chinese revenue, to destroy Chinese printing presses, and to establish a new government in order to protect the nationals of that state? The only difference between Chinese bandits and Japanese soldiers is that the Chinese bandits take only part of the Chinese's goods; the Japanese soldiers take all!

We have tried to show, first, that Manchuria is an integral part of China, and that any invasion of Manchuria is detrimental to China, and second, that Japan's action is detrimental to the peace and welfare of the world, because she has disregarded and violated the

Covenant of the League of Nations, The Nine Power Pact, The Kellogg Peace Pact, all of which were established to protect China and other nations against unjust aggression. Therefore, we believe that the action of Japan in Manchuria is not justifiable.

First Negative Rebuttal, Samuel Barker
Bucknell University

LADIES AND GENTLEMEN: The Affirmative team has attempted to evade Japan's obligations under the League of Nations' Covenant and the Nine Power Treaty by contending that China is no longer a sovereign state and has no responsible government. At the same time Japan claims that the Chinese government is responsible for the economic boycott and also insists on direct negotiations with the Chinese government. Sovereignty is recognized by all authorities of International Law as an attribute to statehood. China has been recognized as a state by the members of the League of Nations and by Russia and the United States. As a member of the League she is upon a parity with Japan.

We must realize that China is now going through a period of social and political adjustment. Every other major country has gone through a similar period. The French Revolution, the Civil War, and the Industrial Revolution are being enacted in China at one time.

Japan, the one country which contends that China cannot govern herself, has not been able to control her own army and navy, for these forces have violated international treaties and solemn pledges of their government.

Our Opponents claim that the presence of Japanese troops has been a stabilizing influence. Yet an analysis of this contention proves it to be fallacious. Before 1931 Japan controlled less than one-half of one per cent of the whole territory of Manchuria, in which she had stationed some 15,000 troops. At present Japan has some 35,000 troops in Manchuria and yet, according to the Gentlemen of the Affirmative, robbery and banditry are increasing daily. The Japanese themselves contradict each other on this point. On November 11, 1931, the Japanese ambassador to France, in attempting to justify Japan's action said, "We have succeeded in transforming Manchuria into a country better governed than the rest of the world." The following day, General Honjo declared that the reason Japan was fighting in Manchuria was that frequent murders and riots were prevalent!

Our Opponents would have us believe that Japanese control over Manchuria would "save" that territory for the world. The Japanese action toward Korea is a good example of their intentions to "save" weak provinces. In 1894 after a rebellion had broken out in Korea, as a protest against Japanese interference, China was asked to assist the Korean Emperor. Japan immediately declared war on China and forced her to recognize the independence of Korea. Five years later, Prince Ito, in a public address said, "The annexation of Korea has no part in the purpose of the Japanese government." One year after this fine proclamation, Japan annexed Korea and has kept her under strict control ever since. That is how Japan bears "Self-denials" and "hardships" to "save" her neighbors!

Japan is not interested in the welfare of the inhabitants of Manchuria. While the use and sale of narcotics are prohibited by law in Japan, her attitude toward this trade is exactly the opposite in Manchuria. According to reports recently published by the National Anti-Opium Association of China, no less than seventy-five per cent of the Japanese nationals residing in South Manchuria are directly or indirectly connected with the drug traffic. These statistics were furnished the Association by Mr. U. Kikucii, Secretary of the Association for the Prevention of Opium Evils of Japan.

Not only are the members of the Affirmative saving Manchuria for the world but they are also preventing the spread of the Red Menace, by making China so weak that she will be the prey for any covetous nation. As Sherwood Eddy pointed out,

"Japan must face the terrible responsibility of being the cause or occasion of the break-up of China and the forming of a large Communist state in the heart of the Far East, a war with Russia followed by internal revolution in Japan, and a world war which may again draw into its seething vortex all the principal nations of the world."

And yet the Gentlemen of the Opposition maintain that the breaking up of China by Japan will benefit the world!

We have seen that China is recognized as a sovereign state not only by the other powers of the world, but also by Japan herself, since she insists on direct negotiations with the Chinese government. We have seen that Japanese force has not succeeded in Manchuria, and we firmly maintain that the way to help China is not to invade her territory but to counsel and coöperate with her.

First Affirmative Rebuttal, Harald E. Kenseth
Bucknell University

LADIES AND GENTLEMEN: The speakers for the Negative side admit that Japan needs her special position in Manchuria and then they say that she shall leave Manchuria. This leaves us with the dilemma consisting of Japan's having to be there and get out at the same time. They claim that she should leave Manchuria because her treaties with China are illegal. May we point out that the very nations the Negative cites as being opposed to Japan's present policy have recognized the treaties in question. We feel that the legality of Japan's position has been established, and on that basis we are discussing her immediate policy.

The Negative also asserts that the Japanese will not settle in Manchuria, and that Manchuria cannot, therefore, be considered as a safety valve for her surplus population. Large numbers of Japanese have not settled in Manchuria because the Chinese officials have kept the Japanese out, and because Japan has been taking care of her excess population by increased industrialization. The time will come shortly, however, when Japan will not be able to care for nearly a million newcomers a year in her small islands. The Japanese will have to emigrate in large numbers. Shall they force their way into the United States, or shall they move into Manchuria where they have a legal right to live?

Is Manchuria really an integral part of China as the Negative contends? We have already shown this contention to be unsound. May we add here that when China declared herself neutral during the Russo-Japanese War, this neutrality did not include Manchuria. If Manchuria were an integral part of China would not China's declaration have included Manchuria? Amos S. Hershey, an eminent authority on International Law, states that "Manchuria is a case of double or ambiguous sovereignty." This evidence in addition to what we have already presented should impress you with the fact that since the rise of the republic, Manchuria has been virtually independent of China proper.

Another contention of the Negative is that Japan has violated the sovereignty of China. They argue that sovereignty is an inherent attribute of statehood, and that since China is a state she is sovereign. We will admit that all states are *theoretically* sovereign over certain lands and peoples, but, as Hershey reasons, a state to persist must exercise sovereignty *in fact*. Sovereignty *in fact* means that a government controls its territory and its peoples. We have shown you that China has been capable of doing neither of these. The Lytton report shows that the granting of League membership to China was based on the hope that the theoretical sovereignty of the central government would become actual. While the powers maintained a "hands off" policy in China this government did not improve. In fact, matters grew progressively worse until by the fall of 1931, the central government was actually sovereign only in the Yangtse valley. Meanwhile a war lord was running—or should I say ruining—Manchuria. Since China is only theoretically sovereign, and since Manchuria is not an integral part of China, we fail to see how Japan has in any way violated China's integrity.

The Negative feel that Japan should have arbitrated with China. But when we perceive this lack of real sovereignty on the part of China, we can see why it was impossible for Japan to make an amicable settlement with her. In fact, Japan went from government to government in China seeking one that would accept the responsibility for the actions of the Chinese. Not one of them would accept it.

The Negative quoted from two pacts to prove that Japan is not fighting in self-defense, and then disregarded them by asking us to show a good case for self-defense according to International Law. We have already done this, but if they wish, we will give additional proof. We believe Japan's case is better than England's in the *Caroline* case when she intervened in American territory, or the *Danish Fleet* case in which England seized the Danish fleet in 1807 to keep it out of Napoleon's hands. The leading authorities on International Law held that these two cases were justifiable actions in self-defense.

Although the Negative has given you the Chinese

version of the particular events leading up to Japan's intervention, we will not counter with the Japanese version, for we do not wish to quibble over minor details. On the other hand, we will show you by analyzing the background of the conflict in Manchuria that the situation there was very dangerous to Japan's existence. In the first place, you know that the Chinese have always hated foreigners since the time China was opened to trade with the modern world. You know that the Boxer rebellion was not fiction, and that it took the concerted action of the great powers to quell the attacks on their nationals at that time. You know that every leading nation keeps troops in China to protect its people and interests. You know that Great Britain had to intervene in 1927. We have shown you how chaotic the condition in Manchuria was, with a war lord in power and Communism and anti-foreignism rampant. The boycott was only one of the direct attacks on Japan arising from this inflamed anti-foreign feeling. It was a cause and not a result of the present trouble. Many were the coercive forces at work undermining Japan's position in China. Will you deny then that the fuel for the fire was there? You can see that Japan's position in Manchuria, on which her life depends, was in imminent danger, and that the policy she is pursuing is one of self-preservation, and fully as justifiable as the cases I have cited.

Moreover, we repeat the fundamental thesis that no nation has the right to question the actions of an independent nation either internally or externally. Nor does any judge who was sitting comfortably in Geneva when the trouble started have the right to question Japan's policy. If your life were threatened you would act, for you would probably be killed if you didn't. So it was with Japan, and we say that her action is justifiable for that reason.

We, the Affirmative, deny the suppositions of the Negative that Manchuria is an integral part of China, and that Japan has violated China's sovereignty. We believe that her positive action in defense of her nationals and of her economic life is just, and is to the interest of humanity, and we ask you to approve with us this measure.

Second Negative Rebuttal, Robert N. Cook
Bucknell University

LADIES AND GENTLEMEN: Our Opponents have tried to justify the action of Japan in Manchuria by citing the economic dependency of Japan upon Manchuria, the right of a nation to fight in self-defense, and the benefits which are supposed to accrue to the rest of the world. The fact that Japan is economically dependent upon Manchuria does not justify the controlling of Manchuria by Japan. The United States, and every nation in the world, is dependent upon other nations. The world is an economic unit.

The fact that the United States depends upon other countries for her tropical fruits, raw rubber, nickel, and other necessary products would not justify the invasion of these countries by the United States. Although our country in the past has invaded Nicaragua,

Haiti, and the Philippine Islands, we would like to remind the Affirmative that the United States has withdrawn her troops from Nicaragua, has voted to free the Philippine Islands, and is withdrawing her troops from Haiti. The signing of the Kellogg Peace Pact outlawed war and made illegal its use to decide any international dispute. The United States has recognized the benefits which will come from a policy of peace and has changed her entire foreign policy. We are in a new era. Japan cannot justify her action by appealing to old precedents which have become obsolete because a new principle and a new law has been established with the signing of the Kellogg Peace Pact of 1928. Our Opponents have based their case upon practices which were formerly recognized as legal and just, but which have now been condemned by practically every nation in the world. Our Opponents have forgotten that actions which may have been legal and justifiable before the signing of the Covenant of the League of Nations, the Nine Power Pact of 1922, and the Kellogg Peace Pact are no longer legal or justifiable.

The Members of the Affirmative have cited the rapid increase in the population of Japan, claiming that she needed Manchuria as an outlet for this surplus population. They forget, first, that the population of China is also increasing very rapidly, and, second, that the Japanese refuse to go to Manchuria. Although the Japanese government has tried to colonize Manchuria, there are today only 220,000 Japanese there. These Japanese are business men, not colonists. On the other hand there are thirty million Chinese in this area. The second speaker of the Affirmative has stated that by our reasoning the southeastern part of Pennsylvania should be a part of Germany because a majority of the inhabitants are descendants from German parents. Proof by analogy is very dangerous and often misleading. Our Opponents have forgotten, first, that these descendants from German parents are American citizens; second, that they speak the English language; third, that they constitute a majority of the population in only a few localities of Pennsylvania, and fourth, that Pennsylvania is not a part of Germany. On the contrary, the inhabitants of Manchuria are Chinese citizens, speak the Chinese language, follow Chinese customs, are ninety-seven per cent Chinese, and live on Chinese soil. The conditions in Pennsylvania are not analogous to the conditions in Manchuria, and therefore, to use such an analogy is misleading. Manchuria should belong to China because it is an integral part of China the same as Pennsylvania is an integral part of the United States.

Our Opponents have tried to justify the invasion of Manchuria by Japan by referring to the historical fact that the Manchus conquered China and were therefore not a part of China. If this logic were true, Japan could justify an invasion into the thirteen original states of the United States, claiming that these thirteen are not a part of the United States because they conquered and acquired the land which now belongs to the United States. In fact, Japan could justify Japanese control of Prussia, because Prussia conquered the other provinces of Germany. No one would be so foolish as to say that the northern states of the United States are not an integral part of the United States, simply because they conquered the southern states in the Civil War, or that Prussia is not a part of Germany because she conquered the other German provinces. We believe that the logic of our Opponents is equally absurd when they say that Manchuria is not a part of China because Manchuria conquered China.

Throughout this debate our Opponents have been using Japanese logic to justify the policy of Japan in Manchuria. What is Japanese logic? Japanese logic is the mingling of true and false statements so that one cannot detect which statements are true and which statements are false. They say that the Manchus conquered China. We admit this. Therefore, they claim, Manchuria is not a part of China. We have shown that this conclusion cannot be drawn from the previously mentioned fact, and furthermore, we have presented evidence to show that Manchuria is a part of China and is recognized by practically every nation as a part of China.

They state that Japan is economically dependent upon Manchuria. We also admit this to be true. Therefore, they say, Japan has a right to invade Manchuria. We deny that Japan has such a right, showing the absurdity of such a conclusion by citing the fact that every nation is dependent economically upon other nations.

They claim that Communism is spreading rapidly through China. We admit this fact. Therefore, they say, Japan's invasion into Manchuria to halt the rise of Communism is justifiable. This conclusion is misleading, because the Japanese invasion is not halting the spread of Communism but is aiding its rise as we have shown. They maintain that every nation has the right to fight in self-defense. We recognize the truth of this statement; however, they have not proved that Japan was threatened with an attack, and one cannot legally defend himself unless he is attacked or threatened with irreparable damage. We have shown that Japan was not attacked nor threatened with irreparable damage. We hope that you will not be misled by these half-truths which our Opponents have presented to you. The burden of proof rests upon the Affirmative to show that the action of Japan in Manchuria is not detrimental to China nor to the general welfare and peace of the world, for no action which is detrimental to the interests of China and a threat to world peace can be called justifiable. We believe that the policy of Japan in Manchuria is not justifiable.

Second Affirmative Rebuttal, Franklin H. Cook
Bucknell University

LADIES AND GENTLEMEN: The previous speaker made three outstanding assertions in his rebuttal. First, that Manchuria need not be a part of Japanese territory to enable Japan to benefit from Manchuria; second, that Japan does not need Manchuria for her excess population because of the small number of Japanese in Manchuria; and third, that a new era of International Law has arisen.

We agree that Manchuria need not be a part of Japanese territory in order that Japan may benefit from Manchuria. But when we agree to this proposition we insist also that Manchuria is not necessary for China's existence. Manchukuo is an independent state. She is not related to Japan as Haiti, the Hawaiian Islands, and the Philippine Islands are to the United States. Japan entered Manchuria to aid in the establishment of an independent, sovereign, stable government. The previous war lords had been unable to protect Japanese lives and property, for economic discrimination had been made against the Japanese and Koreans. Even the inhabitants themselves have testified to the evils of the *status quo ante*. The League of Nations condemns this *status quo ante*. Yet in spite of the protests of the inhabitants and the League of Nations the Negative wishes the former conditions restored. Manchukuo is an independent state just as the League desired. As an independent state it can establish just trade relations with both China and Japan to the economic benefit of both nations.

In refuting the second point of the previous speaker in which he denied Japan's need for Manchuria as a reservoir for her excess population may we repeat that Manchuria is an independent nation; and may we further assert that under the Manchukuo government Japan is not forcing her people to enter Manchuria, but by driving out a disorganized government she has made it possible for her inhabitants to settle freely in Manchuria and for her economic interests in that land to be as safe as investments of the United States are in England and France. Under the Chiangs, because of discrimination against the Japanese, this race was barred from emigrating freely to Manchuria. This fact accounts for the comparatively small number of Japanese settlers there. Further, freedom from the former dangers of war lords, bandits, and Communists will enable the Japanese-owned industries to send a steady flow of the necessary raw materials to Japan's industrial population.

Lastly, may we refute the argument that a new era of International Law has arisen. This argument, by the way, was the main contention in the second Negative speaker's constructive speech. With a great amount of emotionalism the Negative supported the sacredness of treaties and their inviolability. We of the Affirmative recognize the power of Treaties as organs of Peace; but we disagree with the Negative's assumption that Japan has violated the Nine Power Pact and the Kellogg Pact. International Law maintains that a state's first obligation is to preserve its own existence. A treaty is not binding when the preservation of the state is endangered. In our first constructive speech we showed that Japan's national existence was threatened. Further, under the Kellogg Pact and the Nine Power Pact, Japan has a right to enter Manchuria to protect her "nationals." Chief Justice Hughes of the United States Supreme Court in a lecture at Princeton in May 1928 said: "On our part there is no disposition to forego our right to protect our nationals when their lives and property are imperiled because the sovereign power for the time being and in certain districts cannot be exercised and there is no government to afford protection." We have shown the danger to Japanese lives and property which precipitated the Japanese intervention. Legally, Japan has a right to be in Manchuria.

Japan is not subjugating Manchuria. The United States subjugated Haiti, Hawaii, and the Philippines. To date, thirty-five years after the Spanish-American war, none has gained independence; yet the Negative compares Japan's aid in establishing an independent state in Manchuria to the United States' conquest of the Spanish territories. These cases are not analogous. Has the United States ever recognized the independence of the ex-Spanish possessions? She has not. Yet Japan has recognized Manchukuo's independence; she, who would seem to frustrate her own ends by recognition according to the Negative, was the first state to recognize the sovereignty of Manchukuo.

In the closing remarks of the debate let us review the two cases. The Negative established two main contentions. First, they asserted that historically and economically Manchuria is bound to China. This argument we refuted by showing that historically Manchuria has been independent of China; and that economically both China and Japan will benefit from the stable government of Manchukuo. Second, they dwelt upon the sacredness of treaties. We, although recognizing the power of treaties for peace, assert that every nation has the right to fight for her self-preservation.

By showing Japan's need for the safety of her industries in Manchuria and by demonstrating the unjust and unfair treatment of the Japanese, in violation of the open-door policy, we proved our first contention that Japan is fighting self-defensively in Manchuria. Our second argument, that Japan's policy in Manchuria is beneficial to the world was supported by showing the effectual barrier that Japan will be to the formation of a Communist Revolution in the Far East, by illustrating the benefits to the world from the establishment of a stable, sovereign government in Manchuria, and finally, by pointing out that the freedom of the Japanese to enter Manchuria has removed Japan as a threat to world peace. A preponderance of evidence shows that Japan's policy in Manchuria is justifiable.

BIBLIOGRAPHY: JAPAN'S POLICY IN MANCHURIA

Books

Condliffe, John Bell.—*China Today: Economic.* World Peace Foundation, Boston. 1932.

Eddy, Sherwood.—*The Challenge of the East.* Farrar & Rinehart, N. Y. 1931.

——— *The World's Danger Zone.* Farrar & Rinehart. 1932.

——— *The Challenge of Europe.* Farrar & Rinehart. 1933.

Hall, W. H.—*International Law.* Clarendon Press, Oxford, Eng. 1880.

Hornbeck, Stanley K.—*China Today: Political* World Peace Foundation. 1927.

Hershey, Amos S.—*Essentials of International Public Law and Organization.* Macmillan. 1929.

Kawakami, K. K.—*Japan Speaks.* Macmillan. 1932.

Lattimore, Owen.—*Manchuria, Cradle of Conflict.* Macmillan. 1932.

Lawrence, T. J.—*Principles of International Law.* 7th ed. D C. Heath.

Meng, Chih.—*China Speaks.* Macmillan. 1932.

Moore, John Bassett—*International Law Digest.* Vol. 11, Sec. 215,

216, 217; pp. 402-14. Government Printing Office, Washington, 1906.
Orchard, J. E.—*Japan's Economic Position*. Whittlesey House. McGraw-Hill, N. Y. 1930.
Willoughby, W. W.—*Foreign Rights and Interests in China*. Rev. and Enl. Ed., Vol. 11. Johns Hopkins Press, Baltimore. 1927.
Woolf, Leonard.—*Economic Imperialism*. Swarthmore Press, Ltd., London. Harcourt, Brace, & Howe, N. Y. 1920.

Magazines

American Journal of International Law.—27 38, January 1933. *The Meaning of the Pact of Paris*. Quincy Wright.
Annals of American Academy.—152:329-35, November 1930. *Japanese Expansion in Manchuria*. J. E. Orchard.
Current History.—35:345-52, December 1931. *Issues in the Manchurian Crisis. Japanese and Russian Interests. Weakness of Chinese Control*. A. N. Holcombe.
Foreign Affairs.—8.52-68, October 1929. *Russo-Chinese Conflict in Manchuria*. K. K. Kawakami.
Fortnightly Review.—April 1933. pp. 453-62. *A British Policy for China*. Owen M. Green.
Forum.—88:262-8, November 1932. *Storm Over Asia*. Paul Hutchinson. 87:194-9, April 1932. *What Japan Really Wants*. Paul Hutchinson.

Official Documents

Manchuria.—Report of Commission of Enquiry Appointed by the League of Nations. United States Government Printing Office, Washington. 1932.
Treaties, Conventions, International Acts, Protocols, and Agreements Between the United States of America and Other Powers.—Vol. 111 (1910-1923), pp. 3120-3140. United States Government Printing Office, Washington. 1923.

Bulletins

Japanese Chamber of Commerce, Bureau of Information, 90 Broad St., N. Y.—*Background of the Manchurian Trouble*.

Background of the Shanghai Trouble.—New York Office of Japanese New York Office of Japanese National Committee of International Chamber of Commerce.—*Background of the Shanghai Trouble.* 1932.

Press Union, Shanghai (P. O. Box 455).—*The Shanghai Incident Misrepresented.*

Rea, George B.—*The Highway to Hostilities in the Far East.* Japanese Association in China, Shanghai. 1932.

Itok, Takeo.—*China's Challenge in Manchuria.* South Manchurian Railway Co. 1932.

Saito, Hirosi.—*Manchukuo, the New-Born State.* Japanese Chamber of Commerce. 1932.

Research Office, South Manchurian Railway Co., Dairen.—*Brief History of Japan's Rights and Interests in Manchuria.* 1932.

Japanese Delegation to the League of Nations, Geneva.—*Manchurian Question, Japan's Case.* 1933.

Ishi, Kikujiro.—*The Permanent Basis of Japanese Foreign Policy.* Reprinted from *Foreign Affairs*, an American Quarterly Review. January 1933. 45 East 65th Street, N. Y.

Rea, George B.—*Fundamentals, The Sino-Japanese Question from a Different Angle.* Reprinted from the Far Eastern Review, Shanghai.

NEWSPAPER CLIPPINGS

Close, Upton.—*Jehol: A Struggle Colored with Opium.* New York *Times.* January 15, 1933.

———— *Forgotten Men of Manchuria.* New York *Times.* November 27, 1932.

Fisher, Sterling, Jr.—*Japan, by Vigorous Measures Binds Manchuria More Closely.* New York *Times.* December 11, 1932.

Nanking Is Facing Civil War Threats.—Philadelphia *Public Ledger.* April 8, 1932.

Fact, Not Treaties, Is Manchurian Key, Says Tokio Savant.—Philadelphia *Inquirer.* March 27, 1932.

Soklosky, George E.—*The Manchurian Issue Grows and Thunders.* New York *Times.* January 15, 1933.

Editorial.—*China and Jehol.* Philadelphia *Public Ledger.* March 18, 1933.

A PRESIDENTIAL DICTATORSHIP
An Extension Debate

A PRESIDENTIAL DICTATORSHIP

COLGATE UNIVERSITY AFFIRMATIVE VS. NEW YORK UNIVERSITY NEGATIVE

This debate is the annual one between two old rivals on the gridiron and on the forensic platform. In spite of the great differences in the makeup of the two institutions, debating between the two has formed a link that is carefully preserved by each. Colgate is a small university of a limited enrollment of one thousand men, located in the Chenango Valley at Hamilton, New York. New York University, as every one knows, is a large metropolitan university, co-educational, and as urban, at least in location, as any university in the country.

The debate here produced was held before the Jewish Community Center of Stamford, Conn. The audience numbered about two hundred fifty. The then recent persecutions of the Jews in Germany by Hitler gave this audience, composed largely of people of Jewish extraction, a special interest in the question.

The debate was originally planned on the question, "Resolved: That in the present state of world affairs, dictatorship is preferable to democracy." This question seemed rather large for a single debate; consequently, the question was narrowed to read, *Resolved: That the United States should establish a dictatorship.*

The bibliography was prepared by Miss Lida C. Vasbinder, Reference Librarian of the Colgate Library, and the speeches were assembled and contributed to this Volume by Professor J. V. Garland, Director of Debate at Colgate University.

First Affirmative, A. William Christopher
Colgate University

LADIES AND GENTLEMEN: On behalf of the Colgate Debating Team I wish to thank the members of the

Jewish Community Center of Stamford for their kind reception. I also would like to take this opportunity to thank the members of the New York University Debating Team for the kindness which they have shown us. We sincerely hope that the debating relations between the two Universities may be continued in the future.

You know, the word "Dictator" is one which is abhorrent to most people; yet I believe that this is due to the fact that they do not understand that there are varying kinds of dictators. The first thought which comes into our minds at the mention of this word is the kind of dictatorship which Mussolini has established in Italy—that of the "mailed fist" type. We also think of Mr. Hitler and the dictatorship which he has recently established in Germany. We may find, however, that this form of government is in reality an old one; that the first dictatorship on record was established in Rome in the year 501 B.C. This type of dictatorship was of a more limited nature. In truth, it was just such a government which called Cincinnatus from his fields. The Roman dictator took over the reins of government for only a designated period of time. He was limited in his powers; for example, in some cases the dictator did not have any control over the treasury. And so we see that this sort of dictatorship is much different from that with which we most commonly associate the word. Then, too, the dictatorships in Poland, Hungary, Russia and the Latin American States are all widely different.

It is extremely fortunate that we are able to discuss

this topic this evening in view of its timeliness. We find that the people of the United States are faced with certain fundamental problems which demand our immediate attention. These problems faced Franklin D. Roosevelt when he took office on the fourth of March. He found it absolutely necessary that some solution be brought about for these problems. He was faced with the question of unemployment, the matter of the railroads, the distressing condition of the farmer, the question of interallied war debts. He must start some governmental reorganization and probably the most immediate problem was that of the banking situation. President Roosevelt recognized the need for immediate action when he took office and it is for that reason that he asked Congress to grant him powers of a dictatorial nature. What he asked Congress to grant him was not something entirely new to the people of this country. We find that Abraham Lincoln and Woodrow Wilson both received powers of this nature. They were faced with a crisis; so was Roosevelt. The leaders of this country granted Roosevelt the powers which he desired because they realized, as did he, the necessity of an immediate solution.

We have seen the record of Capitalism. It has been successful in helping the United States to grow, to become one of the most powerful nations in the world; yet, in the last seventy-five years our economic structure has tottered twenty-two times. Are we going to save our economic order, or are we going to scrap it? We might substitute some other order and then again, if we are convinced that the capitalistic system is worthwhile, we must take steps to save it. Daniel Willard, President of the Baltimore & Ohio Railroad, believes that it is certain that a system in which millions of people, through no fault of their own, are thrown out of work and remain out of work for many months and have no income in the meantime, cannot call itself perfect. Certainly, with millions going hungry while warehouses are stuffed with food, and with bankruptcies and foreclosures multiplying even though there is plenty of money in the banks, there must be something radically wrong with our capitalistic system.

The capitalistic system stands on trial. We must mend it, no matter at what sacrifice to individualism or the tremblings of Pollyannas. That era of rugged individualism so widely advocated by a past administration has come to an end. Collective effort and collectivism is the order of the day for President Roosevelt. America has come to the end of an era—the era of unplanned, uncontrolled and wasteful production—and we are now enduring not a slump but the breakdown of a system.

Albert G. Milbank, a prominent New York banker, shows the way by saying that capitalism must be "humanized, mutualized, socialized, and stabilized." Our essential job, then, is to bring these wild, undisciplined forces of capitalism into order for the services of Society. We hear the cry for a governor for our capitalistic system. We must have planning and, according to the Institute of Politics Report for 1932, "planning will involve a movement toward an intelligent and efficient democracy under the control of an intelligent dictatorship."

Our ship of state needs a skilled pilot and as a commander turns over his ship in dangerous waters to an experienced pilot, so should we turn over our ship of state to a capable pilot, a man like our President, to bring us safely into port.

First Negative, Daniel Levy
New York University

LADIES AND GENTLEMEN: It is indeed a pleasure to meet the debating team from Colgate this afternoon and, on the behalf of New York University, I bid you welcome, most heartily.

We are now facing extraordinary times, critical conditions, and in view of the current situation, it is not at all surprising that there are many who would advocate radical, and in many ways, illogical and unwarranted changes. Democracy has been challenged by a theory of government which has diametrically opposite theorems. It is proposed that we change *government by consent* to *government by force*. In view of these proposals it seems most pertinent to decide this afternoon as to whether or not in the present state of world affairs dictatorship is to be preferred to democracy.

The Affirmative has attacked democracy. Their case is an easy one for every existing political institution is imperfect. Their difficulty is to substitute an institution for the present one that will work more effectively and just as fairly. That difficulty the Affirmative must overcome or else their case is shattered and the burden of proof has not been met.

Our worthy Opponents are advocating dictatorship, a form similar to, and descended from the monarchical scheme of government which our forefathers decisively rejected when our Constitution was framed. In short, they would have us adopt that rejected form today. We have heard this afternoon of the evils of democracy, but the evils of dictatorship are not only more numerous, but more deeply imbedded in the institution. What is this elusive, high-sounding, fashionable word called dictatorship? What specifically is this form of government, which to exist, must deprive us of representation, of a voice in government, of the freedom of speech, press, or assembly, of the right to hold property? What is there in dictatorship which makes for security of life, liberty, property, and the pursuit of happiness—all characteristics of a democratic régime. A dictatorship has all the features of a monarchy. I will repeat them so as to combat those who would foist upon us reactionary ideas and philosophies, beliefs which we in the United States have tried to avoid.

Dictatorship stands for transference of authority to a ruler who is entirely independent of any public opinion, a man who comprehends within himself executive, legislative, and judicial power, and is above restraint of law or popular opinion. Dictatorship, then, is an authoritarian form of government, centralized in one man, one person independent of all checks, either popular or legal—whose wish is entirely his own.

The first principle of a dictatorship is that it be independent of any public opinion, be that opinion favorable or unfavorable. Being based on force and action it must be entirely independent of popular check, and so we do not find measures referred to any representative assembly, ballot or referendum. A dictator may, and usually does, use the force of the State to suppress dissenting opinion. Criticism is stifled and the organs of government which are supported by the taxes of all the people, are used to suppress and injure those same taxpayers. The police force, instead of being an arm of public protection, merely becomes the iron fist of the dictator to perpetuate his own policies and power. We have current testimonials of what power placed in the hands of one man can do. In Italy we find the people unable to nominate representatives—they merely vote "yes" or "no" upon the names submitted to them by Mussolini. Italian elections are mute proofs of how illegally the ballot can be conducted. In the last election held in Italy, which was in 1925, a time when there was considerable dissatisfaction with the Fascist régime, the official count as handed out by the Mussolini controlled election board read: eighteen million for Mussolini, and twenty thousand against him. Witness the recent German elections, when all anti-Nazis were beaten, jailed, or otherwise intimidated so that Hitler might claim a surprising increase in "Nazi sentiment." In Russia we find the Soviet party numbering two million holding in subjection one hundred and sixty million people, and actually refusing work, lodging and food to all those who oppose the Communist party. In a dictatorship we may look for, but seek in vain, such devices as a Bill of Rights, fair trial, freedom of speech, press and assembly. Old Law is suppressed, and the new law is the will and whim of the dictator, who can either violate established nostrums or set up new dogma as he, and only he, wishes.

Yet our Opponents claim that dictatorship justifies its use of force because it is a government of action. But there are two questions we would like to put. First, what guarantee is there that the action of a dictator will best promote the community welfare? Will this strong dictator of ours use his unlimited power to promote the social good? And second, how will he know what the public welfare is, if he has forcibly closed the channels for the expression of that opinion? Let us take up the first question—the problem as to whether or not an incoming dictator will rule for the public welfare. Let us consider the fact that a man of this sort rules with no checks of any sort upon him. Dictators are always minority dictators, and his group or party, if they master the State, will master him. He is human, and the itching palm has been reached in the loftiest heights of political power. Even if he were of unimpeachable integrity and not susceptible to the easy money of interested men and groups, a dictator still has friends and a party—he has a faction that has placed him in power—a minority faction that has been rejected by a majority of the country. Hitler, in spite of threats and punishments to all opposition, could not poll a majority of the German vote. Mussolini never was able to secure a popular majority in the Italian Chamber of Deputies, but had to dissolve that body to establish and perpetuate his power. How can a dictator consistently think of the public welfare when he has been repudiated by the public? How can he possibly think of the community advancement when he has been placed in power by a minority faction with peculiar beliefs and dogma, ideas that in many cases are for party advancement rather than for the good of all? How can anyone say that the current persecution against the Jews of Germany is promoting national welfare? Are we to believe Hitler when he says that the Jews are the causes of German poverty and depression? This unbelievable outrage of modern times is but a single example whereby we can see how the paramount concern of a dictator is individual and party advancement decidedly more than the public welfare.

But let us assume that this dictator of ours is a most extraordinary individual, and for some strange reason of his own, desires to forget his party so that he can fully promote the community welfare. How can he possibly carry out this most Utopian desire when he has forcibly suppressed all the organs of opinion by which the people can possibly express themselves? As long as these channels of popular opinion are closed there is no true index of what is proper or what the populace wants. And once these channels of opinion are opened, dictatorship can no longer exist, for then it is open to popular check and democracy is in existence once more. Today in the United States, if there is sufficient popular clamor for a law, we are sufficiently able to express ourselves and we must be listened to, for not only have we the power of the ballot to change previous law or the Constitution if necessary, but our representatives, anxious to keep their positions, must listen sooner or later. The long awaited anti-prohibition movement is at last gaining momentum and its eventual success cannot be doubted. However long it may take, it is the will of the people being carried out, and if the people are so inclined, Prohibition *must* be repealed! As long as the people have any say, dictatorship cannot exist for then it is no longer a government of force and action.

As a result we will find stagnation in a dictatorship where ideas of the community are suppressed. All the political advances of the world have come through democracy. Direct election, the initiative, referendum, and recall, popular assembly, women's suffrage, and thousands of other political rights have been carried to completion in democratic states. A dictatorship must, of necessity, crush such enlightenment as that is opposed to an authoritarian form of government. Referring again to our classic examples—women have no right to vote in Italy. In Germany a Communist, Jew, or liberal thinker has as much opportunity of expressing his opinion at the polls as a Republican candidate has hopes of being elected in a solid and staunch Tammany district! How can there be any political advancement when the people cannot express themselves?

We of the Negative do not believe it possible for one man to know completely all that is necessary for the public welfare. The history of the entire world has never revealed a man who was a capable expert as well as a practical politician. If our dictator be an expert, he will have the proper ideals in mind, but not being a politician, he will not have the practical knowledge to carry out his plans. If he is a politician, as all of our present dictators are, he will be merely interested in the promotion of his party and in his personal advancement. If it has proven most difficult to get the proper combination of the expert and politician in political institutions, how can that combination ever be successfully achieved in one human being?

But again let us assume that there can be found somewhere in the world a man who is a great expert as well as a most practical politician—there can be no denying of the fact that this most extraordinary individual is still a human being. Being but human he is susceptible sooner or later to the pangs of sickness, injury, mental feebleness, and eventually death itself. What guarantee can there possibly be that Hitler's successor, Mussolini's apostle, or Stalin's disciple will have that same unusual breadth of vision, power, and personality that their predecessor so strangely had? And furthermore, how can such unusual successors exist when, during the life of a Hitler for instance, all the thinking for Germany has been done by Hitler. All others who have any notions of what proper government should be, are either driven into exile or suppressed, which is another reason for the present war on culture and religion in Germany and Russia. We will find after the death of such extraordinary men that dictatorship must give way to either anarchy or mob rule. We find, going back to historical examples, that after the eighteenth century sway of the "enlightened despots," who were purely monarchical dictators, that the greatest of bloodshed and revolutions took place. The historic French Revolution came as an aftermath of the despotism of Louis the Fourteenth; Austria and Prussia were involved in several bloody struggles after the deaths of Joseph and Frederick. And Russia felt most helpless after Catherine the Great had passed away. We will find that when our current dictators leave this mortal world, either nobody or everybody will rule, and all the advantages that could have resulted from dictatorship will more than be wiped out.

The Affirmative has said that there are evils in democracy. History as well as reason shows us that the evils of dictatorship are a thousand times greater. Before we change let us be careful into what we leap.

Second Affirmative, Ellery B. Haskell
Colgate University

LADIES AND GENTLEMEN: Mr. Christopher has described to you the present critical state of affairs in the United States. He has pointed out that there is an urgent need for immediate action by the government. He concluded by expounding the definitions of dictatorship and democracy.

We believe that the present situation's demand for immediate governmental action is so urgent that our present democratic system of government will be unable to meet that demand. The chief point of weakness in our present system is Congress. It is Congress which retards action. The extreme slowness of this body can be easily explained. The mere fact of its parliamentary procedure is a cause for delay. It took a week and a half to two weeks to organize the two houses of the present Congress. A glance at the recent daily issues of the *Congressional Record* will demonstrate clearly the inevitable drag on all attempts at speed by a normal Congress. There are necessarily rigid rules on debate, but despite them members are able to hold the floor for a long time. In the last few weeks of the Hoover administration, Senator Shepardson held the floor of the Senate for eight hours in order to prevent any attempt at a repeal of the Eighteenth Amendment. Huey Long conducted a superb filibuster of five or six days in order to prevent some banking legislation proposed by Carter Glass. In addition to this, members are constantly interrupting each other to ask questions, to obtain speaking time, and sometimes to find out if a quorum is present. The fate of the country hangs upon the speed with which a governmental body acts which constantly has to interrupt its work to discover whether it is all there or not. Every now and then some enterprising Congressman suggests that the rules of the House or Senate be modified. This happened in the midst of our crucial time in the House on March 14th. The only way to remedy this great difficulty is drastically to limit debate as to the length and nature of it.

The nature of a parliamentary body, such as Congress, and its duties are detrimental to action. There may even be a question of the status of certain members. In this special session of Congress, there has been a lengthy argument concerning the unseating of a member because of felony. There has been delay and incompetence because of the lack of knowledge on the part of Congress. Representative Dunn, on March 11th, stated that the new members had had no time to study the Economy Bill. Senators in the hurly-burly of the rush in which Roosevelt has forced Congress, admit their lack of knowledge about proposed amendments which they are discussing. Senator George said at one time: "I am not familiar with the exact terms of the Amendment." The vast number of bills and the minute character of most of them make it physically impossible for Congress to act quickly. The same body that acts on the most important legislation of the crisis, like the Economy Bill, is also bombarded by innumerable others. There are some 3,125 bills before the House and in addition to these, are the ones which originate in the Senate. These bills deal with almost every conceivable thing under the sun. Some of the bills are: Relief for Agnes M. Angle; Relief for Daisy Anderson; Relief for Holy Family Hospital, St. Ignatius, Montana; and Bill for conveying certain land in the County of Los Angeles, California. The House was obliged to devote not a little time recently to the discussion of a bill enacting a memorial postage stamp for A. J. Cermak. Thus we can readily understand why the vast and diverse legislation in conjunction with such a body as Congress renders swift action physically impossible. The only alternative to this difficulty is to limit drastically the character of bills to be discussed.

The conflict of interests and opinions within Congress is one of the most important features holding up action. We may note that in the last long session of Congress, from December, 1931, to July, 1932, very little was accomplished. The most important bills had to do with the present crisis and embodied the ideas and messages to Congress of former President Hoover. These most important bills, having to do with the Reconstruction Finance Corporation and the Federal Home Loan Banks, were pushed through in the very last few days of Congress, late in July. The short session, from December, 1932, to last March 4th, accomplished nothing. In the New York *Times* for December 29th, we read that there was a lack of cooperation due to wide divergence of basic views on every subject among political leaders. All action on basic issues would be deferred until after March 4th. Congress would do nothing about the budget, war debts, farm relief, prohibition, and granting of administrative efficiencies to President Hoover. It became a do-nothing session.

The reason for this inability to act is not simply the political party fracas, but also that particular interests and opinions are at work. That the trouble is not due alone to party lines is evident from the fact that in recent emergency legislation more Democrats voted against the bills than have Republicans. The other factors making for inaction are quarrels of opinion and interests. There are countless lobbies capable of exercising great power which influence Representatives and Senators. Their methods are to influence the Congressmen themselves and especially to propagandize the public which forms the constituencies of these representatives of the people. They also present their case before committees. The chief function of the lobbies is to secure the interest of the particular group. The trade association's chief interest in government is due to the fear that Congress may enact legislation regulating industry. Representative Burton of Ohio has said: "In nothing is there greater danger to the body politic than in the power of the persistent and well-organized groups to secure the enactment of measures which are contrary to the interests of the aggregate body of citizenship. Washington is filled with lobbyists who seek to overawe Congress for matters of individual and local concern." The effect of the lobbies cannot be doubted. For example, very recently in the Senate, Senator Tydings heroically said that the Senators must balance the question of the country's welfare over against death, politically. Senator Tydings also admitted, to a question by Senator Borah as to where the pressure came to drive out certain items in an Economy Bill, that the pressure had come from business interests. The effects of lobbying interests can be seen in the fights over the very important economy legislation in Congress. The veterans gave a stiff opposition. Representatives and Senators spoke lengthily in defence of them. What may happen about the Farm legislation can be seen by the fact that the McNary-Haugen Farm Relief Bill was passed under the wing of lobbies. There are signs of storms of opposition for every move that President Roosevelt makes from now on. There is a welter of interests concentrated upon a great number of Congressmen dependent upon these interests for their jobs.

In order to avoid the difficulty of debate, of the mass of bills and of conflicts of interest, Congress will have to limit debate drastically, to limit the kind of bills to be discussed, and to delegate power to the President. The recent Congress is doing this. Is Congress saved? Is Democracy saved? The function of Congress is to produce legislation which is the result of integrated opinion of representatives of the people. Cutting down debate cuts out the possibility of an integrated opinion. Delegating power to the President to change bills cuts out the power of Congress. We have, then, a Congress shorn of power and simply doing what Roosevelt wants it to do. The Negative is presented with the following dilemma: Either Congress should be allowed plenty of time to debate and obtain an integrated opinion, or, in the present crisis, the time allowed should be drastically limited and no integrated opinion obtained or the value of Congress lost.

We believe, then, that the present crisis calls for immediate action by the government. We advocate a dictatorship which need not be absolute but at least have very great powers. We believe it is necessary, for Congress or parliamentary democracy is incapable of swift action in a crisis. We ask the Gentlemen of the Opposition to admit or deny the following: the need for immediate governmental action; in order to avoid quibbling, the definition of a limited but powerful dictatorship, and the following dilemma: either Congress acts slowly and we derive value from it, or it acts swiftly and is of no value.

Second Negative, Sanford Solender
New York University

LADIES AND GENTLEMEN: It is an exceedingly significant fact, that on a cold, rainy, and bleak evening such as this, so large a group of people are sufficiently aroused by the suggestion of the establishment of a dictatorship in America, to attend this discussion. We, of New York University, welcome this opportunity which our American democracy so firmly guarantees us, of discussing the comparative merits of a dictatorship and of a democracy, with all the freedom that we desire.

The tremendous evils of a dictatorship have already been indicated. Insecurity, arising from indefiniteness of succession; the danger of the system becoming permanent; complete concentration of power in a single organ who is entirely free from constitutional restraint; and a form of government which is entirely free of popular control, all characterize the type of system which the Gentlemen from Colgate offer. We feel, however, that this system is entirely contrary to the most fundamental factors in our American government, and it is my duty to point out that our system, as a result of certain unique features which it possesses, is entirely capable of coping with the present problems.

In order to see more clearly how adequate our present system is for coping with these problems, it will be necessary to turn for a moment to the background of our government.

From the very formation of the union, all those freedoms, rights, and liberties embodied in the Bill of Rights have been held sacred. Our government was constructed in such a fashion as to prevent undue exercise of power by any organ and to restrain adequately each department, thus preventing any violation of our democracy and of the security of our rights. Various devices were inserted in our Constitution to provide this. A system of division of powers into Legislative, Executive, and Judicial Departments with a balance of powers functioning, making each department a check upon the other. Frequent elections were provided to insure popular control of the government, and all manner of restraints were placed upon both state and national governments in order to insure the inviolability of the fundamental rights of the people. As Harold Laski states, "The democrative move is not historical accident. It grew out of a realization that if popular well-being is the purpose of government, popular control is essential."

And now, after a century and a half of our existence, we have a system in America that the whole world, so torn by dictatorships and suppression, may look upon with envy. While the people of Germany and Italy are utterly helpless in the face of vicious denials of every fundamental right of man, we in America have absolute freedom. The very fact that we may meet and discuss this problem so freely is indicative of the complete freedom of speech and assemblage in the United States.

Freedom of religion, of the press, and absolute guarantee of fair and equal treatment before the law, are but a few of the fundamental rights which are so completely denied in dictatorship nations but which our American government so carefully guards for us. Yet the Gentlemen from Colgate would forget all these facts, would throw aside the democratic system and adopt a dictatorship with its inherent viciousness.

During this century and a half of our existence, another very important development has occurred. As was quite natural, within a short time after our government began to function, differences arose among our statesmen over the treatment of the various problems facing the new nation. Political parties took root and began a long series of developments which have culminated today with the parties as the most important cogs in our political system. Not only do the parties provide coördination between the state and national governments; not only do they nominate candidates, select platforms and conduct campaigns; but, most important, they have provided a medium for securing complete coördination between the Legislative and Executive Departments, particularly in times of stress such as we are experiencing at present.

We wish, in our discussion, to determine the most adequate system to solve our present problems. We must of necessity, therefore confine our discussion to the present political situation. As it stands today, President Roosevelt's Democratic party maintains an overwhelming majority in Congress. He is thus able, by his readily recognizable ability as a leader, to enforce party discipline within the Democratic organization, and to have his plans for the solution of the present crisis executed in this manner with all promptness. In a few words, the party system, by virtue of its discipline, has enabled us to bring about rapid coördination between the executive and the legislative, and to thus meet emergencies with all the necessary promptness.

One need but examine the amazing record of speed and completeness with which President Roosevelt, within three weeks of his inauguration, has met each of the problems facing the United States. First, faced with an acute banking problem, the President exerted his leadership and initiated adequate legislation to meet the crisis. Then, when the problem of legalizing beer arose, he immediately guided the needed legislation through with all necessary speed. Faced with the need of balancing the budget, he initiated the required legislation, and with all promptness performed the necessary actions to solve this problem. Thus, we have had complete, adequate, and speedy functioning of the government in crises. In other words, we have here actual examples of the fact that under our present political system, the party in power, with its discipline, is entirely capable of executing all necessary governmental action to meet the existing problems.

Yet, the Gentlemen from Colgate would ignore these facts, and would destroy entirely our present system, substituting in its stead, a dictatorship, with all its insecurity, lack of popular control and entire supersedence of the Constitution and fundamental law.

The last few weeks have witnessed a revelation in

political history of the United States. It has been evidenced, beyond doubt, that the executive has set a new precedent in the conduct of affairs, both in emergencies and in normal times. Party discipline has made him the leader in legislation. He decides what is best, initiates legislation and guides it through the Congress with all necessary speed. How could a dictatorship possibly give quicker, more decisive, and yet thoroughly constitutional action such as this?

Thus, because we feel that the inherent evils of a dictatorship are so great that they far outweigh any possible faults of a democracy, and because it is obvious that democracy in America has proven itself, both as a protector of the fundamental rights of the people and as a form of government capable of meeting all situations and emergencies, we urge that the suggestion of a dictatorship for America be rejected and the present democracy be maintained.

Third Affirmative, Carl T. Arlt, Jr.
Colgate University

LADIES AND GENTLEMEN: In the course of the discussion there are several important points which gain prominence. First of all, there is the severe economic crisis which demands coördination and planning. In order to preserve the present system we need action. However, when we look over our governmental machinery we find that this representative government, this democracy, does not satisfy that particular need. Democracy is a form of government in which everyone knows what to do but no one has the authority to do it. Thus, we are faced with the question—What shall we do to be saved?

It is the contention of the Affirmative that dictatorship is the answer to the need. Dictatorship would be that form of government in which our dependence is no longer placed on the legislature but rather on a very strong executive with unlimited power. He would then be able to deal courageously with problems of tariff, war debts, economic planning, and taxation. In other words, he would eliminate that problem of deadlock which is not unlike the problem faced by the equally hungry and equally thirsty donkey, equally hesitant and equally inhibited between a bag of oats and a bucket of water. Torn by conflicting forces, dumb in the presence of the equality of ideas and opportunities, the donkey starves. We must answer the need with action.

This idea of concentrating the power in the hands of one individual or a few individuals, when regarded from the standpoint of efficiency and action, is inevitable. We note that we have never had a pure democracy even in the early beginnings of democracy in the Greek state. It was deemed impossible and impractical that every individual should have an active participation in government. Another shining example of this concentration of authority lies in the make-up of a corporation. Although that particular business unit may be owned by thousands and thousands of stockholders, the control and management lie in the hands of a few directors. In the field of taxation it has been considered very practical to centralize the taxing authorities in the state administration. Those states which have been most successful in administering their income tax have been those which have had centralized tax authority controlling the activities of many units. One has merely to glance at the branch banking system of Canada to realize the soundness of centralized control and, as has been mentioned previously in this debate, the Institute of Politics, meeting at Williamstown, Massachusetts, recognized that power is passing into the hands of small groups of competent men. Thus, in analyzing all these examples, we may justly conclude that an economic dictator is consistent with the trends of the present time.

The histories of outstanding democracies bear witness to the fact that in times of emergency they have become less democratic and more dictatorial. In 1925 the Belgian Parliament abdicated so that her problems of taxes, economy, and public debt might be dealt with directly by a single individual or a small group of individuals. The results attained favored this dictatorial action. In 1926, when the French finances were in a precarious position, Monsieur Poincaré was given the reins of the government. Through his actions the French finances were restored to normalcy. In England, the stronghold of Parliamentary procedure, we find the House of Commons relinquishing its control over the purse-strings and abdicating in favor of a strong cabinet which acted, not by parliamentary process, but by Orders in Council.

One of the most outstanding grants of dictatorial

power rendered by democracy is found in no other country than our own United States. In the recent World War, when the country was faced by a world crisis, Congress granted extraordinary powers to President Wilson, and working with President Wilson was a War Industries Board which was in effect a dictatorship. It controlled production by encouraging it in some sections, limiting it in others; by directing the administration of fuel and food; and supervising the operation of our transportation facilities. Action was needed and the War Industries Board restored order out of chaos.

It is not for me to say definitely that these examples are examples of dictatorship. Some may call them dictatorships, others may call them efficient democracies. But regardless of the name which you choose to give them, the fact remains that when action is needed in times of emergency, organization becomes less democratic and more dictatorial.

A glance at the existing dictatorships and their origin shows very clearly that when chaos reigns, people have resorted to dictatorial action. Battagalia, editor of that book, *Dictatorship on Trial,* says this:

"Dictatorship presupposes the failure or disintegration of an older, outworn system; it is chaos and confusion that summon the Alexander of the moment to cut the Gordian knot with his sword. As a rule, the old system goes bankrupt at a critical moment in the domestic and foreign relations of a country. It was thus that dictatorship came to be established in Russia, Turkey, Hungary, Italy, Spain, Poland and Yugoslavia."

Dictatorships of a greater legal character have arisen and do arise in other countries, and yet, like all dictatorships, they are the result of the effort to restore order out of chaos. These dictatorships may be referred to as constitutional dictatorships. In Rome the dictator received his super-legal powers from a legal body. Legal dictatorships occurred for the longest period of time in the so-called Polish Confederation. Sforza, although an opponent of dictatorship, admits that in South America, constitutional dictatorships are in existence because of the need for action.

Thus, one may see that dictatorships may be of various types and degree. Some are more absolute than others. They have varied to meet the needs of the hour. Some are defensive, others are aggressive. In addition, one cannot deny that some of these dictatorships are too tyrannical for the good of the people. However, all these dictatorships point to this one very obvious truth which Mr. Lippmann has expressed so effectively:

"The problems that vex democracy seem to be unmanageable by democratic methods. In supreme crises the dilemma is presented absolutely. Possibly a war can be fought for democracy; it cannot be fought democratically. Possibly a sudden revolution may be made to advance democracy; but the revolution itself will be conducted by dictatorship. Democracy may be defended against its enemies but it will be defended by a committee of safety. The history of wars and revolutions since 1914 is ample evidence on this point. In the presence of danger, where swift and concerted action is required, the methods of democracy cannot be employed."

At the present time Roosevelt has been given dictatorial authority. Indications point to grants of even more dictatorial authority to control more effectively the factors of production. Every day bears witness to a decided tendency to deal less democratically with the problems of the day. It is impossible to deny that. However, there is still too much clumsiness and delay in our governmental functions. Such is the opinion of Babson, the statistician, who has studied the situation very carefully. According to him, we should scrap the Constitution and establish a dictator.

Thus, we may conclude that when the United States is faced by this economic crisis in which chaos prevails; that when our present democratic machinery of government cannot act swiftly with efficiency; when we see that trends point to dictatorial action; that outstanding democracies bear witness to dictatorial action; we of the Affirmative naturally advocate that in the present state of world affairs a dictatorship is preferable to a democracy.

Third Negative, James Keller
New York University

LADIES AND GENTLEMEN: Our Affirmative friends base their plea for dictatorship upon one great argument—America needs action!

The answer to their argument is that we already *have* action, that ever since the inauguration of President Roosevelt we have had nothing but action. From Capitol Hill has come a series of rapid fire decisions, of swiftly enacted legislative measures. Bank Bill,

Economy Act, and Reforestation Measures, have followed each other in rapid succession. Congress has not been abolished, but it has coöperated, so much so that the action our friends desire has become the keynote of present administrative policy. What you wanted, Gentlemen from Colgate, you now have; and your wishes have been granted without scrapping the Constitution, without dissolving Congress, without installing a dictator in the White House.

And now that your wishes have been met, upon what basis do you still complain? Would you be so uninformed as to argue that Congressmen filibuster, and therefore action is impossible? You seek to prove your assertion by remarking that Huey Long and his comembers of the senatorial lunatic fringe filibustered during the last congressional session. You are right. They did filibuster, but that was the last session. Then there was no leader in the White House, then our nation was in that dull interlude which followed the dropping of the curtain on old policies, and preceded the inauguration of the new. But March 4th, Franklin D. Roosevelt took office. Filibustering became a mere memory —a legislature bound by party ties and driven by the manifestations of national will, followed him on every one of his measures. You are right that before March 4th, we lacked action; but today that need is satisfied.

What other fault remains with our present representative, institutional form of government? You present to us a rather queer, and a slightly far-fetched dilemma. Congress, you announce, can either talk or act, it cannot do both. Now, if it spends all of its time in discussion, then the necessary legislation will be impossible; but if it doesn't talk things over, if it acts so hastily as not to have carefully considered measures, it is useless. Let me point out to you that there exists a middle course which is not an impossibility. Congress may spend a moderate amount of time upon a measure, discuss it with moderate fullness, and then vote. Such is in fact the customary practice of representative government. That is a way by which discussion and action can be combined.

There are times when this theory, like every other one, does not work perfectly. It is neither wise nor logical to build a rule out of those exceptions. There is filibustering sometimes, but filibustering arouses comment only because of its infrequency.

There are also times of stress like the present one in which Congress—perceiving that an emergency exists—willingly curtails its right of discussion in order to expedite action. That temporary limitation of discussion is no proof that Congress is worthless. In more normal times freer discussion will be resumed. And, even drastic limitation of debate is far different from dissolution of Congress. Limitation of debate is not the same as permanent destruction of freedom of discussion. Very often, a Congressman can, by removing pompous phrases from his speech, say more in five minutes than he normally does in five hours.

Besides, Congress retains its vote. When the vote is affirmative it is a general declaration that Congressmen believe the measure sound, and believe that their constituents want it. Where the free exercise of such a right to vote exists, there is no arbitrary dictatorial power; representative government is neither abolished nor ineffective.

What then remains, of the Affirmative onslaught against Congress? Well, our friends announce their suspicion that Congressmen may be bribed, that persuasive, slick, unscrupulous lobbyists may bring pressure to bear upon them.

Now it may be that they are right. It may be that some Congressmen will yield to pressure. But this dictator of theirs—what vaccine will they use to inoculate him against bribery and corruption? None has ever yet been discovered. And it is easier for a group to influence one man than it is to control two hundred. All the organs of propaganda, all known instrumentalities for dominating an individual, will be focused on this one dictator. He may be a superman; but after all, there is no guarantee that he will be. A dictatorial glass-house is a poor place into which to toss stones. History does not record that most dictators have stood above all special, narrow interests, and devoted themselves to a furtherance of the general good. Rather, the opposite has generally been true.

Now that our friends have received action, now that their dilemma has been solved, and the great difficulties they feared disposed of, no reason remains for installing a dictator in the White House.

But many, many reasons still remain that make one reluctant to put a Cæsar, a Napoleon, a potential Hitler, or a Nero at the head of our government. All history unites to bid us hesitate. A dictator would possess absolute power, he would control the army, he would control the organs that formulate opinion—press, radio, and motion picture. He could dominate majorities; he could smash minorities; his rule would be limited only by his power to compel obedience, and that power would be great.

Now in that lack of limitation lurks the fatal danger of dictatorship. If the dictator were perfect all might be well. But, there is no guarantee of perfection. Demagogue and cheap politician backed by the propaganda of powerful special interests can win a grant of power, and once in office, forget all promises and brazenly suppress criticism, relentlessly persecute minorities, and rule with an iron hand.

History makes such dangers vivid. This nation rejected monarchy because our Constitution-makers had read history and knew its dangers. Why should we be deluded into the error they avoided? Let us too follow their advice; utilize the advantages inherent in our institutions; and cleave firmly to that we possess.

Before we rush blindly from the institutions that satisfy our needs, let us reflect on the admission which even Will Durant, arch-foe of democracy, is compelled to make:

"To be successful, a dictator must be both a genius and a gentleman, usually, he has been neither."

Negative Refutation, James Keller
New York University

LADIES AND GENTLEMEN: As concluding speaker of the Negative, I want to first remove a few of the minor misconceptions which stud the Affirmative case, and then deal directly with the fundamental issue of this debate.

The first of the misconceptions consists in the vague and slightly naïve statement that not until Roosevelt became dictator was Prohibition abolished. To attribute the abolition of Prohibtion to the benefits of dictatorship is to overlook the fact that Roosevelt is not, according to the definitions we presented and the Affirmative have agreed to, a dictator. If our friends, whenever they talk of dictatorial benefits, are pursuing logic as fantastical as this, then Heaven save us from a dictator.

The second misconception revolves about the Beer Bill now being discussed in the New York State Legislature. To listen to them discuss the temporary delay, in the passage of a State bill regulating the sale of beer, is almost to believe that none will ever be decided upon, that New York State will not have beer on April 7th, and that all of this is due to the breakdown of democracy.

Our friends may rest reassured, for if no State measure is passed on April 7th, there will be beer in New York State, because there will not exist any State law forbidding its sale, and there does exist a national authorization for such a sale after that date.

After all, temporary delay in the passage of this one Bill does not prove the failure of all democracy. It does not even prove that democracy is not functioning well in that one instance. For there is a choice to be made. There are different plans of State control advocated. One is best. It will take long discussion to determine which is best, and out of the conference rooms will come the knowledge that will make enlightened action possible—that will give the people of the State, the beer they want and give it to them before April 7th. Discussion, knowledge, action—such is the process of democratic government.

Let us then sum up the chief issue of debate. For the sake of clarity let us reduce the argument of the Affirmative to a syllogism that will reveal its flaws.

> Action is necessary.
> Only a dictator can give action.
> Therefore, a dictator must be chosen.

If they prove that syllogism, the debate is theirs. If, as the Affirmative team, they cannot maintain their burden of proof, if they cannot prove what they assert, their case collapses.

We admit their major premise. We admit the need for action.

But we challenge their minor premise, because we can have action even though we do not have a dictator.

Our answer is backed by events. While our friends talk of the impossibility of action, under a democratic government, Roosevelt is acting. His deeds disprove their words.

Can they dodge that fact? Well, they argue that Roosevelt will soon become impotent, that a so-called revolt over the Farm Bill is good evidence that soon Congress will cease to follow him.

Note, first of all, that the very argument—Roosevelt will soon stop doing things—implies that at present we are getting action. You cannot stop what has not begun.

Secondly, a temporary opportunity for Congress to have a long discussion of one bill is no proof that Roosevelt has lost all power, and that inertia is about to overwhelm all government. There was a definite reason for prolonging the discussion of the Farm Bill. Roosevelt wanted that discussion, as he frankly announced in the message by which he introduced it to Congress. He is not sure that it is a perfect way to solve the Farm Problem. It is the best way he does know of but discussion may bring new ideas and that is what is wanted. Information may lead to more intelligent action.

If no new information is forthcoming, if Congress does prove recalcitrant, Roosevelt can get results by using the radio to come right into the homes of millions of Americans, and persuade them to write to their Congressmen demanding action. Patronage, party leadership, personal popularity, and the force of necessity will make America follow him when the need for action grows imperative.

Democracy is as effective as dictatorship; it implies no destruction of individual rights, no sheeplike dependence upon the whim of one man. It is more safe.

The stress of necessity is proving its efficiency—why then desert it? Let us repudiate dictatorship and retain democracy.

Affirmative Refutation, Ellery B. Haskell
Colgate University

LADIES AND GENTLEMEN: The Affirmative and Negative have coöperated to make clear the distinction between dictatorship and democracy. The Negative has not pressed the point of absolute power since absolute power is not necessary, although some authorities do state that such a condition is a prerequisite for true dictatorship. However, we have merely to remind ourselves of constitutionally limited Roman dictatorships and of Hitler's limited power as a dictator. Hitler is limited since President von Hindenberg controls the army and can have Hitler arrested if he chooses. I mention these instances since both sides have agreed to call them dictators. On the other hand, the Affirmative recognizes that a dictatorship involves, if not absolute power, a very great deal of power, and has no wish to encroach on the field of modified democracy such as we have in the present crisis under Roosevelt.

The issues of this debate stand out clearly and have been squarely met by both teams. First, is an immediate action by the government necessary? This is admitted by the Negative. Second, is parliamentary democracy incapable of meeting the present crisis? The Affirmative says "yes"; the Negative, "no." Third, is dictatorship the best form of government for this crisis? The Affirmative says "yes"; the Negative, "no."

Let us turn our attention to the second issue, which is the crux of the debate. The Affirmative has pointed out the slowness and ineffectiveness of Congress. The Negative has rejoined by pointing out that the arguments of the Affirmative concerning the weaknesses of Congress refer to the Hoover administration and not to the speedy Roosevelt Congress. This is only partially true. Filibustering was carried on under the Hoover administration only, it is true. However, all the arguments about the parliamentary procedure of Congress, the ignorance of Congressmen, the mass of bills, and the conflict of interests, refer to this session. This special session has trouble over roll-calls, questions, amending of house rules, unseating of members, and limitations of debate. In the House the time for debate for the Economy Bill was four hours for over four hundred men. This means less than three-quarters of a minute per man. How many of you could utter much wise council on an important bill like the Economy Bill in three-quarters of a minute? As a matter of fact, many interests were unheard from and most representatives took up time by getting up and giving their reasons for supporting the President rather than dissecting the bill. This is the body which is supposed to help us out of our crisis. Here the Negative has attempted to answer the Affirmative's dilemma by choosing to make Congress speedy but also making it worthless as a deliberative body. They deny that the conclusion follows, since they try to stand for a middle course: medium speed and some discussion and usefulness. However, the present Congress actually is required by our crisis to operate so fast that it is useless, as I have pointed out. We cannot fix a speed for the efficiency of Congress, we have to fix a speed to meet the present situation, which speed is beyond the power of Congress. The strongest argument for the Negative at this point is the speedy action of Congress at present. Both sides want immediate action by the government. Congress has given it to us. Now the point at issue is, is Congress helpful or not? The Negative nods emphatically, declaring that Congress is passing Roosevelt's suggestions quickly. The Negative, incidentally, has admitted Roosevelt's abilities. We reply: "Precisely. Congress is approving Roosevelt's bills but to anyone who reads the *Congressional Digest*, it is obvious that there is no intelligent discussion of point after point, but rather speech after speech, arguing for or against support of the administration and its increasing power in this time of crisis." We wish to emphasize the fact that, although this is the strongest argument of the Negative—modified democracy and its present speed—it is a very weak procedure to render Congress as a deliberative body practically worthless and, in effect, to allow it to hold up to some extent the bills of Roosevelt which they are passing. We advocate the wiping out of this delay by temporary dismissal of a body useless in critical times. Our essential argument on this most important point is that whereas Congress acts swiftly now, it is of no use to us. The Negative has failed to answer our arguments on the uselessness of that body. In fact, the last speaker for the Negative has admitted that Congress, in order to aid Roosevelt, had to be allowed *time* for discussion. As for measuring public opinion, Roosevelt as dictator has the same sources as Congress: letters, newspapers, and so on. If we want speed, why not drive an Austin at breakneck speed along the highways? This procedure is as relevant and helpful to our present crisis as a speedy Congress.

Moreover, we may be assured that the conflict of interests in Congress will assert itself as more important bills come before it. A Senator has declared that the honeymoon of President Roosevelt has come to an end. The opposition of the veterans to such a necessary bill as the Economy Bill is but a precursor to what follows for more controversial and yet just as necessary legislation. Any attempts of President Roosevelt to deal with the farming situation and especially the industrial chaos, with the planned economy which he favors and which most economists consider necessary, will meet with storms of opposition from general business and farming opinion and the powerful lobbies. This means delay and delay. Instead of an Austin racing along the highways, we shall have a Mack truck with a governor on the engine and a load of backseat drivers. We of the Affirmative point to the slowness of Congress in the past, to the set-up tending toward interference in the immediate future, and to the uselessness of the present hog-tied democracy which amounts to a limping dictatorship. It is for these reasons that we advocate a strong government, a dictatorship to act swiftly and intelligently in the present crisis.

The Negative has been obliged to admit the swiftness of action of a dictatorship. As I have ponted out, it must necessarily admit that a swift-acting dictatorship can perform more intelligently than a swift-acting Congress. The chief criticism by the Negative of dictatorship seems to consist of asserting that it will rob the country of the privileges of democracy. Freedom of speech, press, and religion and so on, will be denied to us. They point to the persecuting of the Jews by Hitler in Germany. First of all, we say that the dictatorship we want is a temporary one, designed to meet the crisis, and hence there would be little point in destroying such benefits of democracy as the Gentlemen of the Opposition have named. Furthermore, the party system will be retained as it is in all modern governments, whether autocratic or democratic. Since our choice for dictator is Roosevelt, elected by a majority of the people, and of whom the Opposition approves, and the president is of the Democratic party, the ideals of the Democratic party will be the essential policy of the dictatorship. Contrary to the Negative, we have the support of political scientists and any dictator is limited in action by the support of the people and especially of his organized backing: his party. Stalin could not act to restore Capitalism nor Mussolini to establish Communism. The Democratic party stands for the democratic things we want preserved. There will be no persecution of Jews, for the Democratic party does not have that as a plank in its platform as does the Nazi party. Hitler does not act so because he is a dictator, but because he is the leader of the Nazi party. Roosevelt's essential policy will be dominated by democratic ideals in a great effort to lift us from our present chaos.

The attacks of the Opposition on personal characteristics of a dictator are unjustified. They have said that the record of dictators has not been good, on the whole. We note a lack of evidence. Time passes quickly, and I can simply reply that the dictators of ancient Rome had a splendid record, and dictators since then in France, England and South American countries have been noted for their success in promoting the national welfare. Also, a dictator would be less susceptible to pressure or bribes for he is not dependent for his job on special interests and all his actions are in the limelight and a matter of personal achievement, whereas those of a legislator are obscure and take place where responsibility is divided.

We of the Affirmative maintain the preferability of dictatorship as a form of government to democracy in this time of crisis on the grounds that immediate action by government is necessary; *second,* that parliamentary democracy is incapable of meeting the crisis since it will either act too slowly due to expression of a world of conflicting interests, or act so swiftly that as a deliberative body it will be unintelligent, parroting the demands of the administration, and useless; and *thirdly,* that a dictatorship acts swiftly, much more intelligently than a swift-acting Congress, and being dominated by party aims and the specific goal of getting out of the present crisis, will act for the benefit of the people.

Dictatorship having saved the people in a crisis, we can then go back to our more leisurely proceeding democracy which at a normal pace is apt to be more just and perhaps wiser. Dictatorship in a crisis and democracy in normal times will then be performing the true function of government—promoting the welfare of the people by whom it was fashioned.

BIBLIOGRAPHY: DEMOCRACY vs. DICTATORSHIP

BOOKS AND PAMPHLETS

Becker, Carl L.—*The United States; An Experiment in Democracy.* Harper, New York. 1920.
Bolitho, Wm.—*Italy Under Mussolini* Macmillan, New York. 1926.
Bonn, Moritz J.—*Crisis of European Democracy* Yale University Press, New Haven. 1925.
Bryce, James B.—*Modern Democracies.* Macmillan, New York. 1921.
Burns, Cecil D.—*Democracy, Its Defects and Advantages.* Macmillan, New York. 1929.
Cheyney, Edward P.—*Historical Tests of Democracy.* (In University of Pennsylvania lectures. 1918-19, p. 189-218)
Cram, Ralph A—*Limitations of Democracy.* Rice Institute. Pamphlet 17, No. 3, 175-199. July 1930.
Forst-Battaglia, Otto, ed.—*Dictatorship on Trial.* Harcourt, New York. 1931.
Herring, Edward P.—*Group Representation Before Congress* Johns Hopkins Press, Baltimore. 1929.
Hobson, John A.—*Democracy After the War.* Macmillan, New York. 1919.
Lippmann, Walter.—*Phantom Public.* Harcourt, New York. 1925.
MacIver, Robert M.—*Modern State.* Clarendon Press, Oxford. 1926.
Myers, Wm. S.—*Socialism and American Ideals.* Princeton University Press, Princeton. 1919.
Nitti, Francesco S.—*Bolshevism, Fascism and Democracy.* Allen, London. 1927.
Rowell, Chester H.—*Challenge to Democracy.* National Conference of Social Work 1927. 13-19.

460 THE YEAR BOOK OF COLLEGE DEBATING

Russell, Bertrand A. W.—*Bolshevism; Practice and Theory.* Harcourt, New York. 1920.
Sait, Edward M.—*Democracy.* Century Co., New York. 1929.
Salvemini, Gaetano.—*Fascist Dictatorship in Italy.* Holt, New York. 1927.
Sforza, Carlo, conte.—*European Dictatorships.* Brentano, New York. 1931.
Spargo, John.—*Bolshevism the Enemy of Political and Industrial Democracy.* Harper, New York. 1919.
Spencer, Henry R.—*Dictatorship versus Democracy in Europe.* (In Institute of Politics, Williamstown, Mass. Report, 1927, p. 28-48.)
Zimmern, Alfred E.—*Future of Democracy.* (In University of Buffalo Studies, v. 8, No. 2.) May 1930.

PERIODICALS

Academy of Political Science. *Proceedings.* 14:592-98, January 1932. *Democracy in the World Crisis.* A. C. Ritchie.
American Journal of Sociology. 24:704-14, May 1919. *Origin of Democracy.* J. L. Gillin.
——— 25:202-14, September 1919. *Ethical Bases of Democracy.* F. G. Henke.
——— 26:545-57, March 1921. *Some Ambiguities in Democracy.* H. L. Stewart.
American Mercury.—19:462-68, April 1930. *Collapse of Democracy.* R. A. Egger.
American Political Science Review.—21:537-51, August 1927. *European Dictatorships.* H. R. Spencer.
American Scholar.—2:187-99, March 1933. *Present-day Forces in European Politics.* W. B. Munro.
Atlantic Monthly.—124;616-27, November 1919. *Basic Problem of Democracy.* Walter Lippmann.
——— 133:456-67, April 1924. *Receding Tide of Democracy.* H. H. Powers
——— 137:825-33, June 1926. *Europe's Bursting Bubble of Democracy.* R. E. Sencourt. pseud.
Century.—103 (n.s. 81):957-60, April 1922. *Democracy at the Crossroads.* Glenn Frank.
——— 104 (n.s. 82):157-60, May 1922. *On Discontent with Democracy.* Glenn Frank.

―――― 112 (n.s. 90):203-12, June 1926. *Democracy's Flat Tire.* C. T. Crowell.

―――― 120 (n.s. 98):170-79, April 1930. *Challenge of Dictatorship.* Jerome Davis.

Commonweal.—17:449-50, February 22, 1933. *Democracy's Self-Dictatorship.*

Current History.—22:345-54, June 1925. *Dictatorship in Spain.* Alphonse Lugan.

―――― 26:175-86, May 1927. *Italy Under Mussolini.* H. G. Wells and T. Sillani.

―――― 26:708-13, August 1927. *Government by Dictators, a New Phase of European History.* Francesco Nitti.

―――― 28:81-84, April 1928. *Defense of Democracy.* V. F. Calverton.

―――― 28:175-204, May 1928. *Is Democracy a Failure?*

―――― 36:641-48, September 1932. *Does America Need a Dictator?* F. A. Ogg.

Current Opinion.—70:788-91, June 1921. *Lord Bryce on the Merits and Defects of Democracy.*

Foreign Affairs.—3:358-70, April 1925. *Italy and Fascism.* Carlo Sforza, Conte.

―――― 5:276-92, January 1927. *Dictatorship in Spain.* R. T. Desmond.

Fortnightly Review.—130:157-64, August 1928. *Democracy Has Not Failed.* W. E. Borah.

Forum.—67:415-21, May 1922. *Shall We Hold to Democracy?* W. G. Brown.

―――― 72:629-35, November 1924. *Despair of Democracy.* G. A. S. Kennedy.

―――― 75:481-95, April 1926. *Is Democracy Doomed?* Shaw Desmond and W. Y. Elliott.

―――― 79:562-73, April 1928. *Democracy's Dilemma.* O. W. Underwood.

―――― 81:34-42, January 1929; Supple. 47-50, February 1929. *Has Democracy Broken Down? With Replies by the Mayors of of America.* W. J. Durant.

Harper's Magazine.—153:555-65, October 1926. *Is Democracy a Failure?* W. J. Durant.

―――― 157:680-91, November 1928. *Democracy Holds Its Ground.* C. A. Beard.

—— 160:144-52, January 1930. *Whom Does Congress Represent?* C. A. Beard.

Independent.—103:338, September 18, 1920. *Strong Man Panacea.* Preston Slosson.

Literary Digest.—99:22, October 27, 1928. *Dictator Defends Dictatorship.*

Living Age.—303:697-700, December 20, 1919. *Danger of American Democracy.* S. Wasshio.

—— 322:15-16, July 5, 1924. *Mussolini on Democracy.* W. R. Inge.

—— 324:633-40, March 21, 1925. *Study in Dictatorship.* Fernand de Brinon.

—— 325:565-68, June 13, 1925. *Difficulties of Democracy.* Albert Apponyi.

—— 332:1060-64, June 15, 1927. *Can Democracy Survive?* J. M. Kenworthy and Chas. Petrie.

Nation.—136 220, March 1, 1933. *Do We Need a Dictator?*

New Republic.—51:36-39, June 1, 1927. *Evolution of the Russian Dictatorship.* H. N. Brailsford.

Nineteenth Century.—98:839-46, December 1925. *Crisis of Democracy.* Stuart Hodgson.

North American Review.—224:646-53, December 1927. *Too Much Democracy.* C H. Bretherton.

—— 226:171-77, August 1928. *Meaning of Democracy.* Reply to C. H. Bretherton, J. S. Dean.

—— 234:484-92, December 1932. *What a Real Dictator Would Do....* Fredericka Blankner.

Open Court.—41:381-84, June 1927. *Democracy and Dictatorship.* Arthur Spatz.

Outlook.—149:43-45, May 4, 1928. *Future of Democracy.* Carlo Sforza, Conte.

Quarterly Review.—235.157-74, January 1921. *Bolshevism and Democracy.* Wm. Ashley.

Review of Reviews.—73 89, January 1926. *Democracy and Its Alternatives.*

—— 73:288-98, March 1926. *Parliamentary Breakdown in Europe.* F. H. Simonds.

—— 82:68-71, September 1930. *Dictators or Democrats?* Roger Shaw.

Saturday Evening Post.—202:22, October 26, 1929. *Government by Propaganda.*
——— 205:3-5, September 24, 1932. *Is Democracy a Failure?* F. A. Vanderlip.
——— 205:20, October 8, 1932. *No Dictator.*
Scribner's Magazine.—83:419-29, April 1928. *Shall We Govern Ourselves?* A. C. Ritchie.
——— 87:500-06, May 1930. *Great Lobby Hunt* F. R Kent.
——— 89:465-76, May 1931. *Twilight of the Dictators.* George Seldes.
World Tomorrow.—16:11-13, January 4, 1933. *Which Dictator?* J. M. Murry.
World's Work.—50:57-62, May 1925. *Does Democracy Fit Most Peoples?* T. L. Stoddard.
——— 60·67-70, January 1931. *Why Dictators?* T. L. Stoddard.
Yale Review.—(n.s. 9):788-803, July 1920. *Democracy at the Crossroads* H. J. Laski.
——— (n.s. 16):1-16, October 1926. *Democracy or Dictatorship?* W. C. Abbott.

RADIO BROADCASTING

A Discussion of Values

RADIO BROADCASTING

OCCIDENTAL COLLEGE VS. THE UNIVERSITY OF ARIZONA

The growing significance of the radio in American life has led inevitably to a discussion of its uses and abuses, of its values and of its baneful influences, of its possibilities and of the forces that are thwarting its benefits. Is the best educational and cultural use being made of the radio—and if not, why not?

The debate which follows deals with some of these considerations. In fairness to the debaters of the two educational institutions it must be said that the debate included here was an extemporaneous debate rather than a studied effort, and was held without the usual period of preparation and research time allowed for the average college debate. The fact that all of the debaters involved were radio announcers or radio workers gives the discussion added interest for it gives opportunity for the expression of ideas gained from participating in the activity discussed.

The proposition was at first stated—"Resolved: That the radio announcer is a public menace." However, as two of the debaters were radio announcers and the other two connected with radio, by common consent the subject was phrased for the actual discussion—*Resolved: That radio, as now operated, is a cultural and intellectual liability.*

The debate was held at Occidental College toward the end of the college year in May 1933, and was afterward written up—the two sides exchanging speeches to produce the present manuscript. To Professor Charles Frederick Lindsley of Occidental College and Professor W. Arthur Cable of the University of Arizona, Directors of Debating at their respective institutions, goes the credit for assembling and contributing the speeches.

First Affirmative, Donald A. Fareed
Occidental College

LADIES AND GENTLEMEN: It is recounted of George Whitefield, the great evangelist speaker, that upon one occasion Benjamin Franklin, a great admirer of Whitefield's voice and style of oratory, paced off a distance beyond which Whitefield's great voice could not be distinguished and drawing an imaginary circle with that distance as its radius, made this statement: "Within this circle are the limits of democracy by the spoken voice." Radio has made the thought, embodied in that phrase, an obsolete curiosity. Today Mussolini's dynamic voice can be heard from Rome to Los Angeles; the spiritual admonitions of the Catholic Pope in the Vatican can be felt and heard by penitent Catholics in Alaska; and Franklin D. Roosevelt has explained why he has closed the banks and inflated the currency to millions of confused Americans. Radio has transformed the world from a barrier of continents to one great amphitheatre wherein all may listen and enjoy. This has all transpired within the last two decades.

Consider the stupendous growth of this infant institution we call radio. From a few scattered transmitters, there has evolved in this country alone over six hundred licensed radio stations, broadcasting from morning until midnight, to an audience of over fifty million people. Let us survey the growth in actual business gains in radio. In 1920 the American people spent only two million dollars. In 1921, with the increased power and range of the vacuum tube, sales increased to six million dollars. The retail sales for 1923 again doubled those of 1922 and attained the astonishing total of one hundred twenty million dollars. Thus did the industry increase by leaps and bounds. By 1928 radio trade realized a retail income estimated at six hundred fifty million dollars. The close of one decade revealed a net revenue of almost four billion dollars. Such has been the growth of radio. Today it is potentially one of the greatest media for cultural and intellectual benefit ever devised by man.

Thus our debate revolves about a pertinent, vital, and epoch-making instrumentality. The question for discussion, as originally stated, was—"Resolved: That the Radio Announcer Is a Public Menace." This statement of proposition we of the Affirmative have interpreted to mean the following: by "radio announcer" is merely signified or symbolized the operation of the radio industry itself, and we shall restrict "public menace," for purposes of argument, to mean a cultural and intellectual liability. Thus, the issue becomes sharply drawn as we discover an intelligible restatement of the question to which our friends of the opposition will doubtless agree—"Resolved: That Radio, as Now Operated, Is a Cultural and Intellectual Liability."

At the outset of the debate it must be noted also that we of the Affirmative are not immediately interested in whether or not radio, as now operated, is a paying business asset to producers. That is waived material. We are not arguing the financial or commercial merits of radio. Our clash of opinion, as set forth in the introduction, revolves about the question as to whether or not radio, as now operated, is a cultural and intellectual liability.

In support of our case, we of the Affirmative advance two main contentions. The first, which it is my purpose to establish, is that radio is dominated by a selfish profit motive and its facilities are ruthlessly commercialized by private industry. The second, which my colleague, Mr. Boardman, will prove is that the general type of radio entertainment is on the whole culturally and intellectually worthless.

I have just cited for you indicative figures which reveal the astonishing growth of the radio industry within the last decade. It is needless to emphasize for, indeed, it is patent that radio is today one of the greatest media *potentially* for the spread of culture and dissemination of knowledge that we have. Why have I said potentially? The answer is discovered first of all in the fact that only one-sixteenth of available radio frequencies is used by educational interests. The great bulk of air frequencies serves the private interests of some commercial concern or business.

This brings us to our first and perhaps basic contention—Radio, as now operated, is dominated by a selfish profit motive and its facilities are ruthlessly commercialized by private industry. Joy Elmer Morgan, Chairman of the National Committee on Education by Radio, has caught the spirit of this argument as he voices protest in the following significant words: "There has not been in the entire history of the United States an example of mismanagement and lack of vision so colossal and far-reaching in its consequences as our turning of the radio channels almost exclusively into commercial hands." Think of it! In California alone, out of thirty-nine licensed radio broadcasting stations, fully thirty-four are owned and operated by private corporations and business men as, for example, KFI by Earle C. Anthony, KHJ by Don Lee, KFWB by Warner Bros., KMPC by MacMillan Petroleum, and so down the line. The five remaining California stations are religious outlets, leaving *not one station* in the state of California available completely for education. Now it logically follows that the businesses owning these radio channels are concerned above all else with the exploitation of those rights for their private benefit. In other words, the basic underlying motive in radio today is not how a station's programs will affect the intellectual and cultural tone of the radio audience, but what kinds of programs will hold the largest audience so that a business may market its product. The underlying motive is the desire for *private profit*.

This argument might well be fortified by using as analogy the case of the motion-picture industry. Of course the basic similarity between radio and moving pictures is that both are superb potential media for educational instruction, political propaganda, and the dissemination of culture. Yet the same thing has happened in the motion picture industry that is occurring in radio, namely, its facilities are manipulated by private, commercial owners to extract the highest possible profit. In the motion picture industry this means producing entertainment that will pander to the lusts, passions, likes and propensities of the man in the street. It means producing anything that will translate itself into fat, huge box-office receipts. In radio this has come to mean the presentation of a general type of entertainment that will appeal to the great mass of the people and sell the producer's soap, toothpaste, refrigerator, or pills. In both, the vast educational and cultural possibilities of the instrumentality are utterly lost sight of in the mad scramble for profits through organized commercialization.

We may argue still further by analogy. Whenever important national resources have been turned over to private interests, they have been *exploited* for private profit and not for public welfare. Consider cases in business history of waterways, oil fields, forests, and so on. Radio today with its tremendous influence on the millions of people who listen to it each day, has assumed the proportions of a great national resource, a potent, mighty instrumentality. Both England and Germany as well as other lesser European nations have recognized this fact. The result has been that in both countries, radio has lent itself to the dissemination of political propaganda, to the crystallization of an organized national political policy, to the broadcasting of good music, and so on. However, we of the Affirmative are not arguing for state control. All we contend is that as long as radio is subjected to operation and control by business interests, there will be that incurable, natural, yet sometimes shortsighted *profit motive;* and as long as there exists the profit motive, the desire for profit gains, there can be no true forward progress in the use of radio for education and culture of the people.

An editorial appeared in the *Christian Science Monitor*, February 28, 1931. Among other things the writer declared: "Radio channels have often been likened to the highways of the air. Today, in America, like the motor highways, the ether routes are filled with advertising billboards, spoiling the musical scenery which is their normal charm. Seated at the dial of a radio set, the seeker of beauty finds himself in a position analogous to the driver of a motor car. A splendid road is found. It is called 'Hungarian Rhapsody' by Liszt. Suddenly a vocal billboard breaks in upon the satisfying mental picture the rhapsody has brought and announces that unless you eat 'Piff's Particular Pickles' you have known only a dismal world. If you haven't tried Piff's Pickles, you ought to stop listening and hurry down to the nearest grocer—" After reading such a comment we see a justification for the indignant outburst of the very man who was in great part responsible for the growth of radio—DeForrest, inventor and perfector of the radio tube. He says in an irate outburst: "Why should anyone want to buy a radio or new tubes for an old set when nine-tenths of what one can hear is the continual drivel of second-rate jazz, sickening crooning by degenerate sax players, interrupted by blatant sales talk, meaningless but maddening station announcements, impudent demands to buy or try, actually imposed over a background of what might alone have been good music? Get out into the sticks, away from your fine symphony orchestra pickups, and listen to what eighty per cent of American listeners have to endure twenty-four hours a day. Then you'll learn what is wrong with the radio industry. It isn't hard times. It is *Broadcaster's Greed*, which is worse."

To recapitulate, we have demonstrated by definite statistics and by analogy that underlying all radio, as now operated, is the *desire for profit*, that upon the altar of the profit motive is being prostituted the cultural and intellectual potentialities of radio. My colleague will further establish the case for the Affirmative by concrete demonstration of the effect of this commercial spirit in the general character of the programs, proving to you that they are culturally and intellectually *not an asset but a liability*.

First Negative, William S. Dunipace
University of Arizona

LADIES AND GENTLEMEN: We of the Negative are more than glad to be participating in a debate with the representatives of Occidental College and wish to offer our sincere appreciation for the welcome which we have received here today. The nature of an extemporaneous debate makes it rather impossible to anticipate all the various angles of the question which are likely to be discussed by the opposing team. However, my colleague, Mr. Taylor, and I had surmised that in the question, "Resolved: That the Radio Announcer Is a Public Menace," our opponents would be forced to discuss the whole radio industry under the heading of "The Radio Announcer." Judging from their first speech, this surmise was correct; that in indicting the radio announcer they have meant to include the entire field of radio. So far, their main contention seems to be that the radio, as an influence in American life, is more of a detriment than a good.

It so happens that the members of the Arizona team are more than casually interested in this question. My colleague, Mr. Taylor, has had some professional experience as a radio announcer, and I have spent some time making a survey of radio advertising for the Percival White Company of New York City. It is our conclusion that radio, both as a contribution to culture and a stimulus to industry, has made a distinct contribution to American life.

Of course, the members of the audience are quite familiar with the book which my colleague and I have here on the platform. *The World Almanac* for 1933 has proved to be a lifesaver for statistical proof in many debates which we have had this winter, and no doubt our opponents will quote from this same book before the conclusion of this debate.

It will be my purpose, as the first speaker on the Negative, to present a few figures from this book showing the importance of radio in the United States. According to information submitted by the Federal Radio Commission in 1931, radio has become one of the foremost industries in the country. There were 558 stations with a total investment of $36,900,000. Considering the radio question from the chain station standpoint, the National Broadcasting Company had an investment of $6,200,000 in its stations. Columbia, with $4,500,-

000, was a close second. Other chain stations smaller in size raised the grand total to $11,000,000.

According to the 1930 census, there were 12,000,000 families in the United States owning radios. That amounted to 40.3 per cent of all the families in the United States. Totaling the members of such families, the estimated number of listeners was 50,000,000 people. Thus, from two angles we see that radios must wield an important influence, both from the amount of money invested and the number of stations, and from the number of radios in actual use. It is only fair to suggest that, in view of the decline of prices since 1930, many more families have been able to invest in a radio since that time, and thus make themselves a part of the large group of people so served.

How has radio made itself important culturally? Only twelve years ago radio as an agency for the presentation of such cultural programs as are now common on the air, was in its infancy. The speaker can well remember the reverent hush of the small group clustered about an old earphone set on the occasion of President Harding's inauguration in 1921. School teachers dismissed students from classes so that they might listen to far-away Washington and learn in a most practical manner the significance and importance of a President's inauguration. At that time there were only a few large stations in the country. KDKA, Pittsburgh, which had a habit of fading and fluttering in its transmission, was the goal of all amateur radio enthusiasts. Since that time the policy of other stations has been much the same as that which KDKA inaugurated during its first broadcasts. Listeners were asked to send in their comments and requests for the type of programs they most enjoyed, and as a result of that policy radio became more and more popular through the intervening twelve years, until at the present time the annual expenditures for talent, programs, and other incidental expenses attendant thereto, amounted in one year (1931) to $78,000,000. Considering the fact that only twelve short years ago there was no market at all, so to speak, for this talent and for those connected with the various programs, we are safe in concluding that radio has created for art a new market worth $78,000,000 each year. Of course, to the aesthetic mind anything so gross as money in connection with art is not to be thought of. Nevertheless, doesn't it seem that since every man must live, radio must be responsible for giving those who wish an artistic chance an opportunity to develop their talents? Our opponents will probably tell you in the course of this debate that radio programs are an atrocious type of pseudo art and that as such they should not be called a true contribution to higher thought and musical expression. They will probably insist that since radio is a commercial proposition and since advertisers must be found to sponsor such programs as are given, such programs are not, as a whole, truly artistic but merely cater to the desires of the sponsors' advertising managers. My colleague will show in his speech that such restrictions as are placed on programs by their sponsors have been dictated by the request of their listeners and not by the unlearned and egotistical desires of some advertising manager.

It will be the duty of our friends from Occidental to show that radio is a definite menace to the cultural, to the intellectual, and to the commercial life of this country, and they must present such facts as are necessary to discredit the part that radio has had in stimulating artistic efforts, as well as the large amount of new business which radio has created for all types of industry connected with it. They must refute the Negative contention that the large majority of this business has actually been created. They must show that the other advertising mediums have suffered in proportion to the amount that radio has gained. They must do this by quoting the number of advertising lines in prominent publications throughout the country before radio entered the field and comparing those figures with those of the present day, making due allowance for the present economic situation. They must show, too, that the type of talent now being presented on the air would have had an equally advantageous market had radio never existed in its present form. They must disprove the fine work now being done by such institutions as our various Universities throughout the country which now offer courses of instruction by way of the radio loudspeaker, and which present daily high-class programs of splendid variety and merit. They must disprove the statement of a certain well known research worker in a speech who said that, due to the radio, the speech provincialisms of various remote sections of the country have largely been eliminated.

It is doubtless known to our Affirmative friends and the members of this audience that men and women who aspire to announcers' jobs with the large chain systems must undergo a course in speech training in order that they may better present the part of the program for which they are responsible. This in itself seems to have had a definite effect upon the problem which we have just been discussing. Does it not seem reasonable that if our friends who oppose radio must ridicule radio as a means of improving the cultural background of its listeners, then they must submit, from those plans already proved effective, one that has a better and more far-reaching means of achieving the same ends, and must support its asserted superiority by factual information? In order that clear-cut comparisons may be made, we request such information.

Second Affirmative, True Boardman
Occidental College

LADIES AND GENTLEMEN: The gentleman from Arizona has intimated that he and his colleague are entitled to speak with added authority on the subject of this debate since he, himself, is a radio announcer, and his colleague has worked in the commercial department of an Arizona Broadcasting station. Under such circumstances it might appear that in contending that the radio announcer is a public menace we were in effect launching a personal attack on at least one of our opponents. To eradicate any such an impression, I must make a confession—make it on behalf not only of myself but also for my handsome and distinguished young colleague, Mr. Don Fareed. Ladies and Gentlemen, despite the frank open countenance of the first speaker for the Affirmative, he is in reality leading a double life—for not alone is he a student here at Occidental but he is likewise a radio announcer outside of school hours. And as for myself, if it were not for a very small portion of the large amount mentioned by the first speaker of the Negative as the radio payroll for last year, I know of one student who would probably have been unable to pay his tuition for this college year. So not only the gentlemen of the Negative, but also those of the Affirmative have found in radio their means of livelihood. Therefore, if affiliation is a test of authority, we are all on common ground.

Speaking quite seriously, I should like very briefly to consider at the outset the argument of the first speaker of the Negative in regard to the economic value of radio. Thousands, millions of dollars, he has told us are invested in radio; it is a source of employment for a considerable group of our citizens. True—indisputably true. And the argument would be completely valid in this debate if we of the Affirmative were proposing the abolishment of radio altogether. It seems to me, however, that my colleague showed that our intention was rather to point out the evils existent in the present use of the air and the need for reform. We contend that the caliber of the average radio program can be improved both culturally and intellectually without necessarily having an adverse financial effect on radio in general.

My colleague has discussed the rabid commercialism of the radio of the present day. It is my purpose to show further the effect this commercial emphasis is having on society—in other words, that radio as now organized and operated is a cultural liability.

Before considering the deleterious effects produced by the radio on any especial class or group, suppose we look to the general way in which it harms all society. Unquestionably under this heading we may place fake ballyhoo advertising. Night after night, hour after hour, the "tuner-in" is bombarded by sales talk after sales talk in behalf of quack patent medicines, "bunko" oil schemes, and a long and varied assortment of gold bricks. And since the breadth of the radio selling field and the possibility of lucrative returns have lured many of the most efficient salesmen into the ranks of the radio "pluggers," many an individual who started by wasting a half hour listening to the Tin Panners Royal Andulasian Orchestra ends by buying a hundred shares in the Kreuger match works or a half interest in the company which holds the exclusive franchise to construct submarines for the Bolivian navy.

The harm of such advertising, however, is more economic than cultural. While it is a fault, it does not represent that the greatest fault of which the radio of today must stand indicted. The danger is not so much to our pocket book as to our intellect. Further, cheap advertising counts its chief victims among adults, but those really harmed the most from the cultural viewpoint are children. The grown man or woman is not apt to be influenced greatly by a radio program. Habits of thought, artistic tastes, and general philosophies of life are already settled. Certainly poor grammar and cheap jazz music does not elevate the adult mind. In many cases it may lower it. But the harm to Mr. and Mrs. American Citizen of Today is negligible by comparison with the harm to Mr. and Mrs. American Citizen of Tomorrow. Psychology has proved within recent years that by the time the child attains his sixteenth year, his speech patterns, his tastes in the arts and the general tenor of his emotional reactions are well established. The development of character is largely (completely, say the behaviorists) dependent upon the contacts made during the formative years. And in these days the radio is an almost omnipresent contact for the greater proportion of the younger generation. Yet that same omnipresent radio brings stimuli that are anything but healthful for the juvenile mind. To a considerable—a very considerable—proportion of programs being sent over the ether objection may be made on at least one of the following grounds:

1. They are conducive to the use of poor grammar.
2. They instruct in details of crime.
3. They are over-stimulating and emotionally unbalancing.
4. They tend to create vulgar tastes (in music, drama, and so on).

In the light of these categories consider the daily log sheet of radio fare. There are far too few which may be granted a clean bill of health when we consider the above faults as diseases. Particularly offensive are many of the crime and horror serials. In this latter regard the Washington *Evening Star* has expressed an editorial opinion to the effect that:

"Parental complaint is heard against a surfeit of blood and thunder in commercial radio programs designed especially to intrigue juvenile interest. Parent-teacher associations are discussing the effects of that sort of mental diet on child minds. An adult revolt seems brewing.

"It is alleged that at the twilight hour, when eight-year-old Jimmy tunes in, the serenity of the home is assailed by the raucous growls of desperate hoodlums, shrill screams of terrified victims, rattle of gunfire, and groans of the dying. In an atmosphere shivery with stealthy plotting and sanguinary with violent deeds, the temperature of Jimmy's imagination rises to fever heat. Later he kicks off the bedclothes and rouses his slumbering parents with yells of nightmare panic. In the days when crime is a social problem of the first magnitude, feeding crime thrills as leisure time enjoyment to infant minds is surely to be deprecated, and good homes are justified in resenting an invasion of the undesirable, so easily made and so difficult to prevent."

Even so called children's programs are not exempt from criticism. In fact the Minneapolis College Women's Club went so far as to issue a formal protest against two of these "kid" programs on the grounds that they encouraged the use of poor grammar, were cheap, artificial, melodramatically sensational, and generally undesirable for children.

As for the development in children of a taste for good music, it seems self-evident that the great preponderance of cheap jazz which issues forth from the majority of stations can only be said to be directly counter to the music appreciation study of our public schools.

All these things considered—and especially as far as children are concerned—we of the Affirmative contend that the radio today is a cultural and intellectual liability.

It is inevitable that the gentlemen of the Negative should laud the virtues of radio, should point out the fact that there are programs on the air of real merit and which are a genuine source not only of entertainment but also in certain cases, of instruction to the listening public. In reply to that argument, we ask our opponents to look again at the log of programs for the day—any day. What proportion of the broadcast time is devoted to really worth-while features and what proportion—considering stations large and small, urban and rural—is consumed by cheap commercialized programs of the sort to which we have made objection.

The fault is a fault of emphasis, say Mr. Fareed and myself. Rather it should be constantly held in mind that the radio is a public utility rather than a field of exploitation. Regulation of the air to prevent these evils we have pointed out should be progressively stronger, and the emphasis should be placed to an increasingly greater extent on the value of radio as a public servant. True, it may be argued that it is not the purpose of the radio to serve as a sort of free school to the public (I say "it may be argued" because that question in itself is worthy of lengthy debate), but certainly the radio has no right to work in diametric opposition to the interests of education.

In conclusion, then, there is unbounded hope for radio. In saying that the radio announcer of today is a public menace, we do not mean that he is inherently so. It is only that his aims have been perverted; he has sold out, or, let us hope, leased his patrimony for a handful of silver. Our nation, criticized before for the wasting of her natural resources, has been no more wary in her use of the one most newly utilized—the air. But the waste is by no means inevitable. Radio can become the most useful of public utilities. It may well be the means of completely altering human relations. The chief requirement in order to bring about such a consummation is a change of attitude as to the fundamental purpose of radio. When such a change occurs, the radio announcer will no longer be a public menace, but the symbol of public benefaction.

Second Negative, Leslie Taylor
University of Arizona

LADIES AND GENTLEMEN: It is with extreme regret to me that we approach the close of this most interesting verbal tilt with our opponents and friends, Mr. Fareed and Mr. Boardman.

The question, according to the interpretation placed upon it both by my colleague and opponents, would read something like this if printed—Resolved: That the Present Radio Industry is a Cultural and Intellectual Menace to the American People. Now, before I proceed any further, I should like to make one or two statements with regard to the Affirmative stand on this question. My most worthy opponents have taken a burden of tremendous responsibility upon their shoulders in interpreting this question as they have. How is it possible for them to define culture as it exists in the United States? Culture can only be defined through comparisons. You people of California undoubtedly think that Arizonans are tremendously uncultured, from your standpoint. Similarly, we Arizonans would think the backwoodsmen of Arkansas uncultured. To reverse the order, the people of Boston would frown with distaste upon the synthetic culture of California. In other words, I am trying to say that it is an impossibility to set up a universal standard for or to define culture in terms of radio programs.

Throughout the entirety of this debate both Mr. Boardman and Mr. Fareed have seen fit to attack that sort of radio program which appeals to the largest number of its patrons. Now, it is all very well to talk about the radio being a danger to the American public, but we must also bear in mind that the sort of program which is most popular with the radio listeners is the kind of program that is going to be broadcast most frequently. Remember the policy developed by radio in its infancy —that of asking its public to indicate the kinds of programs it liked best, and of featuring that kind of programs. The policy is still followed. The point we are trying to make is this: if a large portion of the American radio public do not desire Beethoven's *Unfinished Symphony* or a dissertation on the Gobi Desert, they are not going to listen to that type of program and we cannot force it down their throats, so to speak. And to say that such a program is a cultural menace is a gross mis-statement. According to Webster, "Culture is the characteristic attainments of a group of people." The American people have shown by their popular acclaim that modern radio entertainment programs are the characteristic attainments of the radio which they desire, therefore such programs are indicative of American culture and not harmful or menacing to the American public mind at present.

The Affirmative arguments were summed up by Mr. Boardman in four points. Radio programs are a menace: first, because they are conducive to the use of poor grammar; second, because they instruct in the details of crime; third, because they are over-stimulating and unbalancing; and fourth, because they tend to create vulgar tastes in music, drama, etc. Now I, like Mr. Boardman, ask you to pick up a radio log-sheet of any popular radio station. In it you will find listed every variety of program—programs which appeal to all types of minds—and very few of them, I am sure, you will find appearing in any of these four categories which he gives. How Mr. Boardman can stand on this platform and say that he is a radio announcer and, in the same breath, assert that radio programs are conducive to poor grammar is astounding to me. If Mr. Boardman has, as I presume he has, ever seen or passed a radio-announcer's examination, he will readily agree with me that a prospective announcer who uses poor grammar has little or no chance of ever realizing his ambition.

And how such programs as "The Life of Little Orphan Annie," "Skippy," or "High Lights of History" can instruct in crime or be detrimental to the American public, remains another mystery. The radio provides and is utilized as an excellent medium for education against crime. Would our opponents have us believe that an address by a government official against crime instructs in the details of crime? Are not the talks and stories of Captain Don Wilkie very good object lessons in the time-worn adage that "Crime does *not* pay?" It is quite evident that our opponents were thinking of the "Life of the Borgias" or "Murder in the Rue Morgue" or some other *cultural* classic when they made this statement.

The third count, that radio programs are over-stimulating or emotionally unbalancing, is rather weak, inasmuch as such a remark might be applied even to those programs which our opponents uphold so valiantly as being cultural. Good music or a good play which grips one is emotionally stimulating, but it is also cultural.

The fourth count, that the modern radio program in the United States tends to create vulgar tastes in music and drama, has already been answered. As we stated before, those programs and only those programs which meet the test of popular approval are given to the radio public; and if these are characteristic of American attainments, then they represent the culture of the American people and are not detrimental.

Mr. Fareed says that radio, as now operated, is dominated by a selfish desire for profit and that the facilities of radio are ruthlessly commercialized by private business. But, if this be true does it indict radio as a public menace? Does not the menace, if there is any, lie rather in the type of hands into which some of the radio stations have fallen? Clearly, the indictment is misplaced; it should be charged, if at all, against the manipulators of the agency, not against the agency itself.

But, may I ask you, what is wrong with the desire for profit on the part of an investor in a radio station? Men who invest money in private schools of all types, in medical clinics and private hospitals, in banks and stores and shops and factories, in railroads and steamships and transportation airplanes, all look for a fair degree of profit from their investments. It is a custom in our economic society that men and women must support themselves financially; those with money try to do it by investing that money wisely. The schools, the clinics and hospitals, the banks, stores, shops and factories, the transportation lines render much service to society and thereby do a great deal of good. But they also should make money for their owners and those who have invested in them, and the world regards this as a legitimate and laudable return. Isn't it a bit ridiculous to contend that an investor in a radio broadcasting station, that newest wonder of this amazing world, in which incredible miracles are performed before our astounded ears every minute of the day round and round this planet—isn't it ridiculous, I say, that he cannot look for a reasonable profit without contumely being heaped upon him? And if the owners of broadcasting stations are justly entitled to a fair degree of profit from their investments, one-half of the case advanced by our opponents falls, for you will remember that half of their entire case was dependent upon the charge of a profit motive.

And now may we notice this question of an alleged cultural and educational menace. What constitutes a menace, anyway? I wish our opponents had told us that. Does the radio industry threaten to inflict a calamity upon America? Is an impending calamity imminent, because some radio programs are not all that we wish they were? I do not know whether our Occidental friends mean to decry all entertainment programs, or only a portion of them; but it is being said by the men on the street and by the man in the office and shop that entertainment is a necessity, while culture is a luxury. Those who devote their working time to radio say that less than ten per cent of the vast radio audience of America is cultured. And yet roughly one-third of all the radio broadcasting done in the United States is of a cultural or educational nature, says the Federal Radio Commission. Isn't that a dangerous ratio for the Affirmative to consider: one-third of the broadcasting designed for less than ten per cent of the radio public? Where is the menace in these figures? And when we remember that, by tuning from one station to another, a person can go straight through the entire day and can continue day after day, with nothing but a cultural or an educational program—that it becomes a matter of choice with the radio public—the imminence of a national calamity fades materially.

However, there are added considerations bearing on this matter. Of the sixty-three and two-thirds per cent of broadcasts in this country which are classified as commercial, much of them are really of a cultural or an educational nature. Home economics programs are classified as commercial, but they are really cultural or educational, are they not? So are the majority of programs concerning topics of personal hygiene, as the care of the eyes, and so on. Also, the commercial time decreases greatly from these estimates because the announcer takes a couple of minutes to advertise the goods of the sponsor of the program, and then for the remainder of the fifteen-minute or half hour period the program comes uninterruptedly over the air, much of the time high-class, artistic, and cultural—Seth Parker programs, the Sherlock Holmes detective stories, the Shell Symphony programs, the Standard Symphony hour, and multitudes of others.

Mr. Fareed also says that the present status of radio in California "leaves not one station in the state available completely for education"—I think those were his words. May we remind him that a station need not broadcast programs of a cultural or educational nature all the time in order to be an asset to society. Bear in mind the ratios I have just given you, in which the cultural and high-class bears up favorably and then add to them the five stations—one-twelfth of the total California stations—which, according to their own admission, are maintained for religious broadcasts. I suppose our opponents will agree with us, as you will agree with us, that religion contributes definitely to culture. That fact is so universally recognized that further attention to it seems unnecessary. It is apparent that Mr. Fareed used only theoretical and deductive inference in arriving at his conclusion that, since most of the broadcasting stations were owned by business firms, the broadcasts from them were culturally and intellectually menacing.

These facts place the question of an alleged menace before us in a very different light. In fact, considering the free will which is left to each of us in making choice and the large amount of high-class subject-matter which constantly goes out over the air, the menace fades into unreality—just a nightmare caused by an unwise diet such as our Affirmative friends have been handing us—and the other half of the Affirmative case falls. Therefore, we can only conclude—and are happy to do so—that radio is not a public menace.

There are one or two additional points with which I should like to bring my speech to a close. While the Affirmative members have been most vociferous in their denunciations of the radio as it exists today, they have not given us any explanation whatever as to how they would better these alleged conditions. If they were to revise our radio programs today, in what manner would they do this? Until they have given us a definite plan, they have not established their case. And furthermore, the Affirmative have made no direct statement as to what culture is, or what they would class as a cultural program. Until they do, they have not established any basis upon which to defend or support their contention that radio is a cultural menace to the United States.

We of the Negative have admitted that the radio in the United States is largely a commercial enterprise. We will agree, also, that, like literature, drama, art, and music, there are some programs that are objectionable and perhaps even harmful. But this is not true of the average radio program, and our opponents must take the position that such a condition *is* true of the average program, and they must offer support enough to establish that contention. This they have failed to do, and it is now too late for them to offer such proof, as they have completed all but the closing rebuttal speech, in which no new material is permissible because the Negative would have no opportunity to answer it.

Thus, contrasting Affirmative with Negative arguments, we can only conclude that radio is *not* a public menace.

Negative Rebuttal, William S. Dunipace
University of Arizona

LADIES AND GENTLEMEN: Due to the shortness of time and the desire of most of you, including the speakers, to appease the animal man with a little lunch, we are reminded that much the same urges are governing the real forces in this debate.

Perhaps, as we have discussed this question here this morning concerning the cultural values of the radio, you too, were reminded of those Shakespearian characters, Ariel and Calaban; Ariel always cultural and Calaban just a poor radio advertising sponsor trying to reach the public ear.

Although their speeches have been instructional, our opponents have presented nothing vitally new or unacknowledged by the Negative, and by refusing to state a definite plan, our Occidental friends have definitely embraced the policy of Ariel, which was to prod poor Calaban to distraction but to offer him very little real assistance. It is true enough that our Universities and Colleges should have the national culture well in hand, but, on the other hand, few of them have established radio stations. And if they did, just where would cultural Ariel find the wherewithal to dispense his fine music and educational programs? Did some one mention college budgets? And why has Occidental, this seat of culture from which we speak, no radio station?

If our opponents adopted the taxation policy of England, they would immediately create another barrier against Chaste Culture by the fact that the tax on each radio set would materially lessen the number of people who would be able to avail themselves of such an entertainment luxury. Seventy-six million dollars is a large tax to levy on radio sets each year.

Too, by far the greater number of the people in the country are not educated to culture. By a national survey, taken by the Percival White Company of New York, it was found that the number of people who listen to educative and purely cultural programs is small, which upon reflection, probably would not be considered as news by any member of the audience this morning. The Negative will even be so bold as to suggest that if this audience of college students were given the opportunity at their own firesides, of choosing between a symphony concert and a famous crooner and his band, there would not be an appreciable percentage who would listen to the former. Would it not be fair, therefore, for the Negative to ask if a small group of culturally-minded should have the privilege of dictating to the entertainment tastes of a democratic nation? Isn't radio, a national utility as the Affirmative has said, for the entertainment of all radio set owners instead of a few? And too, as has already been said, hasn't the set owner the privilege of listening or not listening, as he may choose?

In other words, the Negative believes the Affirmative has attempted to blame a public utility for the failure of the Great American Public to have artistic and cultural tastes. It does not seem to us that it is any more the radio's place to educate the public than it is for current literature, the movies, or our system of public education to do so. And if the latter has failed to make the public culture-conscious, why blame radio, which must depend upon commercial support while the schools are supported by public taxation?

The gentlemen of the Affirmative have endeavored to limit the issues of this debate to the cultural and intellectual contributions of the radio industry in this country. But may I remind you that, to the degree to which radio has contributed to industrial advancement in America, just so far that enterprise is proved to be not a menace but a boon to us. And an industry of the magnitude of seventy-eight million dollars a year and upwards, furnishing employment to thousands of people in these grave times of unemployment—to manufacturers, transportation companies, jobbers, retailers, business men, promoters, technicians, and artists of widely different types—who can deny that such an industry is an asset to us economically?

The Affirmative have failed to prove that it is radio's duty to cease being a Calaban to Culture; that radio can do more good in the limited field to which the Affirmative's stand would limit it, than it does now as a commercial proposition. (And their opportunity to submit such proof has passed, as they have but one speech yet to make and we cannot reply to it.) We regret as much as they that it is necessary for commercial advertisers to sponsor our radio entertainment, but we believe the future is bright instead of dark, for we are sure that with such earnest and convincing exponents as our friends of the Affirmative to carry the Torch of Culture into the unappreciative hinterlands, the public's demands to the vulgar radio advertisers will, in the not far distant future, be for educative talks, chamber music, and symphonic concerts without number. Then not even our opponents will be able to say that The Radio Announcer is a Public Menace.

Affirmative Rebuttal, Donald A. Fareed
Occidental College

LADIES AND GENTLEMEN: After our constructive arguments are completed, the last gentleman of the Negative tells us that we must submit a constructive substitute plan, reminding us with glee that we cannot introduce constructive material into the rebuttal speech. That is very much like the case of a drowning man calling frantically for help (being unable to swim) and receiving from the only person on the pier a note attached to a rock telling him to save himself by swimming ashore, the only difference being that in our case, the Affirmative is far from drowning and finds itself on solid ground.

The gentlemen of the opposition have expressed dissatisfaction with our interpretation of the term *culture*. May we remind them of the wisdom of first being consistent within their own ranks. With strange inconsistency, in one breath Mr. Taylor declares that because modern radio entertainment programs "are characteristic attainments of radio which they (the people) *desire*, therefore, such programs are indicative of American culture." While in this assertion Mr. Taylor makes culture the reflection of people's tastes and desire, in rebuttal Mr. Dunipace turns about and quotes a survey showing that "by far the greater number of people in the country *are not educated to culture.*" May we suggest that the gentlemen of the opposition agree among themselves first and then take issue with the Affirmative.

Now let us turn to the arguments of the Negative in the order in which they were presented. First of all our opponents have stressed in constructive argument, even in rebuttal the benefit of radio to industry, quoting figures to show the large amount of business which may be attributed to radio. All their argument on this point may be stricken from this debate as *irrelevant*. We are not arguing the commercial benefits of radio. As a matter of fact we admit these commercial benefits. We are only arguing radio as a cultural and intellectual liability. The industrial argument of the Negative has as much pertinence to the question at issue as the discussion of box-office receipts to the question of whether or not a certain play is of artistic or classic value to the audience.

The gentlemen of the Negative have endeavored to indicate the cultural and intellectual benefits of radio by the following arguments: They have pointed to the University broadcasts over the air. My friends, in answering this argument I appeal to your own experience. How many times can you recall having heard a scholarly or academic university broadcast? In comparison with so-called popular programs (jazz, crooning, serials, etc.), such presentations are almost to be counted on the fingers of one's hands. Again they have cited improvement of speech as a benefit of radio. In intellectual fairness we of the Affirmative will admit that, *in part*, this is true. Yet in this, as in the preceding, the same problem exists. It has been my observation in radio, as Mr. Boardman will likewise testify, that for every program on a large station, with good continuity (embodying a high standard of English), there are a dozen so-called "plug" deals on a small station to "high pressure" some gullible listener into purchasing hokum tablets for his kidneys, or some fantastic reducing lotion for rotund ladies. My experience and doubtless your general observation confirms the fact that on these strictly commercial programs the quality of English used is very dubious. There are frequent grammatical mistakes, slurring of words, though mistakes of pronunciation are kept to a minimum. It must be also remembered that for every fifty thousand watt station there are four, five, or six, five hundred "watters." Thus this observation attains greater significance when considering the effects of radio *as a whole* upon the speech habits of the listening audience. Moreover, since on these small stations, the profit motive is all-important, since commercial sponsors wish to secure the best possible response to their advertising, they therefore *adapt* the vocabulary and style of speech used, to the listener. As a consequence we discover in the continuity of small stations the same limitations and restrictions as in the speech of the average listener. This definitely *does not make for improvement of speech* since the station is adapting its speech to the individual, average listener. Still further, the Negative has selected a few exceptional programs such as the Shell Symphony hour, the Standard Symphony hour, and the Seth Parker programs and on the basis of these exceptions have tried to prove the cultural value of radio. They totally ignore or at least neglect to consider, the great bulk of programs throughout one day on stations throughout the nation; programs of the culturally worthless type that Mr. Boardman mentioned which, though we admit, might be acceptable as entertainment, are a liability from the cultural and intellectual viewpoint.

The Negative has argued that those who are desirous of enjoying cultural programs may tune in to such broadcasts, practically admitting in this argument the small minority of these programs. In the first place, this argument in no way vindicates the cultural worth of radio as a whole but admits the disproportionately small number of worth-while (that is, from the educational standpoint) programs. In the second place, we may reason by analogy that, according to arguments of the Negative, simply because an educated man can attend five or six artistic, classic, or instructive moving pictures in a year, this fact upholds the moving picture industry as a cultural asset. Do you see the fallacy involved in their reasoning? In the third place this argument is not sound because in order to direct cultural influence of radio there must be selectivity at the *broadcasting* end rather than selectivity at the *listeners'* end.

From this point on the gentlemen of the opposition seem to have lost their bearings. When backed up against the wall they say, the responsibility is with the manipulators, not with the agency itself. Of course not, but how is this relevant to the question which considers *"radio as now operated."* The indictment still holds true. They tell us that the first half of the Affirmative argument falls because nothing is wrong with the profit motive in business as in radio. Of course not, but they have missed the point in our argument, the causal relation involved: that the profit motive is subversive to *cultural* progress in radio programs. Thus it is not the profit motive, as such, that we condemn but its *effects*. In his rebuttal Mr. Dunipace has gone so far as to say that since it's not radio's purpose to educate the public why blame radio? My friends, it is not a question of blame, nor of purpose in this debate but one of the *influence* or effect of radio, irrespective of all else, upon the culture and intellect of the public.

To restate our case, we of the Affirmative have proved: *first,* that the profit motive is prostituting the cultural and intellectual potentialities of radio and *second,* as now operated and revealed in its programs, radio is a cultural and intellectual liability. And now —one last word to our opponents—We have enjoyed the debate and may we meet them again at the Radio Announcers' Convention.

BIBLIOGRAPHY: RADIO BROADCASTING

BOOKS

Arnold, F. A.—*Broadcast Advertising.* 1933. Wiley. $3.
Darrow, B. H.—*Radio, the Assistant Teacher.* 1932. Adams, R. G. $1.90.
Kirkpatrick, C.—*Report of a Research into the Attitudes and Habits of Radio Listeners.* 1933. Webb. $1.50.
Lingel, R. J. C.—*Educational Broadcasting.* University of Chicago Press. 1932. $1.50.
Tyson, L.—*What to Read About Radio.* 1933. University of Chicago Press. pa. 25c.

Young, F.—*Shall I Listen; Studies in the Adventure of Broadcasting.* 1933. Constable

PAMPHLETS AND DOCUMENTS

Institute for Education by Radio. *Education on the Air.* Three vols. 1930-1932. Each $3. Ohio State University, Columbus, Ohio. Third volume contains a number of interesting topics related to the debate subject.

Institute of International Education—News Bureau. *International Broadcasting.* F. C. Wilks. March 1933.

Joint Radio Survey Committee. *Appraisal of Radio Broadcasting in Land Grant Colleges and State Universities.* 1933. National Committee on Education by Radio. gratis. 1201 16th St., N. W. Washington, D. C.

Music Supervisors National Conference. *Yearbook* 1932. p. 276-8, p. 263-8.

Music Teachers National Association. *Proceedings.* 1932. p. 124-5. *What May We Expect in Music Education Through Radio.*

National Advisory Council on Radio in Education. *Radio and Education.* 1932. University of Chicago Press. $3.

——— *Proceedings, Second Annual Assembly.* 1932. University of Chicago Press. $3.

National Broadcasting Company. *Analysis of History Making NBC Contributions to the Art of Radio in 1932.* The NBC, 711 5th Ave., New York, N. Y.

United States Office of Education. *Biennial Survey of Education.* 1928-1930. A. Perry. V. 1, p. 619-41.

MAGAZINE REFERENCES

American Teacher.—17:25, February 1933. *Radio Channel Grants and Grantees.* H. K. Randall.

Atlantic Monthly.—150:499, October 1932. *Europe's Air and Ours.* W. Hard.

American Mercury.—29:245, June 1933. *Adding Insult to Injury.* W. S. Howard.

Catholic Educational Review.—30:321, June 1932. *Brief for the Freedom of Radio Education.*

Child Study.—10:187, April 1933. *Movies and Radio Change Old Standards.* S. M. Gruenberg. 10:193, April. 1933. *Radio for Children, Parents Listen in.*

Christian Century.—49:1190, October 5, 1932. *Freedom of the Air and Press.* 50:108, January 25, 1933. *New Year's Eve Here and in England.* 50:579, May 3, 1933. *Uneasy Days for Radio Chains—Why Not a Hearer's Chain?*
Commonweal.—16:229, June 29, 1912. *Education Through the Air.*
Educational Survey.—3:126, March 1932. *International Labor Office and Wireless Broadcasting.*
English Journal (High School edition).—21 757, November 1932. *Announcing and Oral English* G. Fine.
Etude.—50:517, July 1932. *What Do People Listen to on the Radio?*
Foreign Affairs.—11:501, April 1933. *Progress of Socialization in England.*
Grade Teacher.—50:372, January 1933. *New Education for a New World. American Schools Radio Broadcast by N. E. A.*
Harper's Magazine.—165:467, September 1932. *Radio Goes Educational.* T. Hoke. 166:554, April 1933. *Radio, a Brief for the Defense.*
High School Teacher.—8:355, November 1932. *Ohio School of the Air.* 8:302, October 1932.
Journal of Adult Education. 4:234, June 1932. *Revolt of Radio Listeners.* 4:288, June 1932. *International Broadcasting.* J. G. McDonald.
Journal of Education.—115:550, October 3, 1932. *Radio More Than a Commodity.* C. H. Moore.
J-S. High School Clearing House.—7:83, October 1932. *Survey of What is being Done in Radio Education.* M. B. Harrison.
Literary Digest.—114:8, August 13, 1932. *First Aid for Mikemasters.* 114:8, December 10, 1932. *Breaking up the Radio Monopoly.* 115:16, January 7, 1933. *Kind Word for Radio Music.* 115:32, March 18, 1933. *Mother's Fighting Radio Bogies.* 115:14, April 1, 1933. *Child Radio Fans.*
Musician—37:3, November 1932. *Shall We Expose Our Children to Modern Music?* 38:9, January 1933. *Does the Radio Reflect Our Demand for Good Music?* R. Hoylbut.
Nation.—136.128, February 1, 1933. *Selling Symphonies.* 136:362, April 5, 1933. *Children's Hour.*
New Republic.—73:93, December 7, 1932. *Crutches for Broadcast Music.* B. H. Higgin.
Quar Journal of Speech.—18:560, November 1932. *Studies in the Techniques of Radio Speech* H. L. Ewbank. 19:211, April 1933.

Radio Medal of American Academy. Hamlin Garland. 19:219, April 1933. *Radio Influences Speech.* L. B. Tyson.

Parents Magazine.—8:13, May 1933. *Better Radio Programs for Children.* C. S. Littledale.

Pictorial Review.—34:18, October 1932. *Coming up for Air.* C. Lowe.

School and Society.—35:824, June 18, 1932. *Broadcasting Abroad. National Advisory Council on Radio in Education. Same.* The Council, 60 E. 42d St., N. Y. C. 37:93, January 21, 1933. *Radio and the Liquor Problem.* J. E. Morgan. 37:57, January 14, 1933. *Radio Programs in Our American Schools.* 37:612, May 13, 1933. *Educational Broadcasts in California.*

School Life.—17:198, June 1932. *First College Course in Radio Broadcast Advertising.* F. H. Arnold. 18:157, April 1933. *Radio Broadcasting Courses.* C. M. Koon. 18 127, March 1933, 6:30 P. M. Sunday. *When Education Goes on the Air.*

School Music.—32:11, November 1932. *Music That Is Broadcast.* B. H. Higgin.

School Review.—40:646, November 1932. *Civic Education by Radio.*

School Science and Mathematics.—32:776, October 1932. *What to Teach in Radio.* W. E. Smith.

Scribner's Magazine.—93:313, May 1933. *Children's Hour of Crime.* A. Mann.

World Tomorrow.—16:271, March 22, 1933. *Who Owns the Air?*

BIBLIOGRAPHIES

R. Lingel.—*Educational Broadcasting.* Compilation. University of Chicago Press. 1932. pa. $1.50.

U. S Office of Education.—*Good References on Education by Radio.* 1932. M. Koon and M. McCabe.

U. S. Office of Education.—Library Division. *Bibliography of Research Studies in Education.* 1930-31. p. 34.

APPENDICES

APPENDIX I

Topic Index of Debate Subjects Appearing in the Various Volumes of "Intercollegiate Debates"

Volume numbers are indicated after the subjects

Abandonment of Policy of Military Preparedness, *Vol. 12.*
Accident Insurance, *Vol. 4.*
Advertising, Modern, *Vol. 10.*
American Legion Should Be Condemned, *Vol. 14.*
Armed Intervention for Collection of Debts, *Vols. 1, 9.*
Asset Currency, *Vol. 1.*
Athletics, Amateur and Professionalism in, *Vol. 12.*
Banks, Government Control of, *Vol. 14.*
Bank Notes Secured by Commercial Paper, *Vol. 1.*
  (See also Asset Currency.)
Bonus (See American Legion.)
Cabinet System of Government, *Vols. 1, 3, 10.*
Cabinet Officers in Congress, *Vol. 4.*
Cancellation of War Debts, *Vols. 13, 14.*
Capitalism vs. Socialism
  Capitalism Is Unsound, *Vol. 13.*
  Social Control of Production and Exchange, *Vol. 7.*
  Limitation of Wealth, *Vol. 14.*
Central Bank, *Vols. 1, 3.* (See Banks, Gov't Control of.)

Centralization of Power in Federal Government, *Vols. 9, 13.* (See also Control of Industry, Banks, Gov't Control of.)
Chain Store, *Vol. 11.*
Child Labor, *Vol. 8.*
City Manager Plan of Municipal Government, *Vol. 7.*
Closed and Open Shop, *Vols. 1, 3.*
Coal Mines, Government Ownership of, *Vol. 1.*
Co-education, *Vol. 10.*
Commission Form of Municipal Government, *Vols. 1, 3.*
Compulsory Military Service, *Vol. 6.* (See also Swiss Military System, *Vol. 7.*)
Conservation of Natural Resources, *Vol. 2.*
Control of Industry, *Vol. 13.*
Courts and Reform in Legal Procedure.
  Abolition of Insanity Plea in Criminal Cases, *Vol. 10.*
  Judges, Appointment vs. Election, *Vol. 1.*
  Judges, Recall of, *Vol. 2.*
  Judicial Decisions, Recall of, *Vol. 4.*
  Three-fourths Jury Decision, *Vol. 3.*
Cuba, Annexation of, *Vol. 1.*
Declaration of War by Popular Vote, *Vol. 8.*
Dictatorship, Presidential, *Vol. 14.*
Direct Primary, *Vol. 3.*
Disarmament, International, *Vol. 11.* (See Abandonment of Policy of Military Preparedness.)
Divorce
  Divorce Is a Social Asset, *Vol. 13.*
  Uniform Marriage and Divorce Laws, *Vol. 8.*
Education
  Amateurism vs. Professionalism in Athletics, *Vol. 12.*

Education—(*Continued*)
  Co-education, *Vol. 10.*
  Federal Department of Education, *Vol. 9.*
Educational Qualification for Suffrage, *Vol. 1.*
Election of Senators by Popular Vote, *Vol. 1.*
Emergence of Women from the Home, *Vol. 12.*
Farm Relief
  McNary-Haugen Bill (Two debates), *Vol. 9.*
  Fixing Prices of Staple Agricultural Products, *Vol. 13.*
Federal Charter for Interstate Commerce Corporations, *Vols. 1, 4.*
Federal Control of Banks, *Vol. 14.*
Federal Control of the Express Business, *Vol. 5.*
Federal Control of Railroads, *Vol. 1.*
Federal Department of Education, *Vol. 9.*
Foreign Affairs
  Governmental Principles of Mussolini, *Vols. 9, 11.*
  Japanese Policy in Manchuria, *Vol. 14.*
Foreign Loans and Investments
  Armed Intervention for Collection of, *Vols. 1, 9.*
Foreign Relations
  Cancellation of War Debts, *Vols. 13, 14.*
  League of Nations, *Vols. 8, 10.*
  Monroe Doctrine, *Vol. 5.*
  Open Door Policy in China, *Vol. 7.*
  Recognition of Soviet Russia, *Vol. 8.*
Free Trade. (See also Tariff.)
  In Raw Materials, *Vol. 2.*
  International Free Trade, *Vol. 12.*
  Protective Tariff, Abandonment of, *Vols. 1, 2.*

Government, Change in Form of
  Cabinet Form of Government, *Vols. 1, 3, 10.*
  Centralization of Power in Federal Government, *Vols. 9, 13.*
  Educational Qualification for Suffrage, *Vol. 1.*
  Election of Senators by Popular Vote, *Vol. 1.*
  Personal Liberty, Restriction of by Government, *Vol. 9.*
  Power of Supreme Court to Declare Laws Unconstitutional, *Vol. 8.*
  Six Year Term for President, *Vol. 5.*
Government Ownership
  Of Coal Mines, *Vol. 1.*
  Hydro-Electric Power, *Vols. 10, 11.*
  Merchant Marine, *Vol. 6.*
  Telegraph and Telephone, *Vol. 6.*
  Railroads, *Vols. 4, 6, 7.*
Government Policies
  Annexation of Cuba, *Vol. 1.*
  Conservation of Natural Resources, *Vol. 2.*
  Independence of the Philippines, *Vol. 5.*
  Ship Subsidy, *Vols. 1, 6.*
Hydro-Electric Power, Government Ownership and Control of, *Vols. 10, 11.*
Immigration
  Japanese Immigration Law, *Vol. 8.*
  Literacy Test, *Vol. 5.*
  Restriction of, *Vol. 1.*
Income Tax, *Vol. 1, 2.* (See Limitation of Wealth.)
Incorporation, Federal, *Vols. 1, 4.* (See Federal Incorporation of Railroads, *Vol. 1.*)

APPENDIX I 511

Increase in Army and Navy, *Vol. 7.* (Navy alone, *Vol. 1.*)
Independence of Philippines, *Vol. 5.*
Industry, Control of, *Vol. 13.*
Inheritance Tax, *Vol. 1.*
Initiative and Referendum, *Vols. 1, 2.*
Injunction in Labor Disputes, *Vols. 1, 5.*
Insanity Plea in Criminal Cases, Abolishment of, *Vol. 10.*
Installment Buying, *Vol. 11.*
International Free Trade, *Vol. 12.*
Interstate Commerce
  Advertising, Modern, *Vol. 10.*
  Chain Store, *Vol. 11.*
  Control of Industry, *Vol. 13.*
  Federal Charter for Interstate Commerce Corporations, *Vols. 1, 4.*
  Federal Control of Express Business, *Vol. 5.*
  Federal Control of Railroads, *Vol. 1.*
  Federal Control of Banks, *Vol. 14.*
  Government Ownership of Railroads, *Vol. 4.*
  Installment Buying, *Vol. 11.*
  Reduction of Wages Retards Business Recovery, *Vol. 13.*
  Regulation vs. Dissolution of Trusts, *Vol. 4.*
Japanese Immigration, *Vol. 8.*
Japanese Policy in Manchuria, *Vol. 14.*
Judges, Appointment vs. Election of, *Vol. 1.*
Judges, Recall of, *Vol. 2.*
Judicial Decisions, Recall of, *Vol. 4.*
Jury System, Abolition of, *Vol. 10.*

Labor and Capital
  Benefits of Labor Unions, *Vol. 1.*
  Child Labor, *Vol. 8.*
  Closed and Open Shop, *Vols. 1, 3.*
  Exemption of Labor Unions from Anti-trust Laws, *Vol. 7.*
  Forty Hour Week, *Vol. 11.*
  Injunction in Labor Disputes, *Vols. 1, 5.*
  Minimum Wage, *Vols. 3, 6.*
  Reduction of Wages, *Vol. 13.*
Labor Unions, Benefits of, *Vol. 1.*
  Exemption of from Anti-trust Laws, *Vol. 7.*
League of Nations, *Vols. 8, 10.*
Light Wines and Beer, *Vol. 9.*
Liquor Control, *Vols. 8, 9, 12.*
Limitation of Wealth, *Vol. 14.*
Literacy Test for Immigrants, *Vol. 5.*
McNary-Haugen Bill, *Vol. 9.*
Merchant Marine, Government Ownership of, *Vol. 6.*
Military Problems and War
  Abandonment of Military Preparedness, *Vol. 12.*
  Compulsory Military Service, *Vol. 6.*
  Swiss System of Compulsory Military Service, *Vol. 7.*
  Declaration of War by Popular Vote, *Vol. 8.*
  Increase in Army and Navy, *Vols. 1, 7.*
  International Disarmament, *Vol. 11.*
Money and Banking
  Asset Currency, *Vol. 1.*
  Banks, Government Control of, *Vol. 14.*
  Bank Notes Secured by Commercial Paper, *Vol. 1.*
  Central Bank, *Vols. 1, 3.*

Money and Banking—(*Continued*)
  Control of Industry (Credit Control), *Vol. 13.*
  Guarantee of Bank Deposits, *Vol. 1.*
  Postal Savings Banks, *Vol. 1.*
Monroe Doctrine, *Vol. 5.*
Municipal Government
  Commission Form, *Vols. 1, 3.*
  City Manager Plan, *Vol. 7.*
Mussolini, Governmental Principles of, *Vols. 9, 11.*
Old Age Insurance or Pension, *Vols. 4, 13.*
Ontario Plan of Liquor Control, *Vol. 12.*
Open Door Policy in China, *Vol. 7.*
Open vs. Closed Shop, *Vols. 1, 3.*
Personal Liberty, Restriction by Government, *Vol. 9.*
Postal Savings Banks, *Vol. 1.*
Power of Supreme Court, *Vol. 8.*
Power of Government. (See Centralization of Power.)
Prohibition, *Vols. 8, 9, 12.*
Protective Tariff, *Vols. 1, 2.* (See also Free Trade.)
Radio Broadcasting, *Vol. 14.*
Railroads
  Government Ownership of, *Vols. 4, 6, 7.*
  Federal Control of, *Vol. 1.*
Raw Materials, Free Trade in, *Vol. 2.*
Recognition of Russia, *Vol. 8.*
Reduction of Wages Retards Business Recovery, *Vol. 13.*
Regulation vs. Dissolution of Trusts, *Vol. 4.* (See also Federal Control.)
Restriction of Immigration, *Vols. 1, 5, 8.* (See Immigration.)

Ship Subsidy, *Vol. 6.*
Short Ballot, *Vol. 2.*
Single Tax, *Vol. 6.*
Six Year Term for President, *Vol. 5.*
Social Insurance
  Accident, *Vol. 4.*
  Old Age, *Vols. 4, 13.*
  Unemployment, *Vols. 11, 12, 13.*
Socialistic Control of Production and Exchange, *Vol. 7.*
Socialism, *Vol. 14.*
Soldier Bonus, *Vol. 14.* (See American Legion.)
State Government, Reform and Change in
  Abolition of Insanity Plea in Criminal Cases, *Vol. 10.*
  Abolition of Jury System, *Vol. 10.*
  Appointment vs. Election of Judges, *Vol. 1.*
  Direct Primary, *Vol. 3.*
  Initiative and Referendum, *Vol. 3.*
  Recall of Judges, *Vol. 2.*
  Recall of Judicial Decisions, *Vol. 4.*
  State Medical Aid, *Vol. 12.*
  Short Ballot, *Vol. 2.*
  Three-fourths Jury Decision, *Vol. 3.*
  Unicameral Legislature, *Vol. 5.*
State Medical Aid, *Vol. 12.*
Swiss System of Compulsory Military Service, *Vol. 7.*
Tariff (See Free Trade, also Protection), *Vols. 1, 2, 12.*
Taxation
  Income Tax, *Vols. 1, 2.*
  Inheritance Tax, *Vol. 1.*
  Intangible Property Tax, *Vol. 14.*

Taxation—(*Continued*)
>Limitation of Wealth by Income and Inheritance Taxes, *Vol. 14*.
>On Rental Value of Land, *Vol. 2*.
>Single Tax, *Vol. 6*.

Telegraph and Telephone, Government Ownership of, *Vol. 6*.
Three-fourths Jury Decision, *Vol. 3*.
Trusts, *Vol. 4*. (See also Control of Industry, *Vol. 13*.)
Unemployment Insurance, *Vols. 11, 12, 13*.
Unicameral Legislature, *Vol. 5*.
Uniform Marriage and Divorce Laws, *Vol. 8*.
Wages
>Minimum Wages, *Vols. 3, 6*.
>Reduction of Wages, *Vol. 13*.

Working Week of Forty Hours, *Vol. 11*.

APPENDIX II

List of Colleges, the work of whose debaters has appeared in the Various Volumes of "Intercollegiate Debates"

Volume numbers in which the various colleges have had contributions follow the names

Amherst College, *Vol. 1.*
Baker University, *Vol. 1.*
Bates College, *Vols. 10, 12.*
Baylor College for Women, *Vol. 8.*
Baylor University, *Vol. 2.*
Bellevue College, *Vol. 2.*
Beloit College, *Vols. 1, 9, 14.*
Bethany College, Kansas, *Vols. 9, 11.*
Bowdoin College, *Vol. 1.*
British Columbia, University of, *Vol. 8.*
British Universities, Student Union, *Vol. 10.*
Brown University, *Vol. 2.*
Bucknell University, *Vol. 14.*
California Institute of Technology, *Vol. 8.*
Canton College, *Vol. 2.*
Carleton College, *Vols. 6, 10, 13, 14.*
Chattanooga, University of, *Vol. 1.*
Chicago, University of, *Vols. 1, 2.*
Cincinnati, University of, *Vols. 1, 12.*
Colgate University, *Vols. 1, 2, 12, 14.*
College of Emporia, *Vols. 8, 9.*

College of the Pacific, *Vol. 9*.
College of Wooster, *Vol. 14*.
Colorado Agricultural College, *Vol. 6*.
Colorado University, *Vol. 4*.
Columbia University, *Vol. 7*.
Cotner College, *Vol. 2*.
Cumberland College, *Vol. 1*.
Dartmouth College, *Vol. 1*.
Denison University, *Vols. 3, 13*.
DePauw University, *Vols. 12, 13*.
Dickinson College, *Vol. 1*.
Doane College, *Vol. 2*.
Drake University, *Vol. 1*.
Eureka College, *Vols. 6, 8*.
Franklin College, *Vol. 11*.
Franklin and Marshall College, *Vol. 1*.
Fresno State College, *Vol. 14*.
Friends University, *Vol. 6*.
Georgia, University of, *Vols. 1, 13, 14*.
German Universities, *Vol. 12*.
Glendale Junior College, *Vol. 11*.
Harvard University, *Vols. 1, 2, 13*.
Hawaii, University of, *Vol. 10*.
Heidelberg College, *Vol. 9*.
Hillsdale College, *Vol. 6*.
Hope College, *Vol. 9*.
Illinois, University of, *Vol. 1*.
Illinois Wesleyan, *Vols. 1, 3, 4*.
Indiana University, *Vols. 11, 12*.
Iowa State College, *Vol. 13*.
Iowa State Teachers College, *Vol. 4*.
Iowa Wesleyan College, *Vol. 3*.

Johns Hopkins University, *Vols. 1, 5*.
Kansas State Agricultural College, *Vols. 4, 7, 9, 13*.
Kansas, University of, *Vols. 2, 5, 14*.
Kansas Wesleyan, *Vols. 4, 5*.
Kent College of Law, *Vol. 13*.
Knox College, *Vol. 1*.
Lawrence College, *Vols. 5, 11*.
Los Angeles Junior College, *Vol. 11*.
Marquette University, *Vol. 14*.
Michigan State College, *Vols. 9, 12*.
Michigan, University of, *Vols. 1, 14*.
Minnesota, University of, *Vol. 12*.
Monmouth College, *Vols. 3, 5, 10*.
Morningside College, *Vols. 3, 7*.
New York University, *Vols. 1, 14*.
North Central College, *Vol. 9*.
Northern State Teachers College (South Dakota), *Vols. 8, 12*.
Northwestern University, *Vols. 1, 11, 14*.
Occidental College, *Vol. 14*.
Ohio State University, *Vol. 6*.
Ohio Wesleyan, *Vol. 1*.
Oklahoma, University of, *Vols. 2, 3*.
Oregon State College, *Vol. 13*.
Ottawa University (Kansas), *Vol. 3*.
Oxford University (England), *Vols. 8, 9, 13, 14*.
Penn College (Iowa), *Vol. 2*.
Pennsylvania State College, *Vols. 1, 10, 12*.
Pennsylvania, University of, *Vol. 6*.
Pittsburgh, University of, *Vol. 10*.
Princeton University, *Vols. 1, 4, 7, 14*.
Pomona College, *Vol. 5*.

Redlands, University of, *Vols. 6, 7, 8, 11, 13.*
Ripon College, *Vols. 4, 8.*
Rochester, University of, *Vol. 1.*
Rutgers College, *Vol. 1.*
South Dakota Wesleyan, *Vols. 7, 12.*
Southern California, University of, *Vols. 6, 9, 14.*
Southern California Law School, *Vol. 7.*
Southwestern College (Kansas), *Vols. 7, 8.*
Stanford University, *Vols. 10, 13.*
Swarthmore College, *Vols. 1, 2, 12, 13.*
Sydney, University of, (Australia), *Vol. 10.*
Texas, University of, *Vols. 4, 5.*
Trinity University (Texas), *Vol. 5.*
University of Arizona, *Vol. 14.*
University of California at Los Angeles, *Vols. 8, 9.*
University of Iowa, *Vol. 14.*
University of North Dakota, *Vol. 14.*
University of the South, *Vol. 1.*
University of Wyoming, *Vol. 14.*
Vanderbilt University, *Vol. 1.*
Vermont, University of, *Vol. 1.*
Washburn College, *Vol. 1.*
Washington and Lee University, *Vol. 1.*
Washington State College, *Vol. 11.*
Washington University (St. Louis, Mo.), *Vols. 10, 11.*
Whitman College, *Vol. 13.*
William and Vashti College, *Vol. 3.*
William Jewell College, *Vols. 2, 3, 5.*
Williamette University, *Vol. 8.*
Wisconsin, University of, *Vols. 11, 12, 14.*
Yale University, *Vol. 14.*
Yankton College, *Vol. 7.*

INDEX

	PAGE
REVENUES FROM INTANGIBLE PROPERTY	3
Affirmative 5, 18, 31, 47, 53,	59
Negative 11, 25, 38, 45, 50,	56
Bibliography	64

Affirmative
  Fifty Per Cent Tax on Intangibles Necessary

Best means of redistributing revenue	22
Income tax necessary 9, 20, 21, 22, 23,	38
Inequalities under present system 7, 10,	35
Plan is practical 19, 20, 24, 25, 32, 38, 54,	59
Plan is successful in Virginia 24,	31
Plan is successful in Delaware	31
Plan is successful in North Carolina 19, 21, 23, 26, 32, 33,	53
Plan is successful in South Carolina	24
Present Situation Intolerable 6,	49
Produces a More Equitable Situation... 7, 34, 35, 38, 39, 49,	61

Property Tax

Condemned by leading tax authorities	38
Discarded in Europe 11,	32
Places unequal burden on farmer 7, 36,	37
Case of Green County farmer	8
Case of Wisconsin farmer 7, 35, 48, 50,	51
Theory erroneous 9,	38
Unjust 8, 34, 35,	38
Proposed Shift Feasible 6, 21, 34, 38, 49,	61
Results in Total Tax Reduction 33,	34
Sufficiency of	21

Supporting Testimony

Michigan committee	8
Minnesota Tax Commission 7,	49
Model Plan of National Tax Association 20, 22,	55
National Industry Conference 9,	10
National Tax Association 20,	22
North Carolina Tax Committee 21, 32,	33
President Hoover 10,	36
Richard T. Ely	55

Taxation

Delinquency of 19, 37, 49, 50,	54
Federal	12
Fifty per cent should be derived from taxing intangibles	5
	6, 25
Meaning of	5

521

522 INDEX

Revenues From Intangible Property (*continued*)   PAGE
   Present methods 6, 38, 49
   Primary object 13, 19
   Reapportionment necessary 6, 10, 11
   Reduction necessary 10, 11
Negative
  Intangible Property Tax
   Burdens farmer 14
   Inequitable 41, 42
   Impractical 14
   Not fiscally adequate 13, 40, 45
  Not Correlated with Ability to Pay 45
  Results in Delinquency 52
  Results in Tax Evasion 28, 52, 57
  Supporting Testimony
   Michigan 58
   Mississippi 17
   National Industrial Conference Board 40
   New York State Tax Commission 42, 43, 44, 59
   North Carolina 17
   Professor Lutz 13
  Unfeasible in Agricultural States 16, 17, 27, 38, 53
   Mississippi 16, 17
   Missouri 40
   North Carolina 17, 26, 27
   Utah 17, 39
  Unreliable Means of Revenue 14, 16, 18, 26, 27, 28, 29, 45
   Situation in New York 14, 15, 26
   Situation in North Dakota 15, 16, 26, 27
  Unsatisfactory Means of Distributing Revenue 14
                                   28, 29, 30, 31 53

SOCIALISM 77
  Affirmative 78, 95
  Negative 86, 104
  Bibliography 115
Affirmative
  Need for Centralized Control 80
  Need for Centralized Planning 80
  Present Economic Disorder 79, 80
Socialism
  Definition of 81, 82
  Does not give leadership 104
  Failure in Great Britain 99, 102, 103
  Is Marxism 96, 103
  Means annihilation of political freedom 101
  Means annulment of private enterprise 96
  Offers no remedy 86
Success of Private Enterprise
  Achievements under 99, 100
  Allows for planning 97

INDEX 523

Socialism (*continued*) PAGE
    Results in high wages 98
    Results in wealth equality 98
  Negative
    Collapse of Present System
      Failure of distribution 90, 91
      Failure of production 91, 111
      Need for higher wages 93
      Need for planning 92, 108
      Need for productive and distributive control 92, 108
      Need for stabilization 93
    Socialism
      Benefits all 111
      Coördinates production and consumption 109, 110
      Definition of 87, 94
      Is not Communism 112
      Offers a practical economic program 88, 90, 93, 94
      Successful in Kansas 114
      Successful in Milwaukee 114
      Successful in Russia 113
      Would cure speculation 111
      Would cure unemployment 110

CANCELLATION OF WAR DEBTS 121
  Affirmative 122, 134, 151, 158
  Negative 128, 141, 148, 154
  Bibliography 162
Affirmative
  Cancellation
    Effect on United States 123, 126, 139, 140
    Moral justification 134
    Result in unemployment 127, 140
    Will not increase taxation 127, 135
    Will return prosperity 135, 136
    Will stimulate business 127
  Payment is Undesirable
    Bad effect on trade 124, 138, 139
    Cannot pay with goods 138
    Creates unfavorable trade balance 125, 136, 140, 148
    Demoralizes foreign and domestic markets 141
    Depreciates foreign currencies 136, 137, 138, 140, 141
    Disastrous to foreign trade 137, 139, 141
    Payment by crossing off surplus credits 152
    Payment by loan is postponement 124, 148, 159
    Payment by Hoover-Mills plan unfeasible . 152, 159, 160, 161
    Payment impossible by gold 124, 141, 159
    Payment impossible by goods ....·... 138
Methods of Payment 123, 141, 142, 159
  Gold
  Exchange of Goods and Services
  Loans

INDEX

Cancellation of War Debts (*continued*)   PAGE
- Negative
  - Cancellation
    - American industry would suffer 133
    - American taxpayer would suffer 133
    - Definition 128
    - Not preferable to moratorium 147, 150, 157, 158
    - Would decrease purchasing power 133
    - Would increase United States' taxes 133, 156
    - Would ruin world markets 133, 155
  - Payment Desirable
    - Debtor nations are able to pay 145, 148, 150, 157, 158
    - Debtor nations have favorable balance of payments 143
            144, 145, 146
    - Debter nations morally obligated 128, 129, 132, 146, 154
    - Debtor nations received spoils in excess of debts 130, 131
    - France has repaid private loans 131
    - Hoover-Mills plan 145, 148, 158
- War Debts 122
  - Amount Paid 122
  - Average Payment 122
  - Occasion 122
  - Purpose 122

WAR DEBTS 168
- Cancellation
  - American Opinion Against 179, 180
  - Congress Opposed to it 196
  - Economically Sound 178
  - Necessary to
    - Combat British policy 170, 171
    - Decrease unemployment 170
    - Increase employment 178
    - Open European markets 178
  - Public Must Accept 183, 184, 196
  - Relation to Disarmament 186, 188, 194, 195
  - Relation to Political Sentiment 195, 196
  - Relation to Public Opinion 191
  - Would Create Favorable Trade Balance 170, 178
  - Would Destroy Favorable Trade Balance 169, 170, 178
- Payment of
  - Ability of Europe to Pay 188
  - Advantage of Acceptance 198, 199
  - Allies Will Not Pay 180, 197
  - Alternatives
    - Extension 180, 183, 192
    - Repudiation 180
  - Detrimental to Creditor Nation 173, 178, 179, 193, 194
  - Europe Cannot Pay 170, 187
  - Europe Unwilling to Pay 194
  - Germany Cannot Pay 180, 191

INDEX 525

War Debts (*continued*) PAGE
    Loss is Greater Than Gain 194
    Means of Payment 189, 190
        Impossible to pay in gold 190
        Impossible to pay in services 190
    No Method of 197
    Possibility of Future Payment 181, 182, 183
    United States Cannot Accept Payments 185
War Debts
    Confederate 180, 192
    Interest on 168
    Origin of 168
    Payment to Date 168

THE AMERICAN LEGION SHOULD BE CONDEMNED 203
    Affirmative 203, 219, 236, 242
    Negative 212, 227, 233, 239
    Bibliography 246
    Activities of Legion
        Association with schools 207, 216, 235
        Bills passed by Legion 210, 221, 223, 235, 244
        Censorship and suppression of speakers, 206, 207, 208, 234, 238
        Civil service preferment 224
        Conventions 205, 234
        Fostering Americanism 214
        Lobbying and results of lobbying 209
                      210, 211, 221, 232, 244, 245
        Maintaining law and order 213
        Obtaining medical treatment...222, 223, 226, 240, 241, 242, 244
        Promoting peace 214, 215, 216
        Pro-war and anti-foreign policies, 208, 209, 211, 235, 238, 242
        Raiding treasury 205, 229
        Red-baiting 205, 231
        Welfare work 216, 217, 218, 237
    Legion Contrasted with the Grand Army of the Republic 228
                                  229, 244
    Membership of Legion
        Financial status of members 225
        One third actual veterans 205
    Purposes of Legion
        Non-political organization 204
        Original purpose 228
        Preserving comradeship 204
        Stated in Legion Constitution 204, 212, 213
    Stand on Bonus 219, 224, 230, 231, 234, 240, 241, 244, 245
    Stand on Pensions 219
            220, 221, 223, 224, 226, 227, 230, 231, 239, 240, 243, 244
    United States' Veterans Compared with Foreign Veterans 225
                                  226, 243

	PAGE
GOVERNMENT CONTROL OF THE BANKING SYSTEM	251
Affirmative 251, 267, 282, 299, 308,	315
Negative 258, 274, 290, 295, 303, 311,	319
Bibliography	319

Affirmative Plan of Control With Negative Objections
All banks in the Federal Reserve System 255
   268, 272, 283, 284, 289, 297, 298, 299, 303, 305, 306, 309
   Branch banking 256, 290
   Control of investments 257, 305
   Guarantee of deposits, 258, 275, 277, 278, 279, 280, 281, 284, 285
      286, 287, 288, 298, 299, 301, 303, 307, 313, 314, 316
Defects of State Regulation 267, 275, 283, 300, 316
Federal Reserve System 253
Foreign Banking Systems 253, 257, 271, 285, 286, 301, 302, 310
Organization vs. Functions of Banks 261
   262, 266, 275, 282, 283, 291, 292, 296, 309, 311, 317
Past Record of Bank Failures 252
   253, 260, 266, 292, 297, 302, 310
Reasons for Bank Failures
   Competition between banks 253, 261, 301, 306, 309
   Dishonesty of officials 264, 266, 293
   Economic conditions.... 264, 290, 293, 294, 295, 300, 306, 314
   Inability to expand credit 254, 307, 312
   Inability to liquidate 254, 307
   Lack of central organization 253, 261, 266, 284, 306
   Loss of confidence 254, 263, 284, 288, 289, 307
   Under-capitalization 254, 261, 296
   Unstable dollar 254
      265, 268, 269, 270, 273, 284, 296, 304, 305, 307, 308

LIMITATION OF WEALTH	325
Affirmative 326, 337, 349,	360
Negative 331, 343,	355
Bibliography	363

Advantages of Limitation
   Eliminates moral and social wrong 338
      339, 340, 341, 342, 352, 354, 363
   Ends exploitation of public 353
   Practicable 351
   Prevents radical measures 330
   Promotes universal moderation 349, 350
   Raises consuming power 354
   Will not destroy philanthropy or tax income 351
Disadvantages of Limitation
   Cannot be effected 333, 347, 348, 355
   Causes limitation of philanthropies.... 314, 315, 350, 355, 360
   Causes loss of taxes 344, 345, 346, 350, 356
   Disastrous historical precedents 336
   Forces Government administration of property 346, 360

INDEX 527

Limitation of Wealth (*continued*) PAGE
    Inhibits progress dependent upon surplus of capital 332
            333, 334, 335, 336, 337, 343, 348, 349, 360
    No certain cure for economic ills 332, 343
    No immediate benefits 336, 349, 350, 360
    Prevents adoption of more fundamental measures 333, 349, 359
    Will not control credit 357, 358
  Negative Counter Plan
    Abolition of child labor 359
    Control of credit by Federal Reserve System 358
    Minimum wage laws 359
    Old age pensions 359
    Thirty hour week 359
    Unemployment insurance 359
  Unequal Distribution of Wealth—Causes and Effects 326
        327, 328, 329, 331, 337, 338, 339, 340, 341, 342, 361, 363

JAPAN'S POLICY IN MANCHURIA 369
  Affirmative 369, 384, 401, 409
  Negative 377, 391, 398, 405
  Bibliography 413
  History of Manchurian Relations 370
          373, 377, 378, 379, 380, 381, 382, 384, 407, 411
  Japan's Policy Justifiable
    Action beneficial to China, Manchuria and the World.... 387
                388, 389, 390, 391, 412, 413
    Citation of similar cases of intervention 403, 412
    Dictated by law of self-preservation 371
        372, 374, 377, 385, 386, 390, 404, 405, 410, 413
    Establishes bulwark against Communism 370
                 373, 386, 387, 388, 390, 413
    Establishes stable, independent government for Manchukuo 370
                    385, 388, 389, 410, 412
    Japan needs colonies for protection and expansion 372
                    386, 390, 401, 402
    Sanction of International Law 375, 377, 386, 411
  Japan's Policy Not Justified
    Armed force is not justifiable 383, 392, 394, 395, 396, 397
    China has both need for and claim on Manchuria 378
           379, 383, 384, 391, 397, 406, 407, 408
    Japan should have appealed to League 395, 396, 406
    Japan's action violates treaties.... 383, 392, 393, 394, 398, 406
    Korea as an example 399, 400
    Need is no justification 377, 379, 405, 408
    No benefit to Manchuria 399, 400
    Spread of Communism encouraged by Japanese action.... 400
                            408, 409
    Sovereignty of China 376, 379, 382, 384, 398, 402, 403

A PRESIDENTIAL DICTATORSHIP 419
  Affirmative 419, 430, 440, 453

A Presidential Dictatorship (*continued*) PAGE
    Negative 423, 436, 445, 450
    Bibliography 459
    Benefits of Dictatorship
        Dictators less easily bribed 458
        Dictators not absolute 453, 457, 458
        History proves dictators beneficial 458
        History sanctions dictators in crises.... 421, 442, 443, 444, 445
        Promotes efficiency and coördination 441, 442, 458
        Promotes immediate governmental action 430
            431, 432, 433, 434, 435, 440, 453, 454, 455, 456, 457, 458
        Temporary dictatorship will not imperil democracy 457, 459
    Conditions Demanding Immediate Action
        Banking 421
        Farmers' situation 421
        Railroads 421
        Unemployment 421
        War debts 421
    Evils of Dictatorship
        Annuls our progress from monarchial to democratic form
            of government 437, 438
        Bribery of dictators possible 448
        Characters of dictators 426
        Citation of foreign examples of dictators 425
                              426, 427, 428, 437
        Crushes democratic political advances 428
        Dependence upon party 426, 449
        Dictator independent of public opinion 424, 425, 427, 436, 449
        Does not promote social welfare 426, 427
        History warns against dictatorships 448, 449
        No capable successors of dictators 429, 430, 436
        No freedom of speech or press 424, 427, 436, 437, 449
        No representative government 424, 425
        No right to hold property 424
        Not necessary for quick governmental action 439
                        440, 445, 446, 447, 450, 451, 452
    Meaning of Dictator 420, 444
    Precedent for Dictatorial Powers 421, 442, 443
    Record and Results of Capitalism 421, 422

RADIO BROADCASTING 467
    Affirmative 468, 479, 497
    Negative 474, 485, 493
    Bibliography 501
    Explanation of Question 469, 474, 475, 478, 485, 486
    Growth of Radio 468, 469, 475, 476
    Radio Analogous to Moving Pictures 471
    Radio, as Operated, Is a Cultural Liability
        Dominated by profit motive 470, 471, 472, 473, 474
        Encourages use of poor grammar 481, 482, 483, 499
        Industrial benefits not relevant 498

Radio Broadcasting (*continued*)
    Instructs in crime 482, 483
    Lowers artistic tastes
        Of adults 481, 500, 501
        Of children 482, 484
    Over-stimulating 482
    Promotes advertising of worthless products 481
    Small proportion of broadcast time cultural or educational 484, 498, 500
Radio, as Operated, Is Not a Cultural Liability
    Ample broadcast time given to cultural and educational programs 487, 490, 491, 492, 495
    Creates new market for talent 477, 478, 496
    Establishes familiarity with political events 476
    Improves speech
        Of announcers 479, 487
        Of general public 478
    Profit motive necessary and not undesirable 489, 490, 494, 496
    Reflects public's taste 476, 477, 486, 487, 488, 496
    Thwarts crime 488

Speaking! Debating!

Declamations, Recitations, Readings, Dialogues, Debates, Prize Speaking, Orations, FOR ALL OCCASIONS.

Edgerton's *A Speech for Every Occasion*	$2.00
Thomas' A Speech and A Story for Every Occasion	2.00
LeRow's Pieces for *Every* Occasion	2.00
Deming and Bemis' *New Pieces* for Every Day the Schools Celebrate	2.00
Niemeier's *New Plays* for Every Day the Schools Celebrate	2.00
Gunnison's New Dialogues and Plays (*Primary, Intermediate and Advanced*)	2.50
Lovejoy & Adams' Pieces for *Every Month* of the Year	2.00
Ashley's 50 Orations That Have Won Prizes In Speaking Contests	2.00
Blackstone's The Best American Orations of Today	2.00
Esenwein's How to Attract and Hold an Audience	1.50
Scott's Psychology of Public Speaking (*Revised*)	1.60
Neil's Sources of Effectiveness in Public Speaking	2.60
Pearson's *Extemporaneous* Speaking	2.00
Pearson's *Humorous* Speaker	2.00
Pearson's The Speakers' Library (*8 Volumes*) each	2.50
Brownlee's *"Patriotic* Speaker"	1.75
Craig and Gunnison's Pieces That Have Taken Prizes	2.00
McHale's Pieces That Have Won Prizes	2.00
Blackstone's *New Pieces* That Will Take Prizes In Speaking Contests	2.00
Shurter and Watkins' *New Poems* That Will Take Prizes in Speaking Contests	2.00
Shurter's Winning Declamations—How to Speak Them	2.00
Davis' Model Commencement Parts, Orations, Essays	2.50
Skinner's The Bright Side (*Inspirational Verse*)	1.50
Fenno's New Science and Art of Elocution	2.00
Fry's Educational Dramatics	.75
Fry's A Midsummer Night's Dream (*A Dramatic Cast Reading Arrangement*)	.60
Shurter & Watkins' *New Poems* for Oral Interpretation	2.00
Barbe's Famous Poems *Explained*	1.50
Barbe's Great Poems, *Interpreted*	2.00
Shurter and Watkins' Masterpieces of *Modern Verse*	1.50
Hix' Poetry for Each School Year, Grades 1-8 (*Approved Selections*) each	.72
Reynold's Graded Poetry for Memorizing (*3 Vols.*) ea.	.75
Reynold's Graded Poetry for Memorizing, for Junior High Schools, 7th and 8th Years, each	.85
Craig's Both Sides of 30 Public Questions Completely Debated (Pros and Cons), (*Revised Edition*)	2.25
Shurter's Both Sides of 100 Public Questions Briefly Debated (*Revised Edition*)	2.00
Henry-Seeley's How to Organize & Conduct a Meeting	1.50
Howe's Handbook of Parliamentary Usage	.75
Palmer's New Parliamentary Manual	1.00
Nichols and Pearson's Intercollegiate Debates — Year Book of College Debating (*11 Volumes*) each	2.50
Pi Kappa Delta's Winning Intercollegiate Debates and Orations (*3 Volumes*) each	1.50
Shurter's The Science and Art of Effective Debating	2.00

Lightning Source UK Ltd.
Milton Keynes UK
UKOW06n0603070616
275755UK00008B/47/P